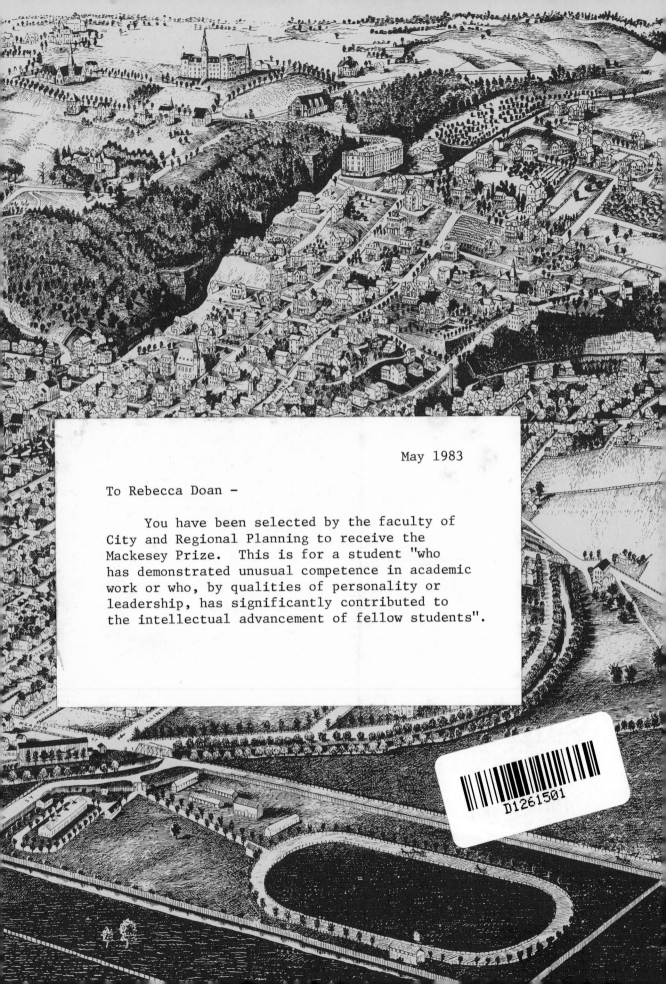

May 1983

To Rebecca Doan –

You have been selected by the faculty of
City and Regional Planning to receive the
Mackesey Prize. This is for a student "who
has demonstrated unusual competence in academic
work or who, by qualities of personality or
leadership, has significantly contributed to
the intellectual advancement of fellow students".

THE CORNELL CAMPUS

A History of Its Planning and Development

On the Quadrangle: Morrill Hall, Uris Library, and McGraw Tower.

THE CORNELL CAMPUS

A History of Its Planning and Development

Kermit Carlyle Parsons

Cornell University Press
Ithaca, New York

Library of Congress Catalog Card Number: 68–12423

PRINTED IN THE UNITED STATES OF AMERICA
BY KINGSPORT PRESS, INC.

To Janice

Contents

Illustrations

Introduction

ONE WINTER DAY EARLY IN 1869 Professor Goldwin Smith, the English champion of Northern interests in the American Civil War, took an exploratory walk on the Cornell campus. He had come to Ithaca, New York, from Oxford to lecture on history at the raw, new University. Smith paused to observe construction at a stone building on the edge of East Hill overlooking the town and lake valley. Inside he saw green wood being used by the workmen and went to report this unhappy fact to Ezra Cornell, the University's founder, benefactor, and construction foreman. Ezra Cornell responded calmly to the news. "Well," he said, "I guess we use our timber greener than you but it will start." Later, Smith wrote his friend Norton at Harvard that he feared Mr. Cornell's response was correct. The wood would start.

Cornell, of course, had in mind only the start of the University. Getting on with the work was much more important than a warped board or two. Two and one-half years before Goldwin Smith's walk, on 1 June 1866, an impatient Ezra Cornell, his wife Mary, and a workman had climbed East Hill from the Cornell farmstead to start the first building. In a simple private ground-breaking ceremony Cornell and his wife turned the first two shovels of earth on the site of South University, later to become Morrill Hall. The building and its two northern neighbors, McGraw and White Halls, still stand. The green wood has cured in their walls for almost a century and somewhere on the campus one could find, with little difficulty, a furtive carpenter nailing more green lumber for a start.

A visitor to the Cornell campus would hardly notice such details. The breadth and power of the campus scene are too compelling to permit it. His eyes are captured by the long vistas at the edge of East Hill, by the rugged beauty of the deep gorges that bound the campus, by the great variety of campus architecture knit together in a vaguely formal order, and by the sharp spatial contrast between broad open quadrangles and courts and the loose informality of nearby groups of buildings.

The Cornellian returned to Ithaca also finds this compelling visual environment, and more. The meaning of his personal experience in Ithaca and at Cornell is symbolized in this landscape beauty, this rich variety of buildings, and this semi-formal order of the campus. For such a person the sight of Cayuga's waters, the Libe Tower, the Giant's Staircase Falls in Cascadilla Gorge, Sage Chapel, the Arts Quad, the Plantations, and the Cornell Crescent are sources of strength. J. S. Finch, Cornellian and Princetonian, recently observed that, on a Saturday afternoon in October at Princeton, football permeates the air, but at Ithaca the air permeates football. Seated high in the Crescent a spectator feels the strength and grandeur of the rolling hills spread before him.

This history of campus planning and architecture—an account of the way those who built Cornell met the varied building needs of a revolutionary kind of university and preserved the remarkable landscape beauty of its site—has been written to help increase our understanding of the interactions among man, purpose, and environment on East Hill. The search for the truth about any human creation has a deep fascination. At Cornell the fascination is heightened by the dramatic circumstances of the establishment of the institution, by the contrasting but amazingly complementary objectives of its founders and leaders, by the "toughness" of the material environment, and by the achievements of its graduates. Speaking of the German universities, Friedrich Paulson said that everyone who joined the community was encompassed by its atmosphere of historic life and took something of it with him when he left. Paulson was, of course, speaking of the intellectual history of the universities, but, from the architectural history of a place, the way men shaped it, we also draw our current perceptions and our conceptions of the future. Romeyn Berry, the "total Cornellian," put it better: "A college can lie about itself in one building but when it rears hundreds of structures through the better part of a century, the truth is bound to come out." "Rym" thought Cornell no exception and "without pretense." He told Cornellians that they could read their family history in their well-kept possessions. "There has never been any attempt to conceal our past or veil our indiscretions."

Passage of the Morrill Act in 1862 established the land-grant colleges and marked a turning point in American higher education. Its passage also marked a new era in college architecture and campus planning. The Morrill Act gave impetus to scientific and vocational education. These new purposes and the limited means available to the new institutions (compared to the relative riches of older Eastern colleges) generated a utilitarian architecture and introduced new types of buildings and campus arrangements. At Cornell, in architecture as in educational policy, there was a blending of the old spirit of the East and the inventive vigor of the West.

Ezra Cornell's purpose was to "place the benefits of higher education at the disposal of the industrial and productive classes of society." Cornell's first President, Andrew Dickson White, had strong convictions that American university curricula needed major reforms to permit more choice of studies, to

elevate scientific and professional courses to the position of the classical course, and to free colleges and universities from secular controls.

In short, in a time when there were only colleges in the land, Cornell and White helped to invent the modern American university. Cornell University was an exciting place in the nineteenth and early twentieth centuries, when Ezra Cornell, Andrew White, Henry Sage, Charles Kendall Adams, Jacob Gould Schurman, Liberty Hyde Bailey, and members of the faculty and student body participated in the evolution of a university that Allan Nevins called "the most remarkable phenomenon in higher education in the post-war decade." What follows here is a historical account of the campus which grew out of and served these educational achievements and which now, as it continues to evolve, symbolizes as well as serves the ideas and ideals of its builders.

The first five chapters are about the founders, their experience in planning, architecture, and building, and their decisions about the location of the campus, its overall plan, and the design of the first buildings. Chapter VI is an examination of the effects of these decisions on campus and community life in the first decade of Cornell. The domestic arrangements of the many Cornell faculty who lived on the campus in the first fifty years and the more imposing homes of the wealthy Ithaca families associated with Cornell in its early years are the subjects of Chapter VII.

Three chapters (VIII, IX, and X) are devoted to an examination of the planning and building activity of the eighties and nineties, including a detailed study of Cornell's most significant architectural symbol, William Henry Miller's library building and tower. The great campus expansion which began shortly after the turn of the century and the emergence of overall campus planning as a force in university development are discussed in Chapter XI. Chapter XII describes a very significant era of campus planning at Cornell, including the contributions of landscape architects Charles N. Lowrie, Bryant Fleming, and Warren Manning, and reviews the emergence of the College of Agriculture as a major component of the University. Chapter XIII is devoted to the realization of Andrew D. White's vision of Cornell and to the evolution of a campus development planning process. A final chapter reports on the major changes in the campus and in campus planning which have taken place during the last thirty years of Cornell's rapid growth.

Campus planning has become a necessary and continuing staff operation for the guidance of growth in most major American universities. The experience at Cornell from the earliest work of Frederick Law Olmsted to the recent organization of a full-time planning staff is but prologue to the continuing fulfillment of revolutions in higher education and campus development initiated by Ezra Cornell and Andrew D. White in 1865.

THE CORNELL CAMPUS

A History of Its Planning and Development

The Founders and a Prophecy

CORNELL WAS IN MANY RE-
spects a prototype for the twen-
tieth-century American university: it was di-
versified in the subject matter taught and in the
interests of students and faculty. It was both
academic and pragmatic, theoretical and
practical, classical and scientific—concerned
with advancing knowledge through research
and providing professional and vocational
training. As this new form of institution developed, its campus became a mirror for the
increasing diversity of American higher education. Cornell displayed all of the architectural and landscape symbols of what
President Clark Kerr of the University of
California has now dubbed the "multi-
versity." [1] Its campus became and is a veritable
museum of the building types, forms, and
styles of American university architecture and
campus planning.

The formative ideas for Cornell's early architecture and campus development were determined by its Founder, Ezra Cornell, and its
first President, Andrew Dickson White. But
Frederick Law Olmsted, the University's first
landscape advisor, prophesied the final outcome. White's radical educational ideas, the

difficult financial circumstances of the early
years, the magnificence of the campus site,
and events we smugly call "historical acci-
dents" all influenced the physical form of the
University. These factors shaped the Cornell
campus through the three men who made the
first decisions about its buildings and plan.

The University in Ithaca began reflecting
its diversity of educational activities in its architecture and campus plan at an early date.
The Founder and first President saw to that,
and Olmsted, who advised them at an important moment, helped preserve order in the
initial key development. In 1867 he told them
they should seek variety within unity in the
arrangement of the campus. Carl Becker, Cornell historian, reviewed the outcome of this
advice seventy-five years later and concluded
that the "variety" part of the recommendation
had been achieved. [2] A subtle unity has been
achieved on the campus, too. To perceive this
unity we must know something of the architectural ideas and objectives of the men who
built it.

Ezra Cornell wanted as many durable, useful buildings as he could get. He wanted to
make it possible for Cornellians to survey the
sweeping landscape of the Cayuga Lake valley, and he wanted the town to see University
buildings on the hill against the skyline. Andrew D. White, though he was a scholarly

[1] Clark Kerr, *The Uses of the University* (Cambridge, Mass., 1963), p. 6. Kerr uses the term to
emphasize the difference between the diffused feder-
ated interests of a large modern university and Flex-
ner's "modern university"—"an organism, characterized by highness and definiteness of aim, unity of
spirit and purpose."

[2] Carl L. Becker, *Cornell University: Founders and
the Founding* (Ithaca, 1943), p. 127.

1

Fig. 1. Ezra Cornell, 1862.

Each of these men was an idealist; each was an innovator; and each was a compulsive traveler. Cornell walked enormous distances in Georgia and Maine selling a patented plow; he also traveled all over the Northeast building telegraph lines; but his true home was in Ithaca, at the head of Cayuga Lake. White's heart and mind and self were constantly returning to Europe and reweaving European ideas and experience. He spent almost twenty years of his life in Europe as a student, traveler, and statesman. Olmsted's travels spanned the continent. His pre–Civil War tours of the South are well known. He also fostered, designed, and built our first great city parks, in New York, San Francisco, Boston, Buffalo, Detroit, Cincinnati, and Chicago. He participated in the invention of suburbia and helped to shape the emerging form of fourteen college and university campuses.[4] At Cornell, in the important first years of campus development, Ezra Cornell supplied the initial order of the plan and a drive to build; Andrew D. White supplied architectural taste and a forceful concern for propriety and beauty; and Frederick Law Olmsted supplied a prophecy of campus form and some practical ideas about the adaptation and achievement of Cornell's basic plan.

Ezra Cornell was a practical man. In his role in the development of the Cornell campus he was controlled by a concern for firmness, commodity, and economy in building. He did care about Sir Henry Wotton's third principle of good architecture—delight —but he was pragmatic enough to place economy in building and savings in architectural fees before what he considered architectural extravagance. He preferred a plain style.

Cornell's experience in building had taught him much about dealing with architects, builders, material suppliers, and building committees. At the age of sixteen he laid out and erected a frame house, and when he came to Ithaca, in 1828, he was a journeyman car-

revolutionist in most matters of higher education, admired the traditional ordered beauty of collegiate quadrangles. He wanted the new University to have a dignified symbolic architecture replete with memorials commemorating the ideals, ideas, and people who made the place. Olmsted's concepts were more subtle and complex. He thought the new land-grant colleges and American communities would assume almost identical forms in which growth and change would require flexible, extendible plans. He also predicted a movement in American society from what he termed a Puritan reaction to "merrie England" toward a new freedom where many men would participate in community affairs, enjoy full family lives, carry on intellectual pursuits, and still have time to make their daily bread.[3] He believed that this new way of life would shape new kinds of communities and new kinds of college campuses.

[3] Frederick Law Olmsted, *A Few Things to Be Thought of before Proceeding to Plan the National Agricultural Colleges* (New York, 1866), pp. 12 ff.

[4] *Frederick Law Olmsted, A Register of His Papers in the Library of Congress* (Washington, 1963), p. 9.

penter. Later, when he worked as the manager, mechanic, and millwright at Colonel Jeremiah Beebe's mills at the foot of Ithaca Falls, he superintended the blasting of a long tunnel through the rock wall of the gorge to tap the water power of Fall Creek, and he built a stone dam at Triphammer Falls to conserve the Creek's water supply. He had built sawmills, and now he built machinery, workshops, and several houses, including his own, near the mills.

In the 1840's and 1850's he managed the construction of Samuel Morse's first telegraph line and of many of his own.[5] Ezra Cornell could organize a building operation from the quarry to the finish trim. So by 1860, when income from investments of labor and salary in telegraph lines made him a millionaire, he was well qualified to superintend as well as finance his extensive philanthropic building projects. His handling of the first of these, the Cornell Public Library, foreshadowed a decade of selfless building, unconventional financing, and conflicts with architects and building contractors.

Cornell first conceived the idea of building a free public library for Ithaca in 1862. He drew rough sketches and had them "perfected" by William Hodgins, an Albany architect. There was no doubt about Cornell's command of the project. His son Alonzo, who assisted his father in business affairs, did not like the first plans produced by the architect. He did not like the elevations, the steeple, or the stairway, and he preferred a plainer style. Although Ezra Cornell must have agreed with most of the criticisms, he did approve the steeple—a $500–$1,000 frill which Alonzo protested cost too much.[6] The approval of the

steeple may have been a symbol of Cornell's refusal to be bound entirely by his frugal Quaker background. Since this was a special community building, a small counterpart of the steeple on the nearby village hall might have seemed to him worth the added expenditure.

There are several indications of Cornell's tendency to innovate in the establishment of the library. He set up a broadly representative board of trustees and he provided for continuing income from the property. The trustees were to include pastors of all seven local churches, the principals of the local academy and public school, three officials of village and county government, six citizens (whose terms were to be staggered), and the Founder or his eldest male lineal descendant. Such composition guaranteed broad, representative control of the library and, one might predict, extended board meetings. The design of the library building provided space on the first and third floors for a bank and commercial offices whose rents would assure income for the maintenance, operation, and growth of the library. As the idea of using the new library building for a community center grew, some features were added: an auditorium seating eight hundred, the Post Office, rooms for the newly formed DeWitt Historical Society, and a "Military Hall" in the basement for the DeWitt Guards. The auditorium, some office space, and part of the library were pressed into service by the space-short Uni-

[5] There are a number of good accounts of Ezra Cornell's life. Becker's in *Cornell University: Founders and the Founding* is brief but perceptive and well documented. The notes for Becker's Chapter II provide a useful guide to materials on Cornell's life. See also Chapter II in Morris Bishop's *A History of Cornell* (Ithaca, 1963). For an extended account see Philip Dorf, *The Builder* (Ithaca, 1952).

[6] MS, "Dedication of the Cornell Library," 5 April 1866, Cornell Papers; Alonzo B. Cornell to EC, 22 March 1863, Cornell Papers. The Cornell Papers, as in

general others of unspecified provenience, are in the Cornell University Archives. William Hodgins to EC, 10, 11, and 24 June 1863, Cornell Papers, Cornell Public Library, Ithaca, N.Y. Hodgins did not visit Ithaca to see the site because of the press of time and the limited fee. In his letter of 11 June 1863, accompanying the finished plans, he refers to the problems which might develop because of this lack of direct information. Several revisions were necessary to incorporate changes, so the architect added $75.00 to the $125.00 agreed fee. Cornell was willing to pay only $25.00 extra and so began what seems to have been the Founder's first debate with an architect over fees. In 1864, Messrs. Nichols and Brown succeeded to Hodgins' practice in Albany. Cornell retained them to design Cascadilla and his new mansion, and to provide design ideas for Morrill Hall.

versity in 1868. Distinguished nonresident professors including Goldwin Smith, John Fiske, Louis Agassiz, James Russell Lowell, Theodore Dwight, and George William Curtis gave their lectures in the auditorium, and tickets were sold to the townspeople. The University faculty held its first meetings there as did the Board of Trustees in the early years when they met in Ithaca.

Cornell took personal charge of selecting and buying materials for the library, a three-storied brick building which, it is sad to say, was demolished in 1961. He also personally supervised construction. Its stone foundation walls were nearly four feet thick. The *Ithaca Journal* commented: "Some of the massive blocks must weigh a ton. There can be no danger of its not standing firm as a rock."[7] Cornell was firm, too, so when on their first day of work Ithaca stonecutters struck for a raise, he went to Syracuse and purchased the necessary stone already cut at a delivered price lower than he had originally agreed to pay the Ithaca workmen.

The Cornell Public Library (Fig. 2) was a

Fig. 2. Cornell Public Library (1863), Ithaca, New York; William Hodgins, architect. This project was one of Ezra Cornell's first major philanthropic efforts.

[7] *Ithaca Journal and Advertiser*, 15 July 1863.

serenely composed, economical red-brick building with a limestone base, horizontal bands of delicate brick ornament, a lightly decorated entrance, a thin limestone string course separating the first and second levels, a noble second public level, and a mansard roof with quiet dormers. The tall windows of the first and second floors were broken into groups of three by brick pilasters. And the brick mullions separating the windows of each triplet were shaped to simulate colonnettes with a single order on the first floor and supercolumniation above. The long areaways reached to the floor level of the basement providing good light and air for the military hall and rental space located there. The library had architectural reserve and dignity in an era when public architecture was often ornate and showy. Its simplicity and compact massing spoke of a client who preferred space rather than rich materials or decoration for his money, yet believed that the durability of the institution would be served by solid construction and that a library building needed to be something more than a warehouse for books.

Early in 1864, Cornell was the principal mover in another civic project in Ithaca, the establishment of a water cure. Its supporters, thirty-two civic-minded Ithacans, hoped it would help make the village a health resort. Dr. Samantha Nivison, proprietor of the water cure at Dryden Springs twelve miles east of Ithaca, had enlisted Ezra Cornell's support for the project, and he carried the principal burden of financing, supervising the design, and overseeing the construction of the building, soon known as "The Cascadilla," in which it was to be housed. Goldwin Smith later (and rather uncharitably) remarked that the building was "so ill-ventilated that as many patients would probably have been killed by the air as would have been saved by the water."[8] He spoke from experience: he lived there on-and-off for three years after the idea of a water cure had been abandoned and

[8] Goldwin Smith, *Reminiscences* (New York, 1911), p. 374.

the University had leased the structure. Plans for "The Cascadilla" were prepared by Nichols and Brown of Albany, successors to Mr. Hodgins' practice.[9] Its ponderous stone mass set the style of Cornell University's first buildings. And its labyrinth of corridors and small rooms was destined to become the University's all-purpose dormitory, faculty apartment, classroom building, and social center—the "family hotel" of the early years. Its designers, Nichols and Brown, were later the "victims" of Ezra Cornell's offhand dealings with architects in the "competition" for the design of the first buildings for the University's quadrangle.

The Cascadilla was and is a useful but ungainly building. An unknown critic of the seventies wrote that it was not a crime "to mistake it for a generously windowed fort." [10] The windows are indeed numerous but quite small in relation to the broad stone walls. Early sketches indicate that the architects intended to provide more windows. If this design had been executed, Cascadilla would have a less forbidding appearance. Stone for the building was quarried from the rocky gorge of Cascadilla Creek in the Giant's Staircase Falls below Central Avenue Bridge. The monotony of its smooth-faced but irregularly cut stone walls and pilasters of the same stone in larger units (Fig. 3) may well have prompted the use of rough-cut stone for the walls and the addition of lighter rusticated medina-stone quoins at the angles of later university buildings on the quadrangle.

Over the years numerous attempts were made to improve the utilitarian and heavy-handed appearance of Cascadilla. An oriel window was added on the south over a secondary entrance, ornament was proposed in

Fig. 3. Cascadilla Place (1866), Nichols and Brown, architects. This building was designed to house a "water cure" establishment, but was pressed into service as a dormitory and faculty apartment building in 1868. Eddy Street is in the foreground.

various combinations, and porches were proposed here and then there, but the building resisted all efforts. Locally published guide books sometimes omitted mention or pictures of Cascadilla, but it endured and still endures such neglect: a solid, serviceable, much-abused but architecturally significant reminder of the vast but austere philanthropic enterprise of the Founder—useful but hardly beautiful.

Ezra Cornell was not insensitive to beauty. He simply knew what he wanted. If the things he wanted in buildings were not always beautiful, it was probably because the service of some social or practical end indicated a need for economy. His discriptions of the landscape in letters written to his wife during extensive travels reveal an appreciation of natural beauty; and his determination to build Cornell University on that portion of his hilltop farm which afforded the best view of the Cayuga Lake valley, rather than a lower site more convenient to the town, has provided generations of Cornellians with dramatic and beautiful views from the campus.

[9] *Albany City Directories* (1863, 1864). Thirty-one of the Cascadilla stockholders gave their collective $16,640 interest to the University for a collective consideration of thirty-one dollars in 1869. The share of the remaining stockholder, Ezra Cornell, was purchased by the University from his estate for $37,100 in 1878 (Cornell University Trustees' *Proceedings,* 8 April 1869 and 18 June 1878).

[10] *The History of Tioga, Tompkins, and Schuyler Counties, N.Y.* (Ithaca, 1879).

Fig. 4. Ezra Cornell's villa, "Llenroc," west elevation by Nichols and Brown, 1865.

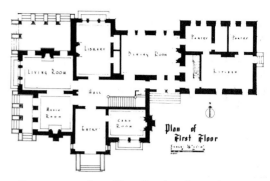

Fig. 5. Ezra Cornell's villa, first-floor plan. Completed after the Founder's death, it was occupied by his family until 1911, when it was purchased by Delta Phi fraternity. The "card room" was the study.

Cornell's villa (Figs. 4–7), built on a large site below the university campus, is Ithaca's most elegant "post–Civil War Gothic" residence. Nichols and Brown, purportedly with the assistance of Thomas Fuller, architect of the Canadian Houses of Parliament and the New York State Capitol, were the architects for this building in 1865.[11] It was Ezra Cornell's only architectural extravagance, but he did not have the pleasure of living in it, since it was not finished until 1875, the year after he died. Construction of the villa was delayed until 1867 because of the press of university building projects and the shortage of skilled masons, but when it did get underway, Cornell took great delight in the progress of the work. Professor Burt G. Wilder made his first trip to Ithaca in the fall of 1867, and Ezra

Cornell drove him in and around the city. Near the Cayuga Lake Inlet, Italian workmen were carving stone for the villa. Wilder observed that the Founder expressed "a genuine and superior artistic pleasure at the execution of the carvings."[12] White remembered that the usually impatient Cornell had no objection if a carver took a month or more to complete a single capital.

The villa was built to last. The limestone facing of its three-foot-thick masonry walls is set in thin beds of mortar and backed up by several feet of local stone precisely laid. The quality of the latter work, which can be seen in the basement, is comparable to the best local exterior ashlar masonry. The building is solid, rich, and somewhat ostentatious. While it is fairly large (110 feet long and 60 feet wide) its massiveness is broken up by an honest exterior expression of the pinwheel arrangement of its principal rooms around a central hall. The resultant rich variety in massing and roof line is further enriched by elaborate and varied ornament. A thin, strongly projected string course at the sill line of the second-floor windows creates a horizontal demarcation between the stories. This separation is reinforced and punctuated by broad, flat, bracketed sills which project

---

[11] Nichols and Brown to EC, 26 May 1865, Cornell Papers. Villa No. 18 in C. J. Richardson, *Picturesque Designs for Mansions, Villas and Lodges* (London, 1870), is in a style very like that of Cornell's villa. Richardson places his design in "the domestic style of the reign of Henry the VII" (1485–1509). This is a late Gothic period and so perhaps not a very proper Ruskinian model. Nichols and Brown's drawings for the house are in the possession of Delta Phi fraternity, which now owns and has beautifully maintained the villa in its original form. When the fraternity purchased the building, Andrew D. White wrote them (7 June 1911) an account of it in which he names Thomas Fuller as its architect. In 1868 Nichols and Brown shared an office with Fuller, who had arrived in Albany in 1865.

[12] Burt G. Wilder, "Reminiscences of Ezra Cornell," in *The Cornell Era* (May 1907). The account was based on Professor Wilder's diaries.

Fig. 6. Ezra Cornell's villa from the south.

from the upper windows of the gable-ends to create deep shadows over the entry and west window of the living room. The carving of the delicate bossy capitals of the porch columns and colonnettes between the windows is repeated on carved brackets set in the walls, on the corner posts at the ends of the column lines and on similar carved brackets set in the window surrounds. Pointed-arch window surrounds and relieving arches terminate in crisply detailed bosses. And the small turrets which terminate the eave lines of the main gables rest upon three-quarter-round carved brackets which embrace the corners of these wings.

The main entry gable (Fig. 7) is an especially lively and well-balanced composition. It has almost all of the ornamental elements described above, and in addition a pair of finely carved roundels is set in the wall below the string course. Unfortunately, the latter are obscured in most seasons by ivy which also, perhaps fortunately, camouflages the chimney just left of the entrance. This chimney, the most playful element of the villa, competed with the entry for attention until the growth of vines sublimated its more vulgar details. It has a short, capped buttress at its base, a

string course, whose outer ends rest on corbeled brackets at the eave level of the adjacent porch, another string course at the second-floor window-sill line, this one broken by

Fig. 7. Ezra Cornell's villa, entrance.

a pointed-arch niche, yet another string course level with the tops of the jerkinhead rooflets of the third-story dormers, a slim deep niche under the chimney cap, and, finally, a broad cap-cornice ornamented with carved bosses and topped by a sloping chimney cap. It is, in all, a very remarkable chimney. The bit of mansard roof behind it, which covers the southwest corner of the villa, is also somewhat remarkable and a little clumsy in relation to the adjoining gable roofs.

The arrangement of the interior is simple and clearly organized. A study for the owner is located to the right of the generous entrance hall. The other principal rooms (a parlor, sitting room, library, and dining room) are located off a long central hall north of the entry hall. The interior finish and ornament are as elaborately and expertly executed as their exterior counterparts. The plaster ceiling of the parlor is especially beautiful. The fireplace mantels are simply but beautifully detailed and the oak paneling and carving in the dining room are a delight.

While the villa was in the main built as designed, the architects later complained that in all the work they had done for Ezra Cornell their role had been to "outline the picture and allow other hands to fill it in without the chance to watch and foster the growth or have a voice in the after treatment." [13] Cornell dealt with the "after treatment" personally and he had an experienced craftsman's appreciation for good workmanship. This appreciation and the general shortage of highly skilled workmen in Ithaca led him to a policy of encouraging the immigration of building craftsmen from Europe. White recalls that Cornell employed German stone carvers who had recently left work on the Cathedral at Cologne to work on his villa. One of the chief recruiters of European workmen was Alonzo Cornell, Ezra's eldest son, who wrote to his father from England in the spring of 1869 that his orders in "looking out for the kind of men you want" were that they should be "young

men, Scotch, English, or German, without families and with money to pay their fares to Ithaca." He was also "to select only such men as will be likely to vote right when they become voters." [14]

One group of fourteen English craftsmen was recruited to come to Ithaca in 1869 when Cornell mentioned the need for such men to Goldwin Smith. They were carefully chosen under the auspices of Aubron Herbert who worked with members of the Parlimentary Trades Union Committee.[15] The committee members were the pioneers of the present English Labor Party and the first labor members of the House of Commons. The departure of the craftsmen was the occasion for a dinner in London. Several lords made speeches at this farewell dinner and the London and New York papers wrote about the migration in the spirit of "hands across the sea" and commended the University's concern for "combining handwork with headwork." [16] One stone carver, Louis Hinton, later remembered that "they went to Ithaca to work on Cornell's villa, and perhaps, it was suggested, serve as trade instructors in the new Agricultural and Technical College." [17]

On their arrival in Ithaca, the workmen were disappointed in two respects: the wages were not what they had expected, and they found their skills were much greater than the work required. Hinton wrote to the *London Spectator* that they "worked at Mr. Cornell's villa [and] the five stonemasons were not the men required, the work for them being nothing but ashlar-work; five London Street

---

[13] Nichols and Brown to ADW, 8 May 1866, White Papers.

[14] A. B. Cornell to EC, 14 May 1869, Cornell Papers.

[15] Louis J. Hinton, MS, "Recollections" (c. 1926), Capitol Papers, New York State Library, Albany. Hinton describes his participation in the parliamentary reform movement including "two full years of intense agitations, mass meetings, radical oratory and street parades . . . in the aristocrats' districts, scaring them rather badly." Hinton was later (1893) foreman of sculptors on the "million dollar staircase" at the N.Y. State Capitol in Albany and the sculptor of much of the carved ornament in the All Saints Episcopal Cathedral in the same city.

[16] *New York Times*, 7 July 1869.

[17] Hinton, *op. cit.*, p. 5.

paviors would have just suited. The care displayed . . . in selecting none but good thorough stonemasons was thrown away, rough and strong-limbed ashlar-wallers being what was wanted." [18]

But the men liked Ithaca and the wage issue was soon settled through Goldwin Smith's good offices.[19] They marveled at local scenic beauty: One of them wrote that "if its like were to be found in Europe, it would have legends, stories, and poems written around and about its countless charms." They liked Mr. Cornell and the way of life—except boarding-house cooking. So, most of them remained for at least a few years. Many went to work on White Hall, the second major building on the campus. A comparison of the quality of its masonry work with that of its immediate predecessor, Morrill Hall, shows the improvement this new talent effected. Some of these workmen settled in Ithaca. Robert Richardson, a stonemason (stone carver) stayed his lifetime and did beautiful work on President White's villa, Sage College, Sage Chapel, the old Armory, Barnes Hall, and many local houses including Jennie McGraw Fiske's mansion (Figs. 10, 11, 55, 69, 101, 110, and 117). John Snaith, a carpenter, became a contractor and worked in Ithaca until 1888. His first major contracts were for building Sage Chapel and President White's villa.[20] Of his adventures after 1888 we will hear later. Will Temple and Francis Dobson,

carpenters, and Noah Kirk, mason, were still in business in Ithaca in the middle seventies. Ezra Cornell recruited some fine building craftsmen for Ithaca and the University, and he brought his own substantial experience in major building projects to bear on the first campus construction.

Cornell supervised the contractor's work personally. In February 1867, he wrote in his report to the Trustees:

In the main the work is progressing satisfactory [*sic*] though a constant watching has been necessary to prevent the masons from setting stones on edge and thus exposing a slab side to the weather. I had occasion also to complain about the lack of suitable ties in the roof to give it requisite strength. [The contractor] assured me that the defect should be properly remedied and I trust that it has been done. If not I will see that it is done.

While Cornell and White shared the ideal of founding a great university, they were strikingly different in personality and interests: Cornell, reserved but at times sharp-tongued, was a builder, mechanic, inventor, businessman, and philanthropist; White, voluble and diplomatic, was a gentleman, scholar, teacher, bibliophile, statesman, and champion of many causes including morality in architecture. Their personalities, ideas, and interests were different but complementary in the building of Cornell University. This was as true for their ideas on architecture and campus development as it was in other matters.

Andrew D. White's earliest interest in architecture was intellectual and emotional. He reacted strongly to buildings and pictures of buildings. He was probably what psychologists might now call a visualizer; that is, one who thinks of situations and places as mental pictures, one who "sees" imaginary landscapes and structures. There is a beautiful passage in White's *Autobiography* [21] in which he describes his first vision of a great university. After reading Cardinal Newman's

[18] Hinton, "The Workingman in America," *The Spectator*, London, 27 November 1869.
[19] EC to ADW, 18 July 1869, White Papers. Goldwin Smith explained the source of the "difference about wages" as a "difference in the trade requirements of the two countries" and "partially a notion [in England] that college buildings must be something ornamental" (Smith to ADW, 12 July 1869, White Papers). Smith had a high opinion of them: "They are also worthy people . . . well spoken of in the village . . . they cling to Ithaca . . . may be a good element there. . . . Mr. Cornell has received them with kindness of which they are well pleased" (Smith to ADW, 15 August 1869, White Papers).
[20] *Proceedings of the Board of Trustees of Cornell University*, April 1865–July 1885 (Ithaca, 1940), Sage Chapel Fund, Ledger, and Check book. Snaith had the contract for "mason and carpenter work" at $19,158; Robert Richardson, for carved stone at $970.
[21] Andrew D. White, *Autobiography of Andrew Dickson White* (New York, 1905), I, 287.

Fig. 8. Andrew Dickson White about 1868.

tiful and dignified buildings like those at Oxford and Cambridge rise in place of the "sordid" architecture of Hobart College, where he was then enduring the role of a disillusioned freshman. The copy of Cardinal Newman's translation of Huber's book in Cornell's Olin Library has a few rather listless illustrations of halls at Oxford and Cambridge. Few exteriors are shown. Perhaps the copy in the Hobart Library was more beautifully illustrated, or perhaps White was capable of great architectural visions with little stimulation. Yet, however stimulated, his youthful visions of a beautiful university campus were powerful and enduring.

In the following year (1850) White transferred to Yale College and there met Daniel Coit Gilman who was having a few architectural visions, too. Gilman, who is perhaps best known as the first President of Johns Hopkins University, and White became lifelong friends. White was probably much influenced by Gilman, who had already joined his interest in university quality to an interest in architectural quality. He had strong opinions about Yale's buildings (Fig. 9). At the begin-

translation of Huber's book on the English university, he says he "saw the handsome home worthy of a great university" with beau-

Fig. 9. "A muses' factory" at Yale, North College (1821). All the dormitories in the brick row except Connecticut Hall were demolished in the last half of the nineteenth century.

ning of White's junior year, Gilman, a senior, delivered an oration in which he asked Yalemen to "adorn and beautify the place; to let art as well as science be cultivated, elegance as well as excellence pertain to everything around." He concluded, "To be sure,

There in red brick which softening time defies
Stand square and stiff the muses' factories;

and yet our efforts . . . may do much to improve as well as adorn." "When," asked Gilman, in the same 1851 issue of the *Yale Literary Magazine* in which his oration was published, "will the sons of Yale [provide her with] a habitation whose architectural appearance will [match] her . . . reputation?" [22]

Gilman would not have long to wait. Many eastern intellectuals were acquiring a taste for the "Gothic" style of building. Now it seemed that even Yale's Congregational builders of a reserved Puritan architecture had come to believe with Pugin and Ruskin that "Gothic" was the true Christian style. Yale's "Gothic" Library had been completed in 1846 and Alumni Hall followed in 1852. Student editor White watched the construction of Alumni Hall with great interest. A new Yale campus was in the making and the plain brick row of "muses' factories" was doomed.

White admired only the new "Gothic Revival" buildings at Yale, and in his senior year, when he followed Gilman as an editor of the *Yale Literary Magazine,* he continued Gilman's attack on the "brick barracks." Most of White's signed articles in the magazine are on historical, political, or governmental topics, but he was developing an increased interest in art and architecture. In "One Suggestion to College Architects," probably written by White, the buildings of Yale's brick row were said to "pretend to nothing except utility" and that "poor stuccoed casket" (Trumbull Gal-

lery) had merit only because "it convinces us never to do it again." [23] The author notes that he has just read Ruskin's *The Seven Lamps of Architecture.* He is thoroughly convinced that architecture should contribute to education and teach lessons in morality.

In December 1853, after White had graduated from Yale and Gilman had completed a year of study in Cambridge, Massachusetts, they left for Europe to study and take up positions in the U.S. Embassy in St. Petersburg. There is some indication in their later correspondence that White and Gilman had started to plan an academic and architectural revolution at Yale. A few years of European study and travel were to prepare them for this effort. Early in 1856, Gilman returned to Yale to be Professor of Geography and Librarian. White stayed a while longer, continuing to make purchases for his architectural library, studying, traveling, and making a special point of visiting the great Gothic cathedrals. But his predilection for this style did not blind him to the building innovations of the age. During a visit to the baths at Weisbaden in 1855 he admired the iron pavilions about the springs and wrote in his diary: "They are beautiful. I am satisfied that the architecture of this age is to be in iron, spite of Ruskin, and these things pleased me." [24]

By 1856, Andrew D. White's plans for a career seemed clear. He was preparing for a professorship in the history of art at Yale. Gilman wrote to him in June that his name had been mentioned "in connection with a professorship of Aesthetics including the History of Criticism of Architecture and other Fine Arts." [25] White returned to New Haven in 1857, studied, delivered a series of lectures, and assisted with an exhibition. One of his lectures, entitled "Cathedral Builders and Medieval Sculptors," was subsequently reworked

[22] Daniel C. Gilman, "The Claims of Yale College to the Regard of Its Students" and "Improvements in College Buildings," *Yale Literary Magazine* XVII, No. 2 (1851). The second article is unsigned but in the copy in the New York State Library (inscribed: "courtesy of A. D. White") Gilman's name is written next to the title in the Table of Contents.

[23] Anonymous (initialed "W"), "One Suggestion for College Architects," *Yale Literary Magazine,* XVII (1853), 240 ff.
[24] Robert M. Ogden (ed.), *The Diaries of Andrew D. White* (Ithaca, 1955), p. 88, 26 August 1855.
[25] Daniel C. Gilman to ADW, 20 June 1856, White Papers.

and delivered on many occasions. The offer of a professorship at Yale did not materialize, however. White supposed that the reason was that he did not have the proper religious views.[26] So, in October 1857, he accepted a position teaching history at the University of Michigan under President Henry Tappan, his friend from European tours. White later credited much of his achievement as a university president to the tutelage of Tappan and indeed many of their views on university reform were almost precisely alike.[27]

In September 1857, White married Mary A. Outwater of Syracuse. With his new wife, his now magnificent library, his grand piano, and his sparkling conversation, White became a center of the cultural and social life of Ann Arbor. His lectures there from 1857 to 1862 made use of much of the illustrative material on art and architecture he had collected in Europe. At Michigan, White continued his personal attempts to beautify the college scene by planting elms in the quadrangle and stimulating the students to follow his example. "Without permission from any one" he began planting trees, "established several avenues and set out elms to overshadow them." He watered them, added some evergreens and "preached . . . the doctrine of adorning the campus." The students joined his enterprise. Finally, the University appointed him "superintendent of grounds" with a seventy-five dollar annual budget.[28] The beautiful academic

grove along the "Diag" at Michigan has resulted from White's efforts.

While White was teaching and planting in Ann Arbor, an 1857–1858 lecture series on art in New Haven was having a sustained influence. "From that time," one Yale historian reports, "there had been firm determination to establish a separate department devoted to it." Mr. Augustus Street turned determination into fact by giving the college an art school building in 1862. In 1863, White sat with Gilman and Noah Porter on the committee which selected the architect, Peter Wight. Street wanted to "establish a school for practical instruction [of professionals] and to awake and cultivate . . . taste for appreciation of the arts among undergraduates and others." The architect, Wight, was a member of the Society for the Advancement of Truth in Art, a band of pre-Raphaelite followers of Ruskin.[29] The second "Gothic Revival" was about to come into its full architectural inheritance at Yale.

White left the University of Michigan on leave in 1862 after having failed to pass the physical examination when he volunteered for service in the Union forces. He represented the cause of the Union in Europe and returned to New York in the fall of 1863. He was elected to the New York Legislature that November. When the Legislature convened in Albany in January 1864, White found there a man "tall, spare, and austere, with a kindly eye saying little, and that little dryly. . . . This was—Ezra Cornell." Soon they began their brief struggle over the disposition of New York's share in the land grant provided

[26] ADW to Clara D. White, 23 July 1857, White Papers, and first draft of White, *Autobiography* quoted in Becker, *op. cit.*, p. 239. White apparently was given an unfavorable reference by a good friend who was "rigid" in religion. White took no interest in prayer meetings which his friend thought "all important."

[27] The reforms suggested in Henry Tappan's *University Education* (New York, 1851) may have been familiar to White even before he taught at Michigan. Many of their views were based on their experience in the German and French universities.

[28] White, *Autobiography*, I, 282–283. See also Walter F. Willcox, "White's Trees," *The Cornell Plantations* (Winter 1956), for an account of White's returning to the Michigan campus in 1912, old planting plan in hand, to inspect the trees planted by the class of 1861 under his supervision; and Albert Bush-Brown, "The Image of a University" (unpublished

Ph.D. dissertation, Yale, 1958). White was not the first to attempt to beautify the Michigan campus. In 1854, Mr. E. Andrews, Superintendent of Grounds and Buildings, proposed the planting of 1,640 trees on the campus. Citizens of Ann Arbor were to plant on the town side of the surrounding streets, students and professors, on the campus side of these streets, and the Regents were to appropriate $50 a year for planting inside the campus (University of Michigan Regents Proceedings, 1837–1864, p. 590).

[29] W. F. Decrow, *Yale and the City of Elms* (Boston, 1882), p. 52. For the views of the American pre-Raphaelite group see their journal *New Path* (1863–1865) and David H. Dickason, *The Daring Young Men* (Bloomington, Ill., 1953).

for by the Morrill Act. Cornell did not object to a proposal to distribute New York's share to a number of institutions. White insisted that the grant should be kept intact and used to establish a great university. Cornell finally agreed to White's position, and they joined forces in securing the grant for Cornell University.

By the spring of 1864, White was beginning to see that he might have to face a choice between the realization of his old plans for teaching the history of art and architecture at Yale and the glimmering possibilities of a role in the future of a great university of a new mold in New York State. The professorship of art at Yale, including the directorship of the Street School of Art, was offered to White in July 1866. By that time he was deeply involved in the affairs of Cornell University. He had led the battle to preserve New York's share of the Morrill Act's land grant intact and to assign it to Cornell University. He was a Cornell Trustee and he had been named a committee-of-one to draft a plan of organization for the new university. He had also received hints from Ezra Cornell that the Trustees might name him as the first President of Cornell. In mid-August Cornell wrote White, who was busily recruiting faculty on the east coast, that he would "occupy a commanding and influential position" if he would remain with Cornell.[30]

Thus, at the age of thirty-four, White found two alternative careers available to him at the same moment in time. He could have been head of Yale's new Street School of Art, which was moving into its new Ruskinian building. There were signs of reform in curriculum and teaching methods at Yale, and there were signs of "Gothic Revival" enterprise on Yale's campus, a place of long traditions and his

alma mater. Or he could be the president of a new university without, as yet, either faculty or buildings but whose goals and plans he was already shaping. On 12 November 1866, Gilman, who was soon to turn down an offer of the presidency of the University of Wisconsin, urged White to return to Yale. He thought White, in "discussing the fine arts in their relation to civilization and history, [could] work out a career of growing usefulness and happiness."[31] At the time White was busily recruiting faculty for Cornell and completing his Report on Organization. On 21 November he presented it to the Trustees and was elected President of the University. He explained to Gilman that he had been "forced to accept the position." He wrote: "It is with no small regret that I turn from the prospects at Yale. . . . I see my old dream of New Haven fading. . . . At some sacrifice, real estate interests were disposed of, Intangling Alliances [sic] severed . . . and a large store of works on art added to my library."[32] All this, done to prepare for a career of teaching the history of art and architecture at Yale, was now sacrificed to work at Cornell.

White's library of books on architecture and art was indeed, as he later maintained, "the best in the country . . . richer better than four times that of the Astor Library, Harvard University, and Yale combined." But the library had been, he admitted, "his pet extravagance."[33] In that last word lies the heart of the matter. Architecture and art were, after all, his second loves—extravagances. His first loves, diplomacy and educational policy, were to carry him to great achievement in the distinguished company of post-Civil War

[30] White, *Diaries*, p. 147, 27 July 1866, *Autobiography*, I, 127. On 27 July 1866, White noted: "Was today notified by Rev. Dr. Bacon on part of Corporation of Yale that they had elected me Professor and Director of Art Department." White must have informed Cornell soon afterward because Cornell soon wrote to White to dissuade him (EC to ADW, 15 August 1866, White Papers).

[31] Gilman to ADW, 12 November 1866, White Papers.
[32] ADW to Gilman, 10 August 1866, Gilman Papers.
[33] ADW to EC, 14 April 1870, Cornell Papers; and *Autobiography*, I, 75. White's architecture library, about 1,200 volumes, lovingly collected in his travels, contained some rare treasures. For another view of White's reluctance to accept the Cornell presidency see George Lincoln Burr's account in *D.A.B.* of Ezra Cornell's threat that he "would not go on with the University without White as President."

Fig. 10. Andrew Dickson White's villa, capital, left entry column. This and other sculpture for the White villa is the first work at Cornell done by Robert Richardson, an English stone carver dubbed *Magister de vivis lapidibus* by White.

Fig. 11. Andrew Dickson White's villa, right porch bracket by Robert Richardson.

American reformers of higher education. It surely must have occurred to him that he might accomplish some improvement in university campus design, architecture, and art at Cornell as a part of general university reform.

In November 1866, the Cornell University Board of Trustees elected White President of Cornell University. For over fifty years, he engaged all comers in a calm but persistent "diplomatic struggle" if he thought they were ignoring or defacing the architectural or landscape qualities he wanted at Cornell. He always had a clear mental picture of what the place should look like. The landscape, buildings, and monuments of the University were, to him, integral parts of higher education. They should recall the ideals and traditions of the institution. He decried the lack of this quality in the older institutions of the East—had been "painfully aware of the lack of . . . commemorative or poetical elements" during his life at Yale. He wrote: "One might frequent the buildings at Yale or Harvard or Brown, as they then were, for years, and see nothing of an architectural sort which had been put in its place for any other reason than bare utility." [34]

The present use of the President's House, which White built and lived in off and on for forty years, as the White Art Museum is the sort of commemorative poetical thing that would have pleased him. He had always wanted, but could never get, an art gallery at Cornell. Now his former home is one. The house itself is full of White's messages: "President Grant stood here"; "I loved books"; "I loved beautifully finished wood"; "By their fruits ye shall know them." The last reminder is illustrated in the richly carved stone brackets and capitals of the entry porch columns (Figs. 10 and 11). The right capital and bracket are carved all over with evil fruits—poison ivy, deadly nightshade—among which lurk rock demons—newts and lizards; the left

[34] White, *Autobiography,* I, 407.

capital and bracket are embellished with good fruits—the leaves and fruit of grapes and figs among which flit stone birds. These carvings are the first work done in Ithaca by Robert Richardson, one of the craftsmen summoned from England by Goldwin Smith for Ezra Cornell.

White preferred the "Gothic Revival" style. The President's House, which he built, is a proper villa built in one of the approved styles of the era. The first designs for it, prepared by George Hathorne, a New York City architect,[35] were an adaptation of Plan No. 33 in Calvert Vaux's pattern book, *Villas and Cottages* (Figs. 12 and 13). It appears that Hathorne's design for a "Gothic villa" was subsequently modified and "drawn up" by Cornell student William H. Miller, later architect for a number of the University's buildings. White later recalled that in 1870 he had admired the lines of an office building in Ithaca, found that Cornell student Miller was the architect, and forthwith hired him to work on the drawings for his house.[36] White probably also saw or heard about Miller's miraculous "Gothic" transformation of Cornell Trustee Francis Finch's house.

The President first contacted Hathorne in October 1869. During the spring of 1870 they discussed the design of a house for Goldwin Smith, who had had enough of Cascadilla, and in May 1870, Hathorne produced designs for a duplex house for Smith and Willard Fiske.[37] Later Professor Smith decided not to build, so Fiske erected half of the house for himself. White knew what he wanted for the President's House but Hathorne had trouble delivering it. He wrote White that he had "endeavored vainly to like the modification of Vaux No. 33." By the fall of 1870 Hathorne sent plans for the President's House and revised plans for a "cottage" for Smith and Fiske. Cottages for Professor Fiske, the University Librarian and Professor of Romance Languages, and Professor James Law of Veterinary Medicine were built in 1871. White met and corresponded with Hathorne through the summer and fall of 1870, but they could not arrive at a modification of "Vaux No. 33" that suited them. The Vaux design (Fig. 12) was varied only slightly in Hathorne's plan of 29 October (Fig. 13). Figure 14 is the plan of the villa White finally built. At the end of the year, White decided that it was too difficult to discuss the design by mail and he could not find time to go to New York to see Hathorne. Besides this, he had decided to resign the presidency. He thanked Hathorne, paid his bill, and filed the plans away. By the next spring the University's prospects and his continued leadership there seemed more assured. William Miller must have been retained in the spring of 1871 to work on the drawings for White's villa.

The President broke ground for his new home on 29 July 1871, but the progress of construction must have been unsatisfactory. In November he discharged his building superintendent, H. J. Smith, and engaged Charles Babcock, the first professor of architecture at Cornell, "to do the remaining architect work and superintend it."[38] By January 1872 the chimneys were capped and the roofs all boarded. The house must have been substantially completed by the spring of 1873.[39] White continued to embellish it. He and Babcock worried about the design of the balcony above the entrance. Babcock wanted to be

[35] Hathorne to ADW, 25 and 29 November 1870, White Papers. W. T. Hewett noted in *Landmarks of Tompkins County* (p. 502) that Miller was the architect for the house, but in his MS notes in a copy of that work used for preparing his *Cornell University: A History,* Hewett writes that on 29 October 1870, Hathorne sent plans for President White's house and on 9 November for Fiske's and Smith's cottage. There is a bill for Hathorne's services in 31 December 1870, White Papers.
[36] Bishop, *A History of Cornell,* p. 97.
[37] Trustees' *Proceedings,* 2 May 1870; S. S. Colt, *The Tourist's Guide Through the Empire State* (Albany, 1871) refers to the selection of a site for a large double house for Smith and Fiske.

[38] W. T. Hewett, *Cornell University: A History* (New York, 1905), I, 313; White, *Diaries,* p. 166, 29 July 1871, and p. 169, 29 November 1871.
[39] Babcock to ADW, 3 May 1873, White Papers. Receipt for payment in full of fee for detailed plans and supervision of house.

PERSPECTIVE VIEW.

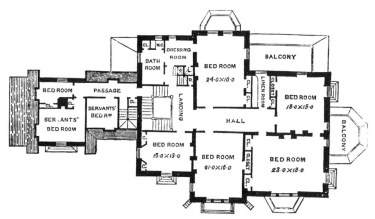

PLAN OF CHAMBERS.

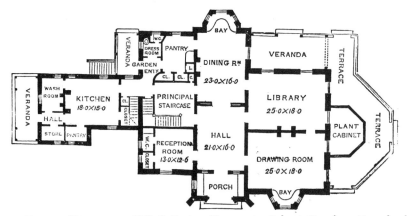

Fig. 12. "Picturesque Villa," Design No. 33, in Calvert Vaux's pattern book *Villas and Cottages* (1865). Annotations made by White about 1870 suggested a larger library and parlor, smaller sitting room and hall, and the addition of a conservatory.

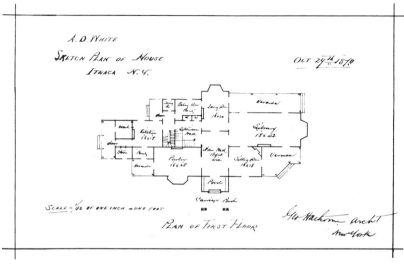

Fig. 13. Sketch plan for Andrew Dickson White's villa by George Hathorne, 1870, based on "Vaux No. 33."

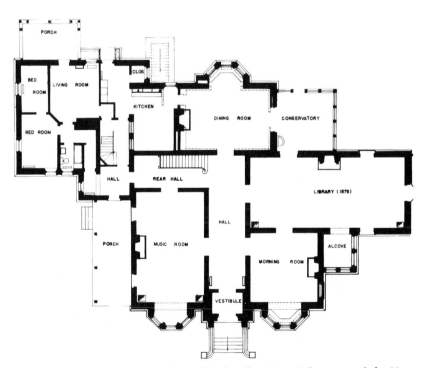

Fig. 14. Plan of Andrew Dickson White's villa, 1871. Refinements of the Vaux prototype are probably by William H. Miller with some final modifications by Charles Babcock.

Fig. 15. Andrew Dickson White's villa, viewed from the west. The south wing (to the right) was added in 1911, William H. Miller, architect.

Fig. 16. Andrew Dickson White's villa, entrance designed by Charles Babcock.

sure that its form and materials gave it a dignity befitting the President's House.[40] In the summer of 1874 carpenters were still setting the mantels and the President was getting his family ready to move in.[41] The long building campaign was partly a result of White's vacillation about his role as President of Cornell, but it may also tell us something about his desire for careful workmanship in the interior finish and embellishment of his villa. Morris Bishop, Cornell's historian, opines that it "still pleases the contemplative eye." Well, that is exactly what White wanted to achieve. The house as he built it and as he lived in it was more than a utilitarian home; it was, in Frederick Law Olmsted's terms, an example of how "an American of considerable responsibility" should live and a symbol of the dignity of the presidential office—a sermon in

[40] Babcock to ADW, 17 January 1872, White Papers.

[41] White, *Diaries*, p. 182, 4 and 23 June 1874. John Snaith was doing the final carpentry work.

Fig. 17. Andrew Dickson White in his library, about 1885.

brick and stone for the educational and moral benefit of Cornellians.

President White's concern for the appearance of the campus had its practical side, too. At least he emphasized this side in his obvious appeals to Ezra Cornell's sense of economy. In 1868, when Cornell announced his intention to erect a temporary wooden laboratory and workshop in the middle of the proposed stone quadrangle, White wrote:

Don't, I beg of you, put up your new building without regard to architectural style or position. . . . The place where we are must be made beautiful and attractive . . . make it beautiful as we can easily do with no great additional outlay and the best of scholars and thinkers will come to us . . . but make it rough and unsymmetrical and we shall gradually find that we can get the best men only by paying extravagant prices.[42]

Cornell built the temporary barnlike wooden laboratory building in the middle of the Quadrangle during White's absence in Europe. It was there, temporarily, from 1868 to 1890. White pestered Cornell to move it. Ezra Cornell's characteristic reply was that he would observe what White said. During the early years of their partnership, Cornell and White managed to balance each other without canceling each other out in most of the affairs of the University. But Ezra Cornell

[42] ADW to EC, 3 July 1868, White Papers (typed copy).

usually had his way in matters architectural.

The President wanted "sermons in stone" and he wanted a "general plan" for the future development of the campus. In the ambiguous and uncertain world of the University's first fifteen years from 1865 to 1880, half a dozen campus plans were prepared.[43] White was never satisfied with them. Then, during the five years of "reconstruction" from 1880 to 1885, everyone was too busy getting things done with the increased wealth from sales of western land to think of a campus plan. When White resigned the presidency in 1885, he made a special plea to the Trustees to prepare a campus plan. He assured them that "the atmosphere of sentiment which gathers about the University is a most powerful factor in its real success." He told them that if the campus was "hard, dry, and unattractive, its buildings mere boxes, its grounds a mere plot of earth for such boxes to stand upon," the University would "fail in one of the highest parts of its mission." He claimed there was educational value in "creating an atmosphere that would make students something more than machines." He urged the University to "enrich itself . . . with buildings which quicken the sense of beauty, in memorials which arouse love and veneration, in works of art which stimulate manliness, and in a general development of the treasures of beauty lying all about." To help accomplish these goals President White asked the Trustees to call in "the best architectural talent obtainable to make suggestions and prepare plans [for] the position of future buildings."[44]

Andrew D. White, who could seldom be accused of over-modesty in regard to his achievements or Cornell's, did not recognize the strength of the plans he and the Founder had already fixed for the campus. These plans, though incomplete on both paper and ground in 1885, were well started and firmly established in the conscience of the University: a broad Quadrangle of stone buildings would crown the brow of the hill; an informal group of red-brick buildings was to be placed south of the Quadrangle in a parklike setting, and a picturesque row of faculty "cottages" would line the edge of the plateau above these groups. The farm fields and buildings would be located farther east (Fig. 18). The first of many "clubhouses" for students on the campus had already been built in 1885.[45] Cornell was already developing in a pattern much like the prophecy of American university campus form made by Frederick Law Olmsted in 1866.

Before we discuss the early development of the Cornell campus, we should examine Olmsted's prophecy of campus form. It was an excellent forecast for Cornell and for American college and university campuses in general. National interest in establishing institutions for higher education in agriculture and "mechanic arts" was at least forty years old when the Morrill Act was passed in 1862,[46] but little thought had been given to the physical form such institutions should take. By 1865, Olmsted, who had been Executive Director of the U.S. Sanitary Commission in the early years of the Civil War, had an opportunity to think through the problems of these new campus forms. In 1864 he had prepared

[43] The early plans: (1) a Quadrangle plan, May 1866, probably by Wilcox and Porter, Architects of Buffalo; (2) a plan by Frederick Law Olmsted, September 1867; (3) a plan by Professor Prentiss, November 1871; (4) a plan by Professor Babcock, April 1873; (5) a plan by Major J. W. MacMurray, July 1873; (6) a plan by J. Widenmann, Landscape Architect and sometime associate of Olmsted, August 1874. Of the plans listed only (3) has been found in the University records. Information on the others is in the following: (1) *Ithaca Journal and Advertiser*, 6 June 1866; (2) White Papers and Olmsted Papers; (4) and (5) Trustees' *Proceedings;* and (6) White Papers and Trustees' *Proceedings.*

[44] White, Annual Report of the President, 1885, pp. 44–46, 67. The Trustees' lack of understanding or

agreement with White's desire to have a campus plan prepared by a skilled designer is shown by the wording of their resolution following his suggestion. It calls for retaining "a suitable architect *or draughtsman* to prepare and submit *for preservation* a plan or plans as contemplated in the President's report" (italics supplied).

[45] *Ibid.,* p. 43. This was the Kappa Alpha House just east of the Central Avenue Bridge over Cascadilla Creek.

[46] Simeon DeWitt, *Considerations on the Necessity of Establishing an Agricultural College* (Albany, 1819); quoted in Bishop, *A History of Cornell*, p. 53.

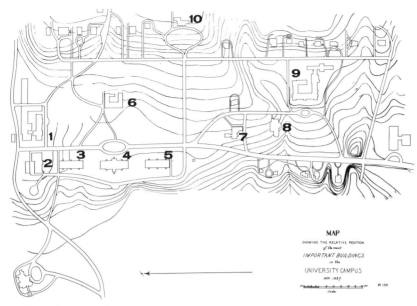

Fig. 18. Map of the Cornell University campus, November 1887: 1—West Sibley Hall (1870); 2—Franklin Hall (1881); 3—White Hall (1867); 4—McGraw Hall (1869); 5—Morrill Hall (1866); 6—Wooden Laboratory Building (1868–1892); 7—Sage Chapel (1872); 8—Barnes Hall (1887); 9—Sage College (1872); 10—President White's villa (1871). Faculty houses are shown above East Avenue at the top and below Central Avenue at lower right. The contour interval is five feet.

plans for a new site for California College, and in 1865 the Trustees of Massachusetts Agricultural and Mechanic Arts College asked him to advise them on a plan for their grounds. He thought his advice might be significant to all of the new Morrill Act colleges, so, the following year he published his report under the title: *A Few Things to Be Thought of before Proceeding to Plan Buildings for the National Agricultural Colleges.* Figure 19 shows a reconstruction of his plan.

The Trustees of the Massachusetts college had decided to house all of their new facilities in a single large multistoried stone building. Olmsted advised a change to "a less formal and rigid plan." He thought a school of agriculture wanted lower, simpler buildings, each designed for an appropriate special purpose. He cited the practice of some recent innovators in another field: the builders of several new institutions for criminals and homeless orphans. Four of the most successful new institutions for "dealing with those classes" had done without large buildings. Why should a

college "for young men of comparatively healthy intellects and unperverted instincts" need them? There was plenty of space on the site and "straight-sided, evenly-balanced, many-storied structures of stone would be in-

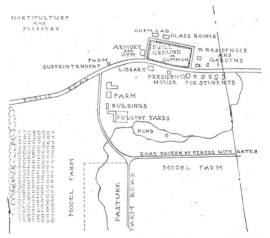

Fig. 19. Reconstruction of Frederick Law Olmsted's plan for Massachusetts Agricultural and Mechanic Arts College, 1866. The plan was reconstructed by Frank A. Waugh from Olmsted's written report.

congruous" in the hilly Amherst landscape. They would "impose unnecessary inconvenience and fatigue." Cottages, farm houses, and "halls for concerts and exhibitions," the buildings that would "meet the ordinary demands of a small town," would be better models than "the time-honored, unmanageable great institutional structures of stone." What Olmsted had in mind for the physical form of the new national agricultural colleges was nothing less than "a model rural neighborhood." [47]

It was Olmsted's conclusion that the ground plan of the new institution "must embrace something more than oral instruction, practical demonstration in the science of agriculture and the practice of rural arts." Arrangements had to be included which were "designed to favorably affect the habits and inclinations of students—to qualify them for a wise . . . exercise of the rights and duties of citizens and householders." To accomplish this he suggested planning the grounds for three educational requirements: first, "those related to the special calling of a farmer" (he seemed to ignore the "mechanic arts"); second, "those related to the affairs of rural communities"; and, third, "those related to rural household affairs." [48] So his three elements of physical structure were vocational training facilities, instructional facilities for the arts and sciences, and living facilities. The accommodations he proposed to meet these requirements were for the first, model farm fields, ponds, and buildings; for the second, a cluster of four simple two-storied buildings, easy to remodel and extend; and for the third, a model villa for the president and "clubhouses" for the students.

The farm facilities were carefully thought out in relation to the landscape, drainage, and soil conditions. Locations for them were outlined. Then proposals were listed for the in-structional buildings. The first would house lecture rooms and faculty studies. The second would house scientific laboratories, lecture rooms, and museums; the third, space for quiet activities—library, reading rooms, and drawing and writing rooms; and the fourth, assembly spaces—gymnasium, armory, and general assembly hall. The second and third buildings would be fireproof; the others, less expensively built. Each type of activity would have an appropriate building. Each could easily be enlarged or remodeled. Each would be detached from the other buildings, set back from the highway, with trees, shrubbery, and turf about it, and accessible by good walks. The provisions of the Morrill Act would also require a parade or drill ground. Olmsted suggested this might as well also be a green, "a ball or playground for the students." He therefore proposed that it be bordered by shade trees and seats. Since it was representative of a rural town hall or courthouse, the general hall of assembly should open onto this green. [49]

Olmsted's third set of building types (those serving needs related to household affairs) would be provided by "model" residential facilities for the president and farm superintendent and "clubhouses" for the students. The former would illustrate what was "best in all respects for the house of any American having to exercise considerable responsibility, and . . . possessed of corresponding means of securing repose from his business cares and labors [in the] health, comfort, and cheerful recreation of his home" [50]—a nineteenth-century country villa. For the students, "the old college barracks and commons" would not be satisfactory. Those who were "acquiring a liberal education should also be established in habits corresponding to those of the ordinary rural household." This, Olmsted believed, might be accomplished in the form of "clubhouses," built as needed, each "a series of rooms . . . common and private for as many students as could be comfortably accommo-

[47] Frederick Law Olmsted, *A Few Things to Be Thought of before Proceeding to Plan Buildings for the National Agricultural Colleges* (New York, 1866), p. 19.
[48] *Ibid.*, p. 14.

[49] *Ibid.*, p. 19.   [50] *Ibid.*, p. 20.

dated and provided for in a domestic way by a family which would undertake the household management." The care of the house— "mowing the lawn, trimming the hedges, rolling and sweeping gravel, training vines, occasional painting, white washing and glazing" would be part of the "duty . . . and education of the students." [51] What a clear vision he had of our suburban (or fraternal) weekend activity!

While we might smile at Olmsted's utopian ideas of a way of life for an agricultural college in 1866, we must marvel at his clear prophecy of the physical plan to be developed during Cornell's first forty years. Until 1905 the Cornell campus developed in a pattern very like the suggestions in Olmsted's report to the Massachusetts Agricultural and Mechanic Arts College. Because he saw the potential need for growth and change in the new land-grant institutions and because he recognized their need for strong links to the society around them, his plan was for an extendable campus with expandable buildings each designed for a special function. Olmsted thought the buildings and the campus design should reflect the functions of a model community. These ideas were perfectly suited to the broad but indeterminate objectives of the new institutions of higher education that were to emerge from the stimulus of the Morrill Act.

[51] *Ibid.,* p. 22.

III

"Upon the Hill"

AFTER A LONG ILLNESS IN the summer of 1863, Ezra Cornell asked his doctor if he would bring his carriage and take him upon the hill. Waterman Hewett, an early Cornell historian, wrote [1] that Cornell had realized as never before the precarious hold that man has on life. "I have accumulated money," he is reported to have said, "and I am going to spend it while I live." Then follows in Hewett's account of the incident the story of a peculiar habit of the Founder. Many people who were in Ithaca during the years 1863–1866 remembered it. Ezra Cornell was continually taking someone upon the hill or through the gorge.[2] He delighted in the beauty of his East Hill farm (Fig. 20), the only land between the Hudson and the Mississippi he thought could take the place of his family's old homestead on the Hudson in Westchester County. As the idea of founding a university took shape during his work in the New York State Agriculture Society and in the legislature in Albany in 1865, Ezra Cornell's accounts of trips upon the hill began to include references to "the buildings which should crown the hillside." [3]

Cornell's discussion with his doctor during the trip to his hilltop farm in 1863 is said to have included mention of his determination to build there "an institution for poor young men [with] no entrance examination [where] they could study whatever they were inclined to." [4] It is hard to believe that Cornell's idea of a school on East Hill was so fully developed in 1863. It seems more likely that the recorded remembrance includes events that occurred at various times.[5]

We do know that by September 1864, Cornell had decided the future use of his farm. He offered it to the Trustees of the State Agriculture College at Ovid along with new college buildings, and a three-hundred-thousand-dollar endowment if they would move the then bankrupt college to Ithaca. The offer was contingent on the passage of legislation endowing the institution with a thirty-thousand-dollar-a-year income from the proceeds of the Morrill Act land-grant. The proposed site in Ithaca, Cornell said, "was within ten minutes' walk of the Cornell Library, the churches, the railroad stations and the steamboat landing." The site he was offering was the lower part of his farm, the area immediately east of the present location of Stewart Avenue.

Ezra Cornell was not the first person to suggest East Hill in Ithaca for educational use.

[1] W. T. Hewett, *Cornell University*, I, 74–75.

[2] Mary Emily Cornell, *The Autobiography of Mary Emily Cornell* (Ithaca, 1929). She recalls a conversation of White and Cornell as follows: White, speaking of a visitor: "What can I do with ———? I have not a moment to spare and we cannot neglect him." Cornell: "I will put him through the gorge before lunch and he will be glad to sleep all the afternoon."

[3] Hewett, *op. cit.*, p. 75. Cornell visited the site with different groups. Accounts of these visits vary considerably in detail.

[4] *Ibid.*, p. 75.   [5] *Ibid.*, p. 77.

24

Fig. 20. A view from West Hill, 1839. Ezra Cornell's East Hill land, in the middle background, lies between Fall Creek Gorge and Cascadilla Gorge. Cayuga Lake is at the left.

The first expression of Ithaca's dream of becoming an educational center had come in April 1822 when the Genesee Conference of the Methodist Church obtained a charter from the legislature incorporating "Ithaca College." Their site was on East Hill below the present site of the main Cornell Quadrangle. The college was to be coeducational and "established on broad and liberal principles . . . a system of instruction adopted without regard to particular religious or political opinions." [6] These educational objectives were much like those held by Ezra Cornell forty-three years later.

A forecast of the coming of higher education to Ithaca was provided by one Hibernicus (DeWitt Clinton) in 1820. In his book on the resources of New York State, Clinton wrote: "The scenery of these lakes is alternately picturesque, beautiful and sublime. Before the revolution of a century, this country will become consecrated to classic inspiration—'live in description, and grow green in song.'" [7] By stretching the point a bit we may interpret

"classic inspiration" to mean higher education.

Solomon Southwick, an itinerant English pamphleteer who "copied some views of Ithaca" in 1836, echoed Clinton's optimistic views of Ithaca's potentials. "This village," he wrote, "is destined to become the resort of fashion, taste and genius." [8] A list of nineteenth-century American villages making such claims would probably include most American settlements of over fifty inhabitants, but Ithaca's dreams came true. It seems likely that Clinton may have stimulated and assisted the idea of the "Ithaca College" on East Hill. The site was Simeon DeWitt's farm. One might almost say that the seeds of the idea of a college planted by DeWitt Clinton and Simeon DeWitt were still in the East Hill land when Ezra Cornell purchased it in 1857. The Methodists had been unable, in 1822, to raise the forty-thousand dollars needed to get the "Ithaca College" started. Ezra Cornell selected his hilltop farm for the new University late in 1864. From then until March 1866, when the specific site for the first buildings was selected, he took many relatives, local friends, and

[6] *Ithaca Journal and Advertiser*, 30 May 1821.
[7] Hibernicus (DeWitt Clinton), *Letters on the Natural History and Internal Resources of the State of New York* (New York, 1822). Letter dated Ithaca, 1 June 1820.

[8] Solomon Southwick, *Views of Ithaca* (Ithaca, 1836).

visitors to see the site. Visitors from out of town were also given the special "Ezra Cornell guided tour" of Ithaca.

Early in the spring of 1865, Cornell conducted such a tour of Ithaca and his proposed site for State Senator and Trustee Andrew Dickson White. The two men were good friends and had become accustomed to working together by this time. Important decisions had to be made about the site for the new university and the design of its first buildings. Both men had an intense interest in these decisions. At one point in their discussion, White championed a Syracuse location: the hill on which Syracuse University now stands.[9] He offered $200,000 additional endowment to the University if this site in his home city were selected. Civic pride seems to have played a minor role in White's desire to find a location other than Ithaca because he also investigated the possibility of a site on a hill overlooking Binghamton, New York. A state "inebriate asylum" competed successfully with the new university for this site.[10] White, no great champion of the American city, apparently recognized some of its advantages as a location for a fledgling university—ease of access to other places and scholars, a greater supply of housing, and the conveniences of city services— which a small village could not afford. According to Goldwin Smith, Ezra Cornell imperiled the success of his enterprise by placing it at Ithaca, then a village with no advantage for the purpose. Smith thought that intellectual exile in Ithaca would be a drawback in attracting professors, which Ezra could not understand, but then Cornell, according to Smith, was "not insensible to the pleasure of seeing his university rise on the hill above the spot where his lowly abode once stood."[11] Cornell's insistence on placing the university in Ithaca gave the institution a typically isolated American college location. But his reason for the choice was civic loyalty, not the usual moralistic reason given for the monastic isolation of American colleges and universities.

To many Americans of the mid-nineteenth century the city was a place of evil. Goldwin Smith reported that Cornell, in his youth, was cheated of his wages in Syracuse and so had a distaste for that place. White believed that "the constant depletion of farming districts of their best men and the over-stocking therewith of city populations was a great evil."[12] Yet he proposed Syracuse and Binghamton as sites for Cornell University. It is probable that if Cornell had lived in a large city, he, too, would have selected it as the site for his university. The superiority of a small-town environment for educational purposes seemed obvious to most nineteenth-century Americans, but Andrew D. White and Ezra Cornell seem to have avoided this prejudice. The ideal college campus site, the kind of place later depicted in countless movies and novels, was a rustic delight, far from the action and strife of the city. And it was always set on a hill. East Hill in Ithaca had the proper qualifications.

The Puritans had consciously located the first American college away from the evil city. The Massachusetts General Courts were horrified at the "moral rot" of Boston, so when they located their new college in 1636, they established it in the outlying village of Cambridge (then Newtown) which was "free of Antinomian Taint . . . spotless from the contagion of opinions."[13] From their choice has followed the American pattern of locating colleges in small towns. Unfortunately, there was no hill, but the school survived that disadvantage and prospered in the cow yard which soon became Harvard Yard.

---

[9] Goldwin Smith, *Reminiscences*, p. 370. See also Ernest F. Huffcut, "Cornell University," in *The University of the State of New York*, ed. by Sidney Sherwood, U.S. Bureau of Education Circular No. 3 (Washington, 1900) p. 330. Huffcut says that a manuscript in possession of Mr. White is the basis of his statement. The population of Syracuse in 1868 was 31,784. Ithaca's population in that year was 5,685.
[10] White, *Diaries*, p. 147, 7 September 1864. The asylum site was developed for a state mental hospital.

[11] Smith, *op. cit.*, p. 370.
[12] White, "Address on Agricultural and Mechanical Education" (Albany, 1869) in *The Cornell University Register* (1870).
[13] Samuel Eliot Morison, *The Founding of Harvard College* (Cambridge, 1935), pp. 182–183.

The preference for small-town locations survived a long time. Two hundred and twenty years after the establishment of Harvard, the distinguished clergyman Horace Bushnell conducted an exhaustive search for an ideal new site for the Trustees of the College of California, then in Oakland. He described one site near Oakland as "quite too convenient for the young men to escape to the city by night and partake of its dissipations." He feared "the young men [would] sometimes get their ship launched before the keel is laid." The site finally selected in Berkeley was said to be "conveniently situated with respect to San Francisco . . . being in full view of the . . . city, and yet sufficiently removed to be beyond objectionable proximity." [14] This is now the campus of the University of California at Berkeley.

The editors of the *Ithaca Journal and Advertiser* seemed also to believe their village was a safer place than the big bad city. In February 1865, the *Journal*, championing the choice of Ithaca as a site for the new University, claimed that "while the students will not be exposed to the temptations and corruptions of a large city they will find [in Ithaca] all the conveniences and advantages of a thriving village." Ezra Cornell and Andrew White were too liberal to have such moralistic views on college location. Cornell, as Goldwin Smith later commented, was simply very loyal to Ithaca. White, as the same commentator noted, believed that they might not be able to attract a high caliber faculty to such a remote spot; but he was not too concerned about the possible effects of isolation. Cornell's senior position, his magnificent endowment, and his magnificent although remote site gave him the privilege of overruling the objections of White and a few other trustees. The Cornell University would be in Ithaca on the East Hill. George Lincoln Burr summarized it beautifully: "Together they drew the charter

of a new university whose site Cornell made Ithaca, whose name White made Cornell." [15]

In May 1865, less than a month after the first meeting of the new university's Trustees in Albany, Senator White wrote to Senator Cornell. He wanted to visit him "to see what sort of place Ithaca really is and above all what site there is for the University." [16] The village lay, busily humming no doubt, at the foot of East Hill as Andrew D. White approached by Cayuga Lake steamer in the last week of May 1865. This urbane young man who had lived in London, Paris, Berlin, and St. Petersburg, could not have been greatly impressed. Later, he recalled that it seemed the place had "sprouted, borne fruit and gone to seed." Ithaca was then very like hundreds of other villages in upstate New York: its broad gridiron streets lined with neat white Greek Revival houses (Fig. 21) and more recent, less stylish workmen's homes, yards fenced to keep chickens and livestock in and dogs out. Here and there a more pretentious town house with a French mansard roof had shouldered its way into the ranks. Goldwin Smith wrote that there was scarcely a house that wore the aspect of extreme poverty, though there were a good many Irish. "There was a good deal of width in the place," he said, "all the dwellings [were] simple and the habits of their owners equally so."

The village's unpaved main street was bus-

[14] William Ferrier, *Origin and Development of the University of California* (Berkeley, 1930), p. 163. The site selected was not one of those recommended by Bushnell. The College became the University of California in 1868.

[15] Chancellor John V. Pruyn of the University of the State of New York, *Address*, at opening ceremonies of Cornell University in October 1868 (Ithaca, 1869); George L. Burr, "Andrew Dickson White" in *The Dictionary of American Biography*. Pruyn said: "I doubted at first whether the place for your university was well chosen. But after visiting Ithaca and looking at the advantages and beauties of the place, I believe it to be one possessing many very desirable points for this purpose." Pruyn was also a Trustee and a personal friend of Goldwin Smith. The New York State Library at Albany houses a presentation volume of photographs of Oxford University buildings sent to Pruyn by Smith in November 1867. Smith had intended to write a history of the buildings but the confused state of his affairs at the time had forced him to abandon the project (Smith to Pruyn 30 November 1867, letter attached to the book; *Ithaca Journal and Advertiser*, 14 February 1865).

[16] ADW to EC, 18 May 1865, Cornell Papers.

Fig. 21. Ithaca in the 1860's, viewed from Prospect Street on South Hill. State Street runs from lower right to middle left with the Wilgus Opera House at the far left. The Cornell Public Library and Village Hall towers are in the middle; Cayuga Lake is at the right.

tling with trade. Farm wagons, goods wagons, buggies, plainly dressed farmers, townsmen, ladies trailing long skirts, and an occasional man on horseback made up the traffic. The creeks had flooded the low-lying village in the spring of 1865, and the stone crosswalks had only recently been excavated from the mud. Ithaca's streets were very like most village

Fig. 22. State Street, 1865, looking west from the corner of Aurora Street.

Fig. 23. Ezra Cornell's home, Forest Park. The house was probably built for Simeon DeWitt, who was the previous owner of Cornell's East Hill farm.

streets in America throughout the nineteenth century; alternately muddy and dusty. When Goldwin Smith arrived in Ithaca "about 6 A.M. on a dreary morning" in the winter of 1868–1869, the streets were "axle deep in mud." Commercial buildings along State Street were unpretentious (Fig. 22). Indeed, many of them would have seemed quite at home on the main street of a western frontier town. One block north of this market place was the newly completed red-brick Cornell Public Library, and across from it on Tioga Street was Alonzo Cornell's white-painted brick, stepped gabled home.[17] White must have stopped there on his tour of Ithaca with Ezra Cornell. A few years later Ezra Cornell moved from his home in Forest Park on East Hill (Fig. 23) into Alonzo's house. His son Franklin continued to live at Forest Park.

If Ezra Cornell followed his usual practice in conducting tours for first-time visitors to Ithaca, there were few preliminaries. Andrew White had to be shown the things which distinguished Ithaca: the new Cornell Public Library, boatbuilding and transshipment of coal

and plaster at Cayuga Inlet, the water-powered mills at the foot of Ithaca Falls, the glacial grooves in boulders at Buttermilk Falls, and, above all, the scenic glories of Buttermilk Falls Creek and the Six Mile, Cascadilla, and Fall Creek waterfalls (Fig. 24). During Goldwin Smith's first winter in Ithaca,

Fig. 24. Triphammer Falls, 1868. Part of Beebe Lake shows at the top of the falls in Fall Creek Gorge north of the campus site.

[17] Ezra Cornell's first family home in Ithaca was "The Nook" near Ithaca Falls. When the income from Western Union stock made him a wealthy man, he bought the East Hill farm but his son Franklin Cornell occupied it after 1867 and Ezra lived in Alonzo Cornell's house on Tioga Street.

Fig. 25. An Ithaca restaurant in the 1870's.

he longed for the coming of summer and observed hopefully that "if waterfalls will make
us happy we shall be blest for . . . we have a
score of them of different shapes and sizes." [18]
Waterfalls indeed comprise one of the most
frequently shown attractions of Ithaca, and
White must have seen his share of tumbling
cascades on his first visit.

The water power of these falls had been the
basis for the village's first industries. By 1865,
when White first visited Ithaca, the early
grist, flour, and plaster mills had been joined
by a tannery, a farm machinery company, a
shoe manufacturer, two iron foundries, five
blacksmiths, five furniture manufacturers, and
six carriage makers. Most of the forests had
been cut over but two lumber merchants still
carried on their operations from Ithaca. One
of them, John McGraw, was to play a major
role in the development of the University.
Ithaca was provided with the usual village
services. There were two bookstores, two

hardware stores, two dentists, two barrel
stores, and two hat stores. These were supplemented by three harness shops, three pho-
tographers, and one painter.

If anyone had bothered to check the 1865
city directory in anticipation of the building
boom about to occur, they would have found
only one carpenter listed. Of course, in those
times almost every workman was a carpenter
of sorts and probably had a few other skills,
too. The English craftsmen who joined the
work force in Ithaca a few years later were
impressed by this versatility of American
workmen. One of them wrote home about a
fellow mason of German descent who owned
a farm where his frau made butter while he
cut stone. He described another fellow who,
besides being a stonecutter in the summer,
was "either a glassmaker, a wheelwright, a
hunter, or a lumberer in the winter. Every one
of the mechanics seemed to have several
occupations." [19]

Ithaca must have been a litigious place in
1865. No group outnumbered the twelve lawyers save the eighteen grocers. Figure 25
shows a typical restaurant of the late sev-

[18] Smith to Norton, January 1868, *New England
Historical Society Proceedings,* December 1915. The
English historian was not quite so happy about the
waterfalls in 1866 when White sent him several photographs of Ithaca scenery as part of his campaign to
lure him to Cornell. Smith then wrote to Norton that
he "abhored waterfalls and American bread."

[19] Louis Hinton, "The Working Man in America,"
in *The Spectator,* London, 4 December 1869.

enties. Two of Ithaca's lawyers were to play significant roles in the development of the University: Francis M. Finch, who was then Ezra Cornell's lawyer, and Douglass Boardman, who became an active Cornell Trustee during the last quarter of the century. A year later Ithaca's lawyers were joined by T. F. ("Teefy") Crane, who in turn joined the Cornell faculty in 1868. In 1865, Ithaca's doctors numbered nine and the drugstores five. In addition to the two hat stores noted above, there were five milliners for the ladies, one dry goods store, seven clothing stores, seven shoe stores, three tailors, two jewelers, and one liquor dealer. The population of Ithaca in 1865 was 7,264, if you believed the *Manual for Use of Legislators,* or 5,685, if you believed the *New York State Census.*[20] Although there were five other hotels in the village, the Clinton House, which had been closed for years, was about to reopen in the spring of 1865 with a newly redecorated club room.[21] Ezra Cornell now owned two-thirds interest in the hotel and was making ready for the influx of visitors who would come to the new university. According to the *Cornell Era,* the Clinton House (Fig. 26) was later used frequently by professors and students for college functions. In 1865 the four local restaurant owners were no doubt also anticipating an increase in business with the coming of the University.

Ezra Cornell, a shrewd strategist, probably saved the best of White's May 1865 tour of Ithaca until last. As they rode up East Hill late on that spring afternoon, the future president must have been excited by the views: the green-walled Inlet Valley winding out to the south; Cayuga Lake, a glistening curved sheet of gray-blue between green hills rising steeply to the north; and the close texture of the slanting roofs of village houses relieved by numerous church steeples. The rich, regular fields and orchards on West Hill sloped away above the helter-skelter collection of shacks, cabins,

Fig. 26. The Clinton House was Ithaca's finest hotel in 1868. Several years after this picture was taken a stylish mansard roof was added to provide more rooms.

and shanties of squatters near the Inlet. When he looked out from what has since often been called one of the most magnificent university sites in the world, he must have, at least for a moment, forgotten the place's isolation from the scholarly world and started mentally building Gothic quadrangles. He was soon expressing concern about where they should be on that terraced hillside.

His companion, Ezra Cornell, had given some thought to the matter but on such occasions usually played the role of a reserved Quaker to the hilt and asked his guests to give their views first. His visitors, falling into the trap, would logically suggest building sites as close to the village as possible—on the plateaus immediately above or next to the village cemetery—two hundred and fifty to three hundred feet above the elevation of the village. Then, so the legend has it, Cornell would take them to the crest of East Hill, four hundred and thirty feet above the village. Turning to the east and facing the gently

[20] N.Y. State Census of 1865 reported in H. E. Abt, *Ithaca* (Ithaca, 1926), p. 82.
[21] *Ithaca Journal and Advertiser,* 31 May 1865.

rolling plateau, he would say "with an appearance of inspiration, 'You do not comprehend the magnitude of the subject you are called upon to decide . . . the locations you have pointed out are inadequate . . . you appear to be considering . . . half a dozen buildings . . . whereas . . . you will live to see our campus occupied by fifty buildings and swarming with thousands of students.' " [22] Cornell, it is reported, would then indicate the upper plateau and say, "Here from Cascadilla to Fall Creek . . . we shall need every acre."

White must have had a similar experience during his first trip upon the East Hill with Ezra Cornell in the spring of 1865. We know that White preferred a lower site, near the village of Ithaca, that would enable students to take room and board with families there. His unhappy experience at Hobart, Yale, and Michigan had convinced him that there was little educational or social value in dormitory life. His good educational experience in European universities, where he boarded in private homes, must have reinforced this conclusion. He did not want to spend money building dormitories at Cornell.

A Building Committee composed of Cornell, White, Francis Finch, Abram Weaver, and William Kelly was empowered by the Trustees in September 1865 to select a site and to provide buildings. Most of the committee agreed with White on the lower location; but Cornell had fixed on the upper site and eventually had his way. Alonzo Cornell, who later wrote his version of one of the discussions that took place on the site, says that eventually the others deemed it useless to discuss the question further. "Their silence," he wrote, "indicated a final surrender and the Founder directed the setting of the stakes" for the first building.

When Professor Hewett prepared his chapter on Cornell University in Selkreg's *Landmarks of Tompkins County* in 1892, President White commented on the manuscript and re-called that at the second meeting of the Trustees, on 5 September 1865, Cornell took the entire board on the hill. All liked the lower site "just above the new Cornell Mansion." "Then," White continues, "we viewed the landscape from [a point west of Franklin Hall]. It was a beautiful day and the panorama was magnificent. Mr. Cornell urged reasons on behalf of the upper site, the main one being that there was so much more room for expansion. . . . All the board agreed with him fully except Finch and myself." White concludes: "I confess freely, that while the development of the University would have been more easy [*sic*] on the lower site, the upper site has, on the whole, proved better." [23]

White had not given in easily. In May 1866, a year after his first visit to Ithaca, he wrote to Cornell that he was "willing tentatively to be guided by the decisions of the committee who are to re-examine the question," but he hoped they would "agree on the second location." By this he no doubt meant the lower site. His continued preference for it is recorded in his brief description of "The Cornell University" in Spence Spencer's guide book, *The Scenery of Ithaca* (1866) where he wrote that "the new university [would] be located three hundred feet above Cayuga Lake." The site finally chosen at a Building Committee meeting upon the hill late in May, 1866, lies four hundred and thirty feet above the lake.

Ezra Cornell's insistence on the upper site did not seem practical to most members of the Building Committee, but he stood firm. By this time, the idea of university use of The Cascadilla was at least being considered.[24] The upper site would be more accessible to the faculty and students who were to live in it. This possibility, the view from the upper site (Fig. 27), and Mr. Cornell's views clinched the matter in the early summer of 1866, but, in a sense, it had really been decided as early as the fall of 1865, when the Building Committee began instructing archi-

[22] Alonzo B. Cornell, MS history of Cornell, C.U. Archives, 47/1/26, pp. 40–41.

[23] ADW to Hewett, 1 October 1895, Hewett Papers.
[24] Finch to EC, April, 1866, Cornell Papers.

Fig. 27. Cayuga Lake valley from East Hill, about 1868. The valley was photographed from the glacial lake delta west of the present site of Franklin Hall.

tects to design the first building with dormitories at each end and lecture rooms in the center section.

The Trustees had authorized the Building Committee to select the university site. Later they confirmed the committee's choice.[25] There being no official record of the Building Committee's decision, we must assume that they finally agreed with the Founder. At any rate, on 1 June 1866, Ezra Cornell and his wife, Mary, went up on the hill with a workman to see how deep the rock was on the site of the first building. Afterward he wrote in his memorandum book: "I then moved the first shovel of earth in digging foundation and Mrs. C. the next. . . . Brot first shovel of earth to house."[26] The campus of Cornell University had been set upon East Hill in Ithaca by its founder.

Thousands of Cornellians and visitors have since enjoyed the spectacular result of Ezra

[25] Trustees' *Proceedings*, I, 8, November 1866.
[26] Ezra Cornell Memorandum Book No. 3, Cornell Papers.

Cornell's perseverance. But in the early years it was sometimes difficult to bear the windy consequences of his selection of this exposed location. Dr. James Morgan Hart, who joined the faculty in 1868 and left in 1873, roundly condemned the choice of a site "pitched upon the crest of a hill, four hundred feet high, and exposed to the inclemency of the weather. By dint of lavish expenditures for planting trees," he wrote, "it is possible that the buildings may be sheltered in the course of a generation from the searching east winds. But nothing can ever screen them from the furious northerly and westerly gales that sweep across the lake every winter and spring." Hart had struggled half a mile through the snow in one such storm, arriving in his lecture room "half blinded and benumbed, scarcely able to collect his thoughts." He wrote, "The cruelest of friendly mockeries" was that of the casual visitor who saw the grounds in June or October, knew nothing of this winter pain and "congratulated the University on its admirable location!" Professor Hart, a Princeton gentleman, thought a fine view on a fine day was "but sorry atonement for months of wearing toil and exposure." "How," he complained, "shall we explain this mania, peculiar to America, of locating public institutions on hilltops?" [27]

In 1890, Professor Hart, presumably by then a tougher and more tolerant man,

[27] James Morgan Hart, *German Universities* (New York, 1874), pp. 349–350.

checked half a generation of tree growth on the campus and returned to the East Hill to teach. He brought with him Dr. William Strunk, who had been his student in a sheltered valley city at the University of Cincinnati. By the time Professor Hart returned to Cornell a stone quadrangle was beginning to take form on the crest of the hill, and it was growing according to the plan developed in 1866 by Andrew D. White and Ezra Cornell.

A Quadrangle of Stone

BEFORE EZRA AND MARY COR-
nell's solemn, private ground-
breaking ceremony took place in June 1866, a
precise quadrangular campus plan had been
adopted for the arrangement of the University's first buildings. No drawing of it survives,
but it was carefully described in the *Ithaca
Journal and Advertiser*. Figure 28 was prepared from this description. The "square" or
quadrangle was to enclose an area of fifteen
acres with internal dimensions of one thousand by one thousand feet (*sic*). A chapel,
with offices for the President and a "picture
gallery," was to be placed in the center of its
western side overlooking the village. This
centerpiece was to be flanked by two dormitory-classroom buildings and by a museum and
a library at the northern and southern corners
of the square. On the other sides of the
square, classroom buildings, laboratories, and
dormitories were to be symmetrically arranged. "Still further east, on a knoll," the
Journal added, "will be an observatory, with a
house nearby for the observor."[1]

While we are not certain about the origin of
the plan, it is probably based on plans for
quadrangles of these dimensions proposed in
1814 by Charles Kelsall in his book, *Phantasm
of An University*. Kelsall advocated the establishment of "a third university" in England. It was to include a college of manufac-
tures and agriculture as well as colleges of
civil polity and languages, fine arts, moral
philosophy, and mathematics. Each college

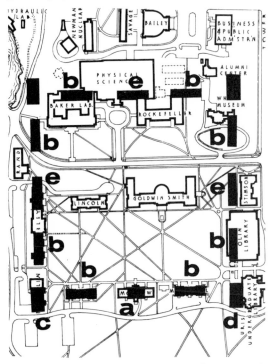

Fig. 28. The first Cornell campus plan, 1866. A
reconstruction of the plan for a "University Square,"
approximately one thousand feet by one thousand
feet, is superimposed on a map of the 1965 campus:
(*a*) chapel, (*b*) dormitory-classroom buildings, (*c*)
museum, (*d*) library, (*e*) laboratory buildings. The
University's first four buildings, Morrill, White,
McGraw, and West Sibley Halls, were located in
accordance with this plan.

[1] *Ithaca Journal and Advertiser*, 6 June 1866.

35

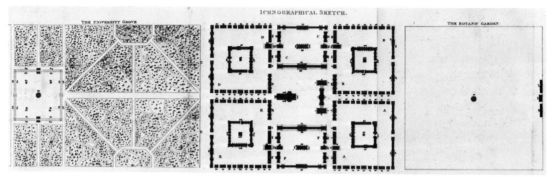

Fig. 29. Plan for a third university in England; "Ichnographical Sketch" by Charles Kelsall, 1814. The large squares in the central portion measure one thousand feet on each side; smaller inside squares, less than three hundred feet—about the size of the Christ's Church Quadrangle at Oxford.

was to have its quadrangle (Fig. 29), and each of the four corner quadrangles was to measure one thousand by one thousand feet with a smaller quadrangle in its center.[2] The parallels of purpose and form in the 1866 academic and campus plan for Cornell and Kelsall's proposals of 1814 may be coincidental, but the concepts are strikingly similar, both in their attempts to revise university goals and organization and in the campus development proposed.

There may also be a connection between Kelsall's vast quadrangles and the plans developed by Charles Bulfinch for Harvard College in 1814 (Fig. 30). Bulfinch's proposal established the outlines for the much-admired form of Harvard Yard. The drawing of Bulfinch's plan probably shows one-half of a square intended to measure seven hundred feet on each side. A square of these dimensions would fit very comfortably within the street boundaries of the Yard.

Andrew D. White referred to the proposed quadrangle arrangement of Cornell's buildings in his article in The Scenery of Ithaca published in 1866. He also referred, perhaps much too modestly, to "much thought given by some of the building committee members to laying out the grounds."[3] White appears to

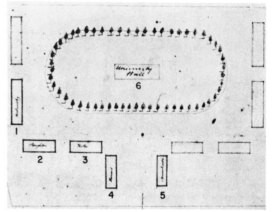

Fig. 30. Plan for Harvard College by Charles Bulfinch, 1814. Bulfinch designed Stoughton Hall (2). The plan may be read as one-half of an eight-hundred-foot square, inside the one-thousand-foot square block bounded by Peabody, Quincy, and Cambridge Streets and Massachusetts Avenue: (1) Holworthy Hall; (3) Hollis Hall; (4) Harvard Hall; (5) Massachusetts Hall; (6) University Hall.

have worked closely with Russell Sturgis, one of the architects who submitted building plans to the Committee. His preference for Sturgis links him to a strong advocate of quadrangle plans for universities. Sturgis, with Noah Porter and White, were the initiators of the quadrangle development at Yale which was eventually to surround and replace all of the buildings of the old Brick Row except Connecticut Hall.[4] White and Sturgis

[2] Charles Kelsall, The Phantasm of An University (London, 1814).

[3] MS Building Committee report, 14 March 1866, Cornell Papers. The manuscript is in White's handwriting.

[4] Russell Sturgis, "College" in A Dictionary of Architecture and Building (New York, 1901), p. 635. White, who continued his interest in Yale affairs, may

would therefore seem possible originators of the idea for a quadrangle at Cornell.

Nevertheless, in spite of this circumstantial evidence, it was probably Ezra Cornell who first conceived the idea of a university square for the Cornell campus. He had visited England in 1862, had seen the older English universities, and was familiar with English ideas on university reform. He may have discovered Kelsall's book during his trip to England or later in the fine New York State Library at Albany, when as a State Senator he was first evolving his ideas for a new university in Ithaca. He also may have absorbed the idea for a large square from President Hill of Harvard when he talked to him in the fall of 1865. That the 1814 Bulfinch plan (Fig. 30) was then still being followed at Harvard is shown by the placement of Grays Hall in the Yard in accordance with Bulfinch's plan. Ezra Cor-

nell's later decision to place a wooden laboratory building in the center of the university square was consistent with Kelsall's plan for smaller quadrangles in the centers of great quadrangles.[5] Finally, Cornell seems the most likely originator of the quadrangle plan because of his dominant position and intensive involvement in university affairs in 1865–1866. Of course, the concurrence of White, and perhaps indirectly of Sturgis, cannot be ruled out. Some years later in a letter to President Schurman, White credited Cornell with the idea of the Quadrangle and said that Cornell thought the space between the buildings on each side of the Quadrangle should someday be filled with fireproof additions that would shield the Quadrangle from winter winds and prevent the spread of fire.[6]

The quadrangle plan for siting Cornell's first buildings was probably adopted sometime during the winter of 1865–1866. Planning for the buildings themselves began in September 1865, with the appointment of the Building Committee. A number of architects were in touch with various trustees long before this. Lawrence Valk, a New York City architect, wrote to Cornell in May 1865 suggesting a competition for the design of the University's buildings. In the same month, Nichols and Brown of Albany wrote that Cornell's villa plans were completed and asked when they could "take that trip on College Business?" Brown later traveled with Cornell to visit Cambridge where they were conducted

have been involved in the 1869 decision to develop a quadrangle at Yale. Noah Porter and Sturgis served on the committee that developed the plan. Russell Sturgis' scholarly predilections, which at this time had expression only in the American Pre-Raphaelite magazine, *New Path,* must have appealed to Andrew Dickson White. Sturgis and Peter Wight, who designed the Street School of Art at Yale, shared an office at 98 Broadway. Sturgis was later author of several books on the history of architecture. White knew both Sturgis and Wight well because of his committee work at Yale and because of their mutual admiration for Ruskin.

We should not assume, however, that White was narrow-minded in architectural matters. Another of his good friends was Arthur Delevan Gilman, New York architect, who was a sharp critic of the American Pre-Raphaelites. In a letter written to White about 1860, Gilman described his recent design for the Grand Central Park Hotel in New York with a "facade 420 ft. long—modern Imperial French in design with high roofs, crested with iron, and with all the full stops of Mansart's [sic], Jean Goujon's and Philibert de l'Orme's Renaissant let out. The 'idiotic and feeble-minded youth' who compose the American Architectural Mutual Admiration Society have retired from the competition in disgust,—and betaken themselves for solace to the Pre-Raphaelite stripes and fizgigs and peaks—poppies on the end of long sticks, and black letter legends cut on forty different-colored stones—in short the exaggerated ecclesiastic's-gingerbread horse-with-a-gilt-tail style, in which Wight and Mr. Wrey Mould are such proficients" (Gilman Papers, American Institute of Architects Library, Washington, D.C., as quoted in the *Journal of the AIA,* February 1958).

[5] Andrew D. White did not like the idea of a building in the center of the Quadrangle. On 19 June 1868 (White Papers) he wrote to EC: "I decidedly demur to the site you have chosen [for the laboratory building]. I fear it will spoil the whole plan on which we have been working. All our plans . . . have been based upon the idea of a large area surrounded by substantial buildings. . . . All this you destroy by planting in the center a great wooden workshop. . . . If not too late I beg you to place the building to one side."

[6] ADW to Schurman, 1909, Schurman Papers. Several of White's sketches of various library sites, including one on the back of a letter to William Kelly (15 November 1869, White Papers) and one to C. K. Adams (11 March 1886), show buildings placed to close completely the west side of the Quadrangle.

around the Harvard campus and through dormitories by President Hill and Frederic Moore. Moore, a former Ithacan practicing architecture in Boston, also asked about the design of the buildings. In June 1865, Russell Sturgis of New York sent White excerpts from circulars which had been provided for architects in several competitions.[7]

Early in August, Building Committee member William Kelly of Rhinebeck, New York, wrote to Ezra Cornell about the skills and economy of another Boston architect, Alexander Esty. Trustee Kelly was amazed at the claims of a University of Rochester professor that the plans for a building recently completed there by Esty were the property of the architect. Kelly continued: "In this idea the professor is clearly starting a new doctrine— one which will hardly gain currency."[8] He wanted to obtain the Rochester plans for inspection and possible use by the Board. The ideas that architectural drawings were instruments of the practice of the profession, belonged to the architect, and could not be used by someone other than the client without compensation being paid the architect were inconceivable to Kelly, a most practical man. Kelly, who was a trustee of Vassar as well as Cornell, urged Ezra Cornell to build with stone in Ithaca. The brick construction used in the enormous and elegant main building at Vassar in the two preceding years must have offended Kelly's sense of propriety.

The Building Committee prepared detailed instructions for the several architects who had expressed interest in the work. Three buildings were to be erected in the first building program: two dormitories, "on a modified Yale plan" in which the entries were separated by a block of lecture rooms and faculty studies in the central part of the building; and a central building for the library and museum. Construction of laboratories was deferred to await the guidance of the yet unappointed heads of the science departments. The two dormitory-classroom buildings were to house sixty students each and were to be designed so that if the University was "able to do away with dormitories, the students' rooms could be laid together with lecture rooms and for several college purposes."[9] The lecture rooms in the center of each building were to be of various sizes, seating from twenty to two hundred. They were located between dormitory rooms to prevent "too much intercourse between students during hours of study." The buildings were to be two hundred feet long, fifty feet wide, and three stories high with a usable fourth floor under the roof. The committee hoped, cost permitting, that the buildings could be built of stone. The museum and library building was to be an oblong structure, fifty by one hundred feet, with its "interior all thrown into one great room . . . surrounded by at least two separate, very broad galleries." It was to be convertible to use as a museum when the library could be removed to a separate building. The need for a chapel or public hall, an observatory, and several houses for professors was noted, but action was deferred.[10]

Less than a week after the appointment of the Building Committee, Eugene Schuyler of Ithaca was discussing dormitory plans with Russell Sturgis and reporting his ideas to White.[11] Schuyler was a Yale graduate ('59), possessor of one of the first two Ph.D.'s granted by an American university, and son of the secretary of the Cornell Board of Trustees. He was a distant cousin of architectural critic Montgomery Schuyler, also an Ithacan. Eugene Schuyler may have been White's accomplice in an attempt to convince the committee that Cornell's first buildings should be done in the "Gothic Revival" style. Sturgis wrote to White sending him a photograph of

[7] Valk to EC, 10 May 1865; Nichols and Brown to EC, 26 May 1865; F. H. Moore to EC, 28 September 1865, Cornell Papers. Cornell must have encouraged Moore to submit a design during his visit to Cambridge; Sturgis to ADW, 30 June 1865, White Papers.
[8] Kelly to EC, 8 August 1865 and 15 May 1865, Cornell Papers.

[9] Building Committee report, 14 March 1866, Cornell Papers.
[10] Building Committee report, 14 March 1866.
[11] Schuyler to ADW, 12 September 1865, White Papers.

Elevation of East Front

Scale
16 feet — one inch

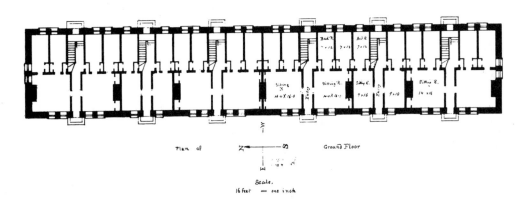

Plan of   Ground Floor

Scale,
16 feet — one inch

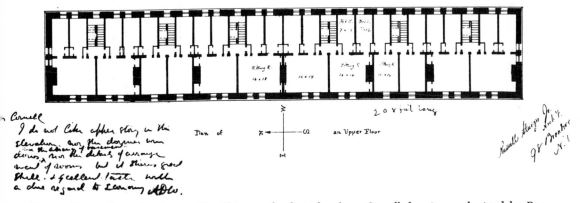

Plan of   an Upper Floor

Fig. 31. Design for a dormitory, 1865. This was the first plan for a Cornell dormitory submitted by Russell Sturgis to White.

his design for a "Fine Arts building." By 18 September 1865, Sturgis had sent plans for a dormitory (Fig. 31). He suggested that the students would feel more at home in a build-

ing divided into six apartments than they would in a building entirely open.[12] A few

[12] Sturgis to ADW, 18 September 1865, White Papers.

years later he used this idea in Durfee Hall at Yale (1870). Sturgis probably had not yet received the committee's specifications for the first building—hence the design for a building with six entries.

The fall of 1865 was a period of intensive architectural research and discussion. Cornell and White visited other universities to inspect buildings. Cornell, with Brown of the Albany architects, Nichols and Brown, measured dormitory rooms in Holworthy and Grays Halls at Harvard and discussed their problem with President Hill. The Founder liked Holworthy better than Grays. Cornell also visited Vassar when his daughter enrolled there in September 1865. It seems probable that the style and large scale of the elegant, recently completed main building there might have influenced Cornell's preference for designs of a similar style at the new university in Ithaca.

Professor Wood of Michigan wrote to White in December 1865, sending a rough sketch of dormitory rooms at Michigan which showed how they could easily be converted into recitation rooms, a plan later followed in Cornell's first two buildings. Sturgis was preparing plans for a library and museum which White rejected. Cornell or White was apparently in touch with Frederic Moore in Boston, Wilcox and Porter in Buffalo, and Nichols and Brown in Albany. During this period of feverish architectural activity, late in 1865, in the correspondence that has been preserved there is no further mention of a competition, but one was obviously underway.

Frederic Moore, Nichols and Brown, Russell Sturgis, and Wilcox and Porter all submitted plans to the Building Committee late in the winter of 1865–1866. The *Journal* reported that "the plans were all of a superior order" and that the committee found "the selection of plans no light task." There may be some exaggeration in the first part of this statement, but the last part rings true. The committee was, in fact, disappointed in the designs submitted for the first buildings; at least, Andrew Dickson White was. In his draft of a report of the Building Committee to the Board of Trus-

tees on 14 March 1866, he crossed out a sentence which read: "The response to the call of the committee by architects of high reputation has not been so general as was expected and wished." It is not likely that White had expected much of any of the designs in the committee's "competition" with the possible exception of the plans by Russell Sturgis. Dormitory designs submitted by the four architects were reviewed and, while the designs submitted by Nichols and Brown of Albany were judged "the most satisfactory," the committee did not adopt any of the plans because they thought "more competition was desirable." [13] The designs of Nichols and Brown were never carried out. Neither was the full plan for a "square" although the present main quadrangle at Cornell is a handsome truncated descendant of this early plan.

Sturgis had completed three sets of plans by early February 1866. He sent them to White, expressing the hope that the committee would decide to entrust the whole matter of the selection of the final design to White "as probably the only person who understands it." He seems to have had the impression that the selection would be made from his designs only. Sturgis also requested White "not to lay his drawings of the exteriors before the committee, but the plans only." [14] Sturgis and White probably feared the committee's (or Cornell's) scorn for their Ruskinian designs. None of the surviving sketches of designs for the first buildings can be attributed definitely to Sturgis except his September 1865 dormitory design (Fig. 31). An inspection of the drawings for the dormitory-classroom building that have survived reveals the indecision of the committee and the stylistic fickleness of the architects. One of the drawings, unsigned but probably a Sturgis revision, was essentially "Gothic Revival" in conception and quite simply and interestingly detailed (Fig. 32). Some elements of this design seem to foreshadow Sturgis' Farnam Hall (1869)

[13] Building Committee report, 14 March 1866.
[14] Sturgis to ADW, 10 February 1866, White Papers. The drawings are in the C.U. Archives.

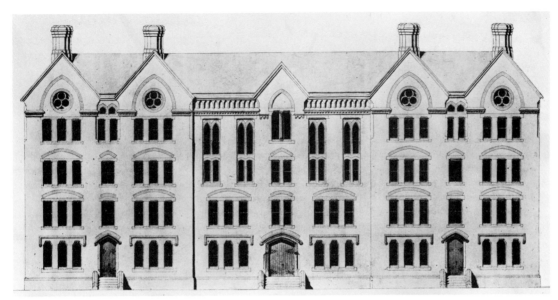

Fig. 32. Design for dormitory-classroom building, 1866. The drawing is unsigned, but it was probably submitted by Russell Sturgis after the Building Committee had established detailed requirements for the first buildings.

and Durfee Hall (1870) at Yale (Fig. 33). This proposal lacked the requisite French roof and on that score alone must have placed low in the committee's rating.

The designs submitted by the other architects were alternative proposals for brick or stone pointed-arch or round-arch windowed buildings or some mixture of the two.[15] The

[15] H. R. Hitchcock in *The Architecture of H. H. Richardson and His Times* refers to one of the mixed styles of the times as "French-roofed, round-arched Victorian Gothic," a type current in London in the late

Fig. 33. Durfee Hall at Yale (1870), by Russell Sturgis.

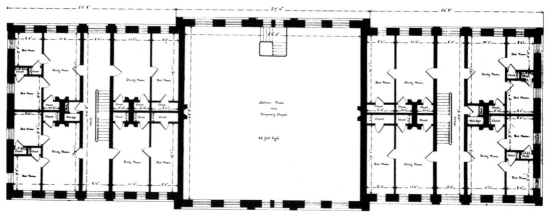

Fig. 34. Design for dormitory-classroom building, 1866, by Nichols and Brown; third-floor plan, brick version.

robust Wilcox and Porter designs which were finally built were later hopefully termed "Florentine Renaissance style." Nichols and Brown offered brick and stone versions of their dormitory design (Figs. 34, 35, and 36), and a design for a library. Most of the plans are dated 1865, and the one attributed above to Sturgis has a rough pencil sketch of a quad-

fifties and early sixties. The building finally built at Cornell seems to fit in this category except for the omission of colonnettes at the windows. ADW refers to the style of the first buildings as "pseudo-Italian." J. A. Morris described the style of the first buildings as "Florentine with French roofs" (Hewett, MS revisions of *Landmarks of Tompkins County*).

rangle on the back. The submissions were all similar in building dimensions, position of doors, and general arrangement of windows; almost all of them have French roofs. Since the committee had prepared such detailed specifications for the building, the final selection of a design was apparently to be made on the basis of the best elevation and internal room arrangement and certainly on the basis of economy of construction. Frederic Moore's rather elaborate proposal must have been given slight consideration along with the most elaborate proposals in the "pointed style" by Nichols and Brown. The latter did not pro-

Fig. 35. Elevation of dormitory-classroom building, 1866, by Nichols and Brown, brick version.

Fig. 36. Elevation of dormitory-classroom building, 1866, by Nichols and Brown, stone version.

vide a basement nor did it make very efficient use of attic space under the French roof.

In March 1866, after the Building Committee stated its preference for the Nichols and Brown designs, it asked the Board of Trustees for permission to use $500 for prizes or direct compensation in order to "obtain more plans and thus give . . . a wider range of choice." [16] It appears that the money was used to pay Wilcox and Porter of Buffalo to develop the

[16] Building Committee report, 14 March 1866.

final design (Figs. 37, 38, and 39). All of this is most mysterious. Erosion of the records, or selective saving of correspondence, has covered the traces of what seems to have been a conflict of opinion within the Building Committee. Ornamented or plain? Brick or stone? White's style or Cornell's? These seem to have been the main points of disagreement. The discussion was no doubt a short one. Speed in getting the buildings erected was important, and the more heavily ornamented designs must have seemed too expensive. By early

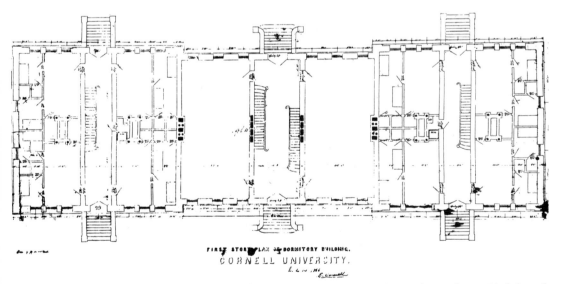

FIRST STORY PLAN OF DORMITORY BUILDING.
CORNELL UNIVERSITY.

Fig. 37. Plan for Morrill Hall by Wilcox and Porter, 1866. Note the similarity of this plan to Nichols and Brown's plan (Fig. 34).

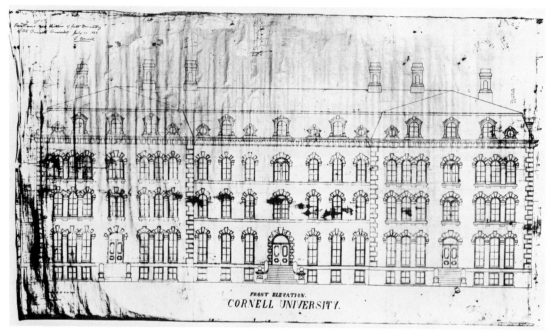

Fig. 38. Elevation of Morrill Hall, 1866, by Wilcox and Porter.

April 1866, the revised Wilcox and Porter plans were sent to Albany for Ezra Cornell's final approval.[17]

The final designs for the first university building present evidence of the pragmatic Founder's skill in combining ideas readily at hand. Since Ezra Cornell probably was not particularly concerned with innovation in building style or arrangement, it is not difficult to trace the origins of his ideas which so strongly influenced the final plans. One has only to look at the arrangement of Grays and Holworthy Halls in the Harvard Yard, which he so carefully inspected before the building specifications were sent to the architects, and beyond Grays at the rugged "Romanesque"

[17] ADW to EC, April 1866, White Papers.

Fig. 39. Morrill Hall in 1966.

exterior of Leopold Eidlitz's Boylston Hall with slightly contrasting quoins at its angles (Fig. 40). Both Holworthy (1811) and Grays (1863) were divided into three sections by masonry fire walls. The students' rooms opened off the center hall of each section and were provided with fireplaces. Hope College at Brown University, which Ezra Cornell also inspected on his trip with Brown in 1868, has a similar tripartite arrangement. The obvious economies of using the mansard roof and high basement to provide inexpensive extra floors in Grays must have appealed to Cornell. Their use at Cornell permitted construction in the "more permanent" stone that White and Kelly wanted and the decorative use of lighter stone quoins at the angles of the buildings. The formal dignity of Boylston Hall's Rockport granite exterior could not be matched with the local Ithaca stone, but the rough cut ashlar walls of Morrill and its neighbors, defined by the massive regularly cut limestone quoins, seems more appropriate to the rustic grandeur of the Ithaca site. The balance of ruggedness and elegance in the walls of the buildings seems to symbolize the balance of practical and academic education the founders wanted at Cornell.

Of the four architectural firms that submitted building plans none seems to have understood that a competition had been conducted.

In April 1866, Nichols and Brown were still working on their designs and were dismayed when Cornell visited them in Albany and took away "the bulk of the work, plans, sketches, and all" after telling them that he "did not think it was the intention of the Committee to engage an architect any further than to secure some general plans leaving the carrying out of the detail of the design to the tender mercies of the local mechanics." [18]

Early in May, Nichols and Brown billed the Trustees $714 for services provided between November 1865 and April 1866. Cornell had paid them $100 when he took the plans in April. They were awarded an additional $250 for the "competition" and in August they submitted another bill for the balance. In December they were still asking Cornell about payment. "We trust you will no longer neglect us," they pleaded, "but give us the means of opening the New Year without debt and with some little money on hand." [19] In May 1867, the Albany architects underlined their confusion about the issue when they wrote to White that they had "fondly imagined at the time the work was done [they] were the architects of the University and that the work

[18] Nichols and Brown to ADW, 8 May 1866, White Papers.
[19] Nichols and Brown to EC, 29 December 1866, Cornell Papers.

Fig. 40. Boylston Hall (1857) and Grays Hall (1863), Harvard.

would pay for any time engaged in perfecting arrangements." [20]

Russell Sturgis was concerned about payments for services, too. He wrote to White in August 1866 that he would be glad to receive the amount of his bill "as soon as it may be convenient." [21] In spite of White's comments on Sturgis' earlier sketches, it seems apparent that he had hoped that Sturgis would be the designer of the first buildings. Sturgis was not as disturbed as Nichols and Brown about the arrangements of the "competition" but there is little doubt that the clients and perhaps the architects had no clear ideas about an orderly, ethical procedure in architectural practice. The clients may have been under the impression that architects provided free sketches. The architects were surely not precise about the nature of the clients' commitments to them. Two years later Russell Sturgis was one of the leaders in the establishment of the New York chapter of the American Institute of Architects. This organization took an early interest in standardizing the forms of agreement for services and payments between architects and their clients.

The practical members of the Board had won the day for a plain style. The first stone buildings on the University's Quadrangle were sturdy, spacious, economical, no-nonsense structures. White, in a later marginal notation on one of the competition drawings, wrote that the plans of Russell Sturgis "were not accepted as they were too Gothic and were especially opposed by John Stanton Gould, our Quaker Trustee." [22] Still later he wrote that though "two architects, who at that time took the lead in American Gothic Architecture, did their best . . . The Trustees would have none of their work and really as I remember it I cannot blame them." [23] In his *Autobiography*, White described his difficulties in promoting the "American Gothic" style for the first buildings.

Alas! I could not reproduce my air-castles. For our charter required us to have the university in operation on October 1868, and there was no time for careful architectural preparation. Moreover, the means failed us. All that we could then do was to accept a fairly good plan for our main structures; to make them simple, substantial and dignified; to build them of stone from our own quarries; and to dispose the buildings [so] that future architects might combine other buildings with them to form an impressive quadrangle on the upper part of the university property. To this plan Mr. Cornell gave his hearty assent.[24]

From this statement and from the design of Ezra Cornell's villa, which was begun in 1867, one may deduce that the Founder was not really opposed to the "American Gothic" style. He just knew when he could not afford it. White's mood at the time is reflected in the Annual Report of the President for 1867 in which he wrote: "The University needs buildings much, a fine faculty more. . . . Buildings never yet made a great university. Some of the greatest are in very poor buildings. Better a splendid and complete faculty in a barn than an insufficient faculty in a palace." Even though the Building Committee had chosen the simplest plans submitted, other economies were necessary. For example, sash weights were left out of the windows to save a few hundred dollars for books and equipment. White, disappointed but always the optimist, thought the buildings "might one day, in the hands of a better architect, be so modified as to produce a thoroughly good effect." [25]

The successful architects in the "competition" were Harlow M. Wilcox and Cyrus K. Porter of Buffalo. After they drew the final plans for Morrill Hall in April 1866, they con-

---

[20] Nichols and Brown to ADW, 16 May 1867, White Papers. In another part of the letter Brown expresses the belief that Cornell must think it dangerous for young men to have money.

[21] Sturgis to ADW, 18 August 1866, White Papers.

[22] Note signed "A.D.W." on an elevation of a proposed Library for the Cornell University, C.U. Archives.

[23] ADW to Hewett, 17 October 1895, Hewett Papers. White must have been referring to Sturgis and Peter Wight.

[24] White, *Autobiography*, I, 337–338.

[25] ADW to Hewett, 17 October 1895.

tinued to provide services for the University through the summer of 1867. In June 1866 bids were taken in their office for the construction of the first building, South University, now Morrill Hall. Their plans (Fig. 37) called for two students rooming together to be provided with a study, two bedrooms, three large closets, a fireplace, and "good substantial furniture." Ash chutes were provided near each room and there were elevators in the corridors for hoisting coal. The central part of the building contained lecture rooms and faculty studies. A large hall in the top floor of the center section seated over four hundred students.

During the first four years of the University's operation the growing library was housed in the first floor of the center section of Morrill Hall. As the library grew, student rooms on this floor were converted for its use. Andrew Dickson White got the shivers when he thought of the valuable books under the same flammable roof with thirty-two stoves and kerosene lamps attended by students. He worked hard to get the library and the students moved elsewhere so the books would be safe and the space could be used for lecture rooms.

Someone in authority must have expressed doubts about the building authorized by the committee. On 2 November 1866, the Trustees passed a resolution which stated that they had "examined with care and attention the location and style of building . . . [and expressed] hearty approbation and satisfaction at the display of great taste combined with due regard to economy in the material, style and ornamentation and elevation of the building." [26] At the same Trustees' meeting Andrew Dickson White was elected President of Cornell University.

A second building authorized by the Executive Committee in February 1867 was "to be duplicate of the first" in style, external finish, and appearance and be located in accordance with the quadrangle plan.[27] Wilcox and Porter

made a few changes in interior arrangements and Ezra Cornell instructed his brother to start the quarry and engage all the masons he could find. Cornell had decided to erect the second building (White Hall) himself by force account but was finally persuaded to let contracts. He did not trust Thomas, the contractor for Morrill Hall, and watched his work like a hawk. Cornell suspected collusion in the bidding for the job,[28] regularly delayed progress payments, and thought he could do the work better at lower cost himself. President White had some ideas about the second building, too. In May he wrote to Cornell about sketches of it "as I believe you prefer it and as I like it myself." [29] Andrew D. White was embarking on the second in a lifelong series of efforts to better the environment of the University's campus.

By late spring 1867, the construction of Morrill Hall was well advanced and the revised plans for the second building were almost complete. A *New York Evening Post* article of 11 June 1867 described the Cornell situation hopefully:

The first of the Cornell University buildings is now nearly finished. It is an enormous edifice of bluestone and Medina sandstone not unlike in its architectural features the palaces of Italian Florence. Five other similar edifices are to be erected [the west row]. The grounds are much varied in their surface and offer an admirable scope for the genius of the landscape gardener. Frank Law Olmsted [sic] . . . is now here and to his skillful hands will be entrusted the arrangement and decoration of the University estates.

White contacted Olmsted in May 1867 after a discussion with Ezra Cornell about the appearance of the campus. He persuaded Cornell that it was important to get the advice of

[26] Trustees' *Proceedings*, I, 8.   [27] *Ibid.*, I, 11.

[28] EC to ADW, 9 July 1866 and 15 August 1866, White Papers; MS "Report of the Building Committee," 26 September 1867 (written 23 September 1867), White Papers. South University (Morrill Hall) cost $60,000. North University (White Hall) cost $63,000. The stone for both buildings, except for the Medina stone quoins, came from the University quarries on the slope west of the site. EC thought he could build the first building, himself, for $40,000.

[29] ADW to EC, 23 May 1867, Cornell Papers.

a landscape gardener. After inspection of the university grounds and plans for their development, Olmsted recommended abandonment of the quadrangle idea. He believed that if the buildings were placed as proposed, the same mistake other colleges were then repenting would be made at Cornell. He was certain that to have a regular plan was an error. His statement echoes advice he had given Yale and Amherst and his published recommendations on campus planning for Massachusetts Agricultural and Mechanic Arts College and California College.[30]

He wrote to White:

You ought to anticipate such a growth of the University as will eventually require ten times the building accommodation that is provided for in your present plan. Do you doubt that far finer buildings than those you are now proposing to construct will be erected for university purposes in the course of a century or two? I do not. And if so—that is to say if the university is to be a great success, . . . is to draw out the affection, the gratitude, . . . and the benevolence of other noble men and women besides its founders—then your proposed line, complete in itself or the "quadrangle" (which is not a quadrangle) complete in itself and with but one front of dignity, will be simply another monument of shortsightedness, inconsideration and complacency with an [sic] little present, like those at Yale and Amherst.[31]

Olmsted explained at length the error of adopting a regular plan for the layout of the buildings. He described the difficulties of siting later structures in a manner befitting their importance when a rigid plan pre-empted the

possibilities of flexible adjustment. He urged a freer disposition of the buildings more in keeping with the rugged topography of the site and the unforeseeable demands of later generations. He believed a "free, liberal, picturesque" arrangement to be best suited. Two stream valleys crossed the campus between the present sites of White, McGraw, and Morrill Halls and immediately north of White Hall the ground rose to the height of the second story. The site was well adapted to Olmsted's skills in picturesque, informal landscape design. "Don't," he advised White, "begin by tying yourself to formality and straight lacing."

But the recommendation came too late. White thanked Olmsted for his "kind letter" and said that his statements regarding the buildings had greatly influenced him. The difficulty posed at the moment, he wrote, was that the University was in a hurry to start the next building and he had no time to "talk up a new plan."[32] The President's diplomacy and optimism are amazing: "[We] must," he wrote, "take one more step in what you regard as a wrong direction; but this done there will be breathing time and though the problem for another architect will be somewhat more complicated it will be all the more honor to have solved it. If there be mistake we must trust to future rectification." President White believed in the triumph of good over evil! "Don't," he begged Olmsted, "lose faith or hope on account of this doubt regarding our buildings. You must take an interest in us."[33]

Olmsted understood the difficulty. He wrote White: "In all that I am good for I am at your service."[34] He was good for a great deal at Cornell. Having damned the Quadrangle, he proceeded to save it by insisting on the importance of placing the second building on the same elevation as the first so that the west

[30] Olmsted, Vaux, and Co., *A Few Things to Be Thought of before Proceeding to Plan Buildings for the National Agricultural Colleges* (New York, 1866); *Report upon Projected Improvement of The Estate of the College of California at Berkeley near Oakland* (New York, 1866). The College of California site was transferred to the University of California several years later. This is the Berkeley campus of the University. The Massachusetts Agricultural and Mechanic Arts College at Amherst became the University of Massachusetts. Olmsted also advised on the campus plan at Amherst College.
[31] Olmsted to ADW, 13 June 1867, White Papers.

[32] ADW to Olmsted, 22 June 1867, Olmsted Papers, Library of Congress, Division of Manuscripts.
[33] ADW to Olmsted, 22 June 1867, Olmsted Papers.
[34] Olmsted to ADW, 27 June 1867, White Papers.

line of buildings on the Quadrangle would form a dignified composition unified by a terrace. He wrote to White:

The site of your second building having been determined against my judgment, it seems to me to be very important that nothing should be done which shall make the suggestion which I offered to you in regard to a terrace impracticable and especially if the first building is duplicated, that its roof lines and base lines should be on the same level with those of the first.

If it is to be almost a duplicate, it should be precisely a duplicate otherwise (especially with a difference of two feet elevation on the horizontal sky-lines), it will look as if any variation has been accidental and a mistake arising from the carelessness or stupidity of the builders. I am surprised to think that Mr. Cornell would entertain such a project; the expense to be saved by it is very trifling.[35]

White responded like a shot. In his letter to Cornell, enclosing Olmsted's letter, he sounds like a man threatened with physical punishment:

Now I beg of you asking it as a favor that the water tables and all the lines including sky lines be put absolutely on the same line.

Mr. Olmsted's remark is, to me, conclusive. We shall at some time erect a central building to give character and unity to the whole mass. If the main architectural lines of the two buildings are not in the same plane we cannot tell what sort of trouble will be produced. But I am certain that we shall deeply regret it. A central building must harmonize with one or the other side buildings. How you can make it harmonize with both I do not see.

Moreover I fear lest we impair the effect of the terrace which if properly carried out will be a noble feature. We risk too much for the small gain.

Even if the differences in the lines of the buildings is not detected at once, it seems to me that the erection of a central building will bring it out.—We are building for centuries and should not subject ourselves to the charge of stupidity from those who come after us.

Now you had your way about the site—yield to the majority in regard to this slight matter of level. I hope you will concede this point. Every college so far is in the main an architectural failure. Do not let us risk the same failure by disturbing the combination between the leading features of our place as I feel we should do by this difference of grades and architectural lines. Don't do it.[36]

Cornell replied calmly: "I will observe your suggestions." And so White Hall was set on the same level as its twin, Morrill Hall. Olmsted's concept of a great terrace unifying the west front of the Quadrangle was not and still has not been carried out, but it reappeared in Cornell campus plans for the next eighty years. It is still a valid idea awaiting execution by some future generation of Cornell campus planners.

With the symmetry of the Quadrangle's west front preserved, Olmsted and White proceeded to develop ideas for its central building and for the rest of the campus. By September 1867, Olmsted had "blocked out a tolerably complete plan for the general subdivisions and formed a theory of the probable progress of closer settlement on the hill outside of the university grounds."[37] This campus and community plan has not survived but was probably very much like Olmsted's studies in 1866 for California College and the Massachusetts Agricultural and Mechanic Arts College. Olmsted's plans were comprehensive, so the one for Cornell probably included an arrangement for the buildings and grounds of the University and proposals for the development of the surrounding community.

As far as the Quadrangle was concerned, Olmsted was in agreement with White about the next step in the development of the west row: "a more important and more advanced [central] building by which the first two buildings would be subordinated and at the

[35] Olmsted to ADW, 10 September 1867, White Papers. In a later accounting of the building cost prepared by Cornell, grading costs are listed at $1,000.

[36] ADW to EC, 12 September 1867, Cornell Papers.
[37] Olmsted to ADW, 10 September 1867, White Papers.

Fig. 41. John McGraw about 1868.

same time assembled." [38] In the original quadrangle plan this central position had been reserved for a chapel and administrative offices. Now the University's great need was for more classrooms, library space, and a museum to house the scientific collections White and Cornell were assembling and buying.

John McGraw of Dryden, New York, and Ithaca (Fig. 41) had made a fortune in lumbering operations. His daughter Jennie presented the University with its first chime of bells at the opening ceremonies in October 1868. They hung in an open wooden scaffolding on the site of Uris Library until 1872. It is said that John McGraw and Henry Sage, a former Ithacan also in the lumber business, were so appalled at the exhausted look of

[38] *Ibid.*

White and Cornell at the opening ceremonies that they committed themselves to the University's cause on the spot. McGraw's first thought was to leave $30,000 to the University in his will. Later he decided (or was persuaded) that he should pay for the central building in the west row of the Quadrangle, and by late October, 1868, the basic ideas for the building had been worked out. It was to be "substantially fireproof" and built in three sections with the middle section one hundred feet wide by sixty feet long and four stories high. Its large galleried halls (Fig. 42), planned for the museum, library, and scientific collections, were inspired by the Albany building of the New York State Historical Society. The end sections were to be "permanent lecture rooms so arranged that apparatus or specimens wanted for instruction [could] be readily carried from the cabinets in the center section." In the west center a tower was specified for Jennie McGraw's chime of bells.[39] The central section was to be designed for temporary use as a library and museum; later these functions were to be housed in separate buildings at the ends of the row in accordance with the original quadrangle plan. The central section of McGraw would then be used exclusively for the science collections.

During the winter of 1868–1869 the University began negotiations with Syracuse architect Archimedes N. Russell, for design services on this central building. Russell had worked in the offices of John Stevens in Boston and Horatio White in Syracuse. In 1868 he opened his own office and carried on an extensive practice until 1915. Russell took his design cues from the detailed building program outlined above, the style of the first two buildings, Frederick Law Olmsted's idea for a

[39] McGraw to ADW, 7 July 1869, White Papers; *New York Evening Post*, 2 October 1868. McGraw signed a contract with Graff and Neis for construction of the building in December 1869. The cornerstone had been laid the previous June. From the correspondence, it appears that it took some pulling and hauling to get John McGraw to pay for the building, by then estimated to cost $70,000. The final cost was over $120,000.

Fig. 42. The McGraw Hall museum in 1878. Scientific collections, located in the center of the building, were immediately accessible from the lecture rooms at either end.

terrace, and White's insistence on a dominant central building, and produced the respectful but insistent mass of McGraw Hall (Fig. 43). Recent generations, unaware of the instructions to the designer, have criticized the first buildings because they face the wrong way. The design was in fact conceived as facing west onto the proposed terrace (Fig. 44). McGraw Hall was designed to complete the composition, and as John McGraw wrote "to give a more ship shape look to the hillside" as viewed from below [40] (Fig. 45). Since the terrace has never been completed these objectives were only partially attained.

Russell's services apparently were satisfactory for he was retained to design the next university building, the first unit of Sibley Hall. For a brief moment William Henry Miller, a young student in architecture being tutored by Andrew D. White, was in the running. White wrote to Vice-President Russel in mid-July, 1870, asking if student Miller had produced any drawings for "the engineers'

building" and threatening to have Archimedes Russell prepare the drawings if he had not. Miller missed the deadline by two weeks and White retained Russell in the middle of July. Late in July both sets of plans were sent to Hiram Sibley, the donor of the building, for approval. Russell's plans were selected.[41] His design for West Sibley Hall (Fig. 46) was a slight but imaginative modification of the style of Morrill, McGraw, and White Halls. The high narrow windows of the principal floor and the larger entrance doors give it a much more dignified character than White and Morrill Halls. Its most significant characteristic, however, is its siting in relation to the first buildings. Here the influence of Olmsted's terrace concept is apparent. By raising the two-storied building on an east-west terrace, its mansard roof is brought into line with that of White Hall. Sibley Hall's two-stories-plus-mansard mass effectively carries the line of the west buildings around the corner

[40] McGraw to ADW 7 July 1869, White Papers.

[41] ADW to W. C. Russel, 13, 14, 16 July 1870, White Papers.

Fig. 43. McGraw Hall, by Archimedes N. Russell (1869), as it appears from the Quadrangle. The campanile which once housed Jennie McGraw's chime of bells faces toward the town on the far side of the building.

of the Quadrangle. Russell continued to provide design services for additions to the Sibley group over the next fifteen years as Sibley and his son advanced funds to provide space for the rapidly growing engineering school.

During the planning and construction of McGraw Hall and the first unit of Sibley Hall, Andrew D. White and Ezra Cornell continued their characteristic roles. In the case of Sibley Hall, White instigated the gift of build-

ing funds by offering to build a President's House if Sibley would erect a building for the mechanic arts. After Sibley had agreed to the bargain, the President spent much time with the architect. He even hovered a whole day in Archimedes Russell's office fending off visitors so that the architect could complete the drawings. White also convinced Sibley that he should add to his gift sufficient money for a second story to house the civil engineering

Fig. 44. Drawing of the Stone Row at Cornell, viewed from the west, by Archimedes N. Russell, 1872. Behind McGraw Hall is the wooden laboratory which Ezra Cornell built in 1868 while Andrew D. White was in Europe collecting faculty, equipment, and books. The connecting walls between the buildings were never built.

Fig. 45. The Stone Row from the village, about 1871. In the foreground, left to right, are Ezra Cornell's Tioga Street house, the Village Hall, and the Cornell Public Library. On the hill are, left, Llenroc, and, middle, the Stone Row.

department. He accomplished this by offering to give an amount equal to the increased building cost for purchase of apparatus, models, and machines for the use of the School of Engineering.[42] President White considered the immediate construction of this building of major importance because of the current criticism of the University's lack of facilities for instruction in the mechanic arts, a charge given to it under the Morrill Act. Speed was important. Sibley saw the first plans late in July 1870, after about two weeks had been spent on the design, and by 10 August, White and Archimedes Russell were staking out the foundations with the contractors, with White carefully measuring off adjacent areas so that they "would divide up properly" for the completion of the north side of the Quadrangle.[43] Early in September, White was negotiating with Sibley for $3,500 for stone quoins in order to dress up the appearance of the building and make it more compatible with its neighbors. The building, which now forms

[42] ADW to Sibley, 22 July 1870, White Papers.
[43] ADW to EC, 10 August 1870, Cornell Papers. White's meticulous reporting to Cornell of the exact location of Sibley Hall and other measurements is additional proof that Cornell was the instigator of the quadrangle plan.

the west end of West Sibley Hall, was completed in June 1871.

White had been given complete authority for the plans and execution of Sibley Hall, but when it came to the practical details of the operations, he relied on Cornell. Soon after the construction began, it became apparent that there was not enough stone coming from the quarry west of White Hall. McGraw Hall and Ezra Cornell's villa were being built with the same stone at the same time. White wrote to Cornell asking him to meet with Russel to "straighten the matter out." White, effective in dealing with broad questions of design and negotiating for funds, sometimes pretended helplessness when it came to the details of the actual work. In this case he relied on the practical builder, Ezra Cornell, to work them out. In this Cornell was assisted by a slacking off in work on McGraw Hall because of the University's poor financial condition. As stone production increased and stone consumption decreased, the rapid pace of work on Sibley Hall was resumed.

With the completion of Sibley Hall in 1871, the Quadrangle began to take shape (Fig. 47). At first in the face of Olmsted's doubts and later with his help, the University's first

Fig. 46. West Sibley Hall (1870) by Archimedes N. Russell.

buildings were sited with dignity and unity on the brow of East Hill. The original plan was still intact. If Andrew White had some reservations about the style of the buildings, they were sublimated by his vision of the successful turning of the corner of the Quadrangle. As he thought about the effect the new building would have, he wrote to Cornell describing his pleasure:

A terrace . . . will form a very handsome feature on our grounds.

This arrangement is especially advantageous since . . . [it] will lift the Sibley building up so that the sky line and roof line generally will be a little higher than the North dormitory—as it ought to be.

I think that standing on the spot, lifted up so as to strike the eye just as one enters the great quadrangle and situated upon a neatly sodded terrace which will break the flatness and monotony of the campus—of the same style as the other buildings—but with a slight modification in trimmings that it will be exceedingly ornamental.[44]

Time and ivy have softened the rugged walls of Cornell's first buildings, Morrill, McGraw, White, and Sibley Halls. These

[44] ADW to EC, 22 August 1870, Cornell Papers.

sturdy monuments have aged well and their siting, massing, and rugged stonework command our respect for the talent of the era. The craggy line of buildings is an appropriately dramatic composition for the dramatic site. The Quadrangle behind them is a calm, orderly, enclosed plain set within an otherwise informal campus composed in part of smaller, less dramatic and less well-defined quadrangles and courts. The Arts Quadrangle is a major unifying element in the Cornell campus and perhaps one of the finest spatial compositions to be found on an American campus.

Olmsted deserves much of the credit for the quality of the Quadrangle. He was willing and able to resolve the divergent approaches of White and Cornell at a critical time in the development of the campus. Also, he first developed the simple system of using terraces which permit unifying horizontal lines on each side of the Quadrangle while the space accommodates a twenty-five-foot rise in grade from west to east. Over the years the Quadrangle has received careful attention, has been furnished with memorial statuary, and has been protected from destructive change. It has become the heart of the Cornell campus. The only significant loss has been the replacing of Boardman Hall with the new

Fig. 47. The Quadrangle in 1873. President's Row has been graded (immediately behind the students in the foreground). At the right is part of the rail fence that divided the campus from Ezra Cornell's fifty acre "reserve" south of the Quadrangle.

Olin Research Library (1962) designed by Warner, Burns, Toan and Lunde, which, though out of scale with its neighbors, none the less respectfully observes the primacy of the first stone buildings.

Montgomery Schuyler thought these first buildings were "on a parity with the Cascadilla" and that "when the time came for their removal, the room of the pioneers would be preferable to their company." He also thought that "there would not be a dog to bark at their going." [45] No one at Cornell has ever seriously proposed their demolition, but a few remarks in their defense on architectural as well as historic and symbolic grounds may be in order. While they by no means represent distinguished architecture, they have much company among college buildings of the same era. Some architects destined for later fame were not doing better work at this time. H. H. Richardson's Agawam National Bank (1869) in Springfield, Massachusetts, approached the same rugged style as the first buildings at Cornell with less surety. In materials and details the Bonner-Marquand Gymnasium and Halsted Observatory (1869) at Princeton were very like the buildings in the stone row at Cornell.

These buildings also had rough gray stonework, bracketed cornices, and deep, arched windows with heavy rusticated arch stones. Bonner-Marquand lacked the power and rhythm of the Cornell buildings, but it somehow escaped the era's ubiquitous mansard roof. Thayer Hall (1870) at Harvard is a simple arrangement of stone-trimmed brick boxes, a dormitory much like Morrill and White Halls originally, but similar in massing to McGraw Hall. Reunion Hall (1870) at Princeton, College Hall (1872) at the University of Michigan, South Hall (1872) at the University of California, and many others share the utilitarian style of Morrill and White Halls, including the heavy mansard roof. South Hall at Berkeley may claim some added quality because of its fine decorative features, but these, alas, are carved in wood painted to look like stone.

Many other college buildings erected in America in the decade following the Civil War were more picturesque in massing than the stone row at Cornell. They were designed in a style sometimes called "Post-Civil-War American Gothic." College Hall (1871) at the University of Pennsylvania, a typical representative of this style, is a picturesque, restless, greenstone building. Charles Babcock, Professor of Architecture at Cornell, developed a somewhat calmer and better propor-

[45] Montgomery Schuyler, "The Architecture of American Colleges," Cornell, *Architectural Record*, XXX, No. 6 (December 1911), 566.

tioned brick version of the genre in Sage College in 1872. George Hathorne's Walker Hall (1870) at Amherst, Potter's Packer Hall (1872) at Lehigh, and Sage College are among the best "American Gothic" college buildings of the decade following the close of the Civil War. Morrill Hall and its twin, White Hall, are about on a par with the best college buildings in the simpler utilitarian style erected in this country from 1865–1875. Their chief claims to admiration lie in their aggressive expression of stone, their dignified simplicity and rhythm, and their appropriate symbolization of Ezra Cornell's rugged determination to build the University of durable materials on the firm foundation of the crest of East Hill.

By 1905 the stone Quadrangle was completed with the construction of Stimson and Goldwin Smith Halls, but even before that the dreams of President White for a less formal campus development as suggested by Olmsted were realized in the design and location of Sage College, Sage Chapel, Barnes Hall, the Old Armory, and the President's House. Both Cornell and White had their way in the end. The contrasting forms of the first buildings on the Cornell campus symbolize the Founder's and the first President's contrasting ideas about architecture. The west buildings of the stone Quadrangle recall Ezra Cornell's rugged, pragmatic approach to building; the informally arranged red-brick Sage College and Chapel, President's House, and Barnes Hall evoke Andrew Dickson White's intellectual commitment to Ruskin's romantic idealism and to Frederick Law Olmsted's landscape ideals.

IV

"Mr. Ruskin Would Be Pleased . . ."

COEDUCATION HAS ALWAYS been a favorite subject of controversy at Cornell. That the first building built on the campus to advance coeducation should also be controversial is therefore appropriate. The intention of the founders was that Cornell be open to all and, although Cornell was not the pioneer in coeducation at the college level, it was the first college in the east to open its doors to women as well as men. Oberlin and Antioch colleges in Ohio and several state universities in the west had admitted women, but before the 1880's, eastern parents preferred to send their daughters to finishing schools and female colleges.

Cornell and White both favored coeducation. Cornell wrote his granddaughter in 1867 that he "wanted girls as well as boys educated in the University." When White wrote his proposal for a new university to Gerrit Smith in 1862, he included a provision that it should be "open to *all*—regardless of sex or color," but when Cornell University opened, White declared that it should be firmly established before introducing coeducation. After the opening ceremonies in October 1868, Henry W. Sage (Fig. 48) quietly told President White to let him know when he was ready to move to provide women with the advantages of higher education at Cornell.

The much publicized innovative character of the new University soon attracted the attention of feminist reformers. Susan B. An-

thony arrived at Cascadilla early in March 1869, "smelt tobacco smoke and saw that ladies were needed there."[1] On 27 March she began her campaign to get women admitted to the University by delivering a lecture in the auditorium of the Cornell Public Library. Goldwin Smith, who was much opposed to coeducation, attended and later reported that "Mr. Cornell pronounced in favor of coeducation after having melted butter poured over his head and down his back by Susan B. Anthony."[2] Mr. Cornell, who called Miss Anthony "the ungentle advocate of the rights of the gentle sex," told her that any woman who passed the examinations for a New York State scholarship would be admitted to Cornell University.[3]

There were several women applicants for admission in the late sixties but none of them appeared on the campus. When Jennie Spencer of Cortland arrived in the fall of 1870 with a state scholarship in hand, she could find no place to live on the hill near the campus and so took quarters in the village. When winter arrived the climb up and down the hill several times a day proved too much for her, and she retired to her home in Cortland. It is said that her trials touched Henry Sage and made him consider more carefully

[1] Hewett, *Cornell University*, I, 259.
[2] Goldwin Smith to ADW, 17 December 1883, White Papers.
[3] Hewett, *op. cit.*, p. 259.

Fig. 48. Henry W. Sage, University Trustee, 1870–1897.

the need to build a "home" for women students.[4] In Brooklyn, where Sage lived, Catherine Beecher was encouraging him to do something about education for women. She was the elder sister of Henry Ward Beecher, the famed pastor of the church Sage attended. Miss Beecher was not a feminist. She disapproved of women's suffrage and believed that women should be trained for their work in the home with the same rigor that men were for their work in the world. Her ideas about women's health (plenty of sunlight, fresh air, and exercise) were to have a marked effect on the design of Sage College.[5] Late in June

1871, Sage repeated his offer to "erect and endow a college or hall for the residence of young women." A committee of White, Weaver, Sage, Andrews, and Finch was appointed by the Trustees to investigate and recommend specific action. Miss Beecher soon wrote to President White (11 August 1871): "Suppose our managers [?] have half a million and should establish in close vicinity to your University and community, a university in which all of the teachers and pupils are in families of from ten to fifteen, all engaged in domestic employment part of each day, and at other hours in study."[6] Her idea, except for the "domestic employment," seems a distant cousin of the coordinate colleges later established at Harvard and Columbia. Miss Beecher's plan was one of the two alternatives studied by the committee during the last half of 1871 and early in 1872 as final recommendations were developed by White and Sage. They visited Oberlin, Antioch, and Michigan to study the facilities and policies of these pioneers in coeducation, and White corresponded extensively with the heads of other institutions to get their views on the subject. Most were favorable.

McGraw Hall was still under construction in 1871–1872 when Henry Sage and Andrew White began work on plans for Sage College. The architectural result is in great contrast to McGraw Hall. Although Sage College is probably one of the best examples in the country of collegiate design of the period immediately following the Civil War, it has also been one of the campus' most controversial buildings. For the most part, this quality springs from the architectural interests of Andrew Dickson White and the architectural talent and the professional poise of Cornell's first professor of architecture, Charles Babcock.

In 1911, Montgomery Schuyler offered some wry but significant praise of the archi-

---

[4] Morris Bishop, A History of Cornell, p. 145.
[5] For an account of the influence of Catherine Beecher on domestic affairs in the last half of the nineteenth century see Russell Lynes, The Domesticated Americans (New York, 1963), pp. 59–64. Miss Beecher's A Treatise On The Domestic Economy, first published in 1842 and reissued in revised form for over thirty years, treated every aspect of housekeep-

ing. Lynes says "she was responsible for getting the curriculum of domestic science accepted, for better or worse, as part of higher education."
[6] C. E. Beecher to ADW, 11 August 1871, White Papers.

tectural qualities of the campus. In the article on Cornell in a series on "The Architecture of American Colleges," he wrote that "visiting alumni of other institutions are reported to agree that Cornell is the second handsomest campus in America." And then he quoted Dean Swift: "It is a maxim that those whom everybody allows the second place have an undoubted title to the first." [7] His high regard for the architectural qualities of Sage College had much to do with this opinion. The story of the design of this building should help us understand some of the reasons for Schuyler's subtle award of first place to Cornell among American college campuses.

After 1870, President White played an increasing role in decisions on campus architecture. Ezra Cornell was busy managing the western pine lands he had purchased to increase the University's endowment and in various railroad enterprises. Henry Sage's offer in 1871 to build and endow a college for women presented White with an excellent opportunity for seeing his personal beliefs regarding university architecture materialize at Cornell. His attempts to achieve "Gothic" buildings in the Quadrangle had failed when the judgment of the "practical builders" prevailed. Once the pattern was set, White had sufficient architectural sense to realize that the Quadrangle should be developed in a simple, consistent style using rough-cut local stone. But White continued to believe that the best collegiate architecture was more picturesque.

His vision of the structures suited to a great university was clear and compelling and it had been developing in his mind since boyhood. In his *Autobiography* he tells of the event that sparked his lifelong interest in architecture.

About my tenth year occurred an event, apparently trivial, but really very important in my mental development during many years afterward. My father brought home one day, as a gift to my mother, a handsome quarto called "The Gallery of British Artists." It contained engrav-

ings from pictures by Turner, Stanfield, Cattermole, and others, mainly representing scenes from Shakespeare, Scott, Burns, picturesque architecture, and beautiful views in various parts of Europe. Of this book I never tired. It aroused in me an intense desire to know more of the subjects represented, and this desire has led me since to visit and to study every cathedral, church, and town hall of any historical or architectural significance in Europe, outside the Spanish peninsula.[8]

White's interest in architecture was further developed and linked to a vision of a great university during his freshman year at Hobart College before he escaped to Yale. Disappointed in the course of study, he spent most of his time in the Hobart Library trying to learn something on his own. He writes of this period:

A room was assigned me . . . and in a neighboring apartment, with charming views over the lake and distant hills, was the library of the Hermean Society. It was the largest collection of books I had ever seen. . . . One day I discovered in it Huber and Newman's book on the English universities. What a new world it opened!

As I read in this new-found book of the colleges at Oxford and Cambridge, and pored over the engraved views of quadrangles, halls, libraries, chapels,—of all the noble and dignified belongings of a great seat of learning,—my heart sank within me. Every feature of the little American college seemed all the more sordid. But gradually I began consoling myself by building air-castles. These took the form of structures suited to a great university:—with distinguished professors in every field, with libraries as rich as the Bodleian, halls as lordly as that of Christ Church or of Trinity, chapels as inspiring as that of King's, towers as dignified as those of Magdalen and Merton, quadrangles as beautiful as those of Jesus and St. John's. In the midst of all other occupations I was constantly rearing these structures on the queenly site above the finest of the New York lakes, and dreaming of a university worthy of the commonwealth and of the nation. This dream became a sort of obsession. It came upon me during my working hours, in the class-

[7] Montgomery Schuyler, "The Architecture of American Colleges," pp. 565–571.

[8] White, *Autobiography*, I, 15.

rooms, in rambles along the lake shore, in the evenings, when I paced up and down the walks in front of the college buildings, and saw rising in their place and extending to the pretty knoll behind them, the worthy home of a great university.[9]

Young Andrew White's "visions" and youthful awakening to the visual world and to imagined environments were somewhat similar to the experiences of John Ruskin. Turner's powerful, romantic landscapes influenced both men. Evidence of White's visual acuity, of the depths to which he was stirred by great architecture, and of his drive to improve the environment is scattered throughout his *Autobiography*. Ruskin's early work had great influence on his architectural conceptions. The influence of Ruskin, his followers, and the English architect William Butterfield apparent in the designs of Sage College and Sage Chapel came through White and the architect, Charles Babcock. A description of the College published in an early edition of the *Cornell Era* concluded: "Mr. Ruskin would be pleased. . . ."[10]

It would have been no easy matter to please John Ruskin with a "Gothic Revival" building of the 1870's. He had preached for years about "truth" in architecture and he felt dismay about the work of architects who attempted to use his ideas in their buildings. Sage College probably came as close to fulfilling Ruskin's architectural precepts as any American college building erected during this period. It had "power" and was "honest" in Ruskin's architectural sense of the words; it used color variations moderately but appropriately, and it was tastefully and sparingly ornamented by craftsmen who used local natural forms for their models. What is more, it was functional and comfortable. It

seems very likely that Mr. Ruskin would have been pleased if he had been able to visit Ithaca to see it.

President White's influence on the design of the structure reveals as much about his statesmanship as his architectural taste. He was never satisfied with achievement of single objectives. He linked them in series to get more power. In this instance he bartered part of his excellent architectural library for an architect who would design in the style he preferred. White had collected one of the best architectural libraries in the country and he now offered to give it to the University *if* the Board of Trustees would establish a school of architecture. He also used the gift of the library to bargain for the purchase of a mathematics library. In June 1871, the Board of Trustees authorized a chair in architecture and Mr. William Kelly purchased a mathematics library for Cornell.

The man appointed to the new post in architecture was apparently destined to become the architect for Sage College. A. D. White probably had thought all of this out ahead of time. After a number of attempts to secure distinguished English architects, including William Fogarty, the chair was offered to Charles Babcock (Fig. 49), a former partner and son-in-law of Richard Upjohn, the architect of Trinity Church in New York City and of scores of "American Gothic Revival" churches in the eastern United States. Babcock had retired from active practice to enter the Episcopal ministry in 1858. Like his model, William Butterfield, he was an active churchman and a high churchman.[11] Babcock accepted the chair in architecture in September 1871. From all indications he was, in fact, accepting two responsibilities: teaching architecture and designing Sage College.

There is some evidence that the University

[9] *Ibid.*, I, 287–288.
[10] *Cornell Era*, "On the Sage College," 17 July 1875. John Rosenberg in *The Darkening Glass: A Portrait of Ruskin's Genius* (New York, 1961) describes Ruskin's tenth birthday gift of Roger's *Italy*, illustrated by Turner, and its influence on his life's work. Ruskin taught himself to see with "extraordinary intensity."

[11] W. C. Russel to ADW, 21 July 1870, White Papers. Russel questioned the value of Charles Babcock's recommendations for a candidate for the chair in architecture. "Babcock is such an extreme high-churchman that very slender acquirements attached to the right dogmas would make any man a suitable candidate in his view."

had considered remodeling or adding to Cascadilla to accommodate men and women students. Preliminary drawings, prepared by Nichols and Brown of Albany, show the old water cure building as having a "women's corridor" on the south and a "men's corridor" on the north.[12] Placing an additional demand on the already overcrowded "family hotel" was seriously considered. Early in December 1871, White suggested that "instead of building Sage College [the University should] take $50,000 to improve Cascadilla by adding a wing and interior repairs—to make it a first class place instead of the . . . ill ventilated, ill smelling, uncomfortable, ill looking almshouse that it now is."[13] But practical considerations, including a shortage of student housing on the hill, forced a decision to build new facilities for the ladies.

The fall and early winter of 1871 was a time of intense, careful preparation for the February 1872 meeting of the Board of Trustees. Early in the fall Mr. Prentiss, the Professor of Botany, had completed a "Map of the Cornell University Estate" (Fig. 50). The University holdings did not at that time include the land south of the present Arts Quadrangle and west of the present East Avenue. Ezra Cornell had retained ownership of this fifty-acre parcel even though as early as 1866 he had stated that eventually the University would need all of this land and the area south of Cascadilla Creek as far as the present line of Dryden Road.[14]

Fig. 49. Charles Babcock, Cornell's first professor of architecture. He was Dean and Director of the College of Architecture until 1897.

In November 1871, Professor Prentiss prepared a plan for new roads and buildings based on his survey of the estate (Fig. 51). He proposed that a building for the "College of Agriculture" be built on the south side of the Quadrangle. In form it would be twin to West Sibley Hall. He also proposed that a conservatory be built on the south side of the agriculture building. Still further south a formal botanic garden was planned. This plan is the earliest drawing on record of campus planning at Cornell and serves as a definite indication that the idea of the symmetrical quadrangle, proposed in 1866, was still fixed in the minds of those responsible for the development of the campus. Prentiss' basic road scheme including Central Avenue, East Avenue, and President's Avenue was adopted with some variations and became the framework for all early campus development. Pro-

[12] These drawings of The Cascadilla are not dated, so it is possible that they are for the building as originally intended for a water cure and so would have provided separate areas for men and women. Dr. Samantha Nivison saw the proposal eventually to establish a college for women as an opportunity to recapture her role in the operation of Cascadilla Place through its use for the "women's department" of Cornell (S. S. Nivison to ADW, undated, White Papers, July 1869 folder).

[13] C.U. Archives, Sage College Undated Material, 43–10–38, letter regarding separate buildings for men and women. ADW to W. C. Russel, 18 September 1871, 7 December 1871, White Papers.

[14] EC to ADW, 28 November 1866, White Papers.

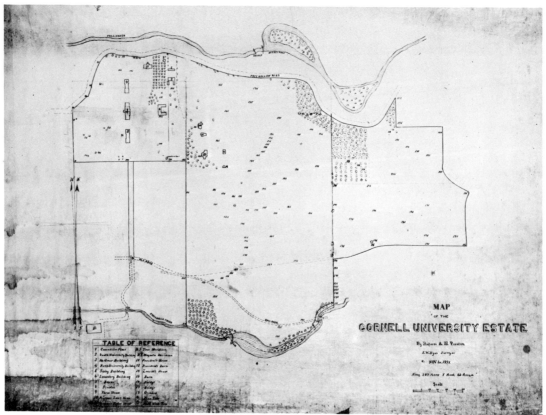

Fig. 50. Map of the Cornell University Estate, 1871, by Professor A. N. Prentiss. Ezra Cornell's "reserve" at the southwest corner is traversed by a right of way from Cascadilla Place.

fessor Prentiss assumed the duties of superintendent of grounds from 1870 to 1885 with little additional compensation from the University. For many years President White personally paid him a small salary for this work.[15]

During the winter of 1871–1872, Professor Babcock worked on preliminary designs for Sage College, and Mr. Sage and President White discussed the location of the building on the land south of the main quadrangle. In December, Henry Sage wrote to White asking for a drawing of the building White proposed. He wanted to examine it and make some suggestions. He believed it should be located north of Cascadilla and south of White's home. He wanted to "get all plans and specifications for building as soon as possible . . .

to put the actual work under way in the spring." He also wanted "a fine site." "Let it have acres," he wrote, "and let them be so used as to give them an odor of Home." [16]

On 3 February 1872, White wrote to Vice-President Russel in a conspiratorial manner: "Can you, without attracting observation, pace off the distance from the front to the rear of Mr. Cornell's lot south of the Campus?" This note of intrigue indicates some fear of opposition to the Sage College venture. But only one of the Trustees, Judge Folger, abstained from voting for the plan recommended in February 1872. President White spoke favorably of a "second plan for Sage College," and Professor Babcock also refers to his preference for the "second plan." This pro-

[15] President's report, 1885, p. 52.

[16] H. W. Sage to ADW, 15 December 1871, White Papers.

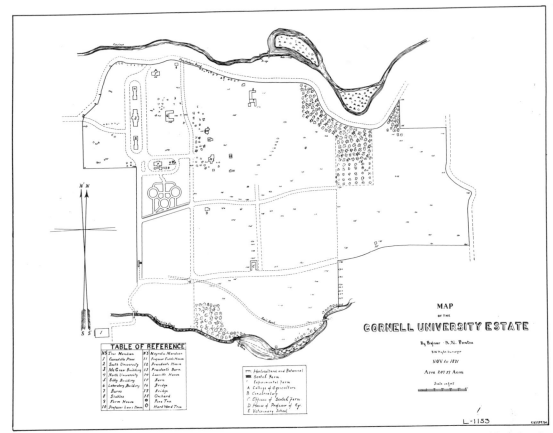

Fig. 51. Plan for the Cornell University Estate, 1871, by Professor A. N. Prentiss. The new building for the College of Agriculture on the south side of the Quadrangle is proposed as a twin to West Sibley Hall.

vided for "a large college building complete in all respects, with lecture rooms, special recitation rooms, infirmary, gymnasium, bathing rooms, and lodging rooms for one hundred and fifty to two hundred lady students . . . a striking architectural feature." The "first plan" was for "a series of quadrangles . . . to be made up of a central building with lecture rooms and a museum connected with the department of botany . . . and of houses, neat and well constructed, which could be afforded at a moderate rent, on condition that each tenant take into the family, a certain number of lady students." This "first plan" closely followed the ideas of Miss Catherine Beecher.[17]

When the Trustees met in Albany on 12 February 1872, the site was tentatively chosen and two alternative building plans were well along. Professor Babcock had thrown himself wholeheartedly into the work on designs to be shown the Trustees when the report of White's committee was presented. On 17 January 1872 he had written to White: "I am working all my spare time on the Sage College." Two days later he wrote that he be-

[17] Andrew D. White, "Report Submitted to the Trustees of Cornell University in Behalf of a Majority of the Committee on Mr. Sage's Proposal to Endow a College for Women," Albany, 13 February 1871; in *Proceedings at the Laying of the Corner Stone of the Sage College* (Ithaca, 1873), pp. 130–133. The chief advantage of the second plan (a large central building with all facilities) was that it "would admit of most complete supervision—that it would tend to satisfy the popular mind in this respect . . . that a separate college building under careful supervision was a matter of absolute necessity." White's survey provides an excellent summary of contemporary attitudes on coeducation.

lieved the Trustees would be pleased with the elevations. By 8 February he was desperate: "I cannot complete the plans . . . before 9 February. . . . I will send them to you in Albany by express." [18] Figure 52, though unsigned, is drawn in Babcock's style and appears to be the west elevation of an early

hall, adding bay windows and a big fireplace to it, and providing a high wainscot on both sides for pictures. To accomplish all of these Oxbridge-like improvements, he proposed enlarging the building by sixty-five feet in the north-south dimension and thirty-five feet in the east-west dimension. Professor Babcock

Fig. 52. Design for Sage College, 1872, unsigned but probably by Charles Babcock.

grandiose scheme for the College by Babcock. It may be the one first shown to the Trustees. The plans arrived on time and the Trustees approved Mr. White's report, accepted Mr. Sage's offer to pay for the building and provide a $300,000 endowment, and adopted the general plan for a single college building.

The new Professor of Architecture had found an ideal, if demanding, client. We judge from President White's penciled comments on a proposed early plan (Fig. 53) that he had as much to do with shaping the design as Babcock. White suggested adding a gymnasium, enlarging the ladies' rooms and placing them all on sunny exposures, widening the central tower, placing an oriel window above the front door, lengthening the dining

followed these suggestions in his revisions, but when preliminary cost estimates came in, White's ambitious program had to be cut back. Babcock wrote to him on 15 February that he had probably "undervalued the estimate of [his] early plans." Instead of being larger, as White had suggested, the building as built (Fig. 54) was some twenty feet shorter in the north-south dimension and thirty-five to fifty-five feet shorter in the east-west dimension than Babcock's preliminary sketches.

After the Trustees approved the gift of the College, Professor Babcock had to fight hard for the design elements he believed essential to its architectural success. Various economies were called for. In his reports to President White, Babcock expresses doubt about leaving off two elaborate, slender end pavilions

[18] Babcock to ADW, 17 January 1872, 19 January 1872, 8 February 1872, White Papers.

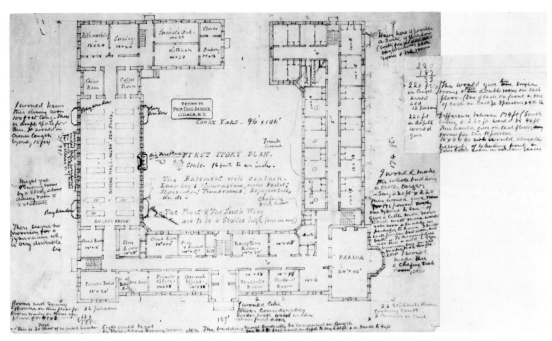

Fig. 53. Early plans for Sage College by Charles Babcock with Andrew Dickson White's penciled comments, 1871. White wanted a much larger building which would include a gymnasium and a larger dining hall and would permit the student rooms to be placed only on sunny exposures.

which his earlier and larger plan (Fig. 52) had included. He was able, however, to enlarge them into the broad-walled blocks that provide the strong terminal masses of the west elevation and so to keep them. Babcock insisted that the central tower roof should "remain as designed in order to have it entirely different from that of McGraw and the president's house." He reported that $300 would be the difference in cost between his design and a "plain one." He had no objection to cutting down the cost but he thought beauty was worth paying for—and worth securing.[19]

Professor Babcock was also concerned about the composition of the Building Committee for Sage College appointed at the Trustees' meeting in February 1872. He wrote to President White suggesting that they "might as well have co-adjutors who will not be *obstructive.*" He said he expected to take

instructions as to cost and accommodations from the committee, but matters of taste and design were his province as architect: "I have the responsibility of producing a building that shall be a credit to the University. . . . I do not wish to be hampered by or compelled to fight with parties who have no knowledge of architecture. I infer from your letter that there will be no trouble of the kind." [20] His inference was correct. The Executive Committee of the Board of Trustees plus Henry Sage were to act as the Building Committee, with full power to act on plans. If we can judge from the style of their Ithaca homes, four of the six committee members must have favored Babcock's approach to design and so would be likely to look with favor on his plans for the women's dormitory.

The house of committee member Francis M. Finch had been remodeled in 1870 by William H. Miller, the first student of archi-

[19] Babcock to ADW, 21 February 1872, White Papers.

[20] Babcock to ADW, 22 February 1872, White Papers.

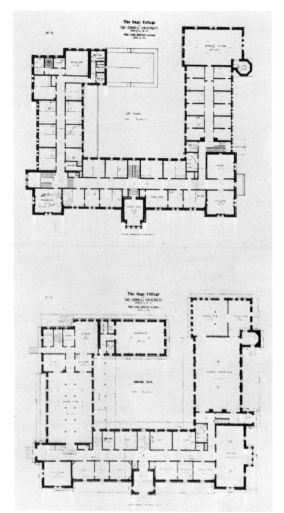

Fig. 54. Final plans for Sage College, 1872, by Charles Babcock. A gymnasium was included and botanical lecture rooms and classrooms were added to the plans, but the size of the building was reduced.

tecture at Cornell. As remodeled, it was decidedly "American Gothic Revival" in style with a rambling porch and gazebo and much "stick work" in the gables. Henry W. Sage was not living in Ithaca at the time, but in 1877, when he decided to move there from Brooklyn, he commissioned Miller to design a great mansion on State Street, now part of Cornell's Sage Hospital (Fig. 93). Although more restrained than Finch's house, Henry Sage's mansion is hardly a calm, reserved design. President White's villa was under con-

struction at the time, and Babcock, as was noted in Chapter I, had been retained to "perfect" some of the details of the design and to supervise construction. It was Babcock's idea that the stone balcony over the porch should be a heavy, dignified, and somewhat forbidding element.[21] He had suggested that "to be consistent with the dignity of [the] house, the balcony platform should be of stone. . . . Something bold and heavy is needed in that position." The effect intended, though not explicitly stated, was to give an approaching student or faculty member a visual reminder of presidential power. Babcock seems to have understood and applied Ruskin's ideas regarding the use of architectural forms as symbols of power. White took his advice.

Another member of the Building Committee, Ezra Cornell, did not seem to be very enthusiastic about the services of the new Professor of Architecture, but his objections were not esthetic ones. Cornell believed the responsibility of architects was to "draw up general plans and leave the details of the design to the tender mercies of the local mechanics," so he was invariably surprised upon hearing the value architects placed on their services. His propensity for trying to reduce their fees caused Professor Babcock considerable difficulty. On 8 March 1872, Babcock wrote to White, who was probably under pressure from Cornell to cut costs:

In answer to your inquiry as to whether I would accept . . . less . . . as compensation for my services as architect of the Sage buildings, I submit the following offers.

I. I will furnish the plans and specifications complete including general and working drawings and all necessary directions to the builders, for $1500.

II. If in addition to the above I am required to superintend the carrying out of the plans, draw the contracts, certify to payments when due, etc., I shall make a further charge of $1000.

In regard to the first offer, you are aware that the usual fee for full drawings is 3½ per cent of

[21] Babcock to ADW, 17 January and 21 February 1872, White Papers. See Figs. 15 and 16.

the cost of the building, which percentage in the present case . . . would be not less than $4000. . . . In making my offer as above I have named the least sum that will pay my own labor [and] defray the expenses of preparing the plans. . . .

As to the charge for the supervision, I cannot take the responsibility involved in directing the work for any smaller compensation. The usual fee is 1½ per cent and traveling expenses, say in this case $2000. . . . I must spend nearly the whole of at least two summer vacations here, at considerable cost, and much against my inclination. I would decidedly prefer that your committee should accept my first offer, for the plans only, and not the second.

If the committee feel disposed to employ anyone else, and think that better terms can be made I shall be glad to retire.[22]

After the difficulty over fees was settled, Babcock prepared the final construction plans with dispatch. On 7 May, the Executive Committee voted to "go upon the hill" the next day and "decide upon a location for Sage College," and by the middle of May an advertisement for building proposals was published in the *Syracuse Daily Journal*. Plans and specifications were to be made available to contractors in the architect's office in Room 19, Cascadilla Hall.[23] But, in fact, the prints of plans for distribution to contractors were not ready until mid-June. Two small difficulties had arisen, and Ezra Cornell seems to have been involved in both of them. The Executive Committee of the Trustees made another attempt to settle the issue of the architect's fees by passing, on 22 May 1872, with only White, Finch, and Schuyler present, a resolution that "the Architect is to be paid in accordance with the understanding existing between President White and Mr. Sage." One can imagine that Babcock might be somewhat reluctant to complete the final drawings when the issue of his fee was still in doubt, especially when the doubt seems to have been Ezra Cornell's.

Another matter seems, in retrospect, some-

what more serious. The University had not yet obtained title to the land on which the College was to be located. Mr. and Mrs. Cornell owned it, and Ezra Cornell apparently was not in full sympathy with the Sage College project nor was he in a financial position to give the land needed for it. In Ithaca at their fifteenth meeting on 26 June 1872, the Board of Trustees authorized the Executive Committee to purchase the fifty acres of land at a price not exceeding $750 an acre ($38,701 for the entire parcel).[24] These fifty acres and Cascadilla were intimately linked in Ezra Cornell's cherished ambition to provide means for the "highest and most useful education for women." We owe his memory an effort to discern this purpose from the few available clues. "Cascadilla Place will . . . be well adapted for a female department of the university" he wrote in November 1866. He thought that the adjoining Giles and Curren properties should be purchased and that the Cascadilla stockholders should donate their paid-up stock "on condition that the University complete the building and *eventually* establish a female department there." Cornell believed that use by the University for temporary accommodations was justified since the stockholders apparently would not or could not support the completion of the water cure building as planned. Rather than have "the work stop and the walls stared at as a laughing stock of folly and irresolution" he thought he would donate his share to the University "on behalf of the ladies of Ithaca for the interest of female education," if others decided to do the same.[25]

So much for Ezra Cornell's ideas on the ladies' rights to Cascadilla. The fifty acres needed for construction of Sage College had been set aside for the use of Cornell's wife, Mary, in furthering women's education. When Frederick Law Olmsted tried to rearrange the campus plan in 1867, he had sug-

[22] Babcock to ADW, 8 March 1872, White Papers.
[23] *Syracuse Daily Journal*, 16 May 1872.
[24] Trustees' *Proceedings*, 26 June 1872. Ezra Cornell was present.
[25] Cornell to ———, 28 November 1866, quoted in Hewett, *Cornell University*, I, 302 ff.

gested shifting White Hall to a location south of Morrill Hall but then withdrew the proposal. "Mr. Cornell," he noted, "might object because it would require him to give up his wife's reserve." [26] Ezra Cornell's ideas about the use of the fifty acres bounded by Cascadilla Creek, the south end of the Arts Quadrangle and the present lines of East and West Avenues (Fig. 50) are nowhere clearly stated, but we can infer from correspondence that the land was intended for the development by his wife of "*a system of industry* by which girls . . . by the application of three or four hours of their time each day [would] provide means for procuring the highest and most useful education." He wrote in this vein to his wife on 16 January 1869, encouraging her to "direct her mind in this channel."

Later, in 1873, we find "a Trustee" (Cornell, no doubt) strongly objecting to the location of professors' houses on the land west of Central Avenue because he planned to "locate there a building for university purposes." [27] Could it be that Cornell's reluctance to give up the fifty acres of land for Sage College and his later attempts to control its use were based on his intention to use it to build a factory for the ladies? He apparently wanted the land for his wife's use in establishing "an industrial system that would help poor young women in securing the benefits of higher education." On this land it would be near the University and near the railroad station, which then was where Hollister Hall now stands. But even Ezra Cornell's energy and fortune had limits. His ambitions for his wife could not be realized at the moment. His

funds were committed to other enterprises (principally railroads connecting Ithaca with the outside world), and if Mary Cornell shared her husband's fervent belief in the need of a factory for the ladies, she failed to record it. The place, the times, and perhaps the idea were not right for such a venture. Ezra Cornell's intended contribution to higher education for women remained a high-minded but vague dream whereas Henry Sage and Andrew D. White were ready to build their ideas into the brick walls of Sage College.

Soon after the land for Sage College was acquired by the University, bids were taken and construction began. Mr. Thomas signed a $93,500 construction contract on 19 August 1872, but soon there were more frustrating delays. First there was a delay while the University piped in the water which it had agreed to provide the contractor. Then there was too much water when late summer rains flooded the excavations. Next difficulties arose in securing stone for the foundations. Later that fall more rain came, and again the foundation excavations were flooded. Finally, there were more delays when an adequate supply of brick could not be obtained. [28]

The Building Committee was disappointed in the progress of construction and Ezra Cornell was more than disappointed in the bill for services received from the Professor of Architecture. News of this reached Charles Babcock in mid-October, 1872, and with restrained rage he wrote to White:

I hear that Mr. Cornell is quite sore about [the] matter of my fees for the Sage College. I sincerely regret that you should have incurred any displeasure in that quarter on account of your kindness to me, and certainly the situation is disagreeable to myself. Probably, however, you mind it as little as I do—and that is hardly worth speaking of. The object of my present writing is to beg that you will not again suggest me as architect for any future University buildings. It is better, I think, that some outside party should do

[26] Olmsted to ADW, 13 June 1867, White Papers. The Samuel Giles property adjacent to Cascadilla Place was to be given to the University. On 29 September 1871, the *Era* reported that the property was being considered as the location of "the building to be erected by the donation of Mr. Sage . . . if the offer . . . be accepted." Defects in the deeds of conveyance to the University were "discovered just before Mr. Giles's death . . . too late for correction." His brother who inherited the land had no intention of giving or selling it to the University and so we have "College Town" in its present location instead of two hundred yards further south.

[27] Trustees' *Proceedings,* 20 July 1873.

[28] Babcock to ADW, 5 July 1872, 22 July 1872, 16 August 1872, White Papers.

the work. I shall then be relieved from any suspicion of using my position for my own benefit. If the Exec. Com., or its chairman [Cornell], think that I ought to render such services as part of my professorial duties, I shall promptly resign the chair I have the honor to fill. I have no reason to suppose, however, that with the one exception referred to, they entertain any such idea. But I cannot consent to work for them at ¼ of the price they would pay for any one else. I should be wronging the profession at large in so doing; and rather than do so, I shall decline altogether hereafter. . . .

For you individually (so grateful am I for your many kindnesses) I will gladly do anything to further your good wishes and help in your work: but my relations to the Exec. Com. are of a different nature and must be governed by the ordinary rules of business. I wish our worthy founder could be made to take that view of the case, but if he cannot it is best that my work here be confined to my duties as professor—I am sure you will understand my motives in speaking as I do.[29]

The quarrel over the architect's fees continued through the winter of 1872–1873, while the meager beginnings of Sage College's foundations lay under the snow. In December 1872, Babcock made his first sketches for the chapel. In March 1873 he was still hopeful about his fees for the design of Sage College and was enthusiastically revising the elevations of the building. He wrote White that he had "overcome all difficulties about the front of the college" and had a new elevation which he liked better than the first.[30]

A new Building Committee was appointed for Sage College and Sage Chapel that spring consisting of White, Cornell, and George Schuyler, and the architect made his peace with the Founder. Babcock's rewards came later. His full fee, $2,609, was paid and, at the cornerstone-laying ceremonies on 15 May 1873, Andrew Dickson White delivered the client's accolade:

[29] Babcock to ADW, 14 October 1872, White Papers.
[30] Babcock to ADW, 10 March 1873, White Papers.

I trust that the modesty of our architect, Professor Babcock, will not be offended when I say that he has planned for us a building admirably suited to the founder's noble purpose. Its arrangement of study and sleeping-rooms; its spacious parlors; its gymnasium, bath-rooms and infirmary; its corridor, open to the southern sun and protected from the winds of winter; its conservatory, its lecture-rooms, laboratory, museum, greenhouse and botanic garden, for the department of botany and horticulture, and other attractions, all combine to make it a healthful and cheerful students' home.

But comfort and bare utility have not been the only things thought of. As a believer in the possibility of "sermons in stones," I rejoice to see that in and about this building there is to be a great deal of crystallized eloquence, very forcible though very quiet, and moreover, perpetual [Fig. 55]. These two examples of the work which has come from the hands and brains and hearts of our stone-carvers—these two sculp-

Fig. 55. Sage College, front entry, column capital by Robert Richardson.

Fig. 56. Sage College viewed from the southwest, 1872. For the prototype of the octagonal tower at the east end of the south façade see Acland's University Museum at Oxford.

tured capitals—with all their crisp leaves and rich fruits and flowers, are to stand among a multitude of others no less exquisite in workmanship, and they testify to you that while utility and comfort are provided for, there is to be a ministering unto the sense of beauty.

And here I cannot forbear a word of acknowledgement. Among the many services, so good, so kind, so quiet, which have endeared to us Professor Goldwin Smith, not the least is his thoughtfulness in bringing over here a body of workmen, skilled in the best practice, and to some extent trained in the best art-schools, of the mother-country. These beautiful sculptures are their work. They have been done with love, and years after we have passed away they will be looked upon with gratitude.[31]

The sculpture was beautiful and the building (Fig. 56) was large and complex, probably the largest building project undertaken in Ithaca up to that time. It was under construction for three years and during that time Babcock supervised the work at no additional fee. He seems to have eventually incurred the displeasure of Henry W. Sage for in 1874 we find Babcock defending his supervisory ability and his building from the donor's criticism. The President's confidence in him continued, however, and later White succeeded in convincing Babcock, against the architect's modest protests, that he should take on the task of

[31] Rough draft of speech for cornerstone-laying ceremonies, Sage College, on 15 May 1873, White Papers, and *Proceedings at the Laying of the Corner Stone of the Sage College,* pp. 8–9. In this speech, White claimed that Sage College was "the finest among the college buildings of the country with possibly two exceptions." He diplomatically fails to name them. His tastes being what they were, the Street School of Art at Yale and Memorial Hall at Harvard seem the likeliest candidates. The Sage College carvings by Richardson cost slightly over $1,600. (See vouchers and Sage Fund ledgers under "Capitols" and "Richardson," C.U. Archives.)

choosing furnishings and supervising the interior finishes of the building.[32] We may conclude that the new Professor of Architecture had proved himself to be a skillful designer and a highly ethical as well as prudent practitioner of the art of architecture.

A Cornell faculty critic is said to have commented that Sage College and Sage Chapel are the only two buildings on the campus that fully reflect President White's taste in architecture and that we are fortunate that the number is so limited. A contrasting view was presented by Montgomery Schuyler, one of the most perceptive architectural critics of the late nineteenth and early twentieth centuries. He thought that the architectural history of Cornell began with the erection of Sage College in 1872 and Sage Chapel in the following year. In our generation we sense a renewed respect, if not the beginning of complete appreciation, for these red-brick creations of Charles Babcock.

Schuyler, writing in 1911, rated the brick buildings at Cornell "among the signal successes of Victorian gothic" and thought them "quite worthy to strike the keynote of a more extensive architectural group than that to which they belong." Of Sage College he wrote:

It is most effectively and commandingly placed on a terrace of its own and suitable provision made in the plantation for its effective visibility. . . . [It] is well worthy of its conspicuousness by

the balance of its masses, the animation of its outline, well within the limit of repose, the successful adjustment and design of its features and the grace of its detail. . . . The Gothic of [this edifice] is unmistakably modern, and, even one may say, Victorian.[33]

Sage College is a fine building of the times and an all too rare example of tasteful design within the general framework of Ruskin's poetical but structurally naïve notions of good architecture. Ruskin was mostly concerned with the symbolic meaning of the ornamental features of architecture, but many English and American architects who tried to put his ideas into practice concentrated on ornamentation to the neglect of composition and structural expression. Matthews Hall at Harvard (1872) and East Divinity Hall at Yale (1872) are contemporary American college dormitories whose designs may be said to fall into this pattern.

Babcock's concern for the building art, his conservative nature, and his long association with Upjohn's practice saved him from such singlemindedness. Nevertheless, the ornament used in the building probably would have pleased Ruskin. As the *Cornell Era* put it: "The capitals of [the] columns . . . tell in stone the great worth of the plea which [Ruskin] so nicely expresses in words, that in architectural ornament every workman should be allowed to fashion his ideas in his own way."[34]

Other Ruskinian elements of Sage College are also striking. For example, the color alternation in the bricks of the arches is meant to emphasize the quality of an arch, that it is made up of individual bricks. These bricks were also meant to symbolize, according to Ruskin, the radiating lines of power of the arch. In Sage College, however, architectural statement is subtle: there are not too many pieces. Ruskin thought horizontal bands of contrasting color were the only correct decoration for a flat wall surface. He believed that

---

[32] Babcock to ADW, 11 April 1874, 9 January 1875, White Papers; Sage College ledgers. According to the 1874 letter, Henry Sage had decided not to build greenhouses (as previously promised) on the Sage College grounds and had given as his reason a lack of confidence in Babcock's professional ability. Babcock explains minor defects in workmanship on Sage College and settlement of some areas ("The building is more stable than any other on the university campus save the chapel") and suggests, "If any of the trustees are dissatisfied with my management of the building let them state their objections openly and give me the chance to defend myself before the Executive Committee." The disagreement between Sage and Babcock must have been resolved, for the architect continued to provide services for the University. In 1882 he designed a public library for Sage in Bay City, Michigan, and he designed four Cornell buildings from 1881 to 1888.

[33] Schuyler, *op. cit.*, p. 568.
[34] *Cornell Era*, 17 July 1875.

such color bands, in suggesting the horizontal spaces of the building on the wall surface itself, would establish in the eye of the viewer an understanding of the total organization of the building. Babcock's use of these bands in Sage College is restrained and tasteful (Fig.

—and somewhat menacing.[35] The tower is obviously a further development of Babcock's design ideas for the tower and balcony of President White's villa and represents a considerable improvement over the earlier work. The second stage finial which topped Sage Col-

Fig. 57. Sage College and Sage Green viewed from Central Avenue, west of the present site of Olin Hall. Babcock's Sage College and Acland's University Museum have suffered similar scientific obfuscations. Restoration of this view would require demolition of the building now occupied by the School of Chemical Engineering.

57). The proportions of wall divisions created by these bands and the window openings are pleasant and varied. This interplay of horizontal and vertical rhythms adds considerable interest.

The Sage College tower and the entry porch are composed in a fine Ruskinian statement of architectural power. At the main entrance to Sage College (Fig. 58), the mass of the tower seems almost ready to fall on the approaching visitor. The oriel window heightens this "threatening" aspect of the tower. Coming up the terrace steps one feels the presence of the building as a thing virtually alive

lege's central tower was removed during repairs in the 1950's. It had provided a fitting and unique climax for the central feature of the college and, if one believes in omens, it provided one, as we shall see.

[35] John Ruskin, *The Stones of Venice*. Chap. 26, Vol. I, provides a discussion of the use of bands of stones of different colors in a wall which "gives opposition to the enclosing power of the wall itself." *The Seven Lamps of Architecture* (2d ed.; London, 1855), p. 69, gives us the best source of Ruskin's idea of a proper tower: "I am inclined . . . to love the vertical, with a solemn frown of projection. . . . This character is always given to rocks by poets; with slight foundation indeed, real rocks being little given

The column capitals (Fig. 55) carved by Mr. Richardson are lovely things. If one pulls away the ivy and examines them, he will find representations of local flora—the orchard flowers, wild flowers, and garden flowers of the Ithaca region. The columns' smooth granite shafts provide another Ruskinian feature. Mr. Ruskin would probably have approved of Sage College's polished red granite columns. He had an explanation for the symbolism of such features in stone. In *The Stones of Venice* he wrote that anyone who maintained that a rusticated wall represented strength was wrong. In his opinion the quality in nature which best expressed the ideas of strength and power was a stone surface that was smooth and slick—"glistening like sea waves"—that looked as if it would "ring under the hammer like a brazen bell."[36] So, according to Ruskin, a polished stone column symbolized strength better than a rough one.

It should be noted here that praise or blame for English literary influences on Babcock's designs for Sage College might also be sought in the pages of the *Ecclesiologist*. This English periodical of the high-church Camden Society published many of the church designs of William Butterfield. Babcock was a subscriber and one supposes that as a high churchman himself he was an avid reader. Although the Octagonal Tower of Deane and Woodward's "Venetian Gothic" University Museum at Oxford (1865) is obviously the model for the south-east stair tower of Sage College, the design seems to reflect even more the influence of Butterfield's Keble College at the same university.

Sage College must have pleased many Cornellians and many Ithacans. The English artisan Robert Richardson and his colleagues,

Fig. 58. Sage College, central tower; a distillation of Ruskinian symbolism: overbearing power, layering of horizontal space, rhythmic movement, and the radiating energy of pointed arch segments.

who carved its capitals, were kept busy carving capitals, corbels, and stone window tracery for Sage Chapel and ornament for many houses in Ithaca. The first women students at Cornell may also have been pleased by the architectural features of Sage College, but the cost of living there and the accompanying restrictions on their independence were too much for many of them. Perhaps Andrew D. White unconsciously sensed the possibility that he and Henry Sage were doing too much for the ladies. Sage had written to White, as we noted earlier, that the building should "have acres so used as to give them an odor of Home." Their concern for the ladies' health and comfort showed in many features of the building. It seems very likely that the President and the donor had provided for every contingency except the fierce independence of those nineteenth-century women who had the courage to enroll at a coeducational university. As it turned out, it was some years before the ladies appreciated Sage College

---

to overhanging; but with excellent judgment; for the sense of threatening conveyed by this form is a nobler character than that of mere size."

[36] *Ibid.*, Vol. I, Chap. 26, vi. "Do not think that nature rusticates her foundations. Smooth sheets of rock . . . that is her preparation for first stories . . . when she needs to lay foundations . . . she seeks the polished surface and iron heart."

enough to fill its one hundred twenty beautifully appointed places.

A circular, prepared for distribution before
the September 1875 opening, described the
glories of the new building. All of the
thoughtful planning by White and Sage dili-
gently executed by Babcock was described in
glowing detail:

The buildings [were] heated by steam, lighted
by gas, provided with water and all the modern
conveniences, with baths on every floor, with a
gymnasium, a sheltered corridor for walking in
bad weather, and an infirmary for the sick. Adjoining the buildings [were] ornamental grounds
and botanical and other gardens, where lady students [could] have practical and healthful instruction in the intervals of their studies under
the guidance of the Botanical Professor and his
assistants.

Large parlors and reception rooms, reading
and dining rooms, and "apartments for literary societies" were part of the facilities.

Though two young ladies occupied an apartment
each [had] her own separate bed. The mat-
tresses [were] of the best quality of curled hair,
supplied by Charmichael and Company of Cortland, New York, and resting on Tucker springs.
Special care [had] been taken in this matter, in
obedience to the express directions of Mr. Sage.

The fine domestic hand of Catherine Beecher
is also evident in these elaborate provisions
for the ladies' health. The parlors, reception
rooms, and reading and dining rooms were
graced with engravings and casts "purchased
at Berlin, Paris, and London, with the intention of surrounding the lady students with

Fig. 59. Sage College, parlor, about 1878. A portrait of the founder of the College in a benevolent mood
surveys the twiggy decor of the seventies.

Fig. 60. Sage College, dining hall, about 1878. Although short of President White's expectations in both size and elegance, the dining hall was far larger than was needed by the number of its occupants until the early 1890's.

objects of real taste and beauty."[37] President White, no doubt, saw to that. As the Cornell *Register* of 1875 pointed out, Sage College was "not a separate department or school, but merely a home or dormitory for women students."

Henry Sage was elected Chairman of the Cornell Board of Trustees on 16 June 1875, and Sage College was formally opened on Commencement Day, 17 June. White gave a reception in the "large and elegantly fitted parlor" (Fig. 59) and Sage was so pleased with the College that he and his family spent their vacation there that summer. Sage and White were certain that there would be a rush of applicants. The circular prepared to an-

nounce the new facility warned, "the maxim will be 'first come, first served.'" Only one hundred twenty ladies could be accepted.

Less than a month after the formal dedication of the building Babcock's two-stage central tower was damaged in an unusual way. Its topmost finial was broken off during a summer storm. It almost seemed a sign that all was not well. Babcock learned of the damage and wrote to White that he had "watched the unfortunate finial with considerable anxiety" during the high winds of the preceding winter and had satisfied himself that all was secure. Professors Anthony and Sweet who witnessed the event believed lightning was the cause. Professor Morris made a replacement, following the instructions of Babcock that the iron shaft which secured the finial to the first wooden stage of the tower be lengthened to counterbalance the force of wind

[37] *Sage College Cornell University* (Ithaca, N.Y., 187–), undated circular issued "in response to various inquiries regarding the Sage College for Lady Students."

Fig. 61. Sage College, entry. The University retained its first full-time gardeners to plant and maintain the grounds of the College.

against it.[38] The architect must have operated under the assumption that wind, not lightning, had caused the damage. Whatever the precise cause, the damage signaled a long series of failures for the College. In its early years, the Sage building proved to be somewhat less than a complete success.

Late in September, 1875, Henry Sage wrote to White, "I shall be glad to see Sage College in working order—it ought to be filled—that small family of 20 will *rattle* in those large halls—but we can wait patiently—woman has a long road before her yet." [39] As it turned out, the road to full occupancy of Sage College was about fifteen years long. In 1882, Moses

Coit Tyler recorded a remark of Mrs. Sage to the effect that her husband had given much for Sage College, but that "it had all turned out a failure." [40] In 1882, White and Sage decided that the building should be remodeled for use by Civil Engineering and Architecture,[41] but the plan was not carried out. Only twenty-five women lived in the building in 1884, but to put this figure in its proper perspective we must note that there were at this

Fig. 62. A view from the vestibule of Sage College, about 1883. In the middle distance may be seen the house built for Major Junius MacMurray and later occupied by Professors Shackford and Oliver.

time only about fifty women students enrolled at Cornell.

In 1881, and again in 1884, the University

[38] Babcock to ADW, 15, 22, and 29 July 1875, White Papers. *Ithaca Journal,* 7 July 1875.
[39] H. W. Sage to ADW, 25 September 1875, White Papers.

[40] Moses Coit Tyler Diaries, 12 January 1882, Cornell University Library (Rare Book Collection).
[41] *The Diaries of Andrew Dickson White* contains the following on the attempted change, 9 January 1882: "with . . . and Babcock on new disposition of Sage Coll." and 11 February 1882: "In afternoon to Mr. Sage's office. W. H. S. offers to give 10,000.00 to

Fig. 63. Sage College, parlor, about 1900, remodeled in the formal style of the era. Note, however, the "art nouveau" decorations in the corners and the stylized flowers in the frieze.

attempted to require the residence of women students in Sage College but this policy was blocked by the ladies' determined independence. The women alumnae protested and the women students published a brochure which proclaimed the new law unnecessary, unwise, and unjust. After a brief negotiation, the rule was withdrawn.[42] White and Sage had done entirely too much for the ladies. In 1875, the President and the Chairman of the Board of Trustees were fifteen years ahead of their time, and at least half of the women students were eighty years ahead of theirs.

Those women students who were less fiercely independent enjoyed the life of Sage College. Anna B. Comstock was among those who lived there in the fall of 1875. She later recalled that it was "a beautiful home . . . and highly appreciated by those who had experienced the difficulties of living in town." Since the Sage dining room (Fig. 60) could not be run profitably with such a small number of girls, men students were given the privilege of boarding there. Dances were held every Friday night, Professor Fuertes led musical evenings, and Professor Corson read from Shakespeare and modern American writers. President White visited the College often to give "talks on various subjects from proper behavior [for ladies] to the art of the Renaissance."[43] Mrs. Comstock also recalled the "inspiring evenings" when the women students were entertained in the Whites' home and "gazed at treasures in the books and pic-

change Sage Coll. into Sage Coll. of Engineering and Architecture. *Laus Deo,* worked over this and other plans."
[42] Trustees' *Proceedings.* On 29 October 1881 the Executive Committee resolved: "All ladies who are students at the University shall be required to room and board at Sage College." On 3 July 1884 the Executive Committee resolved: "All lady students to be required to room and board at Sage College unless specially excused by the Committee on Sage College." On 15 June 1885 fifty-two lady graduates petitioned the Trustees to remove the rule.

[43] Anna B. Comstock, "Pioneers among Women" in *A Half-Century at Cornell* (Ithaca, 1930), p. 72.

tures which President White himself showed and explained to [them]."

By the late eighties the ladies had increased in numbers and had settled down sufficiently to make better use of the building. The grounds were beautifully landscaped and maintained (Figs. 61 and 62). The College was fully occupied and social life there assumed the qualities of a conventional women's dormitory in a conventional university. In fact, Sage College became so successful that in 1896 it was necessary to build a large addition on the northeast to provide a home on the campus for fifty more women. At the same time the parlor was remodeled (Fig. 63). Charles Babcock had designed Sage College in the style which would probably have pleased Mr. Ruskin. Now apparently it pleased the ladies, too.

An Unsectarian Chapel

IN THE DESIGN OF SAGE Chapel, President White, with the services of Professor Babcock, continued the evolution of what he called the "informal grouping at Cornell." Mrs. Henry Sage had expressed surprise at the lack of facilities for religious services at the new "unsectarian" institution in Ithaca. Chapel services were then held daily in the fourth-floor lecture room of Morrill Hall. When Mrs. Sage saw the plans for Sage College in the spring of 1872 and found no chapel, she persuaded her husband to finance the construction of one. Andrew Dickson White again dreamed dreams of "Gothic" buildings. He wrote to the donor:

I would place the building about midway between Sage College and the University Buildings [Morrill, McGraw, and White Halls] *and have it of similar architecture* [the material italicized here was crossed out in draft]. For architectural effect, I would prefer to connect it with the main college building by a covered passage or archway—a sort of cloistered passage perhaps directly from the north lower entrance of Sage College to a south entrance of the chapel, but this I think wise to relinquish in order that it may not appear to be *entirely* for the ladies.[1]

White had included a number of "foundation principles" in his inaugural address. One of them was the principle of "unsectarian education." The University charter provided that "at no time shall the majority of the board be of one religious or of no religious sect" and there were to be no religious tests for admission to the faculty or student body. In his opening address, White had also announced that Cornell would "not discard the idea of worship." He told the audience:

The first plan of buildings and the last embraces the University chapel. . . . We might, indeed, find little encouragement in college chapel services as they are often conducted—prayers dogmatic or ceremonial, praise with doggerel hymns, thin music and feeble choir, the great body of students utterly listless or worse. From yonder chapel shall daily ascend prayer and praise . . . [that] shall recognize in man not only mental and moral but religious want. We will labor to make this a Christian institution; a sectarian institution may it never be.

The location and the source of funds for "yonder chapel" were somewhat vague in the fall of 1868. The first campus plan had called for a chapel in the middle of the west row, but by the time the University opened, this location had been assigned to McGraw Hall. A campus rumor persisted (perhaps in remembrance of the first plan) that the chapel would be located in the center section of the McGraw building. One *Era* editor of 1872 seemed baffled that this plan was not to be carried out[2] and that the library was to oc-

[1] ADW to H. W. Sage, undated draft, White Papers. The words in italics are underlined in the original. The contents indicate that it was written in late summer or early fall, 1872.

[2] *Cornell Era*, 17 September 1872.

cupy the place he thought would be a chapel. Soon afterward Henry Sage's gift of a chapel was announced.

The provision of Sage Chapel was much more successful than Sage College in meeting the immediate needs of the new University. At first, Ezra Cornell insisted that it should be a "Memorial Hall" to hold 2,500 to 3,000 persons. His idea was that the chapel should serve for both religious services and for commencements and other large university gatherings.[3] The University's 1872 report to the Regents of the University of the State of New York (signed by Ezra Cornell) noted that a university chapel was under construction which would seat 500 and could be enlarged to seat 1,200 to 1,500. The fact was that President White and the donor, Henry Sage, preferred a chapel. The idea of building a large hall was soon quieted for lack of sufficient funds. Cornell had remarked that if a large hall should prove to cost more than $30,000 he would "contribute the remainder." As much as he might have wanted to do this it seems unlikely that he could have afforded it at this point in his business affairs.

White was very clear about the size building he wanted: "It should be distinctly a *chapel* for religious services—not so large as to be a great, comfortless, repulsive hall." [4] White's rejection of the idea of the hall was probably colored by the cheerless atmosphere of the large fourth-floor lecture room in Morrill Hall in which Dr. Wilson had held chapel services every morning for the previous three years. Wilson later reported that at least one worshiper had always been in attendance. He refused to give further details when asked if it was sometimes the reader.[5]

Henry Sage's son Dean soon proposed to make the minister as well as the chapel new. In September 1872 he offered to give $30,000 to Cornell, the interest to pay the salary of an Episcopalian chaplain. The offer stirred White to define the purpose of a chapel at Cornell in a fourteen-page letter to Dean Sage. The difficulty with existing college chapels, White thought, was that students were forced to attend under pain of penalty, that they considered it a great bore, that it was difficult to get the "right man" for the job, and that, finally, if a good man was secured, "he gradually lost his hold upon the students." Cornell University faced an added problem in that it was "prohibited from favoring one religion."

White's plan, which he predicted would bring students voluntarily to chapel, was to establish the Sage Lectureship in Christian Ethics or the Sage Chaplaincy which would bring the foremost men in the American pulpit to Sage Chapel on twenty Sundays. White believed that students would crowd in to hear sermons "by the best thinkers and orators in the American pulpit." "Each speaker," he thought, "would be *large* enough, not to say wise enough, to avoid any appearance of proselytization." On the other twenty Sundays of the long 1872 academic year the clergymen of Ithaca would occupy the pulpit in rotation. The visiting preachers, White suggested, might stay a week on the campus with a Sunday at each end for the handsome fee of $200. He even offered to surrender his "beautiful and ample rooms at Cascadilla" to them so they could "live in the very midst of Professors and students." White also proposed to use part of the Sage College endowment for a "Professor of Music" who also would be the musical director for the Sage Chapel so that they could "have music of the best and noblest kind." He outlined the Sunday service

---

[3] ADW to H. W. Sage, undated draft, White Papers (1872). Cornell may have seen or read about Memorial Hall at Harvard; certainly he seemed to have something of the sort in mind. White, however, was sensitive to Henry Sage's objective, which was to provide better facilities for religious services and, incidentally, to give Cornell a religious building, which would project an image of "attendance at chapel."

[4] *Ibid.*

[5] Hewett, *Cornell University*, I, 270. Daily services were at first conducted in the parlor of Cascadilla

Hall and from there moved to the Morrill Hall lecture room in January 1869. Dr. Wilson conducted these services for five years. Daily chapel services on a voluntary basis seem to have been abandoned after 1873.

and suggested that daily services be conducted by "different professors." [6]

Dean Sage was pleased with these ideas, especially having "music of the best kind" in the chapel, and so Cornell has the Dean Sage Preacherships filled by distinguished clergymen of all denominations and the excellent Sage Chapel Choir. Dean Sage's final commitment for the endowment fund was to supply the pulpit "with ministers of different denominations—but good ones; with no restrictions on their actions—but from strong orthodox faiths." [7]

Charles Babcock was willing, not to say eager, to design the chapel. As a partner of Richard Upjohn and later, when he became a clergyman, he had designed numerous churches. The last two were for his own parishes at Greenwood Iron Works (now Arden, New York) and at Ballston Spa.[8] He now

[6] ADW to Dean Sage, 26 September 1872, White Papers.
[7] Dean Sage to ADW, 7 November 1872, White Papers.
[8] Everard Upjohn, *Richard Upjohn, Architect and Churchman* (New York, 1939). Charles Babcock graduated from Union College in 1847. He worked in Upjohn's office from 1848 to 1853. In 1853 he married Upjohn's daughter and became a partner in the firm during the next five years. He was the illustrator of Upjohn's book *Rural Architecture,* published in 1852. In 1859 he returned to his birthplace, Ballston Spa, N.Y., where he designed the Episcopal Church. He was ordained a priest in that church in 1864 and served as pastor at the Greenwood Iron Works (whose church he designed in 1862) from 1863 to 1871, when he accepted the professorship in architecture at Cornell. In addition to his teaching and designing duties at Cornell, he wrote a number of books on architecture, including *A Series upon Elementary Architecture* (New York, 1877) and *Vaulting* (New York, 1884), and several articles on vaulting, including the one in Russell Sturgis' *Dictionary of Architecture.* In 1882 he was a consultant to the N.Y. State Assembly Committee on the stability of Eidlitz's great stone vault over the Assembly Chamber in the State Capitol at Albany. After careful, elaborate measurements and calculations, Babcock reluctantly pronounced the stone vault insecure. It was not taken down until 1888, however, when John Snaith (one of the workmen brought to Ithaca from England in 1869) performed the job and installed a new flat wooden ceiling. Snaith was accused of illegal substitutions of papier mache panels in the work and was tried but not convicted (Cecil R. Roseberry, *Capitol Story* [Albany, 1964]). By a curious coincidence, in

offered to prepare the Sage Chapel plans without charge if Mr. Sage would pay the expense of his draftsman. Late in October 1872, the Trustees authorized the President to have Babcock draft plans for a chapel seating five hundred to be built of "stone dressed in such a manner as to produce the best effect." The simple line drawing he sent the President on 5 December 1872 (Fig. 64) "arranged the

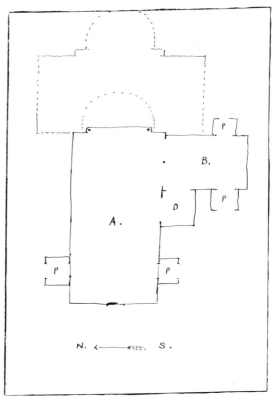

Fig. 64. First sketch for Sage Chapel, by Charles Babcock, December 1872: nave (*A*); small chapel (*B*); organ room and tower (*O*); porches (*P*). Proposed future additions to the east are indicated by dashed lines.

these same years (1883–1890) Louis Hinton, another of Ezra Cornell's craftsmen from England, was foreman of stone carvers on the Capitol's great western staircase (Assembly Documents 1882, Capitol Papers, New York State Library). Babcock became Professor Emeritus in 1897 and died in Ithaca, in his house just east of Sage Chapel in 1913. T. F. Crane recalled him as "a fine Christian gentleman."

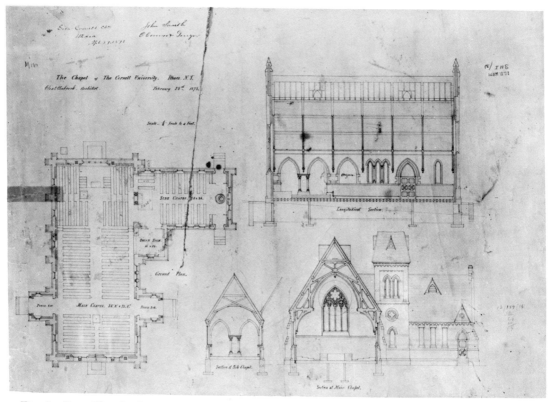

Fig. 65. Sage Chapel, plan and sections, February 1873. Earlier plans for a stone chapel were abandoned because of its high cost.

thing after [Babcock's] idea of what was wanted": a large simple nave extending east and west seating four hundred with a smaller chapel of "100 sittings" forming a south transept. The latter was originally intended for daily chapel services but was never used for this purpose. It provided a convenient worship place for St. Paul's Episcopal Church for which Professor Babcock served as pastor from 1874 to 1892. The small chapel was also to be used together with the large one for Sunday services. An organ room was conveniently located in the re-entrant angle between the chapels and under the tower where it could serve both chapels.

Babcock's plan was adopted, and he prepared drawings and cost estimates. The first estimates of cost must have exceeded the $30,000 available, for in February 1873 we find the architect revising his plans to provide for a brick chapel "to cost less than the esti-

mate for the stone one." [9] While he was at it, Babcock substituted a plain, open ceiling for the previously proposed paneled one in the main chapel, reduced the height of the walls from 24 feet to 18 feet and introduced some white and black bricks in the red-brick walls.[10] With these changes (Fig. 65), he thought "the brick building would be handsomer than the stone one and cost somewhat less." The price was, in fact, very good. Mr. Thomas, who was building Sage College, and John Snaith, the English carpenter-turned-contractor, submitted bids. Snaith was awarded the main contract at $19,155. The cut stone, including carving by Richardson, came to $5,620, for a total cost of $24,775 —well within the budget. This left $5,000

[9] Trustees' *Proceedings,* 14 February 1873.
[10] Babcock to ADW, 15 March 1873, White Papers.

Fig. 66. Sage Chapel, original interior, 1875.

for furnishings.[11] The building was finished in May 1875, and Phillips Brooks preached the first sermon at its dedication.

Babcock seemed pleased with the new design. He probably wanted a brick chapel all along. His earlier church designs and Sage College were in brick, a material used a great deal by both Babcock and William Butterfield, the English architect. It offered, at a reasonable cost, many ways of achieving a picturesque, rule-breaking "noble-grotesque" which, according to the English architectural historian John Summerson, characterized Butterfield's "Victorian Gothic Revival" architecture. In the Chapel, as in Sage College, Professor Babcock's use of colored brick as ornament is much more restrained than similar uses in Butterfield's contemporary church design. The degree of restraint is, of course, relative.

Goldwin Smith thought the Sage buildings "quite equal in merit to the modern Gothic of Oxford" (Keble College and Chapel by William Butterfield). According to Montgomery Schuyler, Goldwin Smith, as a graduate of Oxford's Gothic halls, could claim some qualification as an expert in collegiate architecture.

Schuyler thought Smith's equation of the buildings was an understatement. He believed the Sage buildings were better than Keble College. The "sprightliness and animation of form and color" in the latter acted to "destroy repose," which he thought more valuable. Schuyler thought the polychromatics of Keble, especially the interior, "very trying." [12] Schuyler evaluated Sage Chapel after its present, richly colored interior ornament was in place.

The original Sage Chapel (Fig. 66) was by comparison a chaste, calm building. One of its most beautiful features was the Apostles' rose window in the west end of the nave. It is still there, moved farther west when the nave was extended in 1940. The tower, located in the angle between the south transept and the nave, was the only really unusual feature of the exterior design. It had, like Sage College, a semidetached second stage finial. The Chapel's finial was somewhat larger (Fig. 67) and Professor Corson said it looked like a "four-legged woman holding up her skirts." The roof was of monochromatic slate and the outside walls were decorated with slim bands of black bricks. The inside walls were painted

[11] Trustees' *Proceedings,* 22 April 1873.

[12] *Architectural Record* (December 1911).

Fig. 67. Sage Chapel and the Stone Row about 1880, viewed from Sage College's central tower. Grading and planting in the Quadrangle and around the Chapel were completed in 1878.

pale yellow and were devoid of ornament save Robert Richardson's carved corbels on which the wooden roof timbers rested. The original Sage Chapel was calm, indeed, when compared with the extremes of Butterfield's polychrome geometric ornament in both walls and roof tiles.[13]

To modern taste Sage Chapel may seem overrich in white and black brick banding, overburdened with carved ornament, memorial tablets, mosaics, porches, and the like, and overpowering in the elaborate symbolism of the ceiling decoration. Most of this decoration was added in later years. The first Chapel was a simple church building, inside and out. It was not that Babcock and White might not have wanted to add more adornment. A limited budget and the lack of anything of a

local nature to commemorate at the time forced a decision to leave most of the decoration to the future. When Babcock changed his ceiling design for the main chapel early in 1873, he noted to White that its colored decoration would likely have to wait for several years.[14] As it turned out, thirty years passed before the richly colored designs of the present ceiling were applied.

Succeeding additions to Sage Chapel were all made under the direction of Babcock. One might say he "lived with it" in much the same way as some medieval master masons lived with their cathedrals. He built his house east of the Chapel in 1873 and became the pastor of St. Paul's Episcopal Church, which held services in the small south chapel. Babcock was involved in the protection, embellishment, or extension of the Chapel for the rest of his life. White always contacted him for advice when some new memorial was to be placed in or around the building, and he was the architect for three of the four additions that have been made to the building. Because of this continuity in design, the resulting

[13] John Summerson's "William Butterfield or the Glory of Ugliness" in *Heavenly Mansions* (New York, 1963) is the best article on Butterfield. See also Summerson in *Architectural Review*, XCVIII (December 1948). Upjohn and his student, Babcock, avoided the most striking (distressing?) features of Butterfield's polychrome work except the patterned slate roofs. Kenneth Clark in *The Gothic Revival* (Pelican Books, 1964) concludes that Butterfield had "a good grasp of building and a sadistic hatred of beauty."

[14] Babcock to ADW, 15 March 1873, White Papers.

Fig. 68. Memorial Antechapel (1883) by Charles Babcock. The Antechapel, built with funds from the estate of Jennie McGraw Fiske, is the burial place of Cornell's founders and early benefactors.

structure has unity as well as a great deal of picturesque variety.

In 1883, the Memorial Antechapel was built north of the main Chapel by the Estate of Jennie McGraw Fiske and the University as a monument to Ezra Cornell, Mrs. Fiske, and John McGraw (Fig. 68). In style it is more "correct" than the rest of the building, and according to a description of 1904, of the "Middle French Pointed School." [15] Babcock must have taken especial pride in this addition because he was able to employ his talent in the design of stone vaulting, a subject in which he was a recognized expert. The vaulting ribs of Ohio stone are supported on red marble columns; the ceiling panels are Caen stone. Beneath the north window is a recumbent "heroic size" figure of Ezra Cornell, which was carved in white marble by an American expatriate in Rome, William Story. Elsewhere in the room are similar reclining statues including those of Mary White,

[15] Clark S. Northup, *Sage Chapel: A Description* . . . (Ithaca, 1904).

White's first wife, and Jennie McGraw Fiske. The room, rich in memorials to founders, trustees, benefactors, presidents, and professors of the nineteenth century, has of late been called "Cornell's pantheon" (Fig. 69). It is indeed a treasury of Cornell's "gods" and a thoroughly effective statement in stone and bronze of some of the attractive sentimental aspects of Cornell's founders and their sometimes remarkable taste.

Many of the tragedies and triumphs of the University's early years are recorded in Sage Chapel, but unfortunately in respect to details the symbols are mute. A plaque recording the fact that Professor Willard Fiske's remains lie next to his wife's in the crypt below does not tell us that William H. Sage resigned from the Board of Trustees when Fiske's remains were interred in the Chapel in 1905. The Sage-Fiske feud, a tragic one for Cornell, is discussed in a later chapter. The symbolism of the carved stone Venetian wellhead which stands between the Memorial Chapel and the north transept is also silent until one relates

Fig. 69. Memorial Antechapel, interior. The sarcophagus of Andrew D. White's first wife, Mary, is at the left and that of Ezra Cornell is at the far end of the room. On the bracket at the right is a bronze bust of Hiram Sibley. Interred in the crypt below the chapel are the remains of Ezra and Mary Cornell; Andrew D. and Mary White; John McGraw; Jennie McGraw Fiske; Willard Fiske, the first University Librarian; Alonzo B. Cornell (Ezra Cornell's eldest son); and Cornell's fifth President, Edmund Ezra Day.

this gift of Andrew Dickson White to his excellent biographical sketch of Fra Paoli Sarpi, the Venetian statesman [16] who defended the

[16] A. D. White, *Seven Great Statesmen* (New York, 1910), and *Diaries*, p. 378. White purchased the wellhead in Venice, where he was working on his biographical sketch of Sarpi, in April 1902. He tried (unsuccessfully) to persuade Willard Fiske to purchase one as a memorial to Jennie McGraw Fiske (ADW to Fiske, 9, 11, and 12 April 1902, White Papers). White thought that the one he purchased ("A grandiose one") should have an inscription to Moses Coit Tyler. Babcock, who designed the base and protecting cap piece, did not like the idea of the inscription (Babcock to ADW, 24 November 1902, White Papers). White's gift seems to be directly connected with his work on Sarpi, since the purchase of the wellhead and his renewed interest in the Venetian patriot coincide in time and place. The significant idea White brought from his work in Venice was the importance of Sarpi's courageous resistance to papal control of Venice. Since White believed so strongly in the importance of maintaining Cornell's freedom from sectarian influence, we may view the wellhead as a symbol of this principle.

rights of his city from papal interference; then one suspects that the wellhead may be White's subtle reminder that the Chapel is unsectarian. The wellhead is respectfully covered each winter with a metal coat to prevent frost damage. Would that equal thought were given to reinforcing White's subtle message symbolized in this stone; perhaps some inscription chosen from the works of White or Sarpi could provide a clue.

Succeeding additions to the Chapel were much more extensive. In 1898 the seating capacity was doubled. The south transept, the tower, and the east half of the original nave were demolished and two great parallel north-south transepts covering a space sixty-six by sixty-four feet were added. Rose windows with stained glass of the "Byzantine School" were placed in the four new gables. The nave was lengthened, new porches were built, and the Sage Memorial Apse was added

Fig. 70. Sage Memorial Apse (1898). The Chapel was almost entirely rebuilt in 1898 but much of the stone ornament and glass of the earlier building was reused. Tracery and stained glass from the east wall of the original chapel were moved to the rear window of the apse. The northeast transept at left was not extended to its present length until 1903.

at the east end as a memorial to Mr. and Mrs. Henry W. Sage.

The apse is semi-octagonal, thirty-one feet wide and sixteen feet deep (Fig. 70). On its mosaic walls below the window sills, a procession, forty-two by seven feet, of life-size figures symbolizes the work of the University. A young man and a young woman representing coeducation stand at each end and are separated by eight figures representing the sciences and the arts. The arts stand next to the woman and are led by a figure representing truth. The sciences are next to the man and are led by a figure representing beauty. Philosophy sitting on a canopied throne in the midst of all unites the dual ideas (man and woman, truth and beauty, sciences and arts) and demonstrates the unity of all learning. This allegorical mosaic was designed and supervised by Charles R. Lamb of New York and executed by J. and R. Lamb. Above the mosaic frieze, three memorial stained-glass windows are set in the gray stone walls. They

depict the Christian Graces and record four parables from the New Testament. The smaller side windows have figures of Jesus, the Light of the World, with St. John the Evangelist, and Jesus, the Good Shepherd, with St. John the Baptist. The central window, given in memory of Mrs. Henry W. Sage by her sons, originally was in the old chapel. The smaller windows commemorate Mrs. William H. Sage and her son DeWitt Linn Sage.

In 1903 the north wall of the northeast transept was taken down and the transept extended northward (Figs. 71 and 72). The pine doors at the entrances were replaced by carved oak doors stained dark brown, and gilded wrought-iron doors were installed at the interior entrance to the Memorial Antechapel. The Chapel walls above the wainscot were covered with canvas and colored up to the eaves (Fig. 73), and the cornice boards, roof timbers, and ceiling panels were given their present, elaborate color decoration. The inscription at the cornice line on a striped red

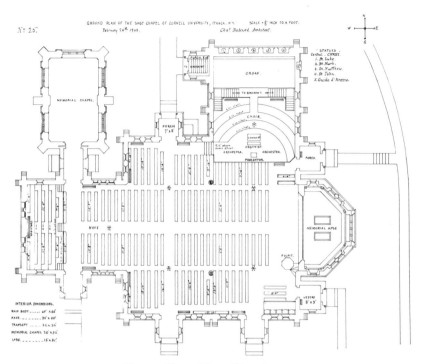

Fig. 71. Plan of Sage Chapel, 1903.

Fig. 72. Sage Chapel from the northwest, after 1903. At the right are the only remaining elements of the original chapel—the three bays at the west end of the nave. A Venetian wellhead, the gift of Andrew D. White, is barely visible below the pine tree in the foreground.

Fig. 73. Sage Chapel, interior, after 1903. Wooden roof trusses (at left) from the nave of the original chapel were used in the transepts added in 1898.

background is a summary of the Law as taught by Jesus. The roof timbers were "relieved" by bands, frets, zigzags, and chevrons of red and blue over a dull brown surface. The ceiling panels, of the same brown and with an ecclesiastical emblem in the center of each, were covered with a spreading pattern of the olive vine and locked in the framework of a deep-blue Latin cross formed by horizontal panels set just below the apex of the roof. In the cross's blue sky were set gilded sunbursts and stars each holding some Christian symbol. The ceiling colors as well as the devices have specific symbolic meanings: white for innocence, purity, faith, joy, and life; red for fire, heat, creative power, and divine love; gray for mourning, humility, and innocence accused; blue for heaven and truth; green for

immortality; and gold for the sun and the goodness of God.[17]

This embellishment of Sage Chapel, foreseen in general terms by its architect in 1873, spread over the walls and ceilings of the enlarged structure in 1903. One would imagine that Babcock must have been especially pleased by the richness and variety of the symbolism and the vigor of its expression in color. As a high-churchman and medievalist of some attainments, the Chapel's architect no doubt played an active role in decisions regarding its decoration. The 1903–1904 enlarge-

[17] Northup, *op. cit.* For those who want to understand the mysteries of the symbolism of Sage Chapel's ceiling decoration and memorial windows, Northup's booklet is the definitive guide.

ment and decoration were gifts of William H. Sage; Babcock was the architect; the decoration was designed and executed by Messrs. Cottier and Company of New York. The work has had its detractors. Burt G. Wilder, Professor of Comparative Anatomy and Natural History, would enter the Chapel only when absolutely necessary after 1903; he was "outraged by the impossible musculature of angels with both wings and arms." [18]

The Chapel's most recent addition was built in 1940 during the administration of President Edmund Ezra Day. Rumor has it that some of the University's leaders at that time wanted to demolish the Chapel and "build a new and adequate one." But respect for Cornell's traditions prevailed, and the nave was extended forty feet to the west to provide the needed increase in seating capacity.

Sage Chapel was and is an integral part of the informally designed south campus, which in itself was one of the loveliest parts of the Cornell campus until the University's growth during and after World War II all but filled this area with buildings. From 1878, when the grading and landscaping around the Sage buildings were completed, until the middle

twenties when Willard Straight Hall was built—for fifty years—the "informal brick group" in the south campus comprised the University's most consistent landscape design. The red-brick buildings in a park, the Sage Green, the winding approach to Sage College, the compatible brick buildings carefully added from time to time—the Armory, designed by Babcock in 1883, and Barnes Hall, designed by William H. Miller in 1887—all contributed to an informal but unified landscape composition of great beauty. Here the original land form, a rolling plateau carved by several small streams, was preserved intact. Here the landscape forms recommended by Frederick Law Olmsted were realized and protected. Now that this quality is only a green memory to a few Cornellians, lost largely because of the growth of Cornell, we should take special care to preserve and enhance its remnants—picturesque red-brick structures, one stream, and a limited area of green lawn. One imagines that when the first structures were completed, Mr. Ruskin would have been pleased. What is more important, we should be pleased to be reminded that the early designers and builders of this part of the Cornell campus had both respect for the landscape and a consistently high standard of taste.

[18] Morris Bishop, *A History of Cornell,* p. 111.

VI

The Campus and the Community, 1868-1880

THOSE WHO CAME TO COR-nell in its first fifteen years never failed to recall the beauty of the place—and the primitive conditions. The site was glorious: bounded by two rocky gorges it looked out over a view which Andrew D. White said was "unrivaled this side of Naples"[1] (Fig. 74). Two of the distinguished nonresident professors were also impressed by the Ithaca landscape. Louis Agassiz thought "Ithaca Falls [Fig. 75] in some respects more impressive and picturesque than Niagara," and Harvard poet James Russell Lowell is reported to have remarked that "if Ithaca's scenery will not make a young lady romantic, there is no hope for her in this world."[2] Several guides to the picturesque scenery of the area were produced in the late sixties and early seventies. Cascadilla Glen provided, one said, "an exquisite bit of scenery scarcely equalled even in the mountains of the Piedmont" (Fig. 76).

The winter scenery was equally striking, "when the rocky sides of the gorge are filled with huge icicles and the overhanging pines heavy with their weight of snow."

The beauties of the University's setting were widely appreciated, but, in the early years, they were dearly bought. For the first five years about 40 per cent of the students and less than half of the faculty lived on East Hill. The rest lived in the village. At first, most of the hill dwellers suffered from the shortcomings of South University or Cascadilla. The village dwellers had to climb the four-hundred-foot hill several times a day: students via the "bone-yard cut" (a path along the north side of Cascadilla Creek Gorge and through the village cemetery) (Fig. 77), and professors, if affluent, by carriage up University Avenue or Buffalo Street. In 1876 omnibus service was provided from the Clinton House to Cascadilla six times a day. The trip took half an hour. Professor Goldwin Smith (Fig. 78) walked from Cascadilla to the Cornell Public Library to deliver his lectures. He soon placed a stone bench for weary hill climbers at the halfway point on Buffalo Street.[3]

[1] ADW to Dean Sage, 26 September 1872, White Papers. President White was proposing that his rooms (with such a view) in Cascadilla be made available for the residence of the Sage Chapel preacher during a week-long stay in Ithaca between sermons preached on successive Sundays. Smith, *The Early Days of Cornell* (Ithaca, 1904), p. 11, remembers how he was stirred by a remarkable scene viewed from his window at Cascadilla Place: below him an eagle was soaring over the lake.

[2] *Boston Transcript,* 1 February 1869; clipping in Cornell Papers (Box 28), C.U. Archives.

[3] *Cornell Era,* 11 May 1870. If (as I suspect) this is the same stone bench which now is in the Arts Quadrangle in front of Goldwin Smith Hall, its inscription, "Above All Nations is Humanity," has topographical as well as philosophical meaning.

Fig. 74. A view from Cascadilla, 1868, looking southwest toward the Cayuga Inlet Valley. The mansard roof under construction at right distinguishes the house on Stewart Avenue formerly owned by John Charles Gauntlett.

Fig. 75. Ithaca Falls, 1868.   *Fig. 76.* Cascadilla Gorge in the 1870's.

Fig. 77. East Hill from the Clinton House, about 1876: White, McGraw, and Morrill Halls can be seen on the skyline at the left; Sage College and Cascadilla Place, to the right. Below them is the village cemetery through which ran a footpath called the "boneyard cut."

The three factors which contributed most toward making life difficult for early Cornellians were rapid growth, scattered facilities, and difficult terrain. The University was unexpectedly successful in attracting large numbers of students. Over five hundred prospective students arrived in October 1868, and after the entrance examinations were completed and graded, 412 were admitted. This was the largest class to enter any university in the country up to that time; 333 were freshmen. The institution and the small village of Ithaca were unprepared for these numbers. There were then only eight or ten houses along Buffalo Street above Stewart Avenue, the halfway point up the hill from the village. There were seven houses along Heustus Street (College Avenue). Apparently very few Ithacans anticipated the possibility that renting rooms to students would be profitable or even that there would be enough students to fill the University buildings. Few of their homes were large enough to have many extra rooms, so crowding was inevitable. The great wooden College Avenue and Eddy Street rooming and boarding houses were yet to be built.

Housing was in short supply in 1868, but

Fig. 78. Goldwin Smith came to Cornell from Oxford in 1868, taught at the University for two years, and returned regularly thereafter to give series of lectures.

the shortage of classroom and laboratory space was desperate. Since there was only one sizable lecture room on the hill, many of the large classes met in the Cornell Public Library downtown. There, too, the entrance examinations were held in shifts in the Military Hall in the basement, and many of the nonresident professors lectured in Library Hall. Other classes were held in the parlor of Cascadilla and in the five or six classrooms of Morrill Hall. Goldwin Smith viewed Cascadilla and Morrill Hall in 1869 and suggested expenditure of some of the University's limited resources for "a little beauty, if it can be had cheap, in the buildings," which he thought "were in danger of being very hideous." [4] There were also some functional problems in Morrill Hall. For example, ventilation for the temporary chemistry laboratory in the basement was partially provided by openings into the library and reading rooms above. The "temporary" wooden laboratory and classroom building, built by Ezra Cornell in the middle of what was to be the Quadrangle, provided much-needed space when it was completed in April 1869. In fact, at that time it provided more teaching space than any other building on the campus. The third building on the campus proper, North University (later named White Hall), was completed late in 1869. This provided eight or ten additional classrooms. Enrollment increased rapidly in these first two years, from 414 in 1868 to 568 in 1870, so the additional space for instruction was put into use immediately.

Sibley Hall provided additional laboratory and lecture rooms for engineering in the fall of 1871, and with the completion of the interior of McGraw Hall in October 1872, classroom space was at last adequate and the University library safely and comfortably housed. Crates of books that had remained in storage because of a shortage of shelf space were now unpacked, and the books were catalogued. With the library moved to McGraw there was room to move the administration offices from Cascadilla to South University, where they remained for seventy-five years until Day Hall was completed in 1948.

McGraw was the first university building to be equipped with central heating, but in spite of this the lecture rooms were cold. One pupil complained about it at the bottom of his examination paper in Professor W. C. Russel's class, and Russel sent the message to White with a sympathetic notation. A neophyte engineer complained that the wind shook the wooden laboratory building (Fig. 79) so hard that it was impossible to draw a straight line, and Professor Hiram Corson complained that his classroom was, at times, full of gas.[5] We must assume, since the record gives no details, that the cause of the complaint was either a faulty gaslight system or the operations of the chemistry laboratory. But these were minor troubles. By 1873 the instructional plant of the University was adequate, if somewhat drafty and occasionally gaseous.

A second cause for discomfort on East Hill was the fact that facilities for living and study were widely scattered (Fig. 80). The lectures given in the Cornell Public Library downtown were easily accessible to students living in the village, unless they had a class the hour before or after on the hill. Attendance by hill dwellers at these lectures required a two-mile round-trip hike which included a 420-foot climb. Goldwin Smith, usually a considerate man, moved his lectures from the Cornell Public Library in the village to Cascadilla in November 1868. He lived there, so the change at least had the merit of making the lecturer's arriving on time more likely. But any of the three hundred students living in South University or the village who attended his lectures had to brave Ithaca's winter storms to get there. These storms were more chilling in the nineteenth century, before the trees on the hill had grown. Cascadilla was only half a mile from South University and the temporary

[4] Smith to Norton in *Massachusetts Historical Society Proceedings,* December 1915, p. 148.

[5] *Cornell Era,* 5 December 1873; Maintenance Order Book, MS, C.U. Archives. In December 1875, Corson noted in this guide for the daily work of the custodian that "Room I was full of gas, at times."

Fig. 79. A classroom on the upper floor of the "temporary" wooden laboratory and classroom building built on the Quadrangle in 1868 and demolished in 1892. The room was photographed about 1878.

Fig. 80. A bird's-eye view of Ithaca, 1873. Fall Creek is at the right bordered by the knob of glacial lake delta on which Jennie McGraw Fiske later built her great mansion. Below is the Quadrangle, bordered on south and east by the Sage buildings and the beginnings of the East Avenue faculty row.

laboratory where most classes were held; but the trip was an adventure. To reach class in the first years on the campus, students left Cascadilla, climbed part way down the Cascadilla Creek Gorge bank, crossed a weak-looking lower-level wooden bridge, rebuilt in 1878 (Fig. 81), climbed up through the pine woods on the north bank, walked through an

Fig. 81. Cascadilla Bridge, north of Cascadilla Place. Completed a few days before classes began in October 1868, this bridge was replaced in 1878 by an iron bridge and in 1898 by the present reinforced concrete and stone arched bridge.

apple orchard, slid down and climbed up the banks of a small ravine where Campus Drive now crosses Central Avenue, and either skittered across the open icy crest of the hill, or slogged through its bogs in fall and spring. To advance education under such conditions indeed required an eager audience quite as much as a brilliant lecturer. Many students and faculty members, including Andrew D. White, wore high boots in the rainy season. John A. Rea later remembered that this attire made White (a man of small stature) look like Puss-in-Boots.[6]

The descent from "the three stately . . . buildings that sat like a triple crown upon the kingly eastern hill" was just as exciting and potentially maiming as the trip from Cascadilla to the campus. One student described such a trip in the course of which he lost control of his heel brakes. Gaining momentum, he plunged headlong through hedges and over rail fences and logs until finally he fell and rolled into the University quarry,

[6] John A. Rea, "The Immortal Eight," in *Fifty Years at Cornell* (*The Cornell Sun*, Ithaca, 1930).

where astonished stonecutters picked him up and, after brushing the dust from his tattered clothes, sent him headlong down the rest of the journey.[7] Those who endured such hardships often sat down afterward to write scathing items for the weekly student paper, the *Cornell Era.* Later, in their memoirs, they would record these same struggles as heroic deeds, but at the time everyone had a surfeit of climbing and descending, marching and countermarching. Students residing in South University at first had no running water nearer than Cascadilla. The military discipline of Cornell's first four years seems in retrospect to have been a necessity.

The third and most telling factor contributing to a rugged outdoor life for early Cornellians was the deplorable condition of the walks and roads needed for easy access and good communication between activities. The thin financial resources of the University were insufficient to cover the expense of the extensive grading and regular maintenance which these routes required. Washouts in gravel paths and roads were frequent on the steep hillsides, and inexpensive wooden bridges were difficult to maintain. The University and her benefactors were reasonably generous in the first decade in erecting buildings, but funds for site improvements were often omitted from the budgets. One thousand dollars was allocated to grading around North University (White Hall) in 1869, but in the first years there were no special appropriations for roads. What road and path grading was done was carried out by the student labor corps, and walks were often built by laying surplus boards parallel on the bare ground (Fig. 82). In October 1870 a motion in the Executive Committee that a good plank walk be built from Cascadilla to South University was lost because there were not funds sufficient to pay for it.

Earthen causeways (Fig. 83) crisscrossed the west part of the Quadrangle between

[7] *Cornell Era*, 13 October 1871, p. 11. The editor claimed that two-thirds of the students used the short cut next to the village cemetery. This account and editorial comment called for an improved direct route from town to hill.

Fig. 82. The Quadrangle looking north, about 1868, showing plank walks in the foreground. Grading of the "University Square" was attacked fitfully by Ezra Cornell's labor corps until 1873 but was not completed until 1878.

Fig. 83. Morrill Hall from the east, 1868. An English visitor in 1873 thought Morrill Hall "a fair specimen of the palaces in which Education holds perpetual levee in this land of thought." Worse has been said of it since; in 1966, however, it was designated a National Historic Monument by the Secretary of the Interior. In return for this distinction the University agreed to love, honor, and tastefully preserve and remodel the building for suitable educational use.

Fig. 84. The Stone Row and West Sibley as they appeared about 1878 after grading and first planting had been completed.

buildings for years before funds were available for the completion of grading. The student labor corps made a road from Cascadilla to the main building in the fall of 1868, and the Quadrangle was rough-graded in the fall of 1871 when McGraw Hall was completed. By late 1871 the roads were at least passable in most seasons. The editors of the *Era* defended their quality with vigor when a miscreant of the class of 1873 circulated unkind statements about them in the national press.[8] But the large-scale grading and road projects needed to make the campus walkable in all seasons were not carried out until 1873, when most of the remaining gullies in the main Quadrangle were filled (Fig. 84). In that same year the right of way and final grade for Central Avenue (then called University Avenue) were established by Charles Babcock and Major Junius W. MacMurray, and the road was graded and graveled. The University was in operation for five years before

adequate provision was made for easy movement from place to place.[9]

Another hazard to improvement appeared in the fall of 1873. In the spring of that year White had personally paid for a plank walk to be built along the Quadrangle side of the stone row. Late in October the walk was torn up by the students in the celebration of Gate Eve (Hallowe'en). President White, although furious at the prank, was undaunted in his efforts to beautify the place.[10] Early in 1874 he convinced the economizing Executive Committee that the services of an expert landscape architect were required. Mr. Jacob Weidenmann, landscape architect and sometime associate of Frederick Law Olmsted, was retained to prepare detailed plans for the Sage College grounds and to prepare a general

[8] *Cornell Era*, 21 September 1871.

[9] Trustees' *Proceedings*, 24 October 1870, 22 April, 30 June, 20 July 1873.
[10] *Cornell Era*, 5 December 1873. White was said to be so "wrathy" about the removal of the walk that he refused to give any money to a group then raising funds to build a student gymnasium.

sketch for the improvement of the rest of the university grounds. Weidenmann recommended a new bridge across Cascadilla Creek and a public road along the western boundary of the University, presently the line of Eddy Street and West Avenue. He thought this new north-south road would require moving the road which provided the existing main approach from Cascadilla to the Quadrangle further up the hill to the east. This change would have placed it directly in front of Sage College, and he proposed extending it to enter the Quadrangle from the center south. He also proposed a circuit drive inside the Quadrangle, now 1,100 feet in length by 500 feet in width.[11] Weidenmann's report to the Trustees also included a detailed design for a terrace west of the Quadrangle. He thought it should be 1,270 feet long and 50 feet wide on the west front with a second elevated terrace on the south side of the building proposed at the northwest corner of the Quadrangle. This higher north terrace, he believed, would lend a picturesque quality to the appearance of the terrace front.

Weidenmann's terrace proposals and all of his other ideas excepting the line he proposed for East Avenue were rejected. His ideas for the terrace and other improvements were regarded as too expensive, but probably more damaging to their acceptance was the fact that he had been tardy in producing detailed plans for the Sage College grounds. The University had recruited a large force of student laborers, but without plans they could not proceed with the work. And the cost of the job had already been financed by a gift of Henry Sage. Weidenmann's tardiness roused Andrew D. White's wrath. The grading and landscaping which were to have started in the spring of 1874 had to be put off until Commencement. By that time the financial crisis caused by Ezra Cornell's illness and imminent death made it impossible to give the work

proper attention. When Weidenmann finally completed his plan in June, White found it "unpracticable in nearly all respects." Professor Roberts did not like the farm layout. White thought that the "botanic garden was not where it was needed" and that roads were "placed where not wanted and none were placed where desired." Weidenmann's services were terminated and the University retained its own engineer so that the work could proceed.

This was a great disappointment to White. He wanted and had retained expert services. Weidenmann, the designer and builder of Bushnell Park in Hartford, Connecticut, was a trusted associate of Frederick Law Olmsted.[12] Time, distance, and other commitments seem to have prevented the landscape architect from giving careful attention to Cornell's needs and time schedule, and so Cornell as well as Weidenmann lost an opportunity to build the great western terrace. Three years passed before completion of final grading, paths, roads, and planting in the Quadrangle, in the area west of the west row, and along East Avenue (Fig. 85). These improvements, carried out in 1876 and 1877 under a plan prepared by Professor Prentiss, were financed by two $3,000 loans from Henry W. Sage.[13]

Student Hallowe'en pranks continued to be a major hazard to campus site improvements. In 1883, in what was probably the most impressive prank during the first twenty years of Cornell pranks, students collapsed the Central Avenue Bridge. Henry Sage thought President White should have stopped this destruction. White was not about to face the "funloving" students.

[11] J. Weidenmann, "Report for Improving and Laying Out Cornell University Grounds at Ithaca," 8 June 1874. MS, C.U. Archives. White Papers, 8 June 1874; Trustees' *Proceedings*, 1 June 1874.

[12] ADW to Weidenmann, 9 September 1874, White Papers. White's letter is quite sharp. The episode must have distressed Frederick Law Olmsted, who had been elected a University Trustee in 1873, but he was probably only indirectly concerned. Weidenmann did the work on his own account. Mr. Olmsted's only recorded attendance at a Board meeting was on October 1874 in Ithaca. He was re-elected Trustee 16 June 1875 for a three-year term in place of George Geddes.

[13] Trustees' *Proceedings*, 1 August 1876, and 30 August 1877.

Fig. 85. The Stone Row viewed from the northwest, about 1878. Here, west of the row, Frederick Law Olmsted and others since have proposed the creation o f a great paved terrace and promenade to exploit the vista of the Cayuga Lake valley and to provide a more dignified setting for the first buildings at Cornell.

All of the early Cornell campus problems—the overcrowding, the long distances between activities, and the primitive road and path systems—would be solved more easily, it was hoped, by the provision of a "closer settlement on the hill." [14] White, however, was much opposed to the dormitory system, and he was very persuasive. Lack of funds for additional academic buildings brought about the gradual conversion of the dormitory rooms in North and South University to classroom use; so, as the years passed, fewer and fewer students lived on the campus.[15] White thought they should live with "genteel families in the village." The latter obliged but at first not in sufficient quantity. The *Era* of 16 March 1869 published an urgent appeal to the people of Ithaca to build more houses nearer the campus and to rent rooms. The author of the plea sounds very like someone who could not wait to leave Cascadilla, the University's "family hotel."

Survivors of the hardships and discomforts

of life at Cornell in early years had as much cause for complaint and reason for pioneer boasting about The Cascadilla as they did about the nonexistent or gullied campus walk system. Cascadilla Place (Fig. 86) was the bête noire of Cornellians in the 1870's and 1880's. Many of the difficulties in "perfecting arrangements" in Cascadilla arose from its confused status as a university building and its split ownership. Ezra Cornell and thirty-one other Ithacans had purchased shares to finance the development of the water cure. When it became apparent that its backers were not going to finance its completion and "temporary University use might be necessary," Cornell, then two-thirds owner, had changed its construction material from wood to stone and the water cure corporation leased it to the University for five years. While the other stockholders gave their shares to the University in 1869, Ezra Cornell and his estate retained an interest in it until 1878.[16]

[14] Olmsted to ADW, 10 September 1867, White Papers.

[15] President's report, June 1885.

[16] Trustees' *Proceedings,* 30 June 1869. The donors of shares for considerations of one dollar each include Schuyler, Rumsey, Finch, Boardman, Titus, Culver, Esty, Thompson, Wilgus, Treman-King and Co., Gauntlett, Wilkins, Mack, Giles, Blood, Stoddard,

Fig. 86. Cascadilla from the village, 1868. Buffalo Street runs diagonally across the picture. Cascadilla Place, as the dormitory-cum-faculty apartment building was known in the sixties and seventies, was the social center for the University in its early years.

After several years of operation by the University, Cascadilla was leased to a private concession and from that time onward, if we can judge from constant complaints in the *Cornell Era*, it was poorly maintained and often incompetently managed. Because of its split ownership, private management, and being frequently damaged during student pranks, it was difficult to identify the responsibility for its poor management and maintenance. However, the *Era* editors, with the clear vision of youth, knew precisely who was responsible for Cascadilla's poor condition. In 1878 one wrote: "In our last issue we made an erroneous statement that Cascadilla had steadily deteriorated under its present management. This is impossible for the building could not be in worse condition than when it was rented to the present lessee. We regard the blame as resting entirely with the Univer-

sity authorities." [17] Meditation upon this condition led the editor to a fanciful solution to the problem which would at the same time provide better walks: "Dump the stones that make up the Cascadilla into the Gorge," he wrote; "wash them for a week and then lay them out for a walk."

In 1881, Chemistry Professor A. Breneman, who was appointed to investigate sanitary conditions in Cascadilla, produced a fourteen-page report. The essence of it was that the building was an unholy, unsanitary mess: among other faults it had poor and antiquated water closets, a poor cellar, and a poor water supply. He recommended more consciousness of sanitary conditions on the part of the University. [18] Expectations were rising rapidly. The sanitary facilities Professor Breneman condemned were the improvements of the preceding decade which had in turn resulted from protests regarding the inadequacy of Cascadilla's outdoor privies.

John McGraw, Jane McGraw, Selkreg and Andrus and several others of lesser local renown. In 1878 the Trustees negotiated the purchase of Ezra Cornell's former interest in Cascadilla from his estate at a price of $37,100. No cash transaction is indicated so it is probable that the amount was credited to his half-million dollar endowment pledge.

[17] *Cornell Era,* 25 October and 22 November 1878.
[18] Executive Committee Papers, 23 March 1881, C.U. Archives.

When the University opened in 1868, most of the doors in Cascadilla had not been hung. The rooms were bare and the means to furnish them quite limited. W. A. Woodward, the business manager, noted in his daybook in October 1868 that Finch had told him the students would have to purchase their own bookcases. Other items were considered absolute necessities. For example, thirty-six spittoons were ordered a month later.[19] The walls of student rooms were bare white plaster, a fashionable decor in the 1960's but a monstrous crudity in the 1860's, when the humblest abode was likely to have figured wallpaper. Ezra Cornell was finally persuaded that the expense of papering at least one hundred rooms could be borne, so in the summer of 1870, after much stalling, the work began. Professor W. C. Russel reported to White, who was away from the campus, that he "dreaded Mr. Cornell's wallpaper . . . expected horrors in every figure." White was not very reassuring. "Ezra Cornell," he wrote, "may be canonized some day but not . . . for such qualities as enrolled Fra Angelico among the blessed. The aesthetic was left out of him."[20]

Because of its primitive qualities and its mixed student-faculty occupancy, at first Cascadilla was an exciting place in which to live. A correspondent of the *Boston Transcript*, a Harvard man it seems, arrived in Ithaca in January 1869, "toiled up the declevity" of East Hill and came upon the Cascadilla House "of rough unmatched stone . . . surrounded by unpainted wooden sheds, huts and fences." A dismantled steam engine was "keeled up near the door. . . . Its rough platform of unpainted boards gave anything but a favorable impression. . . . From the stone structure came the sound of a piano and muffled whooping of young men's voices." Inside he found long, bare corridors with two hundred pairs of white door jambs thickly set on both sides, and, "shocking to the austere Cam-

bridge discipline, . . . evidences of female occupancy and domesticated cats and dogs." Through the open door of Professor Smith's parlor he saw "Mrs. Smith with two or three friends, serving tea and chatting in a cozy way, unmindful of the students' boots overhead, or the sound of students' songs across the hall." The correspondent reported his amazement at this "collocation of the barracks and of the family, this admixture of professor and student in the same house."[21]

The educational benefits of the arrangement were indeed unintentional and short-lived. One hundred and four students and twelve faculty families lived at Cascadilla Place in 1868. Seventy-five students lived in South University.[22] Students who lived in university buildings were subject to semi-military discipline. Rising at 5:30 A.M., they cleaned and arranged their rooms for inspection, wore uniforms to meals, stood guard duty, and asked for a permit when they wanted to leave town. The regulations, said to be "necessary for the preservation of quiet, order, and health," were enforced by the Commandant, Major Whittlesey, who was at Cornell to give

[19] W. A. Woodward's Account Book, p. 1, C.U. Archives.

[20] ADW to W. C. Russel, 14 July 1870; W. C. Russel to ADW, 15 July 1870, White Papers.

[21] *Boston Transcript*, 1 February 1869; clipping in Ezra Cornell Papers (Box 28). The article initialed "C.C." was reprinted in numerous papers, including the *Washington Star*. The correspondent was impressed by the equipment and purposes of the young university: "Chemical apparatus superb, excellent foundations for collections in palaeontology, natural history, physiology . . . library is excellent in its way . . . not an ordinary educational institution, but the beginning of a university embracing a diversity of studies as wide as human industry . . . working with persistence and vigor commensurate with the sagacity, energy and generosity in which it has been planned and endowed . . . to the graduates of Harvard it should be a powerful incentive toward newly endowing and opening out into a generous system of culture adapted to the needs of modern America. The spirit of the age . . . demands some change in the system of higher education."

[22] W. A. Woodward's Account Book, p. 34. Mr. W. A. Woodward was the University's business manager from 1867 to 1869. Woodward was also the agent of Ezra Cornell for locating western lands from 1865 to 1871. He was later involved in litigation with Ezra Cornell, over the costs of his services. Professor Paul W. Gates's *The Wisconsin Pine Lands of Cornell University* (Ithaca, 1943) is an excellent study of the purchase and management of the University's western lands within the setting of U.S. public land policies of the last half of the nineteenth century.

military instruction under the terms of the Morrill Act. Officers were selected from among the students. In his inaugural address the President referred to the system as "government of the students by themselves."[23] In Morrill Hall the officers took the choice ground-floor corner rooms. The privates lived upstairs. This strict military system was abolished in 1872.

All went well at first. Birchard A. Hayes, the son of President Rutherford B. Hayes, wrote home in the fall of 1871, that the board was very good. "We have," he noted, "several kinds of meat for dinner besides soup, sweet potatoes, tomatoes, bread and butter, pie and pudding . . . grapes and apples and coffee, tea and milk to drink." But by February 1872 he was disenchanted: "Board is getting worse and worse." A shopping list for an eighteen-day menu in Cascadilla gives some further idea of the fare. It included pumpkins, apples, butter, eggs, flour, Indian meal, codfish, onions, cabbages, potatoes, beets, carrots and turnips. Business Manager Woodward noted in his account book in the first month that "President White wanted . . . ventilation to Cascadilla Place to carry off savors from the kitchen."[24] The professors and their families had a separate skylighted interior dining room on the second floor, but it was too cold there when winter came, so they moved downstairs into one of the student dining rooms.

These rooms and the parlor of Cascadilla were used for the annual Founder's Day celebration as well as other social events. The entertainments became increasingly Spartan as the University's "floating debt" grew, but the first Founder's Day party (Ezra Cornell's birthday) was a grand affair. It was held in the large two-storied parlor in the west-central part of Cascadilla on 11 January 1869. A blizzard raged outside. Inside, the parlor, dining halls, stairways, and corridors were jammed with members of the University and

Fig. 87. Ezra Cornell in the "President's chair," which was presented to the University by President White for ceremonial occasions.

townspeople. It was a sort of inaugural ball. All Ithacans had been invited, and it seemed as if most of them were there. In the dining rooms large roasted turkeys, uncarved, were placed every few feet along the long tables. The food was very like that served at an old-fashioned New England Thanksgiving dinner. The Founder, seated in a massive chair of state (Fig. 87), held court and was presented a large birthday cake with sixty-two lighted tapers. Later, when the crowds thinned out, there was dancing. The latter was denounced by the local clergy as further evidence of the University's ungodliness: "dangerous" and "destructive to vital godliness." Morris Bishop records that in the following year Ezra Cornell paid for an orchestra to provide music for dancing at his birthday reception.[25]

Although Cascadilla was usually fully occu-

[23] *Register of the Cornell University*, 1868, 1869.

[24] Birchard Austin Hayes to Rutherford B. Hayes, 2 October 1871, 25 February 1872, Hayes Papers; and Woodward's Account Book, pp. 4, 5.

[25] This description is based on the accounts of Professor Burt G. Wilder and Samuel D. Halliday ('70) in the *Cornell Era: Ezra Cornell Centennial Number*, Vol. 39, No. 8 (May, 1907), pp. 389 and 415; and Bishop, *A History of Cornell*, p. 129.

Fig. 88. College Avenue rooming houses in the 1870's. In the foreground is Willow Pond, a long-since-removed component of Otis Eddy's cotton mill, which had occupied the site until 1866.

pied, some of the student rooms in North and South University were empty for years because less expensive accommodations could be found in the village, where eating places were more convenient.[26] When the school year began in 1871, there was a considerable demand for boarding houses in town, and Ithacans were not averse to meeting the need. The *Era* announced that it considered plans for the erection of boarding houses near the University of no small importance. Along Eddy Street near Cascadilla Place and south along what is now College Avenue, scores of big frame rooming houses were erected in the seventies (Fig. 88). Rates at first were as low as $4.50 per week for bed and board compared to the Cascadilla fee which fluctuated between $5.00 and $7.00 a week depending, apparently, on the expenses of the operation.

In the spring of 1871 the Executive Committee voted to close the dining facilities at Cascadilla.[27] The Trustees, especially President White, were more convinced than ever that housing and feeding students was properly a private affair. The business of Cornell was education, and White thought that the proper model was the continental university where students were left to their own devices outside the classroom. The ensuing private management of the Cascadilla dining room must have been disappointing, because boarding clubs run by students began to grow in size and number in the fall term of 1871. By January 1872 there were eleven of them with a total membership of one hundred and forty.[28] Cooperative purchasing was initiated by the club stewards and good quality food was provided at an average price of $2.50 per week. By this time some private boarding houses were charging as much as $7.00 per week for board only. The growth of the clubs, it was hoped, would "keep the rapacity of the boarding house keepers down. . . . Clubs are trump," the *Era* crowed. In 1879 there were still eleven "Hash Clubs" in operation including such exotics as "The Ragout Club, The

[26] Trustees' *Proceedings,* 24 October 1870; White Papers, 28 October 1870; Woodward to ADW, 23 December 1869, White Papers.
[27] Trustees' *Proceedings,* 20 February 1871.
[28] *Cornell Era,* 26 January 1872.

Soup Club, Ye Gourmandizing Troop, The Nail Club, Die Innerberehtnehrsifrissenschelemmere, and the Struggle."

"If any question interests students at Cornell," the weekly *Era* reported in 1871, "it is how to live cheaply and well." As a rule in the early days students were poor. Twenty of them who worked in the student labor corps, Ezra Cornell's work-study program, petitioned the Trustees for permission to build a "cottage" (with removal rights) on the University grounds. The request granted, the establishment was hastily nailed together behind West Sibley. Many of these students worked in the university print shop. David Starr Jordan, who later became the first president of Stanford University, joined several classmates in building a hut south of Andrew D. White's house. Their fellowship was poverty-stricken but garrulous.[29] For students of greater means who could combine high living with the higher learning there were such places as Deschner's Kaffee Haus on Geneva Street where roomers were guaranteed "every facility for acquiring the German language" and lots of wholesome pie, sausage, leberwurst, limburger, pretzels, and cake washed down with the purest Rochester lager.[30]

For most of the students of the seventies life of the sort provided at Deschner's was impossible. One such student, a young farmer who had taken up the study of Sanscrit with Professor Roehrig, lived on $3.00 a week which he earned by working four to six hours each morning on the University farm.[31] Sixty students worked in the labor corps in 1871, earning fifteen cents an hour for common labor and considerably more if skilled. National publicity describing the work-study opportunities at Cornell made the place so attractive that the Cornell *Register* made a point of discouraging unskilled workers from

coming to the University with the expectation that they could support themselves while studying. There simply were not many unskilled jobs available in Ithaca, and most of them were seasonal or short-lived tasks such as roadmaking or landscaping and grading the university square. The last-named, seemingly endless job was finally completed in 1878. A few other unskilled jobs were available: waiting on table at Cascadilla (after the "formal waiters" were discharged), picking up and delivering mail, cleaning the grounds, and cleaning and scrubbing floors in university buildings. The business manager found students so inefficient at scrubbing that he soon asked for women to do the work.[32] For the first five years construction workers were in demand. Skilled carpenters, plasterers, masons, and quarry men had no difficulty finding part-time work; and experienced machinists were in demand at the Sibley Hall shops, but they had to be sturdy to work six hours (a half day) and have sufficient energy left to study.

In 1865, White calculated a typical student's "necessary expenses" for a discussion of the Board of Trustees. They came to $187–$200 for the forty-week school year. Theoretically a sturdy young man who could work thirty-two hours a week at fifteen cents an hour could support himself through his course of study.[33] Ezra Cornell's dream of providing

[29] The Journal of their struggle, kept by Jordan, is preserved in the C.U. Archives.

[30] Advertisement, the *Cornell Era, passim,* fall and winter, 1871.

[31] *New York Times,* 6 November 1871; reprinted in the *Cornell Era,* 1 December 1871. Such stories brought poor but eager young men from all over the world.

[32] W. A. Woodward's Account Book, p. 1. Squads of seven were first used for general labor work such as grading roads. Such work was so popular in the fall of 1868 that the size of the squads soon had to be increased.

[33] In the Trustee Papers of June 1868 in ADW's handwriting are the following calculations and notes:

Approximate Estimate of Necessary Expenses per annum (for students)

1. For state students:
   a. instruction fees   00 to 00
   b. room rent (.60 to 1.10/wk for 40 wks)   24–44.00
   c. board (2.50/wk)   100–140.00
   d. fuel and lights   8–16.00
   e. use of books and stationery   8–18.00
   f. use of furniture, bedding, etc.   7–15.00
   g. washing   10–15.00
2. For students on usual basis: above plus $10.00

an education "which shall prove highly beneficial to the poor young men and poor young women of the country" did come true for a few early Cornellians. But after the first five years the university buildings were completed and the land-poor institution entered into its lean years. The labor corps became too expensive, and a substantial program in agriculture did not materialize. So, when the need for skilled building mechanics declined, only a few jobs in the Sibley machine shops, the print shop, and the farm could be provided by the University for a program of work and education. The Cornell laboring system proved to be a worthwhile and interesting but inconclusive experiment.

Laboring in the University's corps required residence on the hill, so the poor students tended to live there rather than in the village. Indeed, it seemed that a student's intellectual aspirations as well as his economic status might be determined by whether he was a "Dweller on the Hill" or a "Denizen of the Valley." An *Era* editorial (1 December 1876) asserted that those who live near the campus came to study and those who live downtown came to play. The hill dweller, according to the *Era* editorialist, took more advantage of the lectures at night and was much more concerned with the life of the intellect than the valley dweller.

per term for instruction fees—yearly total: $187–208.00.
3. To these must be added traveling expenses, etc.
4. Possible savings to students in voluntary labor corps: a large force can be employed on the farm, in the machine shop, and on the grounds.
5. Special aids to meritorious students: recommends a revision of instruction fees for them: plus $1200 available in scholarships.
6. The location of the university in Ithaca will mean less expense: cost of living less: basic consumer articles less; university itself can raise large number of food supplies; fuel is a cheap commodity.

In conclusion the Trustees pledge themselves to the extent of their power that this shall be made an institution for the people; and that their constant aim shall be to render its advantages more and more accessible to the greatest number at the lowest rates possible.

Cornellians soon came to look on the village in the valley as a prime source of entertainment. Morris Bishop has chronicled many of the students' amusements *in urbe* in *A History of Cornell*,[34] but two characteristic activities, Gate Eve and mock funerals, evoke such romantic pictures of the place that one is encouraged to expand on his descriptions. There were very few student campus celebrations in the first decade of the University. Baseball games, a few dances, the annual rush, an occasional burning in effigy of an unpopular figure, and a few spectacular bonfires including one which consumed most of the outbuildings around The Cascadilla covered much of the range of major campus celebrations. The most exciting student activities were in town, and of these Gate Eve was most likely to stir the blood of the community. All proper Ithaca houses had proper wooden fences and substantial gates. Each fall, late in October, at the appointed hour several hundred young men would emerge from the evening shadows walking briskly down the hill or out of the valley rooming houses. Groups of students, policemen, and special police (plain-clothes) then began an evening of marching and countermarching. The students lifted gates on their shoulders but dropped them quickly at the approach of officers and then outran them. The abandoned gates and others were quickly picked up and borne along by other students, and were stacked for later burning or were floated out to Cayuga Lake along Cascadilla or Six Mile Creek. Sometimes gates were rehung on any convenient gate post. This gleeful childlike destruction often continued until dawn, and throughout the students "sang tremendous songs," while "running the police around."

President White believed that punishment for offenses against the town should be left to the town, but after the gate-lifting episode of 1871, he initiated faculty action which resulted in dismissal of ten students who had already been fined by the local authorities.

[34] Morris Bishop, *A History of Cornell*, pp. 121–142.

Some citizens, including the Chief of Police, petitioned the University to repeal the dismissal, and the students prepared a formal resolution thanking the villagers for their intercession. All of this provided several weeks of entertainment and much grist for the *Era's* paper mill.[35] A few weeks later it was reported that one student, a native of Ithaca, was caught red-handed replacing the gate at his own home. With some difficulty he convinced the police officer who caught him at it that he was not lifting it.

The *Era* viewed the suspension of gate-lifting students as a "wedge that threatened to separate the student body from the faculty" and "end a fine relationship that had been one of the reasons for Cornell's progress." Separate dining rooms for faculty and students were reinstituted at Cascadilla. Finally the air was cleared when the outcast students were brought back. But the gate-lifting continued—a "tradition" had been created. In 1873 three lady students were said to have been seen lifting gates.[36] But traditions were easy to establish and abandon. For example, in 1871 a threat to the "old ball ground" was viewed with some concern by the students of the three-year-old University.

To some extent student ebullience could be channeled along ceremonial lines. In this class was the burial of hated objects. At Yale a mock funeral for Euclid was for years an important and elaborate ceremony.[37] At Cornell

in the fall of 1871 the burial of required freshman caps was a fête of major proportions. The funeral procession assembled by torchlight at the Military Hall of the village library-community civic center. The mourners were mostly dressed in white and were accompanied by a few winged creatures, a red man, a black-robed friar, and a devil. The procession, bearing a casket containing the freshman caps and led by the cadet band on a spring wagon, traveled down Seneca Street, turned over Geneva to State Street, and slowly ascended the hill past Cascadilla, lighted for the occasion—its windows and porches filled with spectators. The procession then proceeded across the Cascadilla Gorge bridge to the campus where the casket of caps was buried in mock-solemn ceremonies with much baiting of town boys and with pun-ridden satirical eulogies.[38]

Student pranks, even those conducted on the scale of Gate Eve, were very minor concerns of the faculty and administration at Cornell in the seventies. The most pressing problems of the decade were financial. The University's objective during this decade was to live on the income from slightly over $1,000,000 while waiting for the value of its western land to rise.[39] The operating costs for new buildings provided by John McGraw, Henry Sage, and Hiram Sibley, the cost of carrying taxes and other expenses on the western lands after the University took them over from Ezra Cornell in 1874, and the ambitious academic plans of President White were more than the University treasury could bear. The new buildings had to be equipped, maintained, and heated; land income did not fully cover the expenses of land ownership, and White's new departments were not usually specially endowed.

[35] *Cornell Era*, October to December, 1871, *passim*. The descriptions of the campaign in the issues of 27 October and 3 November 1871 are particularly vivid.

[36] *Cornell Era*, 7 November 1873. The editor suggested that the young ladies should not have been unescorted on the streets after dark.

[37] Clarence Demming, *Yale Yesterday* (New Haven and London, 1915), pp. 41–50. The burial, generated by student hatred of required mathematics, dated from early in the nineteenth century. In pre-burial ceremonies, Euclid was perforated with a red-hot poker. Thrusting an iron through his covers symbolized that each student had "gone through" Euclid. Then he was held aloft and the class walked below: "He was understood." The burial ceremonies included a costumed procession, Latin prayers, and music and poetry by, for example, Geo. Metry, Cora Lary, Theo. Rem, Polly Gon, and C. Cant. The affairs ended at

Yale in 1863 but were spread by her sons to many colleges. One of Cornell's young faculty or perhaps her young president may have suggested the mock burial "tradition."

[38] *Cornell Era*, 10 November 1871.

[39] Charles K. Adams, "Cornell University, Its Significance and Its Scope," excerpt of an address in the *Cornell Era: Ezra Cornell Centennial Number* (May, 1907), p. 399.

Fig. 89. McGraw Hall, cornerstone laying, 1869. This building, a gift of John McGraw of Ithaca, was the first home of the university library, the Cornell chimes, and the Museum of Natural History; it was also the last home of many a cat awaiting service in Professor Wilder's class in comparative anatomy.

The result of Cornell's initial drive for expansion, in a period when income was static and even declining, was a rising debt. In December 1869, W. A. Woodward, the University's business manager, wrote to White recommending that all building be stopped immediately. The floating debt was $38,000. McGraw Hall's foundations were barely showing above ground level. Its cornerstone had been laid the previous summer (Fig. 89). The architect, Archimedes N. Russell, did some hasty calculations and informed White that $19,000 would be saved if both north and south wings were left off the building. The pace of its construction was reduced considerably but the Executive Committee decided to proceed with the building as originally planned. By October 1870 the debt exceeded $100,000. White wrote his resignation, but the Executive Committee refused to accept it. At the same Executive Committee meeting motions were made that White should give lectures in

agriculture and that a plank walk should be built from Cascadilla to the main building. Both were defeated. All was gloom. In January 1871, President Hayes's son wrote home that the Founder's Day Reception "was a fizzle. Dancing and nothing to eat." Hayes could not have known how land-poor Cornell was at the time. Cake and ice cream for the Founder's birthday party might have made it bankrupt.

By the fall of 1872, the floating debt (a financiers' buoyantly hopeful name for "unfunded short-time debt resulting from current expenses and having no specified date for repayment") exceeded $155,000. Something had to be done about it. So Trustees Cornell, White, Sage, Sibley, and McGraw dug into their pockets and paid it off. With the crisis temporarily over, White became hopeful about expansion. He submitted plans for "enlarging and developing the University" to the Executive Committee in November 1872. The circumstances seemed to give rise to White's hope that this was the time to expand. Sage College was under construction, Henry Sage had just offered $30,000 for the construction of a chapel, and the library was being moved into its fine new room in McGraw Hall. White based his recommendations for further expansion on the assumption that some of the University's pine lands in Wisconsin would be sold for $1,500,000. Mr. Cornell objected. He was pleased with the President's plans and spoke of increasing his endowment from $500,000 to $1,000,000 to carry some of them out. But he was determined that most of the pine land should be held until it increased in value sufficiently to provide a really handsome endowment. Cornell thought as much as $3,000,000 might be realized on it.[40] This turned out to be a wise long-term position but White was impatient to build the University and he was bitterly disappointed at this restraint.[41]

The national recession of 1873 further postponed the growth of Cornell. Demand for lumber declined and the value of the University's western lands declined with it. Ezra Cornell's heavy investment in upstate railroad lines was also threatened by the general economic collapse. He began to replace the solid Western Union stock which secured his endowment to the University with less secure railroad stock and finally he was no longer able to pay personally, as he had for years, the taxes and other expenses required to hold the western pine land. In mid-1874, Ezra Cornell, in poor health and with his business affairs headed for the wall, decided to settle his affairs with the University he had founded. The western lands were transferred to university ownership and Cornell's endowment was secured by various gifts, mortgages, and stock. There was little left in his personal estate when he died at his home on Tioga Street in December 1874. Mary Cornell was comfortably provided for, but most of Ezra Cornell's fortune, once estimated at $2,000,000, had been disbursed. While much of it went to the Cornell Public Library and the University, vast sums had been spent to carry the pine lands and even larger sums had been invested in various railroad and manufacturing enterprises designed to stimulate the growth of Ithaca.

There could be no further thought of university growth in the last half of the seventies. The national and local economy languished, and building ceased on East Hill. No new departments were established, and university enrollment leveled off and began to decline. It dropped from 561 in 1877 to 399 in 1881. Some of the best faculty members left. Professor Crafts of Chemistry, for example, accepted an offer from the Massachusetts Institute of Technology where he eventually rose to the presidency. No new buildings were started for eight years after Sage College was completed in 1874. White asked for a leave of absence in June 1876. He said his health was poor, but, in fact, he was enormously bored with the day-to-day affairs of administration, and travel, as he later wrote, was the best medicine for him. So, Vice-President Russel was made Acting President and White left for Europe in October 1876. He returned to the campus during the academic year 1878–1879, but there was little hesitation on his part when an appointment as U.S. Minister at Berlin was offered him in February 1879. He accepted and in May 1879 left Ithaca for two and one-half years. He later wrote that these long absences from the presidency were really in the best interest of Cornell. They gave the

[40] Paul Gates, *op. cit.,* pp. 242–243, gives an account of the outcome of land sales; $5,000,000 was the net value added to the University's endowment.

[41] Trustees' *Proceedings,* 23 November 1872; ADW to Mary White, 11 January 1873, White Papers. The letter describes a meeting of the Executive Committee: "another of the agonizing times which come perodically in the history of this institution. Mr. Cornell pursued by the demon of unreason, the rest of us struggling vainly against it . . . of all the difficult men to get along with in this world, Mr. Cornell must be the most so." At the meeting White refers to (6 January) a resolution on purchase by the University of the land known as "the Sage College purchase," the building of walks, and administration of the College of Mechanic Arts seem to have been the chief issues.

Trustees and faculty some administrative responsibilities. He had seen great institutions, the University of Michigan and Union College for examples, fall rapidly when their all-controlling presidents went out of office. White's post-flight rationalizations may have had some truth in them but it is also true that he might have successfully preserved some of the ground lost at Cornell in the late seventies.

By 1880 the shrinking university community was fairly well housed on East Hill. Its faculty were twenty-eight, its students were three hundred and ninety-nine. The Ithaca community had now grown to 11,500 persons. There were many serious problems in the academic community of 1880. The physics and chemistry departments were poorly provided for, Russel had not been able to stem faculty tiffs, professors' salaries were low, and community health problems were substantial. In 1878 eight undergraduates died and the fol-

lowing year, six more. Poor drainage and sanitary conditions in the community were blamed. In April 1877, the *Era* growled that "there is probably no worse drained town in the state . . . one half of the sickness here . . . due to that cause alone." Both the University and the community felt their strength ebbing away. Then, in the late seventies, just as the young University began to fade, an almost unbelievably typical nineteenth-century hero, Henry Sage, came to the rescue, ledger in hand and wary businessman's eye on the critical decisions that shape an enterprise. At first, Sage's choice was to economize. From 1875 until 1881, when the first large sales of Cornell's western lands were made, private means provided the small improvements needed to make East Hill in Ithaca a settlement of scholars—privately built houses for students and faculty off campus and a few cottages for professors on leased campus lots.

VII

Cottages and Villas

CORNELL'S FACULTY ROW was born in the deep, dark cavern of Cascadilla in the spring of 1870. The place had always been less than ideal for family living, but that spring must have been extremely trying. The activities of a Mrs. Bailey (no relation to the famous Cornell professor) who tried to take charge of the place were finally too much for Mrs. James Law.[1] Even-tempered Goldwin Smith had had his fill of living there, too, and wanted a house. Several faculty members petitioned the Executive Committee which then appointed Cornell, McGraw, and Finch as a committee to select and lease university land to professors for building houses, "the University to reserve the right to take improvements at an appraisal."[2] "Cottages for professors" had been listed by the Building Committee in their 1866 program but no university funds had been available for them. The idea of building a home on the campus was appealing to White. He had retained his house in Syracuse and roomed in The Cascadilla when he was in Ithaca. Now he decided he would give a President's House to the University.

White immediately wrote to New York architect George Hathorne about plans for professors' cottages and his villa. Hathorne replied that he could furnish plans for cottages at $125.00 for each site and could complete working drawings for $50.00 six weeks after his plans had met requirements of those intending to build. He came to Ithaca in the middle of May, 1870, to discuss house plans with White, Law, Fiske, Goldwin Smith, and anyone who might be interested. The design of White's villa has been discussed. Professor Law decided that he could not afford the services of an architect and proceeded to let a contract for a house based on plans taken from an authoritative architectural pattern book (Woodward's *The House, A Manual of Rural Architecture* by D. H. Jaques). White did not approve. He thought a location on the campus required more careful attention to appearance so he personally arranged for Archimedes Russell, who was supervising the building of McGraw Hall, to prepare a "neat and inexpensive" plan for Professor Law.[3]

[1] Mrs. James Law to ADW, 23 April 1870, White Papers. Mrs. Bailey, who is not further identified, could not have been the wife of Professor Liberty Hyde Bailey, because he did not come to Ithaca until 1888. It would appear from Mrs. Law's letter that this Mrs. Bailey was the wife of one of Cascadilla's managers or employees.
[2] Trustees' *Proceedings*, 25 April and 2 May 1870.

[3] ADW to W. C. Russel, 8 and 9 July 1870, White Papers. Professor Fiske had agreed to house Goldwin Smith if the University would loan him funds to build additional accommodations. White offered to loan one-third of the amount required if Ezra Cornell and John McGraw would each advance the same amount. Plans for a professor's cottage, which may be George Hathorne's plans for Fiske's cottage, are in the 17 June 1870 White Papers. Hathorne's letters to White in the White Papers are 5 May and 17 May, 17 June, 27 September, 29 October and 25 November 1870.

Fig. 90. The gymnasium and professors' cottages from the Sage College central tower, 1874. The gymnasium, financed by student-faculty subscription in the early 1870's, was moved across Central Avenue in 1882 to serve as the gym wing of the Armory. The cottages, from left to right, were built originally for Professor T. F. ("Teefy") Crane, Major MacMurray, and Professor Morris.

Construction of the Willard Fiske and James Law houses was started in the spring of 1871. Professor Fiske moved into his house in the middle of November and so had the distinction of being the first of many Cornell faculty members to live on the university grounds. Rooms for students were provided in a number of the faculty houses on the campus as well as in those being built in town. For example, Tracy Peck, Professor of Latin, built a house at Seneca and Eddy streets in 1872 that included two student rooms.

More house building on the campus began in the spring of 1873. At first it was rumored that the University was planning to build six cottages for professors in the pine woods just north of Cascadilla Creek. In April, the Trustees' Building Committee secured plans for cottages to be built there but, as noted earlier, "a trustee" (probably Ezra Cornell) protested that he planned to erect a university building in the pine woods, so other sites were found. In June 1873 the plans for Professor Babcock's house were approved and construction started on a site just east of Sage Chapel.[4] Some of

the students thought the Professor of Architecture set a rather poor example with his cottage. Birchard Hayes wrote his parents that it was "no beauty . . . being very small and having square windows." "The students," he reported, "easily gulled the freshmen into thinking it was the university barn."[5]

The other faculty cottages originally intended for construction in the pine woods were sited west of Central Avenue and southwest of the Chapel where the Gannett Clinic now stands. Professors T. F. Crane ("Teefy" Crane of Cornell renown), John L. Morris, and Major Junius MacMurray built there in 1873–1874 (Fig. 90). Crane's house was the largest and it was designed by William H. Miller. We know that Crane was quite pleased about the lot-lease arrangement because he noted in a letter to James M. Hart, who had left the windswept hill, that "he would have no taxes, the land cost nothing and he could build a pretty cottage for $4,000."[6] Major MacMurray's diminutive

[4] Trustees' *Proceedings,* 30 June 1873. Professor Babcock's troubles with his house were perhaps typical of those of faculty living on the campus. In 1882, when he wanted to build an addition, he ran afoul the Trustees' $5,000 price limit on cottages and had to agree to sell for not more than that price whenever he left the campus. In 1888, President Adams noted (Adams to Tyler, 28 October 1888) that the football and baseball games then played in the Quadrangle made Babcock's existence miserable. Balls were continually hitting the house. In 1892, the Professor of Architecture successfully protested the extension of

the street railway across the campus. Of Babcock's joys in living on the campus we have found no reports, but such is the nature of things. We seem to record our troubles first.

[5] Birchard Hayes to Rutherford B. Hayes, 1878, Hayes Papers.

[6] T. F. Crane to J. M. Hart, 15 June 1873, Hart Papers. We know the house with the drooping mansard roof was MacMurray's because the Executive Committee reviewed its location and plans on 27 September 1873. There is no record of their approval of MacMurray's house, but on 11 October, J. W. Williams submitted a plan which was approved. He may have built the house for MacMurray because we

house was the subject of an anonymous un-kind cut from a student who wrote to the *Era* that its small size was quite appropriate for its builder. It was probably the best design in this row of three houses—a modest house, almost entirely hidden under the low sweeping planes of a jerkinhead-dormered mansard roof, a fine statement of Victorian outward shyness. But it must have seemed too modest an architectural statement for a military man. After the Major left Cornell, Professor Shackford of English and Professor Oliver of Mathematics were the subsequent occupants of the shy house.

National economic distress and concurrent university troubles stopped cottage building at Cornell for several years after 1873. The next cottage construction on the campus began in 1877 when Prentiss, Professor of Botany and Superintendent of Grounds, built a very large house on the knoll at the northwest corner of South and Central Avenues and Professor Caldwell of Chemistry built south of Morris' house.[7] The Central Avenue row was now complete. Hiram Corson, who lived in the lovely Giles House south of Cascadilla, asked for a lot north of Caldwell's in 1878, but the Executive Committee laid his request on the table, and it was never taken up. It appears that the Executive Committee was saving this site for a university structure, so from 1877 until the late eighties East Avenue became the scene of all faculty cottage building. John H. Comstock built at the north end of East Avenue in 1877. His house (Fig. 109)

was designed by Professor Babcock, as the dominant central tower would lead us to suspect even if we had no other documentation.[8]

Professor Wait built on East Avenue north of Law's house in 1879, and in 1880 Professors Roberts of Agriculture and Bela McCoon of German started building their homes at the same time in the same area at the north end of East Avenue. "Teefy" Crane noted that McCoon's new house (Fig. 91) was enormous and obviously intended to accommodate student roomers.[9] In fact, Professor McCoon's cottage was so large and so expensive that it eventually brought about some new rules for cottage building. The leases of lots to faculty originally included clauses permitting the University to purchase the improvements when a faculty member left the campus. When Bela McCoon left in 1882 his house was appraised at $7,500 and purchased by the University. The McCoon "cottage" later served as a residence for Presidents Adams and Schurman. Figure 92 shows the parlor during Adams' occupancy. The Trustees thought the price was too much to pay very often, so the lease terms were revised limiting the university purchase price for campus cottages to $5,000.[10]

There was nothing to prevent a professor from spending more than this on his cottage, but the practical effect of the revised recapture clause was to discourage the building of very large houses. White thought this a poor policy. When he advised Governor Stanford on university building in 1892, he said he wished Cornell had "favored a somewhat better class of [faculty] cottages." Provision for "commodious, convenient and attractive" homes, he felt, would make the professors less likely to move. "Even the presence of an attractive little veranda or bay-window," he

know that three houses were built along Central Avenue in 1873 (photographs in *Proceedings and Addresses of the Twenty-Fifth Anniversary of the Opening of Cornell University* [plates]). Professors Morris and Crane built two of them and lived there for some years (C.U. *Register,* 1874–1875, which also lists Major Junius W. MacMurray living on University Avenue). And finally, Anna B. Comstock recalled that when she was a student at Cornell in 1874 the "commandants" house was on Central Avenue ("Pioneers at Cornell" in *A Half-Century at Cornell*). *Cornell Era,* 24 October 1873: "The Major's residence will soon be completed. Someone who has no regard for the elemental fitness of things suggests that it is very small."
[7] Trustees' *Proceedings,* 22 February 1877.

[8] See Anna B. Comstock, *The Comstocks of Cornell,* ed. Glenn W. Herrick and Ruby G. Smith (Ithaca, 1953), for an interesting account of the Comstocks' careers and some insights on life on faculty row.
[9] T. F. Crane to J. M. Hart, 14 March 1880, Hart Papers.
[10] Trustees' *Proceedings,* 29 April 1882.

Fig. 91. Professor McCoon's "cottage," probably by William H. Miller (1880). It was later occupied as the President's House by Charles Kendall Adams and Jacob Gould Schurman while Andrew Dickson White was still occupying the "Old-President's House."

Fig. 92. President Adams' parlor about 1885. The entry hall and library may be seen through the opening at the south end of the room.

claimed, "may hold a wife against advanced salary for her husband elsewhere." [11] White, it seems, never missed a chance to turn a romantic architectural idea to the service of practical ends. In this instance, however, he may have failed to foresee Cornell's long-term need for academic space. Within a decade after White's statement to Governor Stanford, several houses in Cornell's East Avenue faculty row were being removed to make room for academic buildings. Fifty years later they all had been removed for the same reason. The cost of this campus redevelopment would have been much higher if unrestricted construction costs had permitted large faculty houses with many student rooms.

There was, of course, no restraint on the building cost of the homes of the founders and university officials. White's villa, which surveyed the campus from a properly commanding knoll, had its value regularly listed in treasurer's reports at $50,000. White gave it to Cornell as a President's house, but the Trustees leased it to him in 1876 for a period of twenty years and renewed the lease in 1896. Ezra Cornell's villa, which also has been described, was located below the campus. It surely cost as much as White's and probably much more. Cornell wrote to his brother-in-law Orrin in 1867 that a newspaper account which reported that he was spending half a million dollars on a mansion was incorrect; someone had slipped in an extra zero at the end of the estimated cost. [12] He did not see why his house should cost more than South University Hall, then estimated at $50,000. After the Cornell villa was completed in 1876, Mary Cornell and her daughters lived in it intermittently for thirty-two years, entertaining village and university friends in a subdued fashion. [13]

For a while Henry W. Sage seems to have considered building a house on the campus. In May 1875, shortly before he was elected Chairman of the Board of Trustees, Sage, who then lived in Brooklyn, was offered a lease for twelve acres of land at the southwest corner of the campus west of Central Avenue and along the north bank of Cascadilla Creek. In June, the Trustees authorized sale or lease of the parcel, [14] but Sage decided against it in favor of a location more remote from the campus. His great red-stone villa (Fig. 93) was built on East State Street in 1877. [15] William H. Miller, Cornell's first student in architecture and later the architect of several important university buildings, was the designer. Sage's son, William Henry Sage, built on an adjacent lot on Seneca Street at the same time. His brick house, also designed by Miller (Fig. 94), was less severe than his father's. Miller's skill in planning, his imaginative and playful disposition of interior space, and the sculptural quality of his exterior masses began to mature in the design of these houses. His clients were very pleased with them. The elder Sage wrote his grandson that he wished

[11] ADW to Governor and Mrs. Stanford, 26 May 1892, draft in White Papers.

[12] EC to Orrin, mid-July 1867, quoted in Philip Dorf, *The Builder* (Ithaca, 1952) p. 330; White, *Diaries*. The President's house cost $56,651 (report to the Regents of the University of the State of New York, 1879). The approval of White's first lease for the President's villa is in Trustees' *Proceedings*, 16 February 1876. The Trustees were at first mildly opposed to the idea of White's building a villa on the campus (see *Diaries*, 29 July 1871, note). The Ithaca Trustees and Hiram Sibley urged White to get a lot in the village. It seems probable that at this juncture White conceived the idea of making the house a gift to the University for use as a President's house. By 1876 he seems to have decided that he wanted to retain possession even though absent from the campus. He returned to it whenever he came back from

travel and work in Europe. This was a source of irritation to Henry Sage, who tried to block renewal of White's lease in 1895. White was deeply hurt (White, *Diaries*, 19 July 1895). His letter to the Trustees requesting renewal of the lease is a masterpiece of diplomatic persuasion delivered under fire. The Trustees approved renewal. Livingston Farrand was the second Cornell President to live in the house and Edmund Ezra Day the third, and last.

[13] Mary Emily Cornell, *The Autobiography of Mary Emily Cornell*, pp. 75–78. Miss Cornell recalled the Sunday evening "pantry teas" in the Llenroc kitchen attended by Professor Estavan Fuertes' son Louis Agassiz Fuertes, Henry Sage's sons, and Emma Cornell Blair's sons, Ezra and Charles. Llenroc was sold to Delta Phi Fraternity in 1911.

[14] Trustees' *Proceedings*, 26 May 1875.

[15] Henry Sage to his grandson Henry Sage, 11 August 1877, Sage Papers.

Fig. 93. Henry W. Sage's mansion (1877) by William H. Miller; it is now part of Sage Hospital, the university infirmary.

Fig. 94. William H. Sage's mansion (1877) by William H. Miller. William Sage's home was built on a shelf of East Hill north of State Street, adjacent to his father's home.

he could take him to Ithaca to see the new house, which he described as a very beautiful home.[16] For Miller these commissions were the beginning of a long and fruitful association with Henry Sage and, therefore, with Cornell University.

Henry Sage's decision to move to Ithaca in 1877 provided opportunities for extensions of his increasingly active role in university affairs. Then and in the eighties his wise and efficient management of Cornell's western lands was the chief factor in the University's realization of an endowment of over $5,000,000 from Ezra Cornell's great land speculation.[17] Sage's drive and his policies also expanded the power of the Board of Trustees Executive Committee at a critical point in the University's affairs. His home, on a shelf of land off East State Street, was the center of his operations. There he maintained his office in the library. Adjourned meetings of the Executive Committee frequently reconvened in this room of Sage's mansion and deliberated late into the night on university matters.[18]

John McGraw, another Ithacan among those considered the founders of Cornell University, had no ambition to live on or near the campus. Trustee McGraw maintained a large, comfortable house on a terrace part way up South Hill beyond the south end of Tioga Street. He had built "Terrace Hill," as the home was called, in the 1850's and seemed content to remain there. When he died in 1877, Jane McGraw, Jennie's stepmother, inherited the property, tore down the house and built a more imposing brick mansion over the old foundation.[19] Jane McGraw's new house

looked like it was designed by Charles Babcock. His trademark motif, a massive central tower pierced by an entrance arch which, in turn, was flanked by contrasting stone columns, was used here in much the same way as at the entrances of Sage College and the President's villa. Even the last curl of Babcock's architectural signature seemed to be present, a stone balcony hanging precariously over the entry. But Dethfelson[20] lists the Jane McGraw house among William Henry Miller's architectural commissions of 1877. All of which proves, not that Miller was a forger, but that in spite of his inventiveness he was still prone to borrow the successful vocabulary of other practitioners.

McGraw's daughter, Jennie, was much more involved in Cornell affairs than was Jane McGraw. In 1877 after Jennie McGraw (Fig. 95) inherited the largest part of her father's lumber fortune, she thought she might use part of it to build a great mansion. In 1878 she inspected a thirty-acre point of land located along the south edge of Fall Creek Gorge at the northwest corner of the campus.[21] This land, ostensibly owned by Mary and Alonzo Cornell, was still tied up in Ezra Cornell's estate. She decided to buy it and began negotiations. The site was one of a series of "hanging deltas" left by a glacial-age stream that emptied into a higher Cayuga Lake, and had once been used by the Cayuga Indians for signal fires. It commanded views of Cayuga Lake, Inlet Valley, and Fall Creek Gorge that were in many ways superior to the prospects from the west front of the university campus. The site was only slightly lower than the campus, projected much further west and sloped off steeply to the south. In the late nineteenth century, when East Hill was almost bare of view-obscuring trees, this spot

[16] *Ibid.*, 13 September 1878.
[17] Paul Gates, *The Western Pine Lands of Cornell University*, pp. 428–430; Morris Bishop, *A History of Cornell*, pp. 211–223.
[18] Trustees' *Proceedings, passim.* December 1880, January 1881. Meetings after December 1880 were frequently held at Henry Sage's house or afternoon sessions at the University were reconvened there in the evening.
[19] Photographs of John McGraw's house in the collection of Ralph Smith, and Dethfelson, "William Henry Miller, Architect," unpublished master's thesis, Cornell College of Architecture, 1956. Jane McGraw

was John McGraw's third wife. He first married Rhoda Southworth, who died in 1847; then Nancy A. Southworth, who died 1857; finally, Jane P. (Turner) Bates, widow of Samuel Bates (genealogy, C.U. Archives, #1580).
[20] Dethfelson, *William Henry Miller*, p. 99.
[21] Jennie McGraw to Judge Boardman, 2 April 1879, Boardman Papers.

Fig. 95. Jennie McGraw Fiske.

had more sweeping, dramatic vistas than most castles on the Rhine.

The quality of the Sage mansions was a topic of much discussion in Ithaca. After Jennie McGraw had heard these reports and observed the progress of Miller's other Ithaca work, she decided that he should be her architect.[22] The site she was trying to buy was an architect's dream opportunity, and Miller was capable of making good use of it. Then, later in 1878, Jennie left for Europe. Her good friends, Judge Boardman, who was her business advisor, and President White, who was by 1879 in Europe as Ambassador at Berlin, tried to persuade her to build in a less remote spot. They suggested the Giles property, just south of The Cascadilla, which the University had acquired; or the "gymnasium lot" just north of Cascadilla Gorge where the Law School now stands; or the orchard between Sage College and Cascadilla Gorge where the

engineering quadrangle now stands. These places did not appeal to her. The Giles property, she felt, was very much depreciated since The Cascadilla had loomed up. And she "never had any fancy for it before the Cascadilla was there." The gymnasium lot was "too public" and too small. It was "enough for a small cottage (Swiss) [*sic*]." But Jennie thought she "would never feel warranted in putting such a house as Mr. Miller [had] planned there." As for the orchard lot, even though Mr. White thought the University would let her lease thirty acres there, she knew she would not be satisfied with it. No, she could think of "nothing else in Ithaca that she cared for" except Mary and Alonzo Cornell's property on the brink of Fall Creek Gorge.[23]

Almost a year passed before completion of the three-cornered negotiations among Jennie in Europe and Judge Boardman and the Cornells in Ithaca for purchase of the latter's land. The Cornells (Mary and Alonzo) wanted to reserve rights to a spring on the property that was their water supply and they wanted to reserve the right to build a road across the land.[24] Jennie, who had offered $20,000 for the parcel, would not agree to these terms. Finally, early in 1880, the Cornells gave in when Jennie added enough to her offer to pay for a water pipe to the University's reservoir. She also gave the Cornells road privileges across the land provided there would be no deep cuts or steep banks.[25] Miller completed the plans for the villa—much improved during the delay, he diplomatically wrote her—and he proceeded with the work. She was an ideal client. She had "confidence most entire" in her architect.[26]

---

[22] *Ibid.*, 29 October 1879. "I hear such glorious accounts of [Miller's] success in mother's and Will Sage's houses."

[23] *Ibid.*, 16 July 1879. Jennie was getting slightly peeved at Boardman's and White's insistence that she consider the lots near The Cascadilla. She compared herself to the little girl who was being urged to try a pickle: "It's a pretty pickle but Sissie don't want it," she wrote.

[24] *Ibid.*, 28 April, 25 May, 3 June, 22 June 1879. Stewart Avenue now cuts the parcel in half. The proposed location of the road the Cornell family wanted across the parcel could not be discovered.

[25] *Ibid.*, 15 January 1880.

[26] *Ibid.*, 16 January and 12 August 1880. After

Miller's elegant villa design (Figs. 96 to 101) was built from July 1880 to the fall of 1881 at a reputed cost of nearly $300,000.[27] While Jennie traveled in Europe and became engaged to and married Professor Willard Fiske, Cornell's first librarian, the house was completed and furnished with fine furniture and works of art. These things (marble and bronze sculpture, paintings, tapestries, wood carvings, ceramics, and embroideries) were purchased in Europe and Egypt by the Fiskes, shipped back to Ithaca, and installed in the mansion. The woodwork, paneling, imported mosaics and carving incorporated in the walls were elaborate and beautiful. For example, a Renaissance chimney piece was built into the drawing room fireplace.

The mansion, sited on one of the most romantic spots in Ithaca, was now filled with romantic works of art. It was a collection of great variety—things that could be assembled only in such a house by such an heiress as Jennie McGraw in the late Victorian era. Exotic carved oak desks and tables graced the library. Intricately carved chairs, settees, and chests from India and Italy were in the drawing room, and some walls were completely covered with tapestries from Spain, France, and Japan. Prints and paintings were everywhere. Professor Fiske's "smoking room" contained Turkish water pipes and a "Cairo chair." The parquet floors were almost completely covered with Persian rugs of all sizes, and shelves and mantels were filled with a varied assortment of minor works of art.[28]

These furnishings were indeed wondrous. The Fiskes must have thoroughly enjoyed buying them. The mansion was a wonder, too, but Jennie McGraw never lived in it. When she returned to Ithaca with her husband in the fall of 1881, she was near death and had no strength to inspect the inside of the not-quite-completed house. But, as her carriage passed it on the trip up the hill from the steamboat landing to Professor Fiske's cottage, she "raised up . . . , looked at it, and said: 'It surpasses all my expectations.' That was all." [29]

The story of the sad decline and tragic destruction of the chateau is best told later, but here we should note that while it was being built and for many years afterward, it was one of the landmarks of Ithaca. Its turrets and many-gabled red-tile roofs could be seen from most parts of the village. Purveyors of stereographs maintained a stock of over fifty views of its exterior, its interior, its art, and its grounds.[30]

The McGraw-Fiske mansion was William H. Miller's most extravagant residential commission and from it he gained a considerable reputation in the East as an architect of some talent for homes on the palatial scale. The extreme dimensions of the great cross-winged plan (Fig. 98) were one hundred ten and one hundred twenty feet.[31] Very few upstate New York mansions of the decade exceeded it in size, and it is unlikely that many surpassed the opulence of its interiors and furnishings.

construction of the house began in July 1880, Miller seems to have argued with Jennie's Uncle James about some aspect of the house. Jennie reported to Judge Boardman that she had written Miller "to *work* steadily on *economically* and *conscientiously*" and that she "would not have trusted him if she had not had faith in him."

[27] H. C. Howe, "Student Life at Cornell," in *Supplement to the Troy Daily Times*, 1898, p. 24. Howe reports that Chi Psi fraternity paid $45,000 for the "castle which is estimated to have cost the builder nearly $300,000, though no individual probably could be found to pay anything like that for it now."

[28] Eagles, photographer, "Views of Ithaca and Vicinity," c. 1886. This is one set in a series of stereographs which includes: views of Cornell campus, various local waterfalls and gorges, Sage's mansion,

President Adams' house, Franklin Hall, the Armory, Sage Chapel, Sage College, Jane McGraw's mansion on South Hill, Wells College buildings, and all of the churches in Ithaca.

[29] Ronald John Williams, *Jennie McGraw Fiske* (Ithaca, 1949), p. 65. The incident was reported by the coachman who brought the Fiskes up the hill from the steamboat landing.

[30] Eagles, *op. cit.* The DeWitt Historical Society has a collection of fifty-two different views. There may have been more. The plan in Figure 98 was prepared from them, from outlines of the house on surveys of the period and from the recollections of pre-fire Chi Psi members Thomas R. Silcox and Gustav J. Requardt, who lived in the house at the time of the fire of 1906.

[31] "Map showing the Relative Position of the Most Important Buildings on the University Campus," November 1887, C. U. Archives.

Fig. 96. The McGraw-Fiske mansion (1880) from the campus, William H. Miller, architect. This house of tragedy was never occupied by its builders. The object of much controversy in the University, it was completely destroyed by fire in 1906.

Fig. 97. The McGraw-Fiske mansion from the west. The house commanded sweeping views of the west front of the campus, of the village, of the Cayuga Lake valley, and of its own thirty-acre private park.

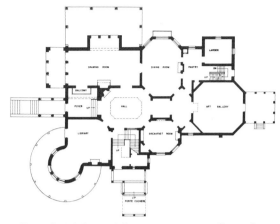

Fig. 98. McGraw-Fiske mansion, main-floor plan.

The arrangement of the plan provided convenience on a grand scale. The large principal rooms were grouped around a great three-storied central "Rotunda." This great hall was served by two entries. A "Grand Entrance" on the west (for formal occasions) brought visitors up a gradual incline with several short flights of steps to a dignified gabled entrance porch. Inside the vestibule one could glimpse the drawing room over a balcony set in a small opening to that room. The rotunda (Fig. 99) was directly ahead up a short flight of broad stairs. At the top of these stairs one could see an art gallery at the far end of the house, its far wall seventy feet away. There, on her pedestal, was Richard Gamble Rogers' sculpture "Merope," the "Pleiade Missing from the Sky," now owned by the Art Institute of Chicago. Morris Bishop has concluded that this quaint symbol of the missing Jennie is probably stored in the basement of the Institute.[32] The other principal entrance was from the south. It led from the "Carriage Porch" and apparently was designed to be used for less formal occasions. It required a sharp left turn by a visitor after he left his carriage. With his dignity somewhat dampened by the maneuver, he then entered the "Grand Staircase Hall" (Fig. 100) and ascended to an off-center view of the rotunda. In this plan Miller had begun to develop some

[32] Morris Bishop, *A History of Cornell,* p. 224.

of the subtle uses of axial and unsymmetrical composition, changes of level with short flights of stairs and changing sequences of

Fig. 99. McGraw-Fiske mansion, rotunda. This great skylighted central hall with its heavy wood paneling and balustrade became an enormous flue in the fire of 1906, drawing the flames up through the building. In the art gallery at the far end of the rotunda stands "Merope," a sculpture by Richard Gamble Rogers.

Fig. 100. McGraw-Fiske mansion, the grand stair-case hall viewed from the foyer balcony off the drawing room. Great quantities of tapestries, rugs, vases, and other furnishings were purchased by the Fiskes in Europe and the Near East especially for the house.

Fig. 101. McGraw-Fiske mansion, entrance porch and drawing-room porch with column capitals by Robert Richardson.

space that he later employed with such excellent results in Barnes Hall, the Cornell University Library building, and Boardman Hall.

The mansion's great round southwest tower gave it the aspect of a Loire Valley chateau. The building was done in a style which used many of the forms and details of early French Renaissance palaces so often employed by the American mansion builders of the early eighties.[33] The masonry and stone carving by Robert Richardson were excellent (Fig. 101). Miller was developing a fine skill in building with stone, a skill that he was to employ later with significant success in his important Cornell buildings. For Miller, the McGraw-Fiske mansion was a relatively calm building. Its many porches, terraces, gabled entries and its

[33] See for example "The Craigs," Mount Desert, Maine, by Bruce Price, 1879–1880 (*American Architect,* 1879), reproduced in Vincent Scully, *The Shingle Style* (New Haven, 1955), Fig. 40.

porte-cochere were kept low or contained in the larger masses. The simple geometric shapes of the main mass and subordinate towers were composed with dignity. The mansion's many and varied roofs when viewed from White, McGraw, and Morrill Halls, had a confused, cluttered aspect; but Jennie McGraw's villa, like McGraw Hall which was given to the University by her father, was designed to be seen from the town below. It was also designed to permit its owners to look out on the town and the curving lake valley. This view was protected by the large expanse of the site and by the steep slopes away from the house in three directions. The McGraw-Fiske front yard on the west was more than one thousand feet deep and it sloped down over 180 feet from the house's west terrace to the top of Lake Street (Fig. 102). Most of this land has since been parceled out for fraternity houses and apartments, but from 1880 to 1900 it was open except for a few strategically

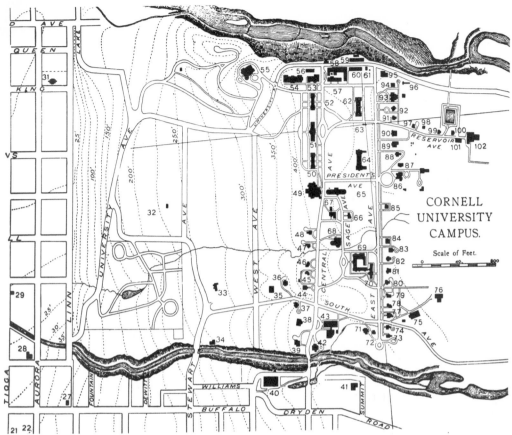

Fig. 102. The Cornell University campus in 1891, showing university buildings and professors' houses: (32) Llenroc, villa of Ezra Cornell; (33) Forest Park, residence of Frank C. Cornell; (34) Chi Phi Lodge; (35) Delta Upsilon Lodge; (36) Prof. Simon H. Gage; (37) Prof. Edward L. Nichols; (38) Sigma Phi Lodge; (39) Psi Upsilon Lodge; (40) Cascadilla Place; (41) Cascadilla School; (42) Kappa Alpha Lodge; (43) Armory and Gymnasium; (44) Prof. Albert N. Prentiss; (45) Prof. John L. Morris; (46) Prof. James E. Oliver; (47) Prof. Thomas F. Crane; (48) Prof. George C. Caldwell; (49) University Library; (50) Morrill Hall; (51) McGraw Hall; (52) White Hall; (53) Franklin Hall; (54) Morse Hall; (55) McGraw-Fiske mansion; (56) Franklin Hall Annex; (57) Sibley College; (58) Dynamo Laboratory, Engine Room, and Machine Shop; (59) Blacksmith Shop and Foundry; (60) Wood-working Shop and Testing Laboratory; (61) Magnetic Laboratory; (62) Lincoln Hall, College of Civil Engineering and School of Architecture; (63) Astronomical Observatory; (64) College of Agriculture; (65) School of Law; (66) Prof. Charles Babcock; (67) Sage Chapel; (68) Barnes Hall, Cornell University Christian Association; (69) Sage College; (70) Sage Conservatories; (71) Prof. J. Laurence Laughlin; (72) Prof. Edward Hitchcock; (73) Prof. Brainard G. Smith; (74) Prof. Harry B. Hutchins; (75) Forcing House of the University Gardens; (76) South or Garden Barn; (77) Prof. Henry S. Williams; (78) Prof. Liberty H. Bailey; (79) Prof. Moses C. Tyler; (80) Prof. William G. Hale; (81) Prof. Jacob G. Schurman; (82) Prof. Herbert Tuttle; (83) Prof. Estevan A. Fuertes; (84) Prof. Robert H. Thurston; (85) Prof. Horatio S. White; (86) Ex-President Andrew D. White; (87) Prof. Spencer B. Newbury; (88) Prof. Waterman T. Hewett; (89) Prof. James Law; (90) Prof. Lucien A. Wait; (91) Prof. Isaac P. Roberts; (92) Prof. Benjamin I. Wheeler; (93) President Charles Kendall Adams; (94) Prof. John H. Comstock; (95) Cornell Farm House; (96) Insectary; (97) Prof. James M. Hart; (98) Prof. Henry H. Wing; (99) The Farm Supt.'s House; (100) The Dairyman's House; (101) Dairy House; (102) University Farm or North Barn.

Fig. 103. Flagg Cottage (1881) by William H. Miller, viewed from the northwest. The residence of Professor Isaac Flagg at No. 1 East Avenue was later occupied in turn by Professors Ralph Tarr and Henry S. Williams. The Alice Statler Auditorium now stands on the site.

placed large trees and was laced with meandering drives and paths in the style of an English country garden.

Miller's practice now began to include a number of public buildings and some very large villas, but he continued to design modest wood and brick cottages for Cornell's faculty row. Four of these, for Professors Webb, Hale, Tyler, and Flagg, were built in the early eighties, near one another along the southern part of East Avenue.[34] They now are all gone, along with the other thirty-four faculty homes which lined East Avenue and spread along Central and Reservoir Avenues in the nineties. But we have the drawings and a number of photographs of Professor Flagg's cottage (Number 1 East Avenue) which Miller designed in 1881 as the McGraw-Fiske "chateau" neared completion. In the Flagg cot-

tage, Miller's residential style seems remarkably up to date when compared to the eclectic "castle" discussed above. The Flagg cottage (Fig. 103) had a steep, massive roof with half timbering in a few gables. Its low brick first story was topped by a shingled second story. In many of its characteristics it resembled the contemporary work of Peabody and Stearns, Wilson Eyre, and William Ralph Emerson, all three among the best contemporary east-coast residential architects. Miller evidently both traveled widely and read his weekly copies of the *American Architect and Building News* carefully.[35] He was also an architect of considerable talent—certainly his work was of regional if not national significance.

The Flagg house design carried a strong low horizontal line completely around at the head of the first-story windows. This, the shingled upper story, and the banks and strips of windows, especially those in the north library wall, were stylistic trademarks of the "Queen Anne Cottage style" as it developed toward the "shingle style" maturity of the early and middle eighties. As was usual with Miller's work, it displayed less exuberance and originality than the most daring designs of the period.[36] Flagg's was an attractive cottage, unpretentious, except possibly for the grand sweep of its steeply pitched roof planes. But here, in the design of the roof, Miller's characteristically picturesque approach to cottage design prevented the development of a unified composition. Many breaks in plan and roof plane, erratic gables, and occasional dormers broke the main roof shape into dozens of smaller elements. But then, this gave the house a variegated form which made it the comfortable companion of other individualist houses in Cornell's faculty row, whose chief quality resembled that of

[34] Trustees' *Proceedings,* 24 June, 18 July 1881; 13 April, 30 May 1882.

[35] Scully, *op. cit.* Figs. 31, 46, 47, and 50 illustrate a few houses published in the *American Architect and Building News* from 1879 to 1881 which bear some resemblances to Flagg's house. These were designs by Potter and Robertson, and William Ralph Emerson.

[36] *Ibid.* Figs. 46, 52, 55, 56, 65, 66, 79, 80, and 97–101 illustrate contemporary work by William Ralph Emerson, Henry Patson Clark, H. H. Richardson, Lamb and Rich, and Wilson Eyre.

southeast where the professor, his family, and guests would be shielded from the northwest winds in the fall and spring. The main entrance was also cleverly shielded from northern blasts. In a sentence: The Flagg cottage was commodious, convenient, and attractive. President White was no doubt pleased to see the Professor of Greek about to be so properly housed when, in the fall of 1881, he returned to the campus from his stint as American Minister to Germany. The President arrived in time to help review and approve the plans at a meeting of the Executive Committee. Professor Flagg, who had taught at Cornell since 1871, enjoyed his new home for seven years until his wife, perhaps in a pique about the relative size of her veranda, made him move elsewhere. Professor Henry Shaler Williams next purchased the house and he and his family lived there from 1889 to 1891 and from 1904 to the mid-1930's. Professor Ralph Tarr occupied the house from 1892 to 1903.

The faculty cottages at Cornell were not all especially excellent works of architecture, but some were much more advanced for their times than suburban homes elsewhere, and

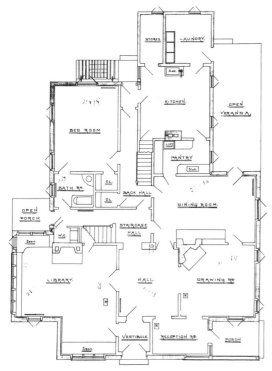

Fig. 104. Flagg Cottage, first-floor plan. The veranda is on the protected southeast side. Ample provision for entry from outside without passing through the hall is provided directly from the reception room and vestibule to the drawing room and library.

their owners who, according to Carl Becker, insisted on the right to be "otherwise thinkers."

The Flagg cottage plan (Fig. 104) was simply and conveniently arranged around a generous central hall. The rooms were not large but they were numerous: five plus a bath and laundry room on the first floor and five plus a bath and a servant's room on the second. Although the house was equipped with a warm-air furnace, Miller also provided three generous fireplaces on each floor. There was one in the drawing room, one in the dining room, and an especially large one in the library, the largest room in the house (Fig. 105). There were also fireplaces in the three largest bedrooms upstairs. This was a generous supply of a rather luxurious creature-comfort for a cottage. The open veranda off the dining room was sensibly located on the

Fig. 105. Flagg Cottage, library.

many were far above average in design and were exceptionally well built. Because their grounds were spacious and cost nothing, and because their owners were reasonably affluent, they represented a very high standard of living for the men who were preparing students for life's work and perhaps for life in the suburbs. We do not know the histories of the designs of many faculty cottages. Many of the plans probably came, as did Professor Law's, from the architectural pattern books of Woodward, Downing, Vaux, and others. Professor Thurston's house seems to have been much influenced by a design by Henry Hudson Holly.[37] We have identified two designs by George Hathorne: White's villa (1871) and Fiske's cottage (1871); two by Charles Babcock: his own house (1874) and Professor Comstock's (1877), and six by W. H. Miller: T. F. Crane (1873), Flagg (1881), Hale (1882), Webb (1882), Tyler (1884), and Newbury (1890) besides Miller's 1891 and 1911 additions to Ex-President White's house. The rest must remain obscure until some diligent architectural historian traces their histories.

Bela McCoon's large house (Figs. 91 and 92) looked like Miller's work and, if so, demonstrated that Miller had the ability to compose calm cottage roof masses when he wanted to. The large front gable controls a clutch of porches, gables, and bay windows. The big gable, an off-center tower, and the large main roof compose well in a simple three-part mass. Miller's residential work at Cornell verged on being distinguished. Babcock's was nothing special, certainly not up to his best "American Gothic Revival" work in Sage Chapel and College. The real significance of the faculty cottages at Cornell lay not in their architectural qualities, excellent as many were, but in the excellent style of campus life they afforded and in the long-term effect their location had on the overall plan of the campus. President Shurman expressed the first point well in his Annual Report in 1892. He wrote:

It is an ideal arrangement that permits professors to have homes on the campus. In reach of urban advantages of the City of Ithaca, they also enjoy the rural delights of one of the most beautiful and romantic situations in the world . . . and the free use of lots and water without charge. Clearly these . . . should not be taken away without a rise in salaries.

The residence of professors in a single community stimulated "cordial social relations" among the faculty, made it easy and likely for professors to entertain visitors and students in their homes, and made it convenient for them to slip back to the library, study, or laboratory in the evening if the press of work so ordered.[38]

For almost half a century, the faculty homes on the campus provided Cornell with a university community reversed from the usual half-measure of American colleges and universities. Although the students at Cornell tended to live more and more in town as dormitory rooms in White and Morrill Halls were converted to classroom use, many of the faculty lived in the midst of the campus. Then after the turn of the century, its nonconformist zeal grown mossy, Cornell began removing the faculty community from the campus and began building student residence halls instead. The space of the cottages was clearly needed for academic buildings. Before this serious dislocation could be carried out, however, the major early development of the University's College of Agriculture was located east of faculty row with the less-than-happy result of creating two academic campuses. The location for Agriculture's new buildings was a subject of much debate in 1904. Some thought the College had a right to a position on the main Quadrangle. A dairy building, later incorporated in Goldwin Smith Hall, had already been built there in 1892. Some of the Agriculture faculty, however, saw a great expansion in their future, wanted room to grow, and wanted to be near their fields. For

[37] *Ibid.*, Fig. 34.

[38] Jacob G. Schurman, *Annual Report* (1892), pp. 51–52.

a time they fought for an upper East Avenue site, but university officials decided that the College would need more room.

The location of the College of Agriculture buildings on the upper campus caused a split in campus continuity that continues to be a somewhat discordant note in Cornell's community of buildings. The two groups will be harmonized some day (one hopes) by the design of stronger links in future landscape and architectural improvements. The location of faculty row caused the lack of continuity. Now all that remains of it is President White's picturesque villa and the memory of an academic community that contributed much of quality to Cornell life for over fifty years.

VIII

The Elegant Eighties

FROM 1881 TO 1893, COR-nell experienced a building boom that more than doubled its physical plant. In this period, which included the last four years of Andrew D. White's presidency, Cornell developed the excellence in faculty, student body, and facilities for teaching and research that mark a great university. On the other hand, the buildings built during this era were a mixed lot. Some were excellent examples of the best in college building design of the times; others barely qualify as architecture. All, however, reflected the elegance and the lack of stylistic consensus of the times. Some of these "Gothic Revival," "Richardsonian Romanesque," and "Beaux-Arts" structures were potential evidence for support of Montgomery Schuyler's remark of 1891 that "American humor has never found full expression except in architecture."

The University was clearly in trouble in the late seventies. In spite of some brilliant national academic and athletic feats, its enrollment, budget, and morale were dropping rapidly.[1] Acting-President Russel made a cool,

rational attempt to explain the enrollment decline. He thought admissions had dropped because of "the erroneous idea that Cornell was irreligious" and the consequent attacks of sectarian schools; because of the well-known fact that "Cornell was falling behind the other great schools in her apparatus and libraries and collections"; because Cornell was no longer "a fashion, a furor" (Harvard, Russel thought, was now the novelty); and, finally, because tuition and admission requirements had been increased.[2]

Some of Cornell's benefactors had begun to lose confidence in her future, too. After President White's departure for Europe, Jennie McGraw wrote Trustee Boardman that "Cornell University as it is now will not long remain a great credit to [Ithaca] or our country. . . . It must have a head that shall be felt as an intellectual and moral force." She hinted that her benefactions might seek other outlets:

Unless all is on a solid good moral and religious foundation I do not care to cast my mite as I have by my papers or by any special identification with it—though I confess to being a miserable sinner myself, I don't propose to help to make others so in a wholesale way. . . . My interest in Ithaca is very different since this change has come.[3]

[1] Morris Bishop, *A History of Cornell*, pp. 135–137, describes Cornell's great victory at public academic contests in New York City in 1874–1875 and the intercollegiate rowing regatta at Saratoga in July 1875. One possible reason for the drop in Cornell's enrollment from 1878 to 1882 which no one seems to have suggested is the fact that this four-year period occurred eighteen years after the Civil War. Lower national birth rates during wartime have frequently had this second-round effect on college enrollments.

[2] William C. Russel, *Annual Report* (1881), pp. 6–10.

[3] Jennie McGraw to Judge Douglass Boardman, 8

It was Henry Sage, Chairman of the Board of Trustees, who acted to reverse the decline. Morris Bishop has written that Sage's timely decisions in the late seventies and early eighties saved Cornell from becoming "a small regional institution." Sage was not only a wise manager of the University's western pine lands; he was a fearless leader who could make difficult decisions and carry them out. In 1880 he insisted that White must return to the campus. White returned. He insisted that Vice-President William C. Russel had to resign. Russel resigned. Sage also used the University's capital for expansion. The latter gamble (not really such a great one considering Sage's knowledge of an upswing in the lumber industry) provided a new prosperity for Cornell and resulted in a major building campaign which lasted over a decade.

A campus symbol of the new prosperity was provided early in 1880 by Professor Anthony of the Physics Department. Anthony had built the first American Gramme dynamo for direct current in 1875 and had provided demonstrations of the uses of electrical power at the Centennial Exhibition in Philadelphia in 1876. At Cornell one of the first practical uses of the dynamo was to power some arc lights installed in the towers of McGraw Hall and Sage Chapel. In January 1880 the intense light of these arc lights was visible for miles around Ithaca. There was, of course, no competition from other light sources.[4] Perhaps Henry Sage's prominence might be similarly

accounted for, although White returned in September 1881, and his energy and ideas were clearly as important to the new prosperity of the University as Sage's initiative and conservative management.

Another mark of the end of Cornell's frugal years was the completion in 1880 of a long-awaited sidewalk. Professor Prentiss termed it "the most important grounds improvement in the history of the University." Finally, after twelve years of mud-slogging and anguished pleas, a $3,200 stone walk was built from Cascadilla to the north end of the north building (White Hall). Coming as it did at the end of years of little building activity on the campus it must have seemed a wonder. There was even "a loop extending from the wooden bridge around by the Sage College and the Sage Chapel to meet the main walk near the South University Building." This walk, Henry Sage's two $3,000 grading projects in 1877 and 1878, and a $15,000 waterworks and reservoir built in 1875 were the only significant new campus improvements between 1872 and 1880.

Now the pace changed. In June 1880, with the report of the glorious new walk in their hands, although, to be sure, it followed Russel's closely reasoned but not very comforting explanation of enrollment decreases, the Trustees took a deep breath and plunged. They resolved that White must return. Russel demurred. In January, the Executive Committee asked for Russel's resignation. White protested.

The Committee also set aside $100,000 for building: $50,000 to erect and equip a "Physical Laboratory"; $10,000 to erect and equip a building for the veterinary and anatomical section of Dr. Wilder's department; $10,000 to erect a greenhouse for the Botanical Department; $20,000 for the Library, and $10,000 for Civil Engineering and other departments.[5]

September 1879, Boardman Papers. This note of no confidence was written shortly before White had left the campus for his post as U.S. Minister to the German Empire. White tarried in Ithaca past the beginning of the academic year to entertain President Grant at his home on the campus. During this visit occurred the often-told incident of White's inability to find liquor in his house late in the evening. A bottle of cooking sherry was finally discovered. General Grant happily carried it off to his room.

[4] Trustees' *Proceedings*, 10 and 29 October 1879. Charles Hull, "First Dynamo Runs" *Alumni News*, 22 October 1931. G. S. Mohler and E. L. Nichols ('75) assisted Professor Anthony in the construction of the dynamo. They returned in 1931 to turn on the dynamo to light the Willard Straight Hall Memorial Room for the sixtieth anniversary of Sibley College.

[5] Trustees' *Proceedings*, 16 June 1880, and 18 December 1880. The building for Dr. Wilder's Anatomical Department was an absolute necessity. On 25 September 1880, the Executive Committee resolved "that Dr. Wilder be informed that this Committee does not consider it expedient to continue the practice

The total authorized was only $5,800 less than the amount spent the previous year for operating expenses. This large expenditure for buildings was possible only by use of a somewhat novel method of financing. Cornell's Wisconsin pine lands, it was decided, were a capital investment, and the University was justified in drawing a reasonable "interest" on them from funds now available from increased sales. Under the circumstances of the incipient decline of the University and the rapidly rising values of the pine lands, this slight audacity was entirely justified. Soon, the Trustees became even more audacious. Less than a year later (September 1882) the cost of the same improvements was estimated at $175,000. But the Board did not flinch. By November 1882, the University Treasurer announced that during the year, 133,704 acres of Cornell pine lands had been sold for $2,105,787 and pine timber on 4,883 acres had brought $50,272 into the treasury. In the great reconstruction of the eighties at Cornell, the grim risks of deficit financing disappeared.

White's first reaction to the Trustees' request to return to Ithaca was to resign the presidency. But by early September 1880, pressure from Sage, Boardman, and others persuaded him that the survival of the University depended on his return. Finch had written: "Something strong . . . must be done or Cornell is dead." Henry Sage pleaded, "Make Cornell your life's work." By early fall White had decided to resign from the Ministry at Berlin in the summer of 1881 and return to Ithaca.[6] He immediately began applying pressure on the Board to increase the faculty and facilities of the University. By the end of September, Trustees Sage and Humphrey reported that a new physical laboratory would cost $35,000, and in the middle of December the Executive Committee made the large appropriation described above. Thus began the first plans for the second major building cam-

paign at Cornell. White soon began making academic plans, too. He projected a new school of history and political science. Moses Coit Tyler, who had been White's colleague at the University of Michigan, was offered a chair in American history early in 1881 and White asked for additional nonresident professorships in history and political science for Henry C. Adams and Herbert Tuttle. In January 1881, Henry Sage was added to the committee on the physical laboratory, and Professor Anthony began his preparation of a detailed program for the new building.

Meanwhile, Henry Sage had been conducting extended sessions of the Executive Committee in his new home on East State Street. Late in December 1880, Vice-President Russel stopped attending. The Executive Committee, as noted earlier, had asked for his resignation as Vice-President and Professor of History. President White objected at first but finally yielded. Russel asked for the Executive Committee's reasons for requesting his resignation and apparently told them that if they would not give any they would have to discharge him. He received a brief reply: The Committee would "accept his resignation as a voluntary act." On 11 April 1881, the Executive Committee accepted and filed Russel's resignation.[7] On 17 March, White had drafted a letter resigning his position in the University again, perhaps over the Russel affair, but he seems to have thought better of it, for on 29 March, he wrote his final letter of resignation of his Ministry to the Secretary of State[8] thereby confirming his intention to return to Ithaca.

Late in March 1881, Henry Sage told Professor Babcock that the question "whether it is or is not the duty of the Professor of Architecture to furnish drawings, etc., for University buildings" would probably be raised in

---

of keeping cats and other live animals in any of the University buildings occupied by other departments."

[6] Francis M. Finch to ADW, 18 June 1880; Henry Sage to ADW, 13 August 1880, White Papers.

[7] Trustees' *Proceedings*, 3 January 1881, 25 February 1881, and 11 April 1881.

[8] White, *Diaries*, 29 March 1881, p. 212. The first diary reference to the "complications" at Cornell is 5 February 1881. White wrote to President Garfield three days later informing him that his resignation (as Minister to the German Empire) must be accepted.

the Executive Committee. Sage apparently intimated that, since Babcock had very few students, he should be willing to provide architectural services for the University without additional compensation. Babcock fired off a clear negative answer in an open letter "by way of facilitating the discussions" of the Executive Committee. He recalled his understanding with White that he would act as "advisory architect" but that they could employ him or not on building design as they saw fit, that he could accept or refuse the work, and that, if he accepted, he was "to do the work at less than other architects commonly charge." He had received "extra pay for extra services" before and now he frankly stated that he "preferred someone else should furnish their plans" and he be "left to fulfill the duties of [his] professorship in peace." He argued that the reduced numbers of students made no difference in his teaching responsibilities. He lectured "to two as fully, frequently and faithfully as he would to fifty." [9] The letter was tabled and arrangements were made for Professor Babcock's fees.

While the "Russel Affair" was boiling, Professors Anthony and Babcock started to work on plans for the new physics and chemistry building. On 24 May 1881, Henry Sage wrote to White that Tyler had been in Ithaca and had accepted the chair in American history, and that the plans for the physical laboratory (Franklin Hall) had been approved "first by the committee of Schuyler, Humphrey and Sage and then by the full Executive Committee." The Board Resolution stated that Babcock's plans for the laboratory building were approved on 24 May and that he was then appointed architect for the building. This would seem to indicate that other architects had submitted plans, but we have found no record of them. Sage wrote that "Babcock and the professors were delighted with the building and plan." The location west of Sibley Hall and the general layout of the building were apparently substantially the same as

those suggested by White, but the material was to be "brick like Sage College with some brick trimmings." Babcock, Sage wrote, thought it would be a "handsome contrast to the factory-like stone row and much better—cheaper by about $6,000 to $8,000." Sage tried to foresee White's objections: "In this [the brick], there is a difference from your views, but I think if you were here, you would agree with us." [10] White was not there and he did not agree. On 24 June 1881, the Executive Committee voted to postpone "further action in the erection of the physical laboratory . . . until President White returned." For once in his career at Cornell, Andrew Dickson White was opposed to the erection of a permanent building. He had written to Fiske in February: "It is not the buildings that make a university, necessary as they are, but the instructors and investigators." Now he wrote to Sage suggesting that the laboratory building be built of wood and be one story. Sage thought this poor economics. He pointed out that such a building would require four times more foundation and four times more roof than the four-storied building they had planned. He also noted that the savings and insurance cost for a masonry building would make it less expensive than a wooden one. [11] It is difficult to imagine Andrew White pleading for a wooden building at the corner of the Quadrangle he always insisted was to be of stone, so it seems possible that his suggestion to Henry Sage was a diplomatic ploy. It seems likely that he would have wanted a stone building on this site and his tactic seems to have been to encourage Sage's desire for a well-built structure by requesting that less money be spent for a wooden one. In answer to White's idea, Sage wrote that the University had "lived through

[9] Charles Babcock to Henry Sage, 6 April 1881, Executive Committee Papers.

[10] Henry Sage to ADW, 24 May 1881, 27 May 1881, White Papers. In the second letter Sage notes that he has received White's plan for the building and that "the building will be sufficiently specified to solicit bids next week" on the plan sent to White three days earlier. White's plan was given to Anthony, and Sage had no objection to their "adopting any part of it instead of their own."

[11] Sage to ADW, 24 May 1881, White Papers.

its shantie stage." White was a careful student of human nature and of Henry Sage.

On 25 July 1881, White wrote to Sage and Babcock to "set the laboratory right." [12] The President spent several days with Professor Anthony, late in the summer of 1881, visiting various physics laboratories at German universities and attending an electrical exposition in Paris. Professor Anthony's trip to Europe was paid for by the Trustees and he was authorized to purchase equipment for the new building. Later that year the Trustees authorized him to offer the first course in electrical engineering in America. On 19 August 1881, the Executive Committee again voted to postpone the matter of the erection of the new building until White returned. [13] New requirements suggested by Anthony's investigation of European schools and White's campaign to influence the design seem to have been the reasons. The result of the discussions, after White returned to Ithaca in September 1881, was a red-stone rather than a red-brick building. To accomplish this the width of the foundations of the laboratory was increased from twenty-eight inches to thirty-two. [14] White had accomplished what he later said had always been his objective: another unit in the Quadrangle of stone buildings. The choice of red stone set in red mortar may have been a concession to Babcock, who seems to have favored the color, or so it would seem from the evidence of his buildings on Cornell's campus. In his diary on 3 October 1881, White noted that at 7 A.M. he "turned the first sod of the new laboratory excavation for the Physical Dept." Later, looking back on the 1881 debate on Franklin Hall (Fig. 106), White wrote that "it was originally intended that the material should be brick, but this had been changed to stone." He continued:

As I urgently supported this substitution, I desire to put on record my reasons for it. Since the plans of our University buildings have begun to be developed I have always felt it wise to have the upper group . . . in stone and the lower or Sage College in brick: to throw each group into a general quadrangular form, preserving in each unity of effect in material and architecture, without a mere dead uniformity. To have inserted a brick building at one of the most important places in the upper quadrangle would have certainly greatly impaired its whole effect. . . . It is in accordance with this idea also that the new drill hall and gymnasium are to be made of brick thus being brought into combination with the group of which Sage College, Sage Chapel, and sundry cottages on the avenue back of Sage College are part, thus giving with variety a suitable unity with materials and style. [15]

Before the laboratory building was completed in 1883, Professor Babcock's first cost estimate of $50,000 had proved only half enough. In September 1882, the Executive Committee raised the budget to $70,000. In February 1883 it was raised to $80,000, and by mid-summer it was at $90,000. Finally, in December 1883, an additional $3,000 was appropriated for the building and the acting treasurer was instructed to have all work on the building stopped. The building's final cost was $100,923. This higher cost was partly a result of the increasing requirements of Professor Anthony's department and partly a result of White's insistence on stone construction. The President also suggested that a series of medallions representing great men of science be incorporated in the walls and that the names of other imminent scientists be inscribed in the space below the arched window openings (Fig. 106). These examples of White's love for memorials are now during most of the year obscured by ivy—a fact which some think much improves the appearance of the building. The idea of applying the names and medallions of scientific personages to Franklin Hall probably occurred to White

---

[12] White, *Diaries*, 25 July 1881, p. 216. The letter does not seem to be in the Sage Papers.
[13] Trustees' *Proceedings*, 19 August 1881.
[14] *Ibid.*, 22 September 1881.

[15] A. D. White, MS, draft of the Annual Report of the President to the Board of Trustees, 1883, pp. 95–97, White Papers. The published report does not include this statement; perhaps White thought it too brash.

Fig. 106. Franklin Hall (1882) by Charles Babcock. The first Cornell building devoted entirely to teaching and research in the physical sciences, it housed the first department of electrical engineering in the country. In the no-nonsense twentieth century, the tower roof was removed and the present flat, economical, and easily maintained roof was put in its place.

in 1881 in Berlin as he purchased copies of commemorative medals as a peace offering to the University on his return.[16] The Franklin outdoor gallery so inspired includes, besides Benjamin Franklin over the main door, Wheatstone, Van Helmot, Agricola, Stahl, Galileo, Newton, Galvani, Volta, Rumford, Boyle, Regnault, Joule, Maxwell, and a dozen or so others.

Franklin Hall has probably excited as much criticism as any of Babcock's buildings on the Cornell campus. In 1920, President Schurman called Franklin an "eyesore . . . and . . . the darkest most inconvenient building on the campus," but his tendency to overstate the matter may have been due to the fact that he was trying to raise funds for a new chemistry building.[17] The building, in fact, contained many spacious, uncluttered, efficient laboratories and lecture rooms (Figs. 107 and 108). These high-ceilinged (and on the top floor now skylighted) rooms provide excellent studio space for the Department of Art. Franklin Hall's exterior is, without question, a good example of Babcock's liking for the "powerful picturesque" after the manner of William But-

[16] White, *Diaries*, 12 May 1881, p. 212.

[17] J. G. Schurman, *Annual Report* (1920).

Fig. 107. Franklin Hall, laboratory. The building's well-lighted upper rooms are now studios for the Art Department of the College of Architecture.

Fig. 108. The east lecture room of Franklin Hall in May 1889, after a lecture in organic chemistry by Professor Newbury. Rooms for preparing demonstrations were located behind the chalkboard in space now occupied by the Franklin Hall Art Gallery.

Fig. 109. Franklin and West Sibley Halls about 1888. On the slope to the right of West Sibley and beyond East Avenue stand the moved and remodeled Cornell farm tenant house, Professor Comstock's cottage, and President Adams' house. Behind the remains of the Cornell farm orchard at the right, construction of Lincoln Hall is in progress.

terfield. His strong tendency to compose jarring juxtapositions of building elements was fully employed in the new science building. But on the whole the architect tried to make the building compatible with the old stone row and Sibley Hall. In an effort to fit Franklin Hall comfortably with its neighbors, Babcock designed contrasting stone belt courses, quoined corners, articulated, round-arched windows, a steep mansard roof, and a dentiled cornice line to pick up similar details on Morrill, McGraw, White, and Sibley Halls. But the laboratory building's composition and massing are restless and programmatic, reflecting the varied space needs of the building. Its siting and design elements are, however, more sympathetic with its neighbors than one might think at first glance. Franklin's western tower, of late roofless, provided a subtle but definite termination to the stone row and the ornamental roof and balcony outside the large lecture room on the south façade provides a terminal feature of interest for those walking along the walk on the east

side of the stone row (Fig. 109). With Victorian individuality, the height of the building's cornice line rises higher than White and Sibley Hall, but this may be only a reflection of the space requirements rather than an attempt to overshadow the first stone buildings. On the campus in the eighties, the new laboratory building (Fig. 109) asserted itself with great force and in a sense symbolized the strength of the sciences at Cornell. This picturesque, memorial-studded design is all the more remarkable because it is not (as most nineteenth-century college science laboratories tended to be) a "mere utilitarian structure devoid of commemorative or poetical elements." Andrew D. White saw to that. We should recognize this quality in Cornell's first permanent science laboratory, a fitting marriage of the arts and sciences, even if we cannot find that "time has invested it with any hoary beauty." [18]

In April 1881, Henry Sage offered to pay for

[18] Bishop, *op. cit.,* p. 236.

Fig. 110. Old Armory and Gymnasium (1883) by Charles Babcock. The building was designed to harmonize with the so-called "brick group" whose first unit, Sage College, is seen here above the trees of Sage Green.

Fig. 111. Old Armory, interior, set up for the 1883 Commencement, the first held on the campus.

the new conservatories for the Botanical Department which had been authorized by the Trustees. His offer of $15,000 was accepted and the $10,000 previously appropriated for the conservatories was transferred to the Military Department, for construction of the second major building of the early eighties—a new armory or Military Hall. This is the building which later came to be known as the "Old Armory" and which served so long as Cornell's men's gymnasium. It was demolished in 1954 to make room for the Engineering Quadrangle. In April 1882 a building committee of Sage, Boardman, and White was appointed, and Babcock began preparing the Armory design. Though designed by the same architect, the Armory (Fig. 110) offered quite a contrast to Franklin Hall. Its sole ornaments were white brick window arches, some slender bands of white and black bricks at the spring lines of the arches, and seven carved column capitals in the round-arched entry. The first

Armory was a simple, massive building which fit unobtrusively into the landscape of the "informal brick group." Its chief architectural merits were the economy of its structure and the utility of its much-needed large interior space. It provided the University's first suitable room for drills, dances, convocations, conventions, commencements, and large public lectures. A barnlike wooden gymnasium structure, which had been erected in 1874 through student and faculty donations, was moved across Central Avenue and made the north gymnasium wing of Military Hall.[19]

The hall's roof structure, which spanned over sixty feet, employed a simple and appropriate adaptation of the wooden truss designs which Babcock had previously used in his church roofs (Fig. 111). When preliminary bids on the carpentry work came in well

[19] Sage to ADW, 5 August 1882, White Papers. "The gym is across the road and within fifty feet of its final location."

over the first estimates, the architect supposed that its unusually spare, economical construction had frightened local carpenters. Babcock's design work on the Armory was done quickly. Within a month after the appointment of the architect, the Executive Committee approved the plans and an additional $10,000 for construction. Bids were taken in July. The final cost of the new Military Hall and Gymnasium was $31,300 including the gymnastic equipment, which was selected by Major Burbank, a new steam heating plant, and landscaping.[20] Three electric lighting fixtures were installed by Professor Anthony in 1883, making the Military Hall and Gymnasium the first building on the campus to be so equipped. Anthony noted the economy of the electric lights as compared to gas lights: "Once in, the cost [would be] practically nothing" since current would be provided by the dynamo already in operation.[21] In 1883, the Trustees established a new Administrative Council to direct the use of Military Hall and Gymnasium and a new Department of Physical Culture. The search began for a director of the program who was to be "thoroughly trained in Medicine, Hygiene and the best methods of gymnastic instruction." Dr. Edward Hitchcock, Jr., a man who met these qualifications, soon came to Cornell where he organized work uniting clinical medicine, health education, physical education, and mental hygiene. Hitchcock also taught "vocal culture."

Two smaller buildings were completed in 1883. A new foundry for the Sibley School of Mechanical Engineering was built on the north side of University Avenue on three acres of land purchased from Mary Ann Cornell. This simple industrial building is the only surviving reminder of the honest range of shops which once filled the space north of

Sibley Hall. The foundry building is now occupied by the sculpture studios of the Department of Art. The new glass conservatories and botany laboratories added as a southeast wing to Sage College were occupied in 1883. Here, Professor Prentiss finally had all the space he needed for botany instruction and plant collection.

At Commencement ceremonies on 21 June 1883, two of Cornell's proud new structures were dedicated. White asserted that the new physical laboratory building was "in many respects superior to any now existing."[22] The equipment purchased by Professor Anthony here and in Europe provided physics laboratories as good as any in the country. The new Military Hall was the scene of the 1883 Commencement, the first to be held on East Hill. Library Hall in the village had been used previously. The occasion was a grand success but the one thousand new folding chairs purchased for it left something to be desired in the line of comfort. At the meeting of the Board of Trustees the day before Commencement, Henry Sage introduced a resolution directing the Executive Committee to purchase a sofa and two chairs "to be placed in the Hall and reserved for Mrs. Ezra Cornell and such members of her family as may accompany her." At this same Trustees' meeting North and South University Halls were renamed White and Morrill Halls and the cornerstones of two more new buildings were laid. Governor Cleveland laid one for the Memorial Antechapel addition to Sage Chapel, whose design Babcock had completed the previous summer. Professor Fiske was to have laid the cornerstone of the McGraw-Fiske "cottage-hospital," but he had mysteriously left the campus a few days before. His wife, Jennie, had left $40,000 for the construction of the hospital. The cornerstone was laid, but we do not know where nor do we know who designed the building. A few months later work on the hospital ended when expenditures from Fiske funds were blocked pending court

[20] Babcock to ADW, 19 July 1882, White Papers. Cornell's Military Hall was an economy building. Hemmingway Gymnasium at Harvard, an elaborate "American Gothic" structure designed by Peabody and Stearns and built in 1887, cost over $100,000.
[21] Anthony to Executive Committee, 26 December 1883, Executive Committee Papers.

[22] A. D. White, *Annual Report* (20 June 1883), p. 17.

decisions regarding the contest of Jennie McGraw Fiske's will initiated by Professor Fiske.

Charles Babcock, architect for all of the major buildings of the 1881–1884 building campaign at Cornell, must have been both satisfied and exhausted. In a period of slightly over two years he had designed and supervised construction on four large building projects (Franklin Hall, the Military Hall, the Memorial Antechapel, and the Sage College Botany Laboratories and Conservatories). In addition to this, he had carried out his regular teaching responsibilities, provided consultation services on Eidlitz's failing stone vaults over the Assembly Chamber in the Capitol at Albany, completed preparation of a book on stone vaulting published in 1884, and continued his duties as pastor of St. Paul's Episcopal Church in the south transept of Sage Chapel. Babcock was fifty-three when he entered upon these productive years of his career. For the first time, after 1881, he had the assistance of a second faculty member in the School of Architecture, Charles Francis Osborne, a former student of Calvert Vaux.[23]

Andrew D. White was justifiably pleased with the first results of the new building program and said so at some length in his Annual Report to the Trustees in June 1883. He also included a lengthy shopping list. Architecture and Civil Engineering could be housed temporarily in the old wooden laboratory, but White hoped some friend of the University would regard it as "a matter not only of duty but of pride to attach his name to this department . . . by providing a large and well-built edifice." The cost, White thought, would be $60,000 to $80,000. Sibley College needed an annex for the machine shop, pattern shop, and printing shop, so that the main building could be used for instruction. A completely equipped astronomical observatory was

needed, and White thought the advisability of heating the main buildings by steam from one central point must be evident to anyone who considered the "grave defects" of the present system. Then, too, a new fireproof library building would soon be needed. Professor Fiske already wanted the whole first floor of McGraw Hall for library use. And finally, Cornell needed "a gallery illustrative of the fine arts."

An opportunity to acquire an art gallery was now offered. The residual estate of Jennie McGraw Fiske, to which the University was entitled, under the terms of her will, included her mansion and its thirty-acre site. The mansion still contained the art objects she and Willard Fiske had purchased in Europe. The University had received an offer of $10,000 (from White?) for the purchase of a collection of casts provided the mansion was purchased and a suitable gallery added. The President wrote that it would be a "harsh proceeding to sell such property to outside parties . . . to many it would have the look of profanation. Apart from the fact that . . . not one fourth the cost of the building and grounds could be obtained at private sale," it seemed to him that "a sentiment of justice and propriety" should lead Cornell to use the mansion as an art gallery.[24] Trustee Chairman Henry W. Sage and Trustee Douglass Boardman thought otherwise, and White's dream was frustrated: first by their arguments, then by the "will case," and again by Sage and Boardman when this part of the residual estate was sold at auction in 1891 after the U.S. Supreme Court's final decision.[25]

White was able to report in 1883 that "a comparatively small number of students were housed in university dormitories." His preju-

---

[23] Charles Francis Osborne's Notes on the Arts of House-Planning (New York, 1888) is dedicated "by permission . . . to Calvert Vaux, who by precept and example first inspired me with a love for my profession."

[24] A. D. White, Annual Report (20 June 1883), pp. 29–32.

[25] White, Diaries, 29 August 1890; 19 February 1891. Fiske told White that he tried to give the mansion to the University but Judge Boardman thought it would cost too much to keep up. White thought the sale of the house and its contents "most pathetic . . . a staring, gaping crowd in the ruins of so many hopes." Thomas McGraw bought the mansion for $35,000. "Dog Cheap," White wrote.

Fig. 112. Kappa Alpha house (1883) by William H. Miller, the first fraternity house built on land leased on the university campus.

dice against dormitories, developed at Hobart and Yale, was still strong. He thought The Cascadilla now promised "finally [to] become permanently useful . . . [as a] place of residence for professors, assistant professors, resident graduates, and members of the Senior Class." [26] He was in favor of so restricting its use and was happy that the University no longer had anything to do with the boarding arrangements there. White's only recommendation for The Cascadilla was that the "exterior of the building be completed, giving it some proper architectural character." In 1884 the top floor was remodeled and an oriel window and new entrance were added at the south side adjacent to the trolley line. William Henry Miller was the architect. In the same year, White was pleased to report that student accommodations in White and Morrill Halls had been "reduced by the extension of lecture rooms and recitation rooms."

President White thought the most hopeful prospect of the eighties, in the line of housing, was the development of fraternity houses at Cornell. In 1881, Kappa Alpha applied for and received the lease of a lot just north of the Cascadilla Gorge Bridge. Their red-stone house (Fig. 112), designed by William H. Miller, was built in 1883 at a cost of $16,000. The following year, Psi Upsilon's plans, also by Miller, were approved. They began building on land leased from the University west of Kappa Alpha across Central Avenue. White believed such "private dormitories [would] arouse in the students a feeling of responsibility both for the care of the property and for the reputation of the house." He wrote that such a system which "fastens upon [students'] duties and responsibilities similar to those of men in the active world was among the better solutions of the problems [of] . . . housing students in American universities." [27] Shades of Frederick Law Olmsted! But Professor

[26] A. D. White, MS, draft of the Annual Report of the President to the Board of Trustees, 1883, White Papers, pp. 99–101.

[27] *Annual Report* (20 June 1883), pp. 33–34.

Fig. 113. Hiram Sibley, University Trustee by the Charter, 1865–1888, and founder of Sibley College of Mechanical Engineering.

Hiram Corson was upset by the new student "private dormitory" development in the pine grove north of Cascadilla Gorge. He reported to Moses Coit Tyler that he thought the Trustees' "heedlessness concerning the beauty of the campus" was demonstrated by their "sacrificing the pine forest to two society houses." He told Henry Sage that "they never did anything on the campus without slapping nature on the face." [28]

But Professor Corson was prone to dramatize situations. The Trustees had, in fact, great concern for the beauty of the place and they acted on it in 1882 when they purchased Mary Cornell's land along Fall Creek Gorge north of Sibley Hall to the center of the stream "to prevent the erection of unsuitable buildings or bringing in of tenants likely to be troublesome." Here the University built the foundry discussed earlier, and here Professor Prentiss, with the concurrence of White, proposed a moderate expenditure for paths lead-

ing through the ravine. He proposed, for the first time at Cornell, the development of part of an arboretum "useful and beautiful from a scientific, practical, and aesthetic point of view." Trees would be "placed in various parts of [the estate] for adornment and shelter, in accordance to some extent with their scientific grouping, but in due subordination to the demands of landscape gardening." [29] President White enlarged on the idea that the university grounds needed more attention in his 1884 Annual Report. That spring a large program of improvements to the grounds on the north side of the campus had been completed. White noted the need for similar work elsewhere:

So large a landed property as ours ought always to have some special care by an expert, who, when a building is to be placed, a road or path laid, trees cut or drains dug, can at once give an opinion worth having, and bring all improvements made into connection with the original scheme, which regards the whole work as a whole, and not as a patchwork resulting from the whims, or perhaps the ignorance of many individuals. [30]

One of the last building projects to engage White's attention before he resigned the presidency in 1885 was the construction of a large addition to Sibley Hall. Until 1884, the building needs of the College of Mechanical Engineering, in excess of the space provided by the original 1871 structure, had been satisfied by the construction of one-story shops behind the main building. These low-cost brick buildings had been painted gray to reduce their contrast to the main building. In 1881, White convinced Hiram Sibley (Fig. 113) that a small addition to the rear of the main building should be of stone. [31] Then in 1884, Sibley

[28] Moses Coit Tyler, Diaries (Rare Book Room, Cornell University Library), 24 December 1883.

[29] A. D. White, Annual Report (20 June 1883), p. 37.
[30] Annual Report (18 June 1884), p. 34.
[31] Sibley to ADW, 6 October 1881, White Papers. Sibley wrote: "I note what you say and especially observe how modestly you disclose your preference for the stone in place of brick. You must be indulged in this matter. Your return to us renders me powerless if I inclined to differ with you. . . . Go on with your

Fig. 114. West Sibley Hall, extension by Archimedes N. Russell (1884). This extension was the second of four stages in the development of the building.

gave Cornell $35,000 for the construction of two additional bays to the east of the original three-bay main building and for a "range of shops." The new bays were carried on in the style of the original stone building. Sibley, who had great confidence in White, agreed to pay the extra cost of stone construction. To keep the front of the enlarged main building symmetrical, architect Archimedes Russell raised a high dormer over the central bay and in the wall below inserted a stone tablet bearing an inscription with the donor's name (Fig. 114). That was all there was to it: a simple, useful extension of the building which was to continue to grow in like manner into the present fine composition of the north side of the Quadrangle.

Several other minor improvements on the campus marked White's last year as President. Several chimneys were removed from the end rooms of Morrill and White Halls permitting

larger lecture rooms running the full width of the building. This was made possible by the removal of dormitory rooms and the addition of a steam heating system. A "room for the ladies" was provided in Morrill Hall and a small wooden magnetic laboratory building was built behind Sibley Hall for Professor Anthony. The enterprising Professor of Physics extended the outdoor campus lighting system and supervised the installation of electric lights in the University Library in McGraw Hall. President White doubted the "experiment." He did not think the library would be used very much in the evening after the novelty of its opening had passed away.[32]

When Cornell's first President resigned in June 1885, the campus was in excellent condition, reflecting the general prosperity of the University. Many of the trees planted in the late seventies and early eighties had begun to mature, the interiors of the original stone buildings had been remodeled, and the four

work, the extra $1400 I will try to meet as you may require from time to time during the progress of the work."

[32] A. D. White, *Annual Report* (17 June 1885), p. 43.

Fig. 115. Charles Kendall Adams, second President of Cornell, 1885–1892.

major building projects of White's last years in office were completed and landscaped. In his Annual Report for 1884–1885, White wrote a "final" reminder of the value of developing "a proper general plan" for the campus:

The time will come when on the University hill will stand a very large library, a gallery for pictures and casts, a building for the departments of civil engineering and architecture, a hall for the alumni, a laboratory or laboratories for biological and kindred researches in natural history . . . a school of mines, a large special assembly room for University purposes . . . an observatory, a law school, a preparatory medical school, a veterinary school, a conservatory of music, and various other edifices. Certainly, it is none too soon to begin devising a general plan as to the positions of such buildings as these.[33]

[33] *Ibid.*, p. 46. White makes a special plea for a

Charles Kendall Adams (Fig. 115), Professor of History at the University of Michigan and nonresident professor at Cornell, accepted the Cornell presidency in July 1885. White left the campus for Europe the following October. On the day he sailed he noted in his diary that friends had told him they would have nominated him for Governor of New York if he had consented to accept. "What an escape!" he added.[34] After a year in Europe, White returned to the campus to what now became known as the "Old-President's house." After 1885 his concern for the development of the Cornell campus was never less than during his twenty years as President. He soon became a Trustee, and if he was not consulted about campus improvements, he managed to offer his advice anyway. While away on frequent extended trips to Europe, he kept up a stream of correspondence to Ithaca, which often included patriarchal advice on building and landscaping at Cornell.

In June 1887, Trustee Alfred Barnes, the New York publisher, offered a $40,000 supplement to funds raised by students and faculty for a Christian Association building under the leadership of John R. Mott, future leader of the international Y.M.C.A. movement. White, while in deep distress after his wife's death, took time to examine possible building sites. He walked over the campus with Henry Sage, worked an entire day on plans, and telegraphed New York architect Frank Ayres Wright to come to Ithaca to discuss the preparation of designs.[35] Henry Sage talked to William Henry Miller about the same subject and a "competition" ensued. The sequence was typical. About the same time White and

"general plan" at two places in this report: here under the subtitle "Buildings" and on p. 67 as the twelfth and final point under his "Final Statement of Views on General University Policy, Internal and External." This document is well worth republication along with his *Report on Organization* of 1866.

[34] White, *Diaries,* 3 October 1885, p. 248.

[35] White, *Diaries,* 24, 27 June, and 7, 8 July, pp. 265–267. Mary White died suddenly on 8 June 1887. White marked a † in his diary on every anniversary of the date until his own death in 1918.

President Adams were discussing library plans with Henry Van Brunt, a Boston architect, Sage was thinking seriously about asking Miller to design the building. The library design "competition" will be discussed in the next chapter. The decisions on Barnes Hall, the student Christian Association building, were in some ways prophetic of the fate of the library plans. Sage switched the site and favored Miller's plans. Miller had recently completed the Ithaca Congregational Church, a magnificent and modern-looking brick structure (Fig. 116). Wright complained that he did not have enough time to adjust his plans for Barnes Hall to the new site, and Miller was awarded the commission. White, always able to adapt to new circumstances, proceeded to work closely with Miller as the plans were refined.[36]

Miller had prepared a design with two alternative architectural treatments for Barnes Hall: "Romanesque and Gothic." President Adams preferred the "Romanesque," and White and Sage concurred.[37] The plans were approved in September 1887, and the building was dedicated at Commencement ceremonies in 1889.[38] It won considerable acclaim for its architect. White thought it would go well with the "brick group"—quite as well as if it were in the same style as the Chapel. At the dedication ceremonies for Barnes Hall (Figs. 117 and 118), Adams gave a history of the building. After noting the great credit which it reflected on the Christian Association, the University, and Alfred S. Barnes, Adams described how its construction seemed to be "attended from the first to the last by the shadows of mortality." Alfred Barnes had died in February 1888. Miller's superintending architect, Kent, died in the summer of 1888. Sweating, the senior contractor, died in 1889, a few months before Barnes Hall was completed. Robert Richardson, the talented English stone carver whose work graced Sage College and Chapel and the White and McGraw-Fiske villas, caught cold while carving ornament for Barnes Hall and died of consumption. The capitals of the building remain unfinished as he had left them. Finally at the very end of the work, the contractor for the gas fixtures was "added to the list of those who had fallen . . . five times death came, as if to remind [them]," Adams said, "that . . . nothing but the great spiritual work for the promotion of which [Barnes Hall was] erected can . . . claim . . . either stability or permanence."[39]

The building has fared better than its builders. Barnes Hall's elegant architectural qualities have helped it survive many misfortunes. Its simple Latin cross plan prefigured Miller's design for the Library. Its saddle-backed tower roof and handsome rounded walls help make it one of the most memorable landmarks of the Cornell campus. Miller made good use of the sloping site. The main entrance, east of the tower, is located at mid-level between upper and lower floors. Upper and lower entrances are also provided at grade. The building as designed for the Chris-

[36] Rossiter and Wright to Osborne, 3 October 1887, White Papers; Rossiter and Wright to ADW, 19 October 1887. The architects submitted a bill for $300 and told Osborne that if this amount was not paid they would sue Sage for 1 per cent of $40,000. They were paid $323.45, and wrote to White thanking him for his attention to the settlement. They regretted that there was a misunderstanding in the matter and told White "in confidence . . . this [was] only another instance where Mr. Sage has had his way . . . the change of site was especially unfortunate . . . like rubbing everything out and beginning over again. This [they] could not do in the face of a declared preference for Miller's design. . . . [They] did not consider themselves in direct competition this time. [There being no] competition where the designer works upon different data." Henry Sage and President Adams kept White (who was on vacation) informed on the progress of the work. Adams spoke highly of Miller's work (C. K. Adams to White, 9 August 1887) and Sage wrote describing the design in detail and telling White that he had decided that university funds should be used to pay the excess cost over what the donor, Barnes, was willing to pay. Sage wrote: "I don't want to see that plan sheared down" (Sage to ADW, 27 August 1887, White Papers).

[37] Adams to ADW, 9 August 1887, White Papers. ADW to Adams, 18 July 1887, White Papers.

[38] Cornell University Christian Association, *Exercises at the Dedication of Barnes Hall* (Ithaca, 16 June 1889).

[39] *Ibid.*, pp. 8–9.

Fig. 116. The Congregational Church of Ithaca (1884) by William H. Miller, one of the architect's first major nonresidential commissions and perhaps his most significant non-Cornell building. It comprised a prelude to his skillful designs of large interior spaces and their crisp exterior expression in Barnes Hall and Uris Library.

Fig. 117. Barnes Hall by William H. Miller (1887), for the Cornell University Christian Association. This building, the fifth of the "red brick group," was sited on the slope with consummate skill by W. S. Brook. Its tower was the eighth of nine otherwise-looking towers at Cornell.

Fig. 118. Barnes Hall and Central Avenue in the 1890's. The informal southern half of the Cornell campus came nearest to being an expression of Olmsted's landscape ideals during the last decade of the nineteenth century. Since the 1940's this open, informal pattern has provided flexible space for expansion, fulfilling one of Olmsted's purposes in recommending it.

Fig. 119. Barnes Hall, interior of the main student lounge. The University Christian Association building was the first of its kind in the country and the precursor of the Cornell student union.

tian Association was full of useful and beautiful rooms (Fig. 119). In addition to the second-floor main hall, Miller provided a large, well-lit reading room in the west wing. The view from it extended twenty-five miles up and down the Cayuga Lake valley. Also on this floor were Association offices, studies, and a library room. The top floor, originally a large lecture hall, is still a favorite place for special lectures, theatre, and musical performances because of its beauty and unusually excellent acoustical qualities. Originally the room seated more than nine hundred people. Sliding glass doors screened the west part from the main space, providing, when needed, a smaller room for classes. The area is now used for storage.[40] The lowest floor of Barnes Hall was at first divided into rooms for students, and here the changes began. During the First World War, a canteen (the predecessor of the student union) was established on this level. Once Barnes was invaded by this most excellent meeting place, the trend to new uses for the building could not be re-

versed. After the war an improved "coffee shop" was provided. Soon a store selling needed student supplies appeared. Finally, when the new facilities of Anabel Taylor Hall were provided in 1952, Cornell United Religious Work left its first home to the commercial victors.

Now, only the beautiful soft brick and stone exterior (marred by service protrusions and amateurish signs) and the excellent top floor auditorium remain as they were when William Henry Miller completed his first major building on Cornell's campus. Even in its present, somewhat neglected state, the building is a significant element of the architectural and landscape history of the campus. It is one of Miller's best buildings. A competent and imaginative refurbishing, addition, and restoration of Barnes Hall for contemporary use would seem to afford both an opportunity to build on the excellence of the past and an obligation to respect Cornell's early achievements in both student religious work and architecture.

White's next efforts to influence campus building had results much less pleasing to

[40] *Ibid.,* pp. 11–14.

him. In his 1885 Annual Report he had recommended that the civil engineers and architects be provided a new building. White wanted to get rid of the pesky temporary wooden laboratory that had been in the middle of the Quadrangle since 1868. When no donors responded to White's call, the Trustees decided to appropriate $60,000 of the new wealth from the sale of western pine land for the building.[41] White wrote Sage a long letter about the building backing the view of Estavan Fuertes, Director of the School of Civil Engineering, that it should be located at the intersection of East Avenue and President's Avenue (where Stimson Hall now stands). This would add another unit to the "great upper quadrangle" and the drafting rooms could face north. White suggested that the ground floor be kept open for display of architectural photographs and sculpture scattered around the University, and he assured Mr. Sage that the latter "was not easily scared by figures" and should therefore not think of "a building of less size than 200 by 50 feet." [42]

Miller had been suggested as architect and White agreed that this was a good choice. The Ex-President thought that Miller had demonstrated, "in taking up the Barnes building, that he [could] do something outside of house building." But as for selecting Miller to design the library (as Sage had hinted), White thought it better to retain Henry Van Brunt.[43] Sage proceeded to move in the direction opposite to that which White suggested. Miller would be architect for the library, and Babcock would design the engineers' building later named Lincoln Hall. And to add a little salt, Sage decided that the site for the engineers' building should be shifted from the south side to the area immediately adjacent to

Sibley Hall on the east side of the Quadrangle. Babcock and Fuertes had developed plans for the first site, but at an Executive Committee meeting on 15 February 1888 the site was changed. Babcock and Fuertes were directed to prepare new sketches.[44] White was furious and he told his diary about it: "Site . . . changed—a collision narrowly avoided. Lord, how long! This 'bossism' and ring control is becoming almost unbearable." [45]

Shortly after this encounter, White left Ithaca on a tour of the South.[46] When he returned in April he discovered, to his dismay, that the engineers' building had been designed to be built of brick. On the "stone quadrangle!" He told Moses Coit Tyler that Sage was treating the campus like one of his sawmills, but he saved his most heated anger for his diary:

The cheap and nasty policy as to new building is detestable because controlled by two "practical" trustees [Sage and Boardman?]. $3000.00 has been saved by making the new Civ. Eng. Building a mere barrack and the $3000.00 was just 5 p.c. of cost of building—a mere bagatelle in view of importance of the building.[47]

This was too much. The next day White visited some of the Ithaca Trustees, and in May he wrote letters to the other Trustees. At the 20 June Trustees' meeting an additional $7,000 was appropriated for Lincoln Hall "so that it might be made of stone in conformance

---

[41] Trustees' *Proceedings*, 26 October 1887.

[42] ADW to Sage, 30 August 1887, Sage Papers #1388, C.U. Archives. White says the building ought to be large, simple, massive, fitted to the needs of two departments.

[43] ADW to Sage, 30 August 1887, Sage Papers. This critical turning point in the design of the Library is described more completely in Chapter IX of this volume.

[44] Trustees' *Proceedings*, 23 December 1887, 15 February 1888, II, 179, 188. C. K. Adams to White, 22 February 1888, White Papers: "The committee . . . decided upon the north locality although it is admitted on all hands that the long axis of the building should have to be north and south . . . in order to have more extension of the wings it will have to be pushed well down into the campus. . . . Babcock tells me that the plan . . . can be completed for . . . $50,000; but this will require a perfectly plain architecture of brick and destitute of all ornament. The situation is an extremely unfortunate one. . . . Babcock is . . . indifferent."

[45] White, *Diaries*, 23 December 1887, p. 276.

[46] White, *Diaries*, 1 January 1888 to 19 April 1888, pp. 278 ff.

[47] White, *Diaries*, 19 April 1888, p. 283. Babcock's plans had been approved (Trustees' *Proceedings*, 15 April 1888).

Fig. 120. Lincoln Hall (1888) by Charles Babcock was Cornell's first permanent building for the Schools of Civil Engineering and Architecture.

to Ezra Cornell's early wishes." White had won the last battle of his campaign, but not entirely: $7,000 was too little, so the Trustees voted on 23 June that the front and sides only would be stone and the back would be brick.[48] And so Cornell acquired another red stone building on the Quadrangle (Fig. 120). Babcock and Sage liked red and White liked stone ("in conformance to Mr. Cornell's early wishes").

The description of one final round of the Sage-White debates over Cornell building policies will provide some further idea of the intensity of their great debate over Cornell's library. White again left Ithaca for Europe in June 1888. Sage had already "won" an important point on the library issue. Miller's plans were to be executed. Now Henry Sage began plans for a brick building on the edge of the Quadrangle. Professor Anthony's great success in the Physics Department and in the new course in electrical engineering coupled

with the growth of course work and research in the Chemistry Department had filled Franklin to overflowing a few years after it was completed. At first, additional space needs were accommodated in an annex built north of the main building, but by the fall of 1888 further expansion there seemed undesirable. The fire hazard of some of the chemistry operations was a further stimulus to provide a separate building for Chemistry.[49] The site chosen was west of Franklin Hall on the promontory where in 1866 Ezra Cornell had first showed the Trustees why they must build the Quadrangle at this upper level of East Hill. In December, Professor Osborne, who had been teaching in the College of Architecture for five years, asked Henry Sage if he might be considered for architect for a university building.[50] He was retained to provide plans for the new chemistry building and designed a functional, economical, ordinary, unadorned redbrick building for the second most prominent site on East Hill. We do not know if White protested during the design and construction of Morse Hall (Fig. 121) but when he re-

[48] Trustees' Proceedings, 20, 23 June 1888. C. K. Adams was very unhappy about the mixture of materials. He wrote White (13 November 1888, White Papers) that "the Architecture on the whole is pleasing especially the campus side. . . . The great mistake was in making the rear of it brick. It is a matter of constant comment, and is really very unfortunate."

[49] Trustees' Proceedings, 24 October 1888.
[50] Osborne to Sage, 3 December 1888, Sage Papers.

Fig. 121. Morse Hall (1888) by Charles F. Osborne. Though this building provided generous space for instruction in chemistry, it angered Ex-President White, who had insisted that the site be kept open in deference to the wishes of Ezra Cornell. It was partially destroyed by fire in 1916 and totally demolished in 1954.

turned to Ithaca in October 1889 there it was: Sage's (and Osborne's) red-brick building standing reproachfully not only on the corner of the stone Quadrangle, but on the "sacred" promontory where the Founder had pointed out the site, where White and Cornell had communed in early times of trouble, and where Phillips Brooks had sat in awe of the beautiful Cayuga Lake valley landscape.[51]

We are not certain whether Henry W. Sage ever knew or thought about White's desire to keep this site open; he did know, however, of White's desire to build the Cornell Quadran-

gle of stone. How could he escape the fact? White announced it whenever the occasion permitted and sometimes when there was no occasion. White had his way eventually, but only partly so before his death. In 1916, Osborne's massive, useful, schoolhouse-like, hip-roofed, red-brick building burned with the fierce intensity of chemical fires. It was patched up, burned again, patched up again, and stood, half-gone with a temporary roof over its remaining basement and first floor until 1954 when the University at last paid White's wishes the honor of removing it— only to put a parking lot in its place.

American architecture was in a critical period of transition in the 1880's. The era was restless and experimental. The national prosperity which followed the post–Civil War depression stimulated much building. The latent revolution of American architecture evident in the work of Richardson and in the wooden houses of the seventies and eighties was reflected in the architecture of our colleges and universities. A lack of consensus on issues of style was also reflected in the college buildings of the era. Cope and Sewardson designed "correct" and picturesquely composed "Gothic" buildings at Bryn Mawr and

---

[51] A. D. White, *Autobiography*, I, 410. White describes the construction of Morse Hall on this promontory as a "sad mistake," one he felt "bound in self-defense to state was made during an absence of [his] in Europe." The day after Morse Hall burned in 1916 White noted a meeting of the local Trustees in his diary (14 February 1916): "Sentiment unanimous for a new . . . laboratory to be placed on line of Physics [Rockefeller Hall]—northward from it, thus restoring to the campus the site of Morse Hall which never ought to have been covered by buildings utterly out of harmony with all the others on the upper Quadrangle. It was done . . . in defiance—not only of all my wishes and ideas—but of a resolution presented to the Trustees and unanimously passed by them—having been moved by Ezra Cornell. It [the site selection for Morse Hall] was virtually forced through by Judge Douglass Boardman."

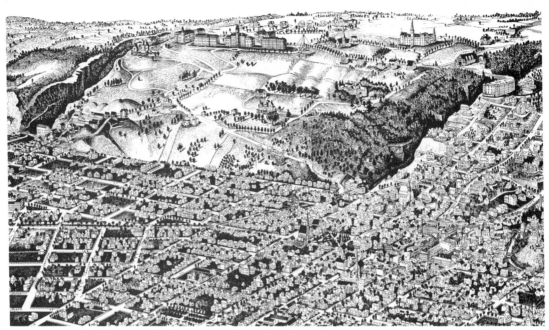

Fig. 122. Burleigh's view of Ithaca, 1882, shows the village, soon to be chartered a city (1888), spreading up East Hill south of the campus. Below the campus and between the gorges, the McGraw-Fiske mansion, Llenroc, and Forest Park stand out clearly on the open slope of East Hill.

Fig. 123. The campus from Sage College tower, about 1888. Beyond the west gable of Sage Chapel the towers of the McGraw-Fiske mansion and the mast of the weather signal station are silhouetted against Cayuga Lake. At the right is Franklin Hall, which provides a strong termination at the north end of the Stone Row.

Princeton in 1886. Ernest Flagg's designs for Annapolis were much influenced by Beaux-Arts traditions and Potter's Alexander Hall at Princeton was, perhaps appropriately, called "Richardsonian Romanesque." Buildings which seemed to fall in the latter category were more likely to be innovative and potentially helpful in the effort to develop a national idiom, even though they ignored the potentials of an emerging industrial technology. With the emergence of William H. Miller's talents, two of the buildings added to the Cornell campus in the late eighties (Barnes Hall and the Library) seemed to be in tune with the most creative trend in American architecture: the casting off of the long dominant influence of Classical and Gothic motifs.

The eighties were prosperous years for the Cornell campus and Ithaca. Early in the decade the village had started to climb East Hill toward the campus (Fig. 122). Now an increasing number of homes were being built near the University. The raw untamed landscape of Ezra Cornell's hilltop farm had been transformed by the grading and planting projects of the late seventies. Now, the trees planted on the campus were beginning to mature and the regular forms of the Quadrangle and the irregular forms of the brick group were enhanced by broad lawns and a well-developed system of paths and drives (Fig. 123). The buildings of the eighties were substantial and well planned. At least one of them (Barnes Hall) was an architectural gem. It showed promise for an improved level of design in campus buildings. The promise was made good in the late eighties in the design of Cornell's Library and Boardman Hall but only after an extended debate between Sage and White over the library building's design. It was, however, a debate whose meanings lay deeper than the issues involved in building.

IX

"Here the Great Library Will Stand"

THE FIRST PLAN FOR COR-
nell's campus drawn in 1866
placed a library building south of Morrill Hall
at the southwest corner of the proposed university square. In the early 1880's this site, the
second highest point of the west front of the
campus, was occupied by a weather signal
station (Fig. 124). With a good glass on a
clear day, the signals hoisted up its hundred-
foot mast could be seen from many miles
away. Sailors far down Cayuga Lake could
check for the latest forecast. This unique university extension equipment had been
preceded on the brow of East Hill by a temporary tower for the Cornell Chimes, a gift of
Jennie McGraw. These bells plus the Great
Maria bell, a gift of Mrs. Andrew D. White,
had been moved to the tower of McGraw Hall
in 1872. The chimes were installed there at
the same time the university library was
moved from its cramped quarters in Morrill
Hall. In retrospect, it seems that the chimes
and the books belong together. The books,
considered a research collection from the
first,[1] with the bells which marked the passage

of the "irrevocable hours" were appropriate
symbols for a modern university. In other colleges and universities, in earlier days, the
chapel was the most significant building and
the community timepiece was often attached
to it, but at Cornell, an unsectarian institution,[2] the bells and books symbolized what
was most important about the place. President White seemed to sense the propriety of
keeping them dramatically before public as
well as university eyes and the best way to
achieve this objective was to place both bell
tower and book house on the high mid-point
of the brow of East Hill.

Although this may seem obvious to us now,
it was not always clear to the people who
made decisions about the location and design
of the structure that is now Uris Undergraduate Library. The stories of romance, intrigue,
and conflict that danced and swirled around
the participants in these decisions would sup-

---

[1] White and Willard Fiske were both skilled book-
men. The special collections purchased for the University denote the building of a scholarly library:
Jared Sparks' collection on American history which
was used as a lure to Moses Coit Tyler; George
Anthon's classical library; White's collections of
materials on the French Revolution and on architec-

ture; and Burr's collection of materials on witchcraft
in New England are typical. There were some complaints from the faculty in the early years that the
library did not contain enough standard works for
undergraduate courses, but there was always someone
who would purchase, for example, a rare volume of
Canina on the Antiquities of Rome or Greece.
[2] White used the term "unsectarian" rather than
"non-sectarian" to identify clearly the fact that Cornell was an institution based on belief in God but free
of any sectarian influences or controls—not against
sects but uncommitted to any one sect.

Fig. 124. The weather signal station about 1885. The station once stood on the future site of Uris Library—a few feet north of the present location of the Library Tower.

Fig. 125. Willard D. Fiske, the first University Librarian and the collector and doner of the core of Cornell's Dante, Petrarch, and Icelandic collections.

ply material for several novels. The marriage of Jennie McGraw and Cornell's first librarian, Professor Willard Fiske (Fig. 125), Jennie's tragic early death, her bequest of most of her fortune to the university library, the drawn-out court battles over her will, Henry Sage's iron determination to get all or none of her fortune for Cornell, his refusal to negotiate with Fiske, and finally his gift for building and endowing the University Library are dramatic events in the Cornell saga. The details of this story are related elsewhere.[3] In this

account we are concerned with the way these events influenced the location and design of the library building. The structure became a pawn in the struggles between White, President Adams, and Trustees Sage and Boardman. The power to make decisions about selection of a site and design of the building symbolized victory for the participants in the larger drama. President White's daughter Karin remembered that he became furious and sometimes trembled in restrained rage as they passed the building during walks on the campus.[4] What angered him was not the library building but the memories it evoked; the fight over the will which he believed un-

[3] See especially Chapter XIII of Morris Bishop's *A History of Cornell*; Ronald Williams, *Jennie McGraw Fiske: Her Influence upon Cornell University*; and Horatio S. White, *Willard Fiske: Life and Correspondence* (New York, 1925).

[4] Statement a'tributed to Miss White in a conversation with Edith Fox, Curator of the Cornell University Archives.

necessary and which he felt had been poorly fought on Cornell's side. He was convinced that the whole affair had done great damage to the University and, but for the stubbornness of the Chairman of the Board of Trustees, Henry Sage, and Trustee Douglass Boardman, had been unnecessary. Although the long-term effect of the struggle was beneficial to Cornell, this was not immediately apparent to its deeply wounded participants.

Jennie McGraw inherited most of her father's lumber fortune when he died in 1877. Her will gave two hundred thousand dollars, and after other bequests to her husband and relatives, the residual estate (another four to five hundred thousand dollars) for "the support, maintenance and increase of the [Cornell] library." She had spent most of her time in Europe after 1877, but in 1880 she began building her great mansion on East Hill. Now she was dying. Professor Willard Fiske had admired her from afar and early in 1880 actively courted her in Rome. The leave of absence required for this romantic activity seems to have been financed, at least in part, by Andrew Dickson White.[5] On their wedding day at the U.S. Embassy in Berlin, in July 1880, Willard Fiske legally renounced claim to any part of her estate. After a honeymoon on the Nile in Egypt and an art- and furniture-buying spree in Europe, Jennie and Willard Fiske returned to Ithaca early in September 1881. Jennie died in Professor Fiske's cottage on faculty row less than a month later.

The fall of 1881 was a significant turning point in the affairs of the University. President White had resigned his post as Minister to Germany and, after the pleas of the trustees, faculty, and student body, he returned to take the affairs of the University in hand. By this time, a brighter future appeared likely for Cornell. General prosperity brought by an upswing of the national economy and in-creased value of the University's western land had quickened the pace of activity on the campus. Salaries were increased, new appointments were made, new departments were in the offing, book purchases were increased, and plans were under way for the physics-chemistry laboratory building and the Armory-Gymnasium described in the previous chapter. Under these circumstances it was natural for White to begin dreaming of a great new library building. On 30 September 1881, Professor Moses Coit Tyler, newly arrived at Cornell from Michigan to teach American history, walked on the campus with White. In the course of their walk the President pointed to the signal station site and told Tyler that he "would rather see a fireproof library building put upon that spot than be a U.S. Senator." That evening, while he was working late in his office, White received word that Mrs. Fiske had died.[6]

On 7 October, Tyler noted that White was cheered by the news of Jennie's gift to the library and believed that "a library building [would] be undertaken at once." White also thought the Fiske mansion would become Cornell property and would be "a magnificent art gallery."[7] Tyler, who had recently heard favorable comment on the plans for a new library at the University of Michigan, passed the information on to White, and the President wrote to Charles Kendall Adams, the source of Tyler's news, asking for copies of plans and more details on the proposed building. He found a willing informant. C. K. Adams was deeply involved in the work of securing a new library at Ann Arbor and was much pleased with the plans of the architect, Henry Van Brunt of Boston. Van Brunt's scholarly achievements as well as his architectural skill and specialized knowledge of library planning had made a lasting impression on Adams.[8] The Michigan history professor

[5] White, "Diaries," MS, 23 May 1880, C.U. Archives. Morris Bishop (*op. cit.*, p. 225) says he thinks that "White regarded his advances [to Fiske] as friendly service, not as a University speculation."

[6] M. C. Tyler, Diaries, 30 September 1881; White, *Diaries*, 30 September 1881.

[7] M. C. Tyler, Diaries, 7 October 1881.

[8] Henry Van Brunt with William Ware was the architect for Memorial Hall at Harvard. Van Brunt

was full of information and enthusiasm about the proposed building and described its arrangements in detail: separate stacks, a commodious reading room, special seminar rooms, storage and unpacking areas, special collection rooms, and a picture gallery. He gave White the dimensions of important spaces and drew a sketch from memory.

The following March, White inspected Michigan's library plans on a visit to Ann Arbor, and two years later, in March 1884, he decided that the building, by then completed, was "admirable." [9] Professor Adams was especially pleased with the Michigan library's seminar rooms. He called the one he used "the historical laboratory" because the specialized collection of books kept there for the students "constituted the furniture of the investigator's workshop." Seven rooms of this type were eventually incorporated in the first Cornell library building and suites of them are located at the end of each stack floor in Cornell's Olin Research Library completed in 1960. Adams, who had studied in Germany in the seventies, had become an innovator in the use of the seminar for instruction at Michigan.[10] When Professor Adams wrote to White describing the Michigan plans, he congratulated him on Cornell's "glorious prospect" but warned him not to "put so much money into the building as to weaken [the] fund for books." The warning was hardly necessary. At the time, White, Henry Sage, and Judge Boardman, the executor of Mrs. Fiske's will, were concerned about a more serious threat: the possibility that Cornell University might not have any rights at all in the McGraw estate.

Within a few months after Jennie's death, Henry Sage and Willard Fiske were disagree-

ing over Fiske's right to live in "the castle," as Sage called the McGraw-Fiske mansion. The almost finished house was part of the residual estate willed to Cornell but, under the provisions of the will, Fiske could live there. He wanted to do so and apparently believed the University should maintain the property. White and Fiske wanted to make the house a University art gallery. Boardman objected and wanted to sell it. Settlement of the issue took three months and left everyone involved feeling very uncomfortable.[11] Sage and Boardman showed signs of bitterness toward Fiske, but their deepest concern was fear of what he might do about the will. A provision in the University Charter limited the amount of property Cornell could own to five million dollars, and conservative accounting placed it dangerously close to that limit in 1881. Early in May 1882 the State Legislature removed the limitation. Later it would appear that Professor Fiske was not informed of the problem or of the Trustees' legislative remedy—most unfortunate errors of omission.

The process of settling Mrs. Fiske's will proceeded slowly. No action was taken on library building plans until February 1883, one month after the judicial settlement of the estate. That month, a library plans committee (Sage, Boardman, and White) proposed that the Executive Committee establish a separate building fund to which specific amounts would be added each year from income. The suggestion was tabled. Professor Babcock suggested a detailed program should be prepared and four or five architects should be invited to an architectural design competition. His letter was referred to committee. In May, after Willard Fiske's return from a journey to

had translated Viollet leDuc's *Discourses on Architecture* in 1878. He had also written on library planning in the *Librarians Journal*.

[9] C. K. Adams to M. C. Tyler, 24 July 1881; ADW to C. K. Adams, 10 October 1881; C. K. Adams to ADW, 12 October 1881; A. D. White, *Diaries*, 3 March 1882 and 27 March 1884.

[10] Charles F. Smith, *Charles Kendall Adams* (Madison, 1924).

[11] White, *Diaries*, 13 December 1881. White notes: "Settled matters as to house between Fiske and University with aid of Sage & Boardman. F[iske] to take house and be custodian." M. C. Tyler, Diaries, 5 February 1882: Sage remarked to Tyler that Fiske "would be very foolish . . . to take the castle and live in it on his income." Sibley to ADW, 18 March 1884: Fiske told Sibley that his only desire in the matter was that the mansion be made an art gallery. Sibley seemed to believe that if the University would do this Fiske would settle out of court.

Europe, the newly established Library Council he chaired requested an appropriation to procure plans of recently erected library buildings. The committee was reminded that only nine hundred dollars remained in the book purchase fund. This laconic attitude is not difficult to explain.[12] The Trustees' library plans committee had deep doubts about the ability of the University to keep the bequest and felt they could not proceed until the matter was settled. Their doubts were realized in July 1883, when Willard Fiske, who had resigned from his position as Librarian and Professor of Scandinavian Languages and who now knew the reasons for the Trustees' concern, brought suit to set aside the provisions of his late wife's will.

So ended the first desultory efforts to build a new university library at Cornell. President White dashed off in disarray pursuing Fiske to London. His five-day marathon negotiation with Fiske in August 1883 was all for nought. The Executive Committee and most especially Henry Sage would have none of it. They cabled the President: "Make no offers." [13] The lines of battle were drawn. Fiske, bitter that he had been treated so badly by Sage and Boardman over the issue of the "castle," the provisions of Jennie's will, and the affairs of the library, and Sage and Boardman, furious at what seemed to them Fiske's frustration of John and Jennie McGraw's desire to endow the library, were facing up for a seven-year struggle over the McGraw fortune.

White's position was typical. He operated between the opposing forces, constantly seeking reconciliation and settlement out of court. He was, according to him, constantly frustrated by the refusal of Sage and Boardman to give an inch.

When President White resigned in 1885, he was in poor health (Ithaca winters were blamed), worn by administrative care (we may assume much of it connected with his struggle for power with Henry Sage), and generally bored with the day-to-day details of the presidency.[14] The Fiske suit (locally known as "the Great Will Case") was in its second full year and fourth volume of testimony. No one had thought seriously about a library building for two years, when Charles Kendall Adams, White's protégé from Michigan and Henry Sage's first choice, became Cornell's second President in July 1885.[15] In August 1885, White, relieved of his responsibilities as President, still dreamed of a great library building for Cornell and sketched his ideas in great detail in a letter to Adams (Fig. 126).

Henry Sage was immediately impressed by the new President's persistent industry and attention to details. He wrote to White: "Adams works like a veritable Giant." [16] In his meticulous way President Adams began to work for a new library building, too. By the late winter of 1886, the Ithaca trial of the Fiske suit was nearing conclusion and the case appeared to be developing favorably for Cornell. Adams quietly began to get in touch with the parties concerned in decisions about the library building. In February 1886, he wrote to White in Italy, suggesting Henry Van Brunt as architect in preference to H. H.

[12] Trustees' *Proceedings*, 24 January 1882, 28 December 1882, 9 January 1883, 27 February 1883, 31 May 1883; Babcock to Executive Committee, 15 March 1883. Fiske sent books to be bound in England without authorization. The Executive Committee voted early in 1882 to require that all future expenses in excess of the $18,000 bill already outstanding be reviewed by the Committee. At the same meeting salaries of the library staff were increased and two additional assistants were authorized.

White was more positive about the plans for a new library building. In his Annual Report in June 1883 he wrote: "A clear opinion [has been] arrived at as to the best mode of procedure . . . we ought to begin preparing plans very soon for a new fireproof structure to hold 300,000 volumes."

[13] Trustees' *Proceedings*, 27 July 1883.

[14] ADW to Fiske, 23 June 1885, Fiske Papers.
[15] Moses Coit Tyler, Diaries, 27 February 1883: "[Sage] has wholly lost respect for White as a president . . . spoke kindly of White personally but felt it his duty to . . . bring matters to an issue. He has a high regard for C. K. Adams for President. The talk was to me sad, yet he is right." (See also Tyler, Diaries, 10 February 1884.)
[16] Henry Sage to ADW, 28 May 1886, White Papers.

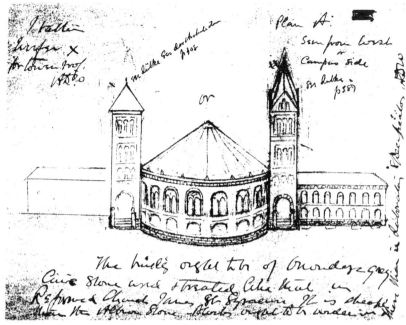

Fig. 126. Andrew Dickson White's sketch for a library on the east side of the Quadrangle, August 1885, was included in a letter to C. K. Adams, who had become President of Cornell the previous month. White's note read: "The building ought to be of Onondaga grey limestone and treated like that in the Reformed Church, James Street, Syracuse. It is cheaper than the Alberine—Joints ought to be wider in these than in [Franklin] Laboratory specifications." White also noted that he rather preferred the left tower roof.

Richardson, whom White seemed to favor.[17] White replied quickly and at some length with detailed suggestions on the building program, possible sites, and architects. He enclosed a sketch (Fig. 127) which indicates he was now vacillating between two sites: one opposite McGraw Hall which would begin to fill in the third side of the great Quadrangle and the other, the recurrent favorite, south of Morrill Hall. A building on the first site would permit a symmetrical scheme. (White seems to have the symmetrical University of Michigan library plan still fixed in his mind and uses its general plan form in his sketch as a symbol for the building.) Use of the east site would have achieved one of White's pet objectives by wiping out the wooden laboratory which he detested. For the second site he sketched a plan which would complete the

west row including a tower to echo that of Franklin Hall to the north. He suggested that Adams consider retaining James Lyman Silsbee of Syracuse to associate with Van Brunt, recommended the exclusive use of stone in the Quadrangle ("I beg of you, resist brick") and directed Adams to take a look at the stone work of St. Paul's Church in Syracuse.[18] In short, he was concerned about and had strong ideas on everything connected with the new library building.

Now that he was free of the overall day-to-day responsibility of the presidency, White simply could not surrender participation in the details of decisions on building. He had a personal stake in the success of the place, was about to give his magnificent historical library to Cornell, maintained his home on the campus, and was soon to be elected to the Board

[17] C. K. Adams to ADW, 12 February 1886, White Papers.

[18] ADW to C. K. Adams, 11 March 1886, White Papers.

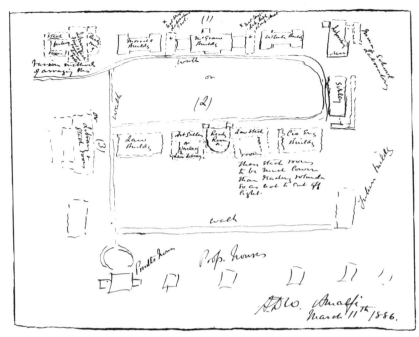

Fig. 127. Andrew Dickson White's plan for library sites in a letter to President Adams, 1886: (1) proposals for additions to McGraw Hall; (2) the preferred library site on the east side of the Quadrangle; (3) an alternate site on the south side of the Quadrangle. At the southwest corner of the Quadrangle is a third alternative next to which White notes, "Various methods of arranging this."

of Trustees. Poor Adams was already receiving rugged training for his seven stormy but fruitful years in the Cornell presidency and his nine calmer but equally significant years in the University of Wisconsin presidency. In matters related to the new library he was caught between titans. He operated as a buffer between White and Sage, trying to keep them from colliding while he worked at getting the building designed and built. Henry Sage's way of looking at it, after a time, was that White was using Adams to have his way on the library and he would have none of it. When White and Adams pushed he would pull, and so on.

In the first days of April 1886, Benjamin Ide Wheeler, a special lecturer on classical philology, arrived on the campus and met with the President. Later he recalled that Adams seemed rather gloomy during their chat. It was evening and they went for a walk over the campus. They came finally to "the brow of

a hill that overlooks the lights of the valley and commands the dim expanse of the lake to the north, and there [Adams] stopped and struck his cane on the ground. 'Here the great library will stand,' he said. His voice had a new ring. The drag and lethargy were gone." [19] President Adams had decided that the library would be on the signal station site. His vision of it there seemed to give him power to proceed. The next move was to bring the Trustee Executive Committee into the work. On 22 April 1886, they acted to appoint a new committee on the library building: Adams, Henry Sage, and Henry B. Lord. Adams was chairman. He wrote to White that he was asking Van Brunt to come to Ithaca and that there might be a "limited

[19] Benjamin Ide Wheeler. Memorial address for C. K. Adams quoted in Charles Foster Smith, *Charles Kendall Adams*, p. 31. The following year Wheeler accepted a full-time appointment to the Cornell faculty where he remained until 1898 when he was elected President of the University of California.

Fig. 128. The campus from the west, about 1891. Henry Van Brunt, the architect retained to design the university library building in 1886, first saw this view of the campus from the Lehigh Valley Railroad station. The experience suggested some way of "reconciling" contradictions of style and color in the existing buildings by the design of a new library building.

competition." [20] This last sounded like an idea Sage might have suggested. A competition was eventually held in 1888 (much to Adam's dismay), but for the next year and a half Henry Van Brunt alone was to study and restudy library plans to his heart's content; or perhaps to his dismay at the University's lack of ability to make decisions.

The architect came to Ithaca late in April 1886. His report of this first visit and his recommendations to Adams on the library building provide a fine statement of architectural principles for the Cornell Quadrangle. Van Brunt first saw the campus from the Inlet Valley railroad station. It crowned East Hill with its four western stone buildings and the spires of the red-brick informal Sage group (Fig. 128). He immediately recognized the great importance of the site south of Morrill Hall as a link between the gray-stone west row and the red-brick buildings to the southeast and as a balance to the red-stone mass of Franklin Hall at the north end of the row. "The new building," he wrote, "should . . . fall in with these gray structures and at the same time serve as a balance or pendant to [Franklin Hall]." This suggested, he thought, "the mass of its walls being in the local greenish-gray or blue random rock-faced ashlar . . . relieved with red sandstone in such proportions as to compose well." Exactly

right, and so it was ultimately built, but by another architect. Van Brunt's conception of the new structure was that it should be "not only perfect in itself, and on a high plane of architectural thought, but should rise to the dignity of architectural peacemaker by placing itself in harmony with the old works and in some sense reconciling their contradictions of style and colour." [21] But, having made this excellent analysis and having arrived at an excellent statement of architectural principle, Van Brunt began pedaling rapidly away from the use of what he termed a very beautiful and very inspiring site. The first site might not, he argued, be the best spot for a library: too many restrictions, all of the façades would be conspicuous (no place to hide a bookstack capable of indefinite extension). The exceptional difficulties of this site, including steep grades, might, he thought, under thorough study, force a brilliant solution. Eventually they did. But at the time Van Brunt saw no obvious solution, so he inclined toward the use of the site on the east side of the Quadrangle opposite McGraw Hall. Here a simple building could be designed without the encumbrances of the first site and the Quadrangle façade could mask the bookstacks.

Van Brunt's scheme (Figs. 129 and 130) proposed the new library as the central feature of a new *corps des bâtiments* on the east

[20] C. K. Adams to ADW, 13 April 1886, White Papers.

[21] Van Brunt to Adams, 1 May 1886, White Papers.

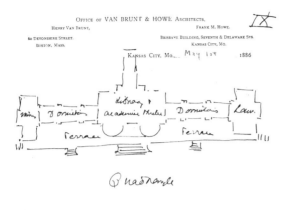

Fig. 129. Van Brunt's first site plan for a library on the east side of the Quadrangle, May 1886.

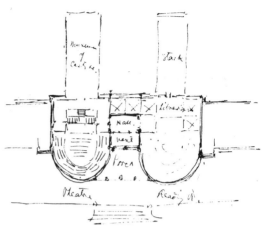

Fig. 130. Van Brunt's first sketch plan for the library, May 1886.

side of the Quadrangle. Adams and White were won over by his arguments. They seemed to have forgotten their predictions of where the great library would stand. Adams was cautious. He advised the architect to proceed with plans but to design the building so that it could fit either site. White was sure Van Brunt was right. In July 1886 he wrote from England to Henry Sage "that [the library] ought to be where the old laboratory [the "temporary" wooden laboratory] now stands, and that it should be of stone," and "that should it be otherwise in material or position you may be sure that future generations will not rise and call you blessed." [22] These dogmatic remarks from White seem almost designed to encourage a man like Sage to build elsewhere and of brick.

By the end of May 1886, the Ithaca courts had decided the Fiske will suit in Cornell's favor. Andrew D. White proposed the University make some face-saving concessions to

Fiske to avoid further litigation. [23] Meanwhile, the library plans were to be provided as rapidly as possible so that construction could begin the following spring. Van Brunt offered to prepare "tentative sketches" for buildings on both sites to help the committee decide on location. He was retained as architect for the building and proceeded with these studies, including some overall campus planning which he described as designed to "enable the committee to reach a deliberate conclusion . . . as to the relation of the library to the present and future buildings of the University." [24] Van Brunt's conclusion was that the site on the east side of the Quadrangle would be best. He drew a scheme for it. Henry Sage was not convinced. Late in June 1886, he had a survey of the site made. And, sure enough, he found that construction of the library as Van Brunt had drawn it would require the demolition of the "Engineering Department House," the "temporary" wooden laboratory. Sage concluded that this site might not, therefore, be available. "If it is not," he wrote, "the one originally proposed is and will be in many respects preferable. . . .

[22] ADW to Henry Sage, 6 July 1886, Trustee Papers. White urged Sage to delay final commitment to Van Brunt's plans. "A building once in the wrong place," he wrote, "is forever a calamity."

[23] Ibid.
[24] Van Brunt to Adams, 17 May 1886, Adams Papers.

Fortunately," he added, "we are in no haste." [25]

Adams spent the summer of 1886 in Europe. In July he wrote to Professor Tyler from Oxford that he was much impressed by the buildings there and regretted that Sage was not with him. He thought "it would have been a grand thing for him and perhaps for the University. Everywhere [he] saw stamped on everything the one idea of permanence." [26] Henry Sage was concerned about a different kind of permanence. He would not budge from his position that the University should make no face-saving concession to Fiske. They had won the McGraw-Fiske law suit and Henry Sage insisted they should hold fast to all of their rights, fighting appeals of the decision through to the U.S. Supreme Court, if that was necessary, and it was. White was furious. He saw the dream of "the noblest structure of its kind ever attempted in our country" fading and with it one of the handsomest library endowments ever held by an American university. [27]

Meanwhile, Van Brunt proceeded with his architectural studies, and late in October 1886, after reviewing them, the Board of Trustees referred the final selection of site to the Executive Committee. They recommended that the "Library Building be located on the site now occupied by the signal station." Adams still preferred the site on the east side of the Quadrangle, but he was outvoted. [28] Adams and White met quietly with Van Brunt in Syracuse early in January 1887, and, according to White, "set [the] plans for [the] library." Van Brunt then developed two designs for the signal station site: one symmetrical and one unsymmetrical. He "strongly preferred" the unsymmetrical one. Why he showed the other, we will never know. Doing so got him into a pack of trouble. Henry Sage

liked the "symmetrical design." It occurred to Adams that this one was suited to the upper site on the east side of the Quadrangle. He asked the architect to adapt his design to this already rejected site. This Van Brunt did, and so it went for many months. [29] Van Brunt drew many alternate plans, and finally all designs were reviewed by the Board of Trustees in June 1887. An "unsymmetrical" design for the signal station site was selected and the architect was directed to prepare a revised design. At some point in these systematic but complex maneuvers, Henry Sage must have yearned for the simple system of the previous decade when the Board of Trustees would march out on the campus in a body and select the site for a building. By mid-summer, 1887, after fifteen months of study and discussion, a site for the great library had finally been selected and a general scheme approved. [30]

But now problems of cost began to plague Van Brunt and Adams as they prepared the revised plans for the building. White had made the provision of a fireproof room a condition of his gift of his 30,000-volume historical library. The plan now adopted provided a semidetached fireproof main bookstack. But the White Library would function effectively only if it were part of the main building. The best solution, therefore, required making the entire building of fireproof construction. Van Brunt was sure this would cost more than the $225,000 budget available. Adams was sure that Sage would call for a general competition if he discovered that their architect had advised that the building could not be built within the budget. [31] Despite their budgetary

---

[25] Henry Sage to Van Brunt, 28 June 1886, Sage Papers.

[26] C. K. Adams to M. C. Tyler, 19 July 1886, Tyler Papers.

[27] White, *Diaries*, 13 June and 31 December 1888.

[28] Trustees' *Proceedings*, 2 November 1886. M. C. Tyler, Diaries, 30 November 1886.

[29] White, *Diaries*, 3 January 1887. Van Brunt to Adams, 5 and 23 February, and 5 March 1887.

[30] *Report of the Library Committee*, 15 June 1887; Trustees' *Proceedings*, 15 June 1887. This was a tragic time in White's life. On 7 June Van Brunt and his wife arrived for a one-week series of meetings on the plans. On the morning of 8 June White's wife Mary died very suddenly. White, grief-stricken, did not participate in the discussions on the library or attend the board meeting, the first since he had been elected a trustee in March, 1887 (White, *Diaries*).

[31] Van Brunt to Adams, 18, 19 July 1887, Adams Papers; Adams to ADW, 23 July, and 5 August 1887,

Fig. 131. Van Brunt's final design for the library on the signal station site, August 1887. It was rejected by Henry Sage, much to the dismay of Adams and White but much to the benefit of William H. Miller, for the ensuing competition offered the great opportunity of Miller's career.

difficulties, Adams, White, and Van Brunt were quite pleased with the new design. At this point Henry Sage and Henry Lord had not seen it. All that survives in the university records is a perspective of Van Brunt's design as it was in early August 1887 (Fig. 131). That month the architect was working out some final economies of arrangement and the final details of the elevations. He lowered the

ceiling in the main reading room to fifteen feet and used the second story over it for seminar rooms. After much study, he developed a composition for the great east gable that pleased him and he asked Adams to provide a suitable classical inscription to fill the pediment.[32]

White Papers. Van Brunt and Adams now believed the building might cost between $270,000 and $300,000. Adams asked White to intercede with Sage. He was "not sure it [was] best for [Adams] to see Sage before [returning Van Brunt's] sketches."

[32] Van Brunt to Adams, 27 July and 15 August 1887, Adams Papers. Van Brunt was preparing final designs to present at the fall meeting of the Board of Trustees. Figure 131 has no title or signature but is unquestionably a perspective of the library design to which Van Brunt refers in his letter of 15 August 1887 to Adams. He describes the "gable end toward

The book house on paper fell before it could be built of stone. On 20 August 1887, the New York Supreme Court reversed the Surrogate Court's decision, and it now seemed probable that Cornell would lose its share of Jennie McGraw Fiske's fortune. Henry Sage and Henry Lord had still not seen the revised library plans. Seven days later (27 August 1887), Adams and White met Van Brunt in Boston to go over the library plans and discuss the next steps.[33] In Ithaca, Henry Sage was already taking them. He must have been rather unhappy that Adams and White were busy being the clients and not consulting him. He also thought that William H. Miller, whose very successful design for Barnes Hall was now under construction, might be a good architect for the library. And finally, at this turn of events in the Fiske law suit, Henry Sage must have started considering the possibility that his own funds would be needed for building and endowing the library. He moved quickly, suggesting Miller as architect in a letter to White written late in August. White demurred: Miller was an excellent architect, had proved in Barnes Hall that he could do more than houses, but a man with more experience with fireproof construction was needed.[34] On the first of October 1887, Sage wrote a very strong letter to Adams criticizing him for proceeding with the library plans without consulting the rest of the committee.[35]

Then at the Board of Trustees meeting late in October the plans of Van Brunt were laid aside. Professor M. C. Tyler told his diary that Sage had "decided against the present acceptance of Van Brunt's noble plans for a library and to have other plans done, probably by Miller." "Adams," Tyler wrote, "has taken a step or two without consulting Sage: Hence the old man disciplines him and lets him know who is Boss here."[36]

By the middle of November 1887, Adams was so disconsolate over the entire library matter that he told Tyler he was ready to settle on almost any plan for the new civil engineering building.[37]

In the middle of December a docile Adams sent architects W. H. Miller and Charles Babcock instructions for the design of a library building. By the end of 1887, Henry Sage had assumed full responsibility for and full control of the provision of the great library. He personally made the arrangements to compensate Miller and Babcock for their services.[38] Adams seems to have surrendered his role in

the East" as follows: "Three romanesque arches [are] flanked by two aisles in the interior; this gives . . . a broad nave in the center and two aisles on each side separated from the nave by a line of columns; the aisles having a flat ceiling." Van Brunt believed, "The Eastern Gable was [the building's] most important architectural feature" and wanted "to occupy the pediment, or triangular area over the three arches . . . with an inscription," which he thought should be "something out of the classics in praise of literature . . . sufficiently voluminous to occupy a large area with many letters, after the manner of the crowded inscription over some of the Roman arches." Could Adams, at his leisure, "look up something suitable and sufficiently monumental for the place?"
[33] White, *Diaries*, 27 August 1887.
[34] ADW to H. Sage, 30 August 1887, Trustee Papers.
[35] H. W. Sage to Adams, 1 October 1887. Adams has called for a meeting of the library committee.

Sage admonishes him: "I consider it particularly unfortunate that we have not met before upon this most important business, so that as the architect progressed with his work it could have been with the sanction of the committee as a whole, instead of that of a single member of it." And again: "Duty and responsibility attach to each member of the committee in equal degree . . . no member of it should be asked to accept and commend to the full board a plan upon which he has never been consulted." And yet again: "Each member of the committee should forever Protest [sic] against having any one member of it assume all responsibility and expect his associates to blindly adopt his conclusions." Sage noted that he had commended Van Brunt's plan to the full board at the June 15 meeting after "the only meeting [the library] committee ever had." But he added that he had put cost limitations on it that he thought made its adoption impossible because he felt then he could not, when White's "sorrow was so fresh, and overwhelming," discuss adversely "a plan to which [he] knew White had given much thought and his own assent."
[36] M. C. Tyler, Diaries, 26 October 1887.
[37] *Ibid.*, 17 November 1887.
[38] C. K. Adams to W. H. Miller, 15 December 1887, Adams Papers; Babcock to Adams, 12 February 1888. Adams' letter to Miller is unusually formal. Babcock writes that he had forgotten to make formal reply to committee chairman Adams' invitation to prepare library plans because all of the arrangements had been made directly with Mr. Sage.

decisions on the library entirely. But as usual Ex-President White was irrepressible in matters architectural. He now began, figuratively speaking, but for all we know perhaps in person, to peer over William Miller's shoulder as the architect sketched his design for the library. In a delightful letter to Miller, White subtly transmitted the main elements of Van Brunt's designs which he considered good:

The more I think of it, the more I am convinced that the main feature on which accent should laid [sic] should be a building for a reading room, and perhaps with seminary rooms above it *extending east and west* on the signal station site and with a great tower just opposite the chapel and looking down the walk in both directions. I dread the effect of any long building, the fourth in a row, with its longest line north and south. This would be disastrous. . . . The same may be said regarding the big tower at the west end of the building, for we should have a regular gradation of three towers [Franklin, McGraw, and the new library tower] which would certainly have a comical look from below, and simply be a case of positive, comparative and superlative.[39]

White's lesson in architectural grammar was not wasted on Miller. He was a brilliant planner, but we should not fail to give credit to Van Brunt, via White, for some of the excellence of siting and the bold composition of masses of the Cornell library building. Miller's scheme was excellent, apparently superior to those of Van Brunt and Babcock. Its greatest merits were in its organization of functions. We do not know if Van Brunt submitted another design. It seems unlikely. We have not found any of Professor Babcock's

drawings for the library. However, since the library committee commented on designs by all three architects in their report and recommendations to the Trustees on final selection of plans, we must assume that these three competed for the commission.

William H. Miller worked on his plans for the library with the confidence of one who knows he has the boss's eye. Early in February he reported to White (who had left Ithaca late in December and was then on a tour of the South) that "Sage often comes in . . . though verry [sic] guarded in what he says, I can see he likes mine better than his (i.e., Babcock's)."[40] Adams was resigned to what would be. He thought Miller's plans interesting and ingenious. His building, he concluded, would be "Milleresque rather than monumental . . . bright and airy rather than dignified and sedate."[41] White returned to Ithaca late in April 1888, and Miller showed him some preliminary sketches of his library plan which White preserved in his papers. These sketch plans were essentially the same as Miller's final scheme except that the size of the building was later reduced—a change which made coat closets of the cloak rooms—and the bay window of the White Library was moved from the north end of the room to the center of the west wall.

All of the library plans, Van Brunt's earlier one and those produced by Miller and Babcock early in 1888, were reviewed by the library committee and the librarian in May and June. At their annual meeting, 20 June 1888, the Trustees received a report on the plans from the committee. It recommended adoption of William Henry Miller's plans. The committee had something good to say about each design. Van Brunt's treatment of the exterior was, they reported, "more successful than either of the others," but they did not like his semidetached bookstack. Babcock's plans were compact, his arrangement of func-

---

[39] ADW to W. H. Miller, 19 January 1888, White Papers. White and Miller were long-time friends. They must have discussed Miller's plans on several occasions before they were reviewed by the library committee. Miller's early study of architecture at Cornell was carried out under White's tutoring, and in February of this year (1888) Miller went to Washington, D.C., where White met him (Adams to ADW, 22 February 1888). Miller was designing a house in Washington for Senator Philetus Sawyer, a Wisconsin business friend of Henry Sage (*American Architect and Building News*, 24 November 1888).

[40] W. H. Miller to ADW, 12 February 1888, White Papers.
[41] C. K. Adams to ADW, 22 February 1888, White Papers.

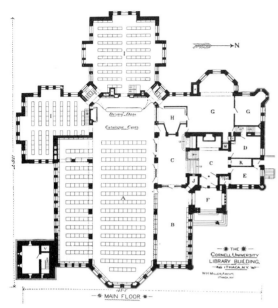

Fig. 132. William H. Miller's plan for the library, main floor, 1888: main reading room (A); periodical room (B); entry hall (C); men's cloak room (D); women's cloak room (E); vestibule (F); work rooms (G); librarian's room (H); stacks (I); storage (J); and (K); lifts (L) and (M).

tions convenient, and his design less expensive than the others, but the reading room was too small (room for only one hundred sixty readers), the stacks were crowded, and they provided no space for desks. Furthermore, the committee thought his utilitarian design for the stack exterior would be unattractive from the south and west. They thought Miller's plans (Figs. 132 and 133) had many advantages: administrative space was ample, the reading room was large and "fortunately situated," the White Library was "commodiously provided for, and the basement provided the largest usable space of any of the plans." Best of all, the bookstack design was excellent: two stacks making imaginative use of the site's steep drop to the west were easily accessible from the main reading room and the White Library. The book resting on its shelf farthest in the stack was only one hundred and twenty feet from the delivery desk. The reading room floors were at the mid-point in the stack levels, further reducing the time

required to deliver books.[42] Miller's plans were ingenious, as Adams had said. He had made excellent use of the sloping signal station site and had provided a very efficient arrangement of interior functions.

Henry Sage now formally announced that he would provide $250,000 for the construction of the building and a $300,000 endowment for book purchases. This was to be repaid him if the University was successful in the Fiske suit. If Sage felt guilty about his handling of the Fiske suit, he gave no sign of it. White was astounded when Sage told him in June 1888 that, "if we lose [the case], we are sure that we have done all in our power to carry out Jennie McGraw's intention."[43]

Adams still preferred Van Brunt's plans and told the Executive Committee that "if the

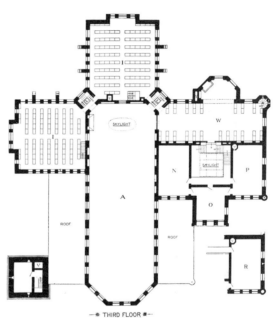

Fig. 133. Library, plan of upper floor: seminar rooms (N), (O), (P) and (R); White Library (W).

matter were his to decide he would select them," but far from being his, it practically belonged to Sage, and therefore Sage's preference should be "all controlling." Later, he

[42] *Report of the Committee on the University Library,* 20 June 1888, typed copy in Trustee Papers.
[43] White, *Diaries,* 13 June 1888.

wrote White that his "encouraging Van Brunt to prepare a general plan for the development of the university was unfortunate" and that some of the Trustees apparently thought he

Fig. 134. Tower of City Hall in Albany, New York, by Henry Hobson Richardson (1882).

was "trying to run away with all earlier plans and consequently that he must be hauled in and kept within bounds." After Adams' reference to the Trustees' "earlier plans," White

made a marginal note on the letter: "They had none." [44]

White now seemed pleased about the outcome—at least he liked the architectural result. He wrote to Fiske in June that Miller's plans were incontestably the finest of those submitted and that Miller had shown genius in his arrangements and in the architectural character of the whole. "The style," he reported, "is Romanesque, the general treatment being first suggested by Richardson in his best buildings at Boston and Cambridge." [45] White might have gone on to mention the debts Miller owed to Richardson's tower in the City Hall (1882) at Albany (Fig. 134) and to the general massing of Van Brunt's design for the library. [46] But White was a gentleman and a good judge of architectural quality. He no doubt was aware of the ingenious inventiveness of Miller's planning, the skillfulness with which he used the slope of the site and the strength and dignity of his composition —a decided improvement over Van Brunt's.

The Miller tower is very slightly attached to a low element of the main building and is much stronger looking and much simpler than Van Brunt's design. Van Brunt's tower (Fig. 131) was jammed against the building at the re-entrant angle of the south and east wings and weakened by being pierced at its base with the main library entrance. While the lack of ornamentation on Miller's tower (Fig. 135) was probably dictated by a tight building budget, its simplicity is much more compatible with the gray buildings of the west row than Van Brunt's. Because the tower is almost detached from the building, it is a stronger element in the composition. To set the tower off further, its masonry was cut narrower and is of a slightly different color

[44] C. K. Adams to M. C. Tyler, 28 October 1888, Tyler Papers; C. K. Adams to ADW, 30 November 1888.
[45] ADW to W. Fiske, 18 June 1888. This was written two days before the Trustees' vote on the final library committee report recommending Miller's plans. The decision obviously was already made.
[46] Henry-Russell Hitchcock, *The Architecture of H. H. Richardson and His Times* (rev. ed., Hamden, Conn., 1961), p. 215.

Fig. 135. Library Tower, renamed McGraw Tower in 1962 when the Miller library building was remodeled for use by undergraduates. The library itself was renamed the Uris Library for Harold D. Uris, whose gift helped to finance the remodeling.

than that of the rest of the building. In the main building the round arch is rather sparingly used (Fig. 135). Arthur N. Gibb, a student of architecture at Cornell when the building was built, decided that the style was "Square Romanesque." [47] The carved ornament was appropriately symbolic. Carved heads on the capitals of the main entry porch columns include "The Four Seasons" on the right and the four great divisions of the globe (Europe, Africa, Asia, and America) on the left (Fig. 136). The small capitals in the north opening of this porch and the carved tympanum of the arch over the north, so-called "women's entrance" are especially beautiful. [48] The initials of Henry W. Sage, Jennie McGraw Fiske, and Andrew D. White are delicately carved in the architrave over the main entrance (Fig. 137). And the essential facts of the University's family feud are inscribed for the ages to read on a bronze plaque within the main entry porch:

THE GOOD SHE TRIED TO DO SHALL STAND AS IF 'TWERE DONE
GOD FINISHES THE WORK BY NOBLE SOULS BEGUN.
IN LOVING MEMORY OF JENNIE McGRAW FISKE WHOSE PURPOSE TO
FOUND A GREAT LIBRARY FOR CORNELL UNIVERSITY HAS BEEN DEFEATED
THIS HOUSE IS BUILT AND ENDOWED BY HER FRIEND
HENRY W. SAGE

1891

The Library's great eastern reading room (66 feet by 166 feet) is the most imposing interior space in the building. It has excellent natural lighting from the twenty-nine windows which rise from a level of eight feet above the floor. These are supplemented by twenty clerestory windows above the low aislelike extensions of the main room. The main elements of library plan (Figs. 132 and 133) are clearly based on the cross form often used in churches with the reading room in the nave and aisles, the main seven-level stack in the choir, the White Library and five-level south stack in the transepts, and the book delivery desk at the altar. The high-ceilinged main room (Fig. 138) is spanned by light iron trusses. Originally this room was very richly

colored with yellow prevailing and the walls above the buff amherstite brick piers in brown and gold. In the White Library the predominant colors were pink and red with a pink marble fireplace. Many of these bright interior touches together with some colorful roofing materials have been lost in various remodeling projects over the years. Originally the main roof was of dark purplish-brown Spanish tiles and the tower roof was covered with cream-colored tiles. But, in general, the building has been treated with respect. Its recent interior remodeling (1961–1962) by Warner, Burns, Toan, and Lunde for use as an undergraduate library retained most of the significant Millerian features, including the intricate cast-iron White Library stacks. The White Library room (Fig. 139), which occupies a space 66 by 23 feet, provided space for 40,000 volumes in its two-storied galleried

[47] Arthur N. Gibb, "The Library Building of Cornell University," unpublished thesis, Cornell University, 1890. Mr. Gibb, who practiced architecture in Ithaca until the 1940's, evaluates the style of the building, and describes the construction and interior finish. He concluded that the style (or lack of it) was not a success, "especially when used for educational purposes." In such a place as a university, he believed it should be "as pure . . . as possible." But on the whole he found this "curious mixture of several transitional styles not unpleasing to the eye." The paper has many photographs of the building under construction and includes an analysis of the light iron trusses of the roof system.

[48] The Library's ornament is very restrained and owes nothing to historical style. The work, especially the style of the heads on column capitals, is comparable to that in the State Capitol in Albany done in the eighties and early nineties during and after H. H. Richardson's and Leopold Eidlitz's regimes as architects there. The names of the sculptors are not known, but it seems probable that some of the same sculptors who worked on the Capitol may have come to Ithaca to do the work on Cornell's library building.

Fig. 136. Library, main entrance, capitals. Carved heads on the left-hand capitals (facing the entry) symbolize the four great divisions of the earth. Shown here are Europe and Asia; America and Africa appear on two other capital faces.

Fig. 137. Library, main entrance. The initials of Andrew D. White, Jennie McGraw Fiske, and Henry W. Sage are delicately carved in medallions in the architrave over the second-story windows. At the left is the periodical room wing. The building is especially notable for its beautifully conceived and expertly executed stone masonry.

stacks. Its upper gallery opened to two seminar rooms on the east, one for European, the other for American history. Another seminar room was provided for the Sage School of Philosophy. It was cleverly slipped in at mid-level between the European history room above and the men's and women's "cloak rooms" below. Below the librarians' rooms, which were on the main level on the west side, were three more seminar rooms then assigned to English, to classical languages, and to French and German. A spacious seminar room for political economy and social institutions was located on this lower level below the periodical room. In all, Miller provided seven seminar rooms and an office for the *Philosophical Review.* A high-ceilinged lecture hall seating nine hundred occupied the space below the main reading room.

The great Library was dedicated at ceremonies on 7 October 1891, twenty-three years to the day after the University was first opened.

Henry Sage spoke first. He described the slow growth of the library from 18,000 volumes in 1869 to 84,000 in 1891. Now, he noted, a library of 30,000 was added by "our late honored President." Sage reminded the audience that John McGraw, who had wanted his fortune to go to Cornell, entrusted it to his only daughter because he knew that she wished to aid Cornell's library as he did. And, he added, had her bequest to the library "been permitted to accumulate without conflict or legal costs," it would then have amounted to more than two million dollars. "Measured by what she tried to do she was by far the greatest benefactor Cornell ever had." But, "all her noble purposes were defeated, and Cornell's hope for a library . . . dashed to the ground!" Sage continued:

Our late president was completely overwhelmed. He has often said he thought it would be his

Fig. 138. Library, main reading room. Catalogues and delivery desk are at the far end of the room. Borrowed light comes from the stack stairs outside the angles at the end of this space. Fluorescent lighting added to this excellent room in the early 1950's did less than one would have expected for the quality of the room. Such as it was, it was dreadful.

death blow . . . when I saw her purposes were in peril I resolved to do what I could to promote and repair them. . . . I was ready to proceed with the construction of this house and to endow it with $300,000, the income to be used only for the purchase of books. I deeply regret that I cannot make it equal to the whole sum lost, but that is impossible. . . .

I have done what I can. . . . It is finished. . . . Jennie McGraw rests with her father in yonder chapel. In full view of it stands and will stand the work I have done, representing a small part only of what she *tried to do,* but could not! [49]

Henry Sage then presented the building and the bronze medallion of Jennie McGraw which is now over its main door. This last, the work of Anne Whitney, Sage thought "a remarkable likeness."

President Adams accepted the building and noted the great number of Sage's other gifts

[49] This and the following quotes from addresses at the dedication of the library are from *Exercises at the Opening of the Library Building* (Ithaca, 1891).

to Cornell (Sage College and Chapel, the School of Philosophy, all endowed) and the excellence of the library gift which fulfilled the two great purposes of such an institution: bringing together sources of information in abundance and making these sources easily accessible to users. The size of Henry Sage's endowment assured accomplishment of the first objective, Adams said, and the skill with which the details of the building were arranged assured the other. "The easy and attractive companionship of books" had at last been provided at Cornell.

"The late" (or Ex-) President White spoke next. He described the growth of the library he now gave Cornell from a small book his father gave him as a boy, "the first I ever looked upon with a sense of ownership," through its increased content of historical works at Yale and in Europe, where he indulged in a "passion for book hunting . . . out of season as well as in season." He described its further increase in works needed for his

Fig. 139. The White Library. Although White's history collection has been disbursed, this is still one of the most delightful rooms in the building. Tasteful remodeling in 1962 left the wrought-iron stacks and added portraits and busts of the first president and his wife. There are striking views of the valley through the west bay window and of McGraw Tower and the first buildings through the great north window.

own historical studies: "a keen hunt carried on in bookshops from Quebec to St. Augustine—from St. Petersburg to Naples—from Edinburgh to Athens—from Constantinople to Cairo" for thirty years in all seasons "all four quarters of the globe [had] thus . . . been laid under contribution." Thus subtly White tells future historians who is responsible for the iconography of the column capitals at the Library entrance. The Ex-President stated his belief that the main means of instruction of men for the future must be a thoughtful study of the past. This had been the formative idea of his collection now given for the use of Cornellians. White had a practical idea for his listeners, too: if they made collections such as his they should remember that the new library was made to keep such treasures for "the highest profit and purest pleasure of future generations of scholars." White expressed his "feeling of deep gratitude

to Jennie McGraw-Fiske [*sic*], and to her friend Henry Williams Sage . . . the man who had provided so perfect and so beautiful a place for the library which had been one of the pleasures of [his] life to accumulate." And finally he said with special pride that the building, designed by a son of Cornell, was such "a marvel of good planning in which fitness is wedded to beauty."

Librarian Harris accepted White's books on behalf of the University commenting that they were "now placed beyond risk of dispersion—that sad fate of so many a noble collection." Harris thought the gifts of the building and its endowment by Sage and the scholarly collection by White had placed the Cornell library "among the great ones of our land" and pledged himself to help make it "one of the great libraries of the world." Harris made good his pledge in the years of his service as Cornell's librarian.

Daniel Coit Gilman, President of Johns Hopkins University, former Yale librarian and White's long-time friend, gave the principal address at the Dedication. It began with a salute to the union of "beauty and utility" which Miller had secured (an example set for American colleges to follow) and continued with a brief but brilliant history of great American and European libraries and the librarians who made them great. This essay deserves republication. To paraphrase it here would be impossible and destructive. Only one of Gilman's references will be repeated: the ideal of Anthony Panizzi, organizer of the British Museum, who said "I would have a public library so complete that a scholar, however rich, will find it a more convenient working place than his own study, however well equipped." Panizzi's ideal must have then seemed a fitting goal for the library of the University whose founder had declared for a place where "any person can find instruction in any study." The new building and endowment, White's library, and the ideals of the men who made these gifts now had established a foundation for seeking knowledge where "the great library will stand." Here, as White remarked, fitness and beauty were joined.

Sage, Adams, and White all were properly pleased by the outcome of their efforts. Each was working in his own way in the best interests of the University. But their sword-crossing could have made a good building and a great library impossible. Fortunately the genius of William Miller came into full play in the design, and high standards had been established for the collection. The building is undoubtedly Miller's masterpiece and Cornell's most significant nineteenth-century building. It is still, and no doubt will be for many years to come, a fitting symbol for the Cornell campus: a magnificent "Romanesque" book house with a very distinguished bell tower whose bell "calls as fly the irrevocable hours."

Within a year after the completion of the Library, William H. Miller was granted a rare

opportunity—the commission to design a building complementing his masterpiece. The State had been forced to pay Cornell $90,000 in improperly withheld service charges on interest payments on the Morrill Act land-grant funds it held in trust. Liberty Hyde Bailey and others insisted that this windfall should be used for the work in Agriculture since the land grant was designed primarily to develop work in this field and the mechanic arts. But the Trustees decided that Cornell's great need at the moment was a building for the Law School, which had been growing rapidly since its establishment in 1887 under Dean Douglass Boardman. President Adams now brought Charles Evans Hughes to the staff. When Judge Boardman died in September 1891, Francis M. Finch was appointed Dean and the Trustees decided to make a major effort to put the school on a more solid basis.[50]

Miller designed a building for the Law School which would complement the new Library structure by closing the south side of the Quadrangle and continuing the mass of the Library's navelike reading room. Boardman Hall (Fig. 140), a simple, massive 200-feet-long three-storied structure, was demolished in 1958 to make room for the construction of the Olin Research Library. The old law school building was a fine neighbor to the Library, quiet and reserved, its only adornment being sculptured heads (some of which are now preserved in the stone walls of the Olin Research Library) and the carved capitals of the colonnettes at the windows and the columns of the entry porch (Fig. 141). In the upper floors of the west end was the law library, an excellent room, which accommodated 40,000 volumes and three hundred readers. It was one of Miller's finest interiors (Fig. 142). Here the widow and daughter of Judge Boardman placed a fine gift to the school, the Moak Law Library, and here Andrew Dickson White placed the portraits of six great jurists: Hugo Grotius, Christian Tomasius, Lord Mansfield, Lord Camden, Chief

[50] Trustees' *Proceedings,* 18 February, 25 April, 21 September 1891.

Fig. 140. Boardman Hall by William H. Miller (1890) with the Library Tower and the main Library, from the Quadrangle. This complement to Miller's great library building extended the massing of the navelike main reading room along the south side of the Quadrangle. Plans of the 1920's called for the extension of the law library located in the upper west end of Boardman Hall along the upper level of an arched gateway to connect Boardman and the Library.

Fig. 141. View from the north loggia, Boardman Hall, showing the main entrance to the Library at the left. President's Avenue and the upper terminal of the trolley line from the village are at the right.

Justice Marshall, and Chancellor Kent. The interior of Boardman Hall was exceptionally spacious. Its three large lecture rooms, court rooms, and offices with fireplaces (never used) were very difficult to surrender when this fine but small building had to give way to provide space where the great library could grow. The new Olin Library, as fine as it is in most respects, does not provide the excellent complement to Miller's library building that was so long a joy for Cornellians. The large and useful new building pays its respects to Stimson Hall, the roof lines of the original buildings and the window proportions, tower roof ornament, and entrance of Miller's building, but it is much too big and insistent to be a thoroughly respectful neighbor.

In the summer of 1892 a strong climber could look down from Cornell's completed Library Tower on two dissimilar campus groups to the north and south and on the now almost half-mile-long faculty row to the east. On the north was the partly completed Quadrangle of gray and red-stone buildings: Morrill, McGraw, White, Franklin, Morse (a brick ringer), Sibley, Lincoln, and Boardman Halls. On the south, among trees now quite mature on the rolling lawns, were the red-brick buildings of the "informal group": Sage College, Sage Chapel, Military Hall and Gymnasium, and Barnes Hall. The tower marked a meeting place of the useful and the beautiful; of the dual ideals of the intellectual and practical men who had done most to build Cornell;

Fig. 142. Boardman Hall, interior. Boardman housed the law library until 1932; after World War II it became the first home of the Collection of Regional History and the University Archives. Law Librarian E. E. Williver is standing in the foreground.

of the formal, regular, traditional, and disciplined hard-edged beauty of the Quadrangle with the informal, irregular, innovative and less-disciplined, soft-edged beauty of the brick group. They met there in the nave of the Library under the shadow of its tower.

X

The Nineties under Schurman

COMPLETION OF THE LI-
brary building at Cornell
marked the end of the Adams era and the
beginning of a period of more rapidly paced
expansion under Jacob Gould Schurman and
Liberty Hyde Bailey. From 1892, when Schurman (Fig. 143) became President, until 1903,
the University's enrollment and physical plant
grew steadily but not spectacularly. Then
Liberty Hyde Bailey, one of the great figures
in the history of the University and of American agriculture, assumed a leading role in
university affairs. After Professor Bailey became Director of the College of Agriculture,
the growth of Cornell and its campus increased rapidly and the institution, its architecture and campus took on some radically
new characteristics.

The 1891–1892 map of the Cornell University campus (Fig. 102) illustrates the extent
of campus development at this point of transition. The partially completed stone Quadrangle included nine major academic buildings
counting the recently completed Library and
Boardman Hall. In addition to these, there
were seven smaller structures north of Sibley
and Franklin Halls: annexes, machine shops,
and the like, a rather untidy collection of
inexpensive one-story structures that had
been built to accommodate overflow from the
very rapidly growing chemistry and physics
departments and the College of Mechanical
Engineering. The "temporary" wooden laboratory had finally been removed from the center of the Quadrangle when the civil engineers and architects moved to Lincoln Hall.
Thirty-five faculty cottages and the President's
villa (the latter occupied intermittently by
the Ex-President) lined the upper side of East
Avenue and the lower side of Central Avenue.
Between these ranks of houses and south of
the Library, Sage Chapel, Barnes Hall, Sage
College, and Military Hall punctuated the
ample grounds of the south campus. The University's estate was only slightly larger than
the original "two hundred acre" farm given it
by Ezra Cornell in 1865. Fifty acres south of
the Library and west of East Avenue purchased from Mary Ann Cornell in 1873 and
three acres purchased from her in 1882 were
the only significant enlargements of Cornell
University's land holdings in Ithaca in
twenty-six years.[1] By 1891 campus development had completely and beautifully transformed Ezra Cornell's farm. Pastures were

[1] Ezra Cornell's original gift of land for the university site appears to have been 207 rather than 200
acres. But he transferred ownership of the south
fifty-plus acres of Lot 167 to his wife. This land lies
between East Avenue and West Avenue and south of
an east–west line bisecting the main reading room of
the undergraduate library. The University bought it
from her when Sage College was built. The three-plus
acres purchased from Mary Cornell in 1882 are located between University Avenue and Fall Creek,
near the Suspension Bridge. They were acquired to
prevent private development along the rim of Fall
Creek Gorge.

now confined to the land above faculty row.

One building indicated on the 1891 campus map in the same black ink as its neighbors was never built. This building, Number 64, is said to be the "College of Agriculture." Charles Babcock had designed it to look like Lincoln Hall from the Quadrangle.[2] It was to be almost an exact duplicate. This was the architectural manifestation of a great and familiar dilemma at Cornell. Enrollment in the College of Agriculture did not justify such a large building but the Morrill Act funds now accruing to Cornell from the sale of unprecedented amounts of western land were designed to promote education in agriculture as well as the mechanic arts. Was agriculture a university subject? If so, was Cornell to build a large building and develop a more extensive educational program with the hope that enrollment in it would increase? In 1891 there were twenty-two undergraduate students in agriculture, half as many graduate students, some "special" students who were not candidates for a degree, and a rapidly growing extension program under the direction of Liberty Hyde Bailey. Bailey, who had joined the faculty in 1888, had not yet begun to work his magic with the New York State Legislature.

During his seven years in office President Adams had done much to improve the caliber of the Cornell faculty. In addition to Bailey, he had been instrumental in bringing to the University Benjamin Ide Wheeler, James Morgan Hart, Carl Becker, and Edward L. Nichols. The adoption of higher admission standards had raised the caliber of students, too. By 1891, Cornell University had achieved economic as well as scholarly success. Her annual income had more than tripled in a decade: from $142,000 in 1881–1882 to $464,000 in 1891–1892. But enrollment had quadrupled in the same period: from 384 to 1537. A year later (1892) the statute requiring women to live in Sage College was repealed. There were 221 women students and the building could no longer contain them. As for the work

[2] Sibley School of Engineering Bulletin, November 1890.

Fig. 143. Jacob Gould Schurman, third President of Cornell, 1892–1920.

in agriculture, no new building was needed, at that time, to contain it. And so, on 30 May 1892, the Trustees decided not to build one. White wrote a bitter entry in his diary: "Mr. Sage forced through his report . . . in favor of abandoning the Agricult. building—they passing it without crossing a t or dotting an i."[3]

In September 1891, shortly after his marriage to his second wife, Helen Magill, daughter of the President of Swathmore College, Andrew D. White had drafted a document called: "A Plan of Development: What Cor-

[3] Trustees' *Proceedings,* 30 May 1892; White, *Diaries,* 30 May 1892. At this meeting of the Trustees, White voted against abandoning the new building for agriculture and against the resolution accepting President Adams' resignation.

nell University Now Needs."[4] Part of this plan was a rather long list of needed buildings. First in priority, White wrote, was a building for agriculture with a museum for implements and the like as the main feature; then more space was needed for Sibley College, "whose success is now imposing a very serious burden on the University"; then Cornell needed "a University Auditorium and Hall for Music" to be "monumental in character . . . in a central position . . . say at the center of the line of buildings forming the west side of the northern quadrangle." A hall of fine arts was listed next followed by a biological and sanitary laboratory between White and McGraw Halls, a Law School building, a medical school in New York City, an observatory, and, surprisingly, Fellows' buildings and dormitories for students. White appears to have been converted (slightly) by President Adams, who thought Cornell should build dormitories so that students could get to and from class more easily and so that the University could gain 6 per cent on the investment.[5] White now favored "small dormitories accommodating fifteen to twenty-five students leased to clubs of students, formed for this purpose and held responsible for each of their members and the good order of the buildings."

Last on White's 1891 list of building needs, but certainly not least, were "public monuments, bridges, gates, and the like."[6] Referring to the new gates at Harvard and the Caius College gates at Cambridge, White asked why Cornell's grounds, "already becoming known throughout the country for their exceeding beauty," could not have enrich-

ment of this sort. He thought Cornell's entrances were "utterly unworthy of the institution and its beautiful campus." In addition to gates at the entries, he thought a "beautiful bridge of stone" might be built across the Cascadilla Gorge.[7] White's dreams of building at Cornell were all to be fulfilled in the next twenty-five years of expansion. He was to see all of them built, although construction of the first one on his list was frustrated by Henry Sage's judgment (probably sound) that the time was not ripe for a new building for agriculture or indeed for any new buildings financed from income funds.

More important matters needed Sage's attention in the interests of the prosperity of Cornell. For one, a new President was to be installed. C. K. Adams, whom Sage seems to have decided was White's surrogate, had been pre-emptorily dismissed late in April 1892. According to a story which Morris Bishop believes authentic, "Sage drove in his buggy to Adams's house [the former Bela McCoon king-sized cottage], summoned him from his lunch, informed him in the vestibule that he was deposed from his office, and drove on, having ruined the President's career and his lunch."[8] On 18 May, Adams' resignation was accepted by the Trustees with one dissenting vote: White's. Then in 1892, Sage's protégé, Jacob Gould Schurman, an eminent Professor of Cornell's Susan Linn Sage School of Philosophy and Editor of the *Philosophical Review*, was unanimously elected third President of the University.

One of the most striking passages in President Adams' last message to the Trustees describes the growth of Cornell's enrollment during his seven years in office. With this growth had come a corresponding growth in the numbers of students exempt from tuition payments. Of a total enrollment of 1,500 in 1891–1892, over six hundred were state scholarship students. Adams made no connection between his pleas for a building for agricul-

[4] A. D. White, MS, "A Plan of Development: What Cornell University Needs," White Papers. In the opening statement White noted that he was writing a "few months less than a quarter century since the first formal meeting of the University Trustees." This would place the date of writing in September 1891.

[5] C. K. Adams, *Annual Report* (1885–1886), p. 36. Adams devoted seven pages of his report to the subject. He proposed a study of the land between Central Avenue and East Avenue south of Morrill Hall as a possible site for dormitories.

[6] White, "A Plan of Development," p. 13.

[7] *Ibid.*, p. 14.
[8] Morris Bishop, *A History of Cornell*, p. 267.

ture, so recently postponed by the Trustees, and the education of New York State students on a tuition-free basis. The bulk of his Annual Report was devoted to an impressive inventory of University achievements during his seven years at Cornell, and concludes with a quote from his Inaugural Address, delivered in 1885, in which he had forecast the "crowning glory of all . . . a great library arising to fulfill the provisions of a noble and *unthwarted* purpose." [9] Henry Sage's blood pressure probably rose a few points when he saw this White-like statement about unthwarted purposes repeated by Adams in June 1892, eight months after the propitiatory library building had been dedicated.

Of course C. K. Adams' career was not really ruined by the struggle with Henry Sage which finally resulted in Adams' departure from Cornell. The fact is that the crowning achievements of his career began a few months after his resignation. He then received and accepted an offer of the presidency from the Trustees of the University of Wisconsin. There, in Madison, he and his second wife, the poetess widow of Alfred S. Barnes, spent fifteen happy and fruitful years. And there C. K. Adams was instrumental in building a third great university library building and in developing the academic excellence of another great university. [10]

During Adams' time of troubles with Henry Sage and White's time of disappointment about the new building for agriculture, the Ex-President and his wife took a "very charming walk behind the library and found a new and very beautiful view of the valley and

lake." [11] They soon conceived the idea of placing a stone seat there so that others might pause to enjoy the view. Later that summer, their year-old daughter Hilda died suddenly. The Whites, who no doubt returned many times that summer to look over the lake valley from the spot they had found behind the new Library, placed a stone seat there (now located between the Library and Morrill Hall) which bears the following inscription:

> To those who shall sit here rejoicing,
> To those who shall sit here mourning,
> Sympathy and greeting;
> So have we done in our time.
> 1892 A.D.W.–H.M.W.

It seems that almost any significant event inspired White to inscribe an appropriate memorial in stone, and Cornell was always richer for it.

President Schurman's list of Cornell's needs was not markedly different from A. D. White's list or, for that matter, C. K. Adams' list, but he did have one revolutionary and successful idea about how the needs should be met. According to Shurman, nothing less than capital appropriations from the State of New York could adequately finance Cornell's expansion. In his 1892–1893 Report to the Trustees he marshaled many logical, statistical arguments to prove his point. There was, for example, the matter of Cornell's education of the holders of state scholarships. Roughly one-third or $150,000 of the annual expenses of the University were chargeable to the cost of education for state scholarship holders. But this was not exact enough for Schurman. After elaborate computations he concluded that: "For the education of State scholars and agricultural students combined the proportionate cost to Cornell University for 1892–93 was $160,138.71." [12]

Schurman's message was, in a sense, documentation and justification for action already accomplished. That winter the State Legislature had recognized Schurman's claims of

[9] *Annual Report* (1891–1892), p. 47.
[10] Charles Foster Smith, *Charles K. Adams.* Smith quotes Benjamin Ide Wheeler's Memorial Address on Adams: "There were many delicate things to be done [at Cornell]. . . . He did them honestly, not always delicately. . . . The Cornell which we know today [1902] was practically the making of those [seven years of Adams' administration]." Wheeler noted that Cornell had grown from a "small college and formless" to an organized University during Adams' administration. Between 1885 and 1892 the enrollment increased from 638 to 1538, the number of graduate students from 61 to 282, the faculty from 38 to 63 (32 of these appointed during Adams' presidency).

[11] White, *Diaries*, 12 June 1892.
[12] *Annual Report* (1892–1893), p. 50.

Fig. 144. Dairy Building (1893) by Charles F. Osborne. The first state-financed building at Cornell, it has now been incorporated as the north wing of Goldwin Smith Hall.

Cornell's right to support from New York by appropriating $50,000 for an agricultural building. Since this was not enough money for the building that had been planned by Professor Babcock, a new design by Professor Osborne was prepared for a building to be erected in stages. Its first increment, the Dairy Building (Fig. 144), was located south of Lincoln Hall and is now the north wing of Goldwin Smith Hall. This location was determined by the need to place the building near Reservoir Avenue so that raw milk could be delivered easily to it from the North Barn.

The Dairy Building's front entrance faced Lincoln Hall, giving it the aspect of a building only tentatively on the Quadrangle, casting a sidelong bovine glance, as it were, at its real home further east near the university pasture. It was ambivalently sited and designed; that is, its location and material recognized the

prestige of being on the Quadrangle and being built of stone but at the same time it was almost expectantly oriented toward the farms to the east. In this attitude its position was prophetic. Professor C. Francis Osborne, the architect of the Dairy Building, was sensitive to the qualities of other buildings on the Quadrangle in this second utilitarian structure of his design on Cornell's campus. The rough-cut ashlar stonework of the first agriculture building is excellent. The proportions and spacing of the windows are in debt to the first buildings of the west row and it pays its respects to the Library and Boardman Hall by use of dentils very similar to theirs under its eaves. The entrance of the Dairy Building seems an even more distant echo. Its delicate-columned, gabled porch looks very like the "Grand Entry" of William H. Miller's McGraw-Fiske mansion. In fact, the Dairy

Building's chief claim to individuality was, perhaps, its red-tiled hip-roof which, in turn, suggested a similar roof form to Carrère and Hastings twelve years later when they incorporated the Dairy Building in Goldwin Smith Hall, although, to be sure, they covered its red roof with gray slate, submerging its little individuality forever.

Osborne's second opportunity to make amends for the disrespect his brick Morse Hall design had shown the stone Quadrangle came in the same year the Dairy Building was started. Hiram W. Sibley, son of the founder of Sibley College, gave Cornell $54,000 for another structure to house the growing classes in mechanical and electrical engineering and a new hydraulic laboratory. Of the 1,700 students enrolled at Cornell in 1893–1894 over six hundred were in Sibley College. Next to the new Law School it was the most rapidly growing part of the University.[13] Director Robert H. Thurston's vigorous new program and the rapidly moving industrialization of the country made Sibley College one of the University's most successful departments. There was little difficulty in arriving at a decision about where the new Sibley College building should be located. In 1886, Hiram Sibley had asked Archimedes Russell to prepare a plan for the future growth of the College, and it had been approved by Mr. Sibley before his death in 1888. The new east wing was almost an exact repeat of West Sibley on the Quadrangle side. Its east end and the north side, facing University Avenue, however, were built of yellow brick; the intention then being to complete a quadrangle with a stone exterior and a yellow brick interior extending eastward, turning northward, then west along the Avenue. East Sibley Hall (Fig. 145) was completed in 1894.

President Schurman had been active in his pleas for funds in the State Legislature, and in 1894 an appropriation of $150,000 was made for the "completion of laboratories, museums, hospitals, and other structures in-dispensable to the State Veterinary College." The Trustees authorized the location of the new State College on Cornell grounds with the proviso that New York State appropriate sufficient funds for equipment and maintenance.[14] C. Francis Osborne was the architect for the Veterinary College buildings, a utilitarian assemblage consisting of one principal building with the college offices, museum, laboratories, and lecture rooms and seven other buildings which housed in turn: a ward for sick animals and another for healthy ones, an operating theatre, a mortuary building, a detention shed, a cottage for the stud groom, and a forge. In 1895–1896 the College was built near the farm fields east of East Avenue and south of the Ex-President's house. Finally, after numerous requests and resolutions of the Board of Trustees, Dr. Law had the facilities he needed for instruction and research in veterinary science.

The last of these first Veterinary College buildings, the main building, was demolished in 1959 when the School of Industrial and Labor Relations took over the newer buildings of the Veterinary College and added some new ones of its own. Previous to this (in 1953) a complete new campus for the Veterinary College was built at the east end of Tower Road. The original buildings, on East Avenue, were an unimpressive lot. The program required numerous small one-story structures reminiscent of Frederick Law Olmsted's suggestions for the Massachusetts Agricultural and Mechanic Arts College buildings in 1866. They were built of brick: light yellow pressed brick and terra cotta on the façades of the main building, three stories in height, and common yellow brick elsewhere. The main building was sited behind a park 140 feet deep, half of which is now a parking lot. They all were very economically constructed. President Schurman reported that their ornamentation was limited to "such portions of the principal building as are clearly important when viewed from East

---

[13] *Annual Report* (1893–1894), p. 16.

[14] Trustees' *Proceedings,* 29 September, 2 October, 13 November 1894, and 13 November 1895.

Fig. 145. East Sibley Hall by Charles F. Osborne (1894). On the Quadrangle side an unabashed copy of West Sibley Hall, it is marked "to be continued" by yellow brick walls on the east and west ends.

Fig. 146. James Law Hall (1894), by Charle F. Osborne, was named for Cornell's first professor of veterinary medicine, White's Scotch horse doctor. In the foreground are the cottages of Professor Horatio White (left) and Robert H. Thurston (right).

Avenue; strict plainness being the rule elsewhere." [15] These were efficient and useful but not very good-looking buildings (Fig. 146). Their loss was not a great one.

Another utilitarian project undertaken about this time was the construction of a hydraulic laboratory in the Fall Creek Gorge at Triphammer Falls. This provided, according to reports of the time, a laboratory building set at the foot of the falls and elaborate provisions for supplying water for the various experiments conducted within it. Topographic conditions for the development of such a laboratory were excellent and it was, perhaps, the finest university hydraulic laboratory in the country.

Late in the summer of 1895, Andrew Dickson White returned from one of his numerous journeys to Europe. He was shocked to find that Henry Sage had decided that the Ex-President would have to leave his "President's House" on the campus. White, deeply hurt, began a campaign to secure the renewal of his lease from the Trustees. This last struggle between White and Sage was very bitter but it had a significant and perhaps symbolic resolution in the summer of 1896 after the Trustees unanimously approved the renewal of White's lease. For sometime the Ex-President had nagged everyone about the appearance of the south entrance to the University at Cascadilla Gorge. Now, in the spring of 1896, Henry Sage's son, William H. Sage, asked William H. Miller to prepare plans for improving this entrance. Sage purchased additional land south of The Cascadilla to straighten up the property line. Miller designed a new roadway closer to the gorge bank, an entrance gate at the end of Eddy Street, and a new stone-arched bridge across the gorge. According to Schurman, "Within 20 days . . . A. D. White, to whom the aesthetic interests of the University have always strongly appealed, came forward with a gift for the erection of the gateway." [16] William Henry Sage made a gift

Fig. 147. Stone arched bridge over Cascadilla Gorge, 1896.

of the stone arched bridge, which still serves Cornell well at the main south entrance to the campus (Fig. 147). The gateway, west of Cascadilla Hall (Fig. 148), is sometimes referred to as "Andy White's chocolate layer cake," because it is built of alternate courses of white Ohio sandstone and reddish brown Berea limestone. The union of white stone and red stone in the gateway seems, in a quaint way, symbolic of William Sage's desire for a cease-fire in the warfare between his father and Andrew D. White. The red and white horizontally striped composition, uniting in the building material the colors most

[15] *Annual Report* (1894–1895), p. 39.

[16] Schurman, *Annual Report* (1895–1896), pp. 74–75. Schurman fails to note that White had proposed such an entrance in his "Plan of Development . . ." in 1891. The gate is not dearly loved by motorists who use this "back door" to the campus from Eddy Street. Morris Bishop reports that Charles H. Hull frankly called it hideous. The antiquarian and anti-automobile fanatic would let it be; or, at most, remove the road; or perhaps relocate the stones to widen the gate.

Fig. 148. White Gateway at the north end of Eddy Street, by William H. Miller (1896), was locally known as "Andy White's chocolate layer cake."

liked by the Trustees' Chairman and the Ex-President, in one way at least brings their architectural ideas together at last.

White, naturally, thought of appropriate inscriptions for the gate: the one on the west wing reads: "So enter that daily thou mayest become more learned and thoughtful. So depart that daily thou mayest become more useful to thy country and to mankind"; and on the east wing: "The Lord bless thy going out and thy coming in from this time forth for ever more." Over the opening between the gate piers is an elaborate wrought-iron arch. In recent years, when the demolition of the gateway was proposed in order to provide greater road width, it was suggested that a more respectful solution to the problem might be achieved by moving one or both of the piers and making a longer wrought-iron arch. If improvements are contemplated there, such an expenditure seems worthwhile in the interest of preserving this reminder of the Sage-White feuds and White's fine sentiment about the entrance to the University.

The reversal of White's policies on student housing at Cornell was not as easily achieved as the integration of the favorite building-stone colors of White and Henry Sage. President Schurman continued to issue pleas for gifts of dormitories.[17] Adams had tried to reverse White's policy on such buildings, too, in his first annual report in 1886. But Adams' and Schurman's urgings that some benefactor of the University erect dormitories were in vain. In spite of this failure, some of the University's student housing problems were solved in 1891 when the Ithaca Street Railway, the second electric trolley line in the country, was extended up East Hill and across Cascadilla Gorge on its own wooden bridge to a point near Military Hall. In addition to affording magnificent vistas, this new facility enabled students living in the village to get back and forth between their rooms and boarding houses in the town and the campus with much-appreciated ease (Fig. 148). At first the Trustees would not permit the extension of the line across the campus.[18] However, the advantages of more direct service were so great that in 1896 the line was extended along East Avenue with a shuttle parallel to Boardman Hall in front of the Library. After the turn of the century when Cornell Heights was developed, the line was extended farther along East Avenue, across Triphammer Bridge, and down Thurston Avenue to Stewart Avenue to form a loop back to State Street. The indefatigable Professor Anthony was the guiding light in the development of the trolley system. It was a typically integrated land-and-transportation-development scheme much like the surburban land company-trolley line corporations organized about this time in many major cities. But, while the extended trolley system opened new land for the construction of faculty cottages and fraternity houses on the north side of Fall Creek, it did not provide a long-term solution to the stu-

[17] *Annual Report* (1895–1896), p. 74.
[18] Trustees' *Proceedings*, 3 May 1892, 28 February, 4 and 14 March 1893. In March 1893 the Board decided by a vote of ten to two against extending the line across the campus.

dent housing problem. President Schurman continued to press the University's friends for gifts for the construction of dormitories near the campus.

In the nineties and the first two decades of the twentieth century most of the men students at Cornell lived in town or in fraternity houses. As enrollment grew, more apartments and rooming houses were created by construction and conversion in the areas south and west of the campus. Ithaca's population increased, too, and in 1888, the village secured its charter as a city. Still, most of its streets remained unpaved until the advent of the automobile. Ithaca's State Street, the main shopping and amusement area, was first paved in 1890 (Fig. 149). The Wilgus Opera House on State Street was replaced by Rothschild's Department Store, and the Lyceum, with its moving floor, became the favorite theatre for vaudeville and more serious entertainment downtown.

With the new charter and powers available to it as a city, Ithaca began a series of major improvements which culminated in the draining and filling in of the last swamps remaining along the southern shore of Cayuga Lake. After the trolley line was extended across Fall Creek Gorge in 1901, the area to the north of the campus developed rapidly. Here were built the fraternity houses of the 1910's and 1920's and here many of the faculty, gradually dispossessed of their cottages on East Avenue, built their new homes.

On East Hill, the development of the campus (Fig. 150) and Sibley College continued with another gift of Hiram Sibley's son, this one for the construction of a tower between East and West Sibley which was to provide a large auditorium in which all students of the

Fig. 149. State and Tioga Streets about 1895. Ithaca's streets were first paved in the 1890's. The Wilgus Opera House by then housed the Rothschild Brothers' Department Store on the ground floor and the Ithaca Conservatory of Music above. The latter grew to become Ithaca College, which in 1966 had an enrollment of over 3,000 and a new campus "higher above Cayuga's waters" on South Hill. Jane McGraw's mansion may be seen at the left beyond the south end of Tioga Street.

Fig. 150. Cornell University buildings, 1898.

College could be assembled, and a museum for the numerous models of machinery which had been collected for use in instruction. Again, there was no problem in siting the new improvement—a tower had been contemplated as a culminating feature for the Sibley group which, in turn, would complete the north side of the great stone Quadrangle. Arthur N. Gibb ('91) was the architect. Gibb had assisted Osborne in planning the Morse Hall chemistry laboratories. He was later to be the principal architect for the laboratories and interior of Baker Hall. During the planning of the new Sibley addition, Gibb came to the conclusion that the tower form originally proposed was not suitable for the large interior space of the auditorium. And so he designed Sibley Dome, the only major manmade campus landmark that is not a tower.

The new Sibley addition (Figs. 151 and 152) is more strictly classical in design than the adjacent wings. We may assume that Gibb designed it on the same principle by which he had criticized William H. Miller's library building, namely, that the style of an academic building should be "as pure as possible." Again economy was stressed, and the rear portion of the Sibley Dome addition was built of brick, now somewhat unhappily exposed to view by the demolition of the Sibley

shops north of it. The dome was fireproof, thus following, in general, the scheme which Andrew D. White regularly put forward for inserting fireproof buildings between the older buildings of the stone Quadrangle. The idea still suggests a simple and effective way of providing additional floor area when it is needed in the colleges around Cornell's Arts Quadrangle.

Another of William Miller's buildings was added to the south end of the Arts Quadrangle in 1900. In that year Dean Sage gave the University funds for a building for the "Ithaca Division of the Medical College." Miller again demonstrated his great architectural talent by designing a building in a style different from that of its neighbor and yet which respected its principal architectural features. In the case of Stimson Hall this was a difficult problem. The Medical College's space requirements were substantial. The building had almost twice the floor area of Boardman Hall, its western neighbor, and was sited on a level some fifteen feet above the Law School. Stimson Hall (Fig. 153) was built of the same gray sandstone as the Law School and the Library. A strong horizontal string course above the ground floor lined up with the eaves line of Boardman Hall. Below this the walls were of rusticated stone with small windows;

Fig. 151. Sibley Hall with Sibley Dome (1902), an addition by Arthur N. Gibb. This central link now houses the Fine Arts Library and the administrative offices of the College of Architecture, which has occupied the remodeled Sibley group since 1959.

Fig. 152. The Quadrangle, White Hall, Sibley Dome, and East Sibley, about 1910.

Fig. 153. Stimson Hall (1903) by William H. Miller, Boardman Hall, the main Library, President's Avenue, and Morrill Hall.

Fig. 154. Stimson Hall from the northeast. The building, a gift of Dean Sage, son of Henry Sage, housed the Cornell Medical School so long as instruction was offered in Ithaca as well as in New York.

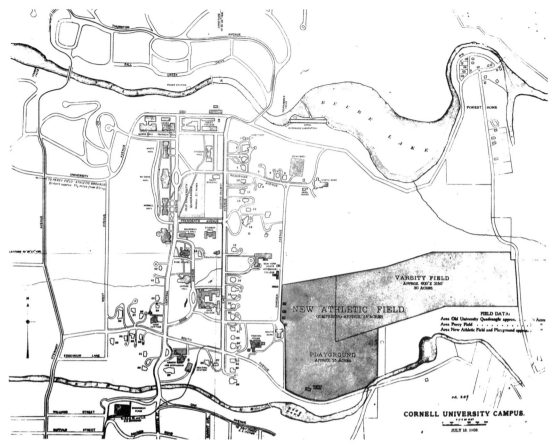

Fig. 155. Map of the Cornell campus, 1903.

above it was a smooth stone wall with a great expanse of very large windows (Fig. 154).

After paying these external respects to its neighbor, Miller proceeded to design a thoroughly functional interior which was beautifully lighted and more flexible than any building previously erected on the campus. For example, the northern side of the second floor is arranged as one large room extending the whole length of the building. Its 160-feet-long space is easily divided into various-sized laboratories and offices with nonstructural partitions. The building was designed to provide for one-half of the space needs contemplated by the Medical School in Ithaca. The service court on the south was eventually to be in the middle of an enclosed court formed by this first U-shaped building and a similar unit to the south. At the time Tower Road had not

been conceived of, and the size of the Medical School development contemplated in Ithaca was much greater than that which finally took place. Miller demonstrated in Stimson Hall that he could design a simple functional building respecting historical styles but free of eclecticism. Its pleasing proportions, the strong rhythms of its window spacing, and the excellence of the interior rooms make Stimson Hall one of the University's most distinguished and useful buildings.

The first decade of President Schurman's administration at Cornell were years of consolidation and re-evaluation. The excellent faculty assembled by President Adams was enlarged and strengthened. The professional schools of law and medicine were established. The student body continued to grow. Graduate work was strengthened. The policy of the

State of New York in regard to financial support of Cornell was reshaped and the University became thereby more public, less private, and more prosperous.

On the campus these achievements and changes were reflected in a number of new buildings and improvements (Fig. 155). Better connections with the community were provided by the street railway; Boardman Hall was completed and occupied—to the delight of the space-pinched law faculty and students; Sibley College was doubled in area; the Medical School in Ithaca was handsomely housed; and two new buildings for instruction in agriculture were built. These last portended new directions for Cornell. The yellow brick buildings of the Veterinary College on East Avenue were, by their location and color, especially good forecasts of things to come in State College architecture, in the growth of research, instruction, and extension in agriculture, and in the expansion of the campus.

XI

Expansion Begins

IT HAS BEEN SAID THAT chance often has much to do with the course of the affairs of an individual or an institution. Such was the case with Cornell in the financing of one of its first turn-of-the-century buildings. On 29 July 1900 Andrew D. White, who had just completed the first half of a seven-year term as U.S. Ambassador to Germany, boarded the *Deutschland* at Cuxhaven to return home. At his table he found Mr. and Mrs. John D. Rockefeller and young Mr. Rockefeller. He found their company delightful. Mr. Rockefeller gave him "some details as to his way of bestowing money on sundry charitable and educational institutions." It seems probable that White might have mentioned some of Cornell's needs to Mr. Rockefeller, although he surely was not so undiplomatic as to mention them on this first meeting. He spent considerable time with the Rockefellers during the voyage and found that he liked Mr. Rockefeller "better and better the more I see of him." Less than a year later, in May 1901, John D. Rockefeller gave the University $250,000 for the construction and maintenance of a new building for the Physics Department, with the condition that the University raise an equal amount for other construction.[1]

President Schurman found it difficult to meet the condition. Early in 1902 he wrote to White complaining that Andrew Carnegie, with whom White had been negotiating about a gift for Cornell, was doing nothing and was absorbed in other affairs.[2] He was, in fact, absorbed in the creation of the Carnegie Institute at the suggestion of Andrew D. White. After several months of indecision and no favorable word from White, the Trustees decided that they would match the Rockefeller gift themselves by financing a new building

[1] White, *Diaries,* 29 July and 3, 5 August 1900. ADW to Schurman, 11 June 1901, White Papers. "The plan as it developed itself in my mind before I saw your presentation of the needs of the Depart-

ments of Physics and of Languages was to propose a building for an auditorium and adjacent halls on a line with the Civil Engineering building, but south of the Dairy building thus forming the eastern boundary of the large upper stone quadrangle and then to divide the great quadrangle thus made into two, running from the east side of the campus to the west, thus giving the long line of drafting rooms with a northern exposure, so much needed by Civil Engineering and Architectural departments. But if money is to be given to you to erect a great building for a Department of Physics I see no place for it except in that same situation, namely a building running from the southwest corner of the Civil Engineering building to the northeast corner of the McGraw building. I would be glad to know where you propose to put your Physical building in case you can get it, for it seems likely that we are to be greatly embarrassed by lack of a proper site."

[2] Schurman to ADW, 24 May 1902, White Papers. Schurman wrote that he was finding great difficulty matching Rockefeller's gift. "This seems to me a very appropriate time to strike Mr. C. . . . There is no one interested in Cornell University who has so much influence with Mr. Carnegie as you have. You have under authority of the Board authority to receive gifts to Cornell University arising in Europe."

for the "academic department." They voted to spend $50,000 of income funds for five years for this purpose.[3] At the same time the University was seeking state funds for additional buildings for agriculture. So, in 1902, the active building proposals were three: buildings for physics, the "academic department," and agriculture.

White suggested sites for two of the new buildings to President Schurman in the spring of 1902. He thought the physics building might bisect the stone Quadrangle, running parallel to Sibley Hall between the south ends of White Hall and Lincoln Hall. He thought the new agriculture buildings should be sited in flanking positions west of the Veterinary College to form a court. President Schurman soon found that Professor Nichols, head of the Physics Department, objected to a Quadrangle site for the physics building. He thought it too near the electric trolley line, which would interfere with his electrical experiments. Nichols wanted the building to be sited on the hill above the Quadrangle on the east side of East Avenue where Professors Hewett and Law had their cottages.[4] The electric trolley issue was to bedevil the decision on the location of the physics building for over a year while the architects made plan after plan for the Quadrangle site.

At first Schurman agreed with White on the location of Rockefeller Hall in the Quadrangle to create two smaller quadrangles but he believed in using experts, so he called in Thomas Hastings of Carrère and Hastings to advise him on the location and design of the new physics building. Hastings' visit was a great success. With President Schurman he devoted the entire day to walking around the campus, measuring off spaces, "his imagination fairly teeming with ideas." Hastings liked White's idea of building across the Quadrangle, but Schurman now thought this prominent site should be reserved for the "academic departments" building. Schurman also began to hear complaints about the location of an agricultural building on the Quadrangle. Babcock had planned one there in 1890 and Osborne had sketched a southern extension of his Dairy Building in 1895. Now both the faculty of agriculture and the faculty of the academic departments believed a building for agriculture should be nearer the farm, perhaps where White suggested next to the Veterinary College, where it "would not be out of sight of the campus."[5]

During his visit to Cornell in June 1902, Hastings also proposed a site for the auditorium which the Trustees, White, and Schurman had been discussing for some years. Hastings proposed it be located on the present site of Day Hall at the intersection of Tower Road and East Avenue, and he proposed that a new gymnasium, which was now also needed, be combined with the auditorium building as had been done at Columbia. Schurman was delighted with Hastings' suggestions. He wrote White: "For ten years I have been thinking a good deal about the development of the campus and discussing it in board meetings and committee meetings. . . . I got better ideas from Hastings during his brief stay than from all the deliberations we have had hitherto on the subject."[6]

The Trustees soon authorized Schurman to select an architect for the new physics building, and he immediately chose Carrère and Hastings. Hastings agreed to bring a general plan for the campus to the June meeting of the Board of Trustees. His ability and willingness to prepare a campus plan in such a short time seems to have pleased and impressed President Schurman. The President noted that Hastings believed that location, grading, flagging, and relation to other buildings and to

[3] Trustees' *Proceedings*, 30 September 1902. Bishop states in *A History of Cornell* (p. 361) that "seven well-wishers" matched Mr. Rockefeller's gift.

[4] Schurman to ADW, 25 February 1902. Schurman Letterbooks, X, 442–447. Schurman thought White's arguments against Professor Nichols' choice of a site for the physics building stated the case "most strongly." He read White's letter (14 May 1902) to the Trustees and they rejected Nichols' proposal.

[5] Schurman to ADW, 14 June 1902, Schurman Letterbooks, XI, 45–51.
[6] *Ibid.*, p. 49.

the campus as a whole were all as essential conditions in the mind of the architect as the purposes for which the building itself was to be built. "For the first time," Schurman wrote, "we shall have an architect who will look at our campus as a whole and study the relation of part to part." The President thought this a good omen for Cornell's architectural future.

Hastings' approach, Schurman wrote, was a special feature with all architects who studied at the Ecole des Beaux Arts.[7] This was so, yet Hastings, like others so trained, sometimes used the overall approach learned in Paris in a way which tended to destroy the inherent landscape qualities of a site and the character of previous improvements. Lacking the access to almost absolute and extended control, often available to French architects, the Americans were capable, perhaps unintentionally, of defiling sites (which should have developed gradually and variously) with a rigidly imposed order which could only be partially achieved.

The Cornell Trustees approved Hastings' ideas for a physics building to be located in an east-west position across the Quadrangle. President Schurman proceeded with the work of assisting him in the preparation of plans, commenting rather casually to White that he believed Sibley would not object to an east-west building across the Quadrangle. He could not foresee, at this juncture, that Sibley would finally change all of their plans by his objections. Sibley had not attended the June Trustees' meeting at which Hastings' plans were presented and apparently was not directly consulted about the decision.[8] On 25

[7] *Ibid.*, p. 31.
[8] *Ibid.*, 13 October 1902. Schurman writes eloquently of the similarity of Hastings' proposal to divide the Quadrangle to the quadrangles of the colleges at Oxford. Both Schurman and White seem to have forgotten the long-standing plan to have a large Quadrangle of stone on the lower campus. And it did not seem to occur to them that Sibley might object to the diminution of the space fronting the College named for him. In this letter Schurman also makes known his determination to increase Cornell's land holdings.

October 1902, Hastings presented the plans for the new building and a more elaborate general plan for the campus to the Trustees. The Executive Committee voted their thanks to Hastings for his "generous donation of a Plan of General Development" (Fig. 156) and approved it and the location in the Quadrangle he proposed for Rockefeller Hall.

Hastings' plan was an attempt to bring the entire campus into a very formal arrangement. The plan was also the first to visualize the extent to which Cornell would grow in coming generations. Unfortunately, because Hastings was dedicated to axial planning, topography was largely disregarded and roads were proposed for impossibly steep grades and monumental widths. His plan did, however, contain some workable ideas for dividing the Quadrangle. The spaces created by its proposals would have been well proportioned, small quadrangles and courts providing striking contrasts to the distant vistas of the valley from the west front of the campus, but Cornell would have lost the spacious excellence of its Arts Quadrangle, one of the most beautiful university spaces in America.

At first Hastings' site for the physics building seemed acceptable, but the faculty of the academic department did not like his proposal that their new building be placed above East Avenue south of Reservoir Avenue. Many of them complained to President Schurman that the site was inconspicuous. They also thought it too closely associated with the technical departments; the over-all campus plan indicated a future wing of Sibley College dangerously near the new academic department building; and it was too distant from the Library. Some of the professors wanted their building adjacent to the Library on the west slope where Hastings had indicated some possible future buildings in his general plan. Several suggested that it might even be connected directly to the Library. Schurman, being a philosopher, philosophized as follows: "I find . . . wherever this or any other building is located there are certain to be objections. The problem is to find a location

Fig. 156. Carrère and Hastings' general plan for the Cornell campus, 1902. The plan was prepared by Thomas Hastings as a gift to the University during the site selection and preliminary design phases for Rockefeller and Goldwin Smith Halls. (1) Sibley Hall; (2) Lincoln Hall; (3) Dairy Building; (4) Franklin Hall; (5) White Hall; (6) McGraw Hall; (7) Morrill Hall; (8) Library; (9) Sage Chapel; (10) Boardman Hall; (11) Stimson Hall; (12) Old President's House; (13) Barnes Hall; (14) Sage College; (15) Armory; (16) Cascadilla Place.

open to the fewest objections." [9] Professor Nichols now, after further study, objected to the connection of the physics building to Lincoln Hall (Fig. 156). He was sure that tremors from the civil engineers' machines would interfere with the delicate experiments of his department. President Schurman immediately agreed with Nichols that the new building could not touch Lincoln Hall, and so instructed Hastings.[10] The President seemed to change his mind easily in the discussion on these buildings, responding almost instantly and automatically to any reasonable suggestion.

On another matter of great importance to

the future of the campus, Schurman moved decisively. He had become concerned about the extent of Cornell's future land requirements after his first discussions with Hastings. So in November 1902, he urged the Trustees to purchase additional land west of West Avenue from Franklin C. Cornell.[11] Mr. Cornell

[9] Schurman to Hastings, 20 October 1902, Schurman Letterbooks, XI, 224.

[10] *Ibid.*, 5 and 6 November 1902, XI, 297–299, 310.

[11] The Cornell family was one of the principal financial beneficiaries of the University's expansion policies after 1902. The following list shows the total amount paid Ezra Cornell and his descendants for land adjacent to the campus:

Land Acquired from Cornell Family 1873–1926

	Date	Acres	Price
Ezra Cornell, s. of Library	2/20/73	50.00	$ 38,700
Ezra Cornell, Fall Creek,			
n. of Sibley	10/13/74	5.90	500

had subdivided sixteen acres of his land there into lots and had started advertising them for sale. Schurman thought this land would not be needed for fifty years or more, but he was convinced that its purchase and reservation would be a wise policy. Thirteen years later the first units of the men's dormitories were built there. Schurman reported his success in gaining approval for the land acquisition to White. In the same letter he sent a copy of the Trustee-adopted Hastings plan, commenting that the *Cornell Alumni News* clipping he enclosed made it unnecessary to describe its features. He then proceeded with a seven-page description of its features: it respected existing conditions (only three faculty residences were to be demolished), the agricultural building group was to be as White had

Land Acquired from Cornell Family (*cont.*)

	Date	Acres	Price
Mary Ann Cornell, s/s Fall Creek Suspension Bridge	6/1/82	3.05	5,000
F. C. Cornell, between Stewart and West Avenues	11/24/02	14.00	73,266
F. C. Cornell, Beebe Lake	6/29/03	37.00	5,500
F. C. Cornell, e/s Snyder Hill Road	7/8/14	9.11	1,024
F. C. Cornell, s/s Snyder Hill Road	7/8/14	4.41	496
F. C. Cornell, e/s Pine Tree Road	7/8/14	13.17	1,481
F. C. Cornell, e/s Pine Tree Road	7/8/14	4.86	547
F. C. Cornell, w/s Pine Tree Road	7/8/14	11.43	1,285
F. C. Cornell, w/s Pine Tree Road	7/8/14	56.90	6,399
F. C. Cornell, w/s Pine Tree Road	7/8/14	11.60	1,305
Charles Cornell and others, Fall Creek e and w of Stewart Avenue Bridge	4/1/20	10.40	5,000
F. C. Cornell, Collegetown boundary and Food Storage Area	11/17/22	1.07	6,250
F. C. Cornell, Stewart and West Avenues	6/7/26	6.90	200,000
Total sum paid to Cornells			$346,747

Source: "Cornell University: Lands and Buildings, June 30, 1963."

suggested, the physics building was to be located across the Quadrangle as White had suggested, "plastic arts" could be located in one flanking wing of the arts buildings above East Avenue, and provisions had been made for the extension of Sibley College across East Avenue to the knoll where faculty cottages were then located.

Schurman also reported that the alumni had petitioned for a "playground of twenty acres to be taken from the farm back of [White's] stable" southward to Cascadilla Gorge.[12] President Schurman was concerned about the resulting decrease in university farm acreage and began negotiation to purchase several farms east of the campus to replace the land to be used for a "playground." Some of the professors of agriculture must have felt threatened by all of these incursions on their domain. Not only was there the suggestion that they be gently nudged out of the Quadrangle, but also much of their farm land further east was about to be taken for sports. But the great expansion of Cornell was beginning and Agriculture's time of growth was soon to come. In an imperialistic era the University was acting imperialistically. In the following decade the University acquired over 700 acres of land, reserving land for its future growth which surely would have been at least partially developed in private uses had no action been taken.

In the last months of 1902, President Schurman began working out the detailed program for the new academic department building with the help of the department heads. Then, early in December, a very disturbing letter arrived from Hiram Sibley objecting vigorously to the location of the new physics building in front of Sibley College. Sibley felt that

[12] Schurman to ADW, 24 November 1902, Schurman Letterbooks, XI, 373–379. White objected strongly to the location of a "playfield" south of his house. Schurman thought White had overstated "the danger of tramps." Schurman's land policy was very ambitious. In this letter to White he wrote that he wanted "to expand the University Estate gradually to Varna [three miles east of the Quadrangle] taking the streams on each side as our natural boundaries."

the effect was to "belittle the College." Schurman referred the matter to the Executive Committee which in turn recommended to the Trustees that they abandon the proposed physics building site "if Sibley's views remained unchanged." They urged him to come to Ithaca to discuss the issue on the ground. Schurman wrote Sibley an eleven-page brief defending the Quadrangle site for the physics building and explaining that the architects had been careful to respect the Sibley College buildings by keeping the new physics building low, by providing an arched entrance from the proposed south quadrangle on axis with Sibley Dome, and by providing for future expansion of Sibley College to the east. Schurman urged Sibley to come to Ithaca to see for himself.[13]

In spite of Schurman's efforts, Sibley remained opposed to the proposed development. Schurman reported his troubles to White: "a new complication arises just after everything is complete . . . [it] has upset us completely." The President telegraphed Carrère and Hastings to stop all work on plans. He was alarmed at the implication that any donor of a building might insist that the ground in front of it be left forever open. What would happen, for example, he wrote, "if Dean Sage insisted that the land in front of Stimson Hall be kept open." If that happened, the Quadrangle never would be completed. He suggested that the University defer to Mr. Sibley on the location of the physics building but reserve its proposed site for the eventual construction of an addition to Sibley College. Schurman, a shrewd strategist, was certain that Sibley's opposition and the Trustees'

deference to his wishes had delayed construction of the physics building for at least another year, but he fought hard to retain university control of decisions on the location of buildings. He asked White if it was not his or Ezra Cornell's plan to have two east-west buildings across the Quadrangle dividing it into three quadrangles. If so, where were the buildings to be built?[14]

By February 1903, the impasse on the location of Rockefeller Hall seemed finally solved when Hastings presented a revised plan for a building parallel to and east of White and McGraw Halls which, with Lincoln Hall, would form a symmetrical court centered on Sibley College (Fig. 157). It seems that Mr. Sibley approved this compromise.[15] Meanwhile, White had been away from his home base at Alassio, Italy, on a trip to Corsica. When he returned to Alassio, he found Schurman's letter reporting the compromise solution. While he seemed very upset at the turn of events, his suave diplomacy did not fail him. He reported to Schurman that he was sure it never occurred to Ezra Cornell that the

[13] Schurman to Sibley, 9 December 1902, Schurman Letterbooks, XI, 443–453. In this very detailed statement the President mustered every argument he could think of to defend the decision. He cites White's suggestion for an east-west building across the Quadrangle and states that White's advice and Hastings' plan influenced him greatly. He cites his defense of Sibley College against "Agriculture's charge" that it is expanding too much. And he describes the long search for other sites for the physics building as well as the great thought and care that went into siting the physics building in relation to Sibley College.

[14] Schurman to ADW, 24 January 1903, Schurman Letterbooks, XI, 631–635. White had prepared some plans of his own from time to time. He had described them to Schurman (ADW to Schurman, 9 February 1898): "It seems to me that pains should be taken first as to the sites of these buildings [dormitories] and that they should be brought into proper relations with existing buildings so as to complete as far as possible the general effect of large squares and quadrangles in obedience to a university tradition founded upon practical as well as aesthetic considerations. I once went so far as to take the plan of the campus and to put upon it a number of papers carefully given to scale representing such buildings. No doubt Mr. Burr could find it for you if you are looking for it. It might afford you some suggestions." And (ADW to Schurman, 9 February 1900): "The blue print with indications of future buildings to which you refer is I think in the little document room opening out of the library at the Old President's House and I will immediately ask that it be hunted up and placed in your hands. It was the result of much thought on the subject and I should be exceedingly glad to have you glance over it. Its purpose was to range our buildings in appropriate courts and quadrangles which would be most conducive to the interests of the various departments and effective architecturally."

[15] Schurman to Hastings, 6 February 1903, Schurman Letterbooks, XII, 2–3.

Quadrangle would ever be divided by buildings running east and west: "I do not think he ever dreamed this was desirable or possible." White indeed had "thought of such a line" (and a second line extending east from the space between McGraw and Morrill Halls). After reflecting on the matter, especially in view of Mr. Sibley's objections, he suggested that they study other sites: east of Garden Avenue (where the Agriculture College quadrangle was built a few years later) or the west side of Central Avenue where Professor Prentiss' cottage stood. (The Prentiss Cottage later became Sage Cottage, and still later, the University Club; the Campus Road now runs through the spot.) He thought a fine brick building in the "Romanesque style" would go quite nicely there and would be compatible with Barnes Hall and the "informal group." Either plan, White noted, would "adjourn indefinitely the running of buildings across the Quadrangle, which adjournment, I think, all of us would rejoice at." [16] In a draft of this letter which is in the White Papers, the Ex-President crossed out the last two words of this sentence which had ended: "I think all of us must regret" and substituted the words "would rejoice at." He was that close to continuing his support for an ultimate division of the great Quadrangle.

White wrote Schurman that he had tried to convert himself to the idea of east-and-west building across the Quadrangle and had for a time succeeded, but in view of the "impressive building which Mr. Sibley has given us," his old doubts and misgivings had returned. The Ex-President requested that they postpone any decision on new buildings until the annual Trustees' meeting in June. He would like to be there and he hoped Mr. Sibley would be present, too. He had some ideas on the resolution of their debate and sent some sketches, asking that Schurman cable him about the site decisions either "deferred" or "not deferred." [17]

[16] ADW to Schurman, 12 February 1903, White Papers.
[17] *Ibid.*, 12 February 1903.

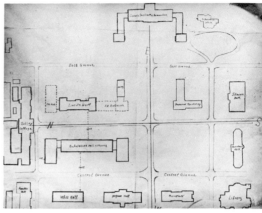

Fig. 157. Hastings' second proposal for locations of Rockefeller and Goldwin Smith Halls, 1903, was developed in response to Hiram Sibley's objection to covering the view of Sibley Hall from the Quadrangle. This proposal was strongly and successfully opposed by Andrew Dickson White.

On 6 March, Schurman cabled White, "not deferred." He thought the building parallel to White Hall provided "a very happy compromise" and proceeded to instruct Hastings to develop final plans. Then White stepped up his campaign to defer the decision. He wrote letters to various Trustees including Samuel Halliday and Schurman. [18] About this time a serious typhoid epidemic occurred at the University and most of Schurman's attention was directed toward the problems that ensued. Further work on plans for the academic department building was deferred, and plans were developed for a new water filtration plant to be financed by Trustee Andrew Carnegie. White was greatly pleased with Carnegie's gift, but he pleaded with Schurman to defer action on Rockefeller Hall. He hoped that the President would not consider him "crotchety or hypocritical" when he expressed a fear that "they would all regret this latest change in plans." White requested "a hearing" before the Trustees. [19] At the Trustees' meeting

[18] Schurman to Hastings, 23 February 1903, Schurman Letterbooks, XII, 101. White, *Diaries,* 17 March 1903. ADW to Schurman, 26 March 1903, White Papers.
[19] ADW to Schurman, 3 April 1903, White Papers. White protests that a building parallel to White Hall will bisect McGraw Hall, result in a view of the end

on 18 April, it was voted that "in view of the high cost of building at present . . . the erection of proposed new buildings at the University be postponed." When Schurman wrote this news to Hastings on 22 April he noted that the physics building plan they were then considering (parallel to White Hall) had provoked some criticisms and that now Hastings' campus plan was also meeting some opposition. The criticism and opposition were White's. Schurman sent Hastings a copy of a letter from "a gentleman somewhat prominent in art circles and also deeply interested in the future of the University." [20] It must have been White's most recent letter to Schurman in which he had expressed serious doubts about many of the proposals of Hastings' "Plan of General Development" for Cornell.

At the Trustees' meeting on 17 June 1903, White had his hearing. That evening he told his diary that the Trustees had given a great athletic field to the students and had bought new land adjoining the university estate. He does not mention the discussion of a site for Rockefeller Hall. This matter was not yet settled, but over the summer and the following fall, Schurman gradually arrived at the conclusion that no building could go astride the Quadrangle. He suggested to Hastings that they reconsider the site originally recommended by Nichols on the hill above East Avenue. After fifteen months of discussions they had come full circle to where they had started, Professor Nichols' recommendation of June 1902.

On 24 October at a Trustees' meeting which White described as "large and successful," the positions of Rockefeller and the building for the academic departments were finally decided, White thought, "most happily." [21] Rockefeller Hall was to be located south of Reservoir Avenue and east of East Avenue; the second building, now named Goldwin Smith Hall, was to be located on the east side of the Quadrangle opposite McGraw Hall. Everyone seemed pleased with the solution. The scholars would be near the Library, the scientists would be outside the menacing circuit of the electric trolley line, and the stone Quadrangle would be completed. Why had not this excellent solution occurred to someone sooner? Perhaps it was too simple.

A few weeks before this October decision of the Trustees, White may have persuaded Schurman that a more refined and subtle plan for campus improvement should be developed. Early in October 1903, Schurman discussed this need with Charles N. Lowrie, New York landscape architect, who was doing several other campus plans at the time. Within two months, Lowrie had developed a detailed plan for landscaping the campus (Fig. 158). His *Report on the Landscape Improvement of the Cornell University Campus* was sent to President Schurman on 15 December 1903. [22] Its proposals were limited to the lower campus area. At the time it was done, the sites and general outlines of both Goldwin Smith and Rockefeller Halls had been determined and at least a tentative decision had been made to place agriculture buildings as

of the building on entering the Quadrangle, and obscure almost as much of Sibley Hall from the southwest corner of the Quadrangle as would an east–west division of the Quadrangle. He says he would "infinitely prefer" a return to the former plan of a divided Quadrangle but thinks locating "Physics on some other site up the hill" would be the best solution.

[20] Schurman to Hastings, 22 April 1903. Schurman Letterbooks, XII, 539–540.

[21] White, *Diaries*, 25 October 1903. Schurman to Hastings, 28 October 1903. Schurman Letterbooks, XIII, 320–322. Schurman says it will not be necessary for Hastings to spend any more time on *general* plans.

[22] White, *Diaries*, 2 and 4 September 1903. White wrote a memorandum to the Trustees' building committee regarding the physics building site and discussed the problem with Schurman. We have no evidence that White suggested bringing Lowrie in to work on the plan, but he was pleased with it. White comments on it in his *Autobiography*, I, 410–411: "In my view one of the most important things to be done by the Trustees is to have a general plan most carefully decided upon which shall then be strictly conformed to in the erection of all future buildings. . . . This has been urged from time to time but deferred." Then he notes: "It has now—1904 [the publication date of Lowrie's plan] been very intelligently developed."

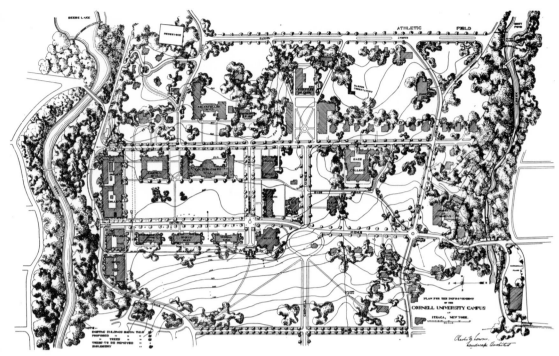

Fig. 158. Lowrie's plan for landscape improvement, 1903, marked the beginning of a fifty-year period of skillful development of the landscape assets of the campus by a series of talented designers working for sympathetic clients. The era was characterized by concern for all elements of the landscape, ranging from the broad vistas offered by East Hill to the smallest details of planting and paving.

flanking wings adjacent to the Veterinary College.

Lowrie believed that through minimum investment in a number of small improvements the University could make much more advantageous use of its landscape potential. His report discussed four major landscape features: driveways and avenues, paths, vistas, and planting. He developed a refinement of Hastings' proposal for an east-west road across Central Avenue by making a double loop south of the Library to permit easier negotiation of the steep grade. He also proposed a broad loop road around the agriculture court above East Avenue. The objective here, as in Hastings' plan, was to provide an improved means of east-west access to the campus, thereby removing some of the traffic from the single southern approach on Central Avenue. Lowrie's other road proposals included shifting University Avenue to the edge of the Fall Creek Gorge. He referred to the

eventual removal of some of the shops behind Sibley and his plan showed the closed quadrangle then intended for Sibley College. Lowrie also proposed that a road named Sibley Avenue be developed from East Avenue down the slope to University Avenue on the south side of Sibley College. This seems to have been a concession to Mr. Sibley after the latter's protest about the "belittling" of Sibley College in Hastings' plan. Lowrie proposed that the College be made more public by a new road. Part of this proposal was built as a carriage road, but with the appearance of the automobile this and many road redundancies of the nineteenth century have been removed from the Quadrangle. For example, Reservoir Avenue, which extended across the Quadrangle to Central Avenue (then also located within the Quadrangle) was removed in 1906 when Goldwin Smith Hall was completed.

The landscape architect also proposed a number of improvements which could be

Fig. 159. The Quadrangle from the Library Tower, 1906.

effected by new paths. He suggested that the path east of the stone row be moved so that it would line up with the Library Tower and that a broad area running the entire length of the east side of Morrill Hall from the building to this path be made a terrace. This improvement was carried out in 1905 (Fig. 159). He also proposed several paths in the gorges, including one from the top of Ithaca Falls to Central Avenue. This was developed a few years later. He listed other new walks and paths needed throughout Fall Creek Gorge, "making frequent connections with campus paths." Many of the present gorge trails and campus paths were located in accordance with Lowrie's plans. Lowrie's later (1915) plans for development of walks and steps in Fall Creek and Cascadilla Creek gorges are masterpieces of informal design which carefully integrate the natural features of these deep rocky chasms with the man-made trails. Everyone who has had the delightful experience of climbing up the side of a waterfall in Cascadilla Gorge is deeply in debt to Lowrie. In these ideas, as in his other suggestions, he had the assistance and support of Professor Willard W. Rowlee ('88), who had taken over the responsibility for the university grounds formerly borne by Professor Prentiss.

Some of Lowrie's most interesting and enduringly useful proposals were those designed to open vistas from the campus to the Cayuga Lake valley. By the time Lowrie came to Cornell to do his work, the ambitious tree-planting programs of the seventies and eighties had contributed much to the appearance of the campus, but they had also blocked off from the central campus all but two of the major vistas of the valley. Lowrie listed eighteen places at which he thought selective tree cutting was needed to make more extensive outlooks available to Cornellians. One of the perennial favorites among the many views of this sort was open then as it is now. This is the view from Central Avenue opposite Barnes Hall where, in 1903, Lowrie found an "extensive view of Cayuga Lake, very slightly interfered with." Between Morrill Hall and the Library he found the long vista of Newfield valley entirely hidden by young trees. At the north end of Central Avenue where he proposed a waiting place for trolley cars, one of the best campus views of Lake Cayuga was then open. In recent years this view had been almost entirely blocked by tree growth, and only a few years ago extensive cutting in the Fall Creek Gorge in connection with the reconstruction of the suspension bridge reopened this magnificent vista. Every one of the fifteen other distant views listed by Lowrie was blocked to some extent by tree growth. Many of these views are still unavailable for the same reason. It has been rumored that one of Cornell's later presidents suggested to the superintendent of grounds that he do some midnight lumbering to open a few views while tree lovers slept. Unfortunately, the superintendent seems not to have had enough courage to carry out the much-needed weeding.

The last points of Lowrie's 1903 report concerned planting and unplanting on the campus. He suggested that the rows of trees along campus avenues needed thinning: every other tree was to be removed to permit high arching growth in those remaining. He also suggested several new rows of trees. He proposed plantings to screen service areas and some of the less attractive buildings, using native shrubs and small trees: thorns, dogwood, viburnum, redbud, and witch hazel. The principle of using natural plants of the region, outlined in 1866 by Olmsted, was again receiving attention. Lowrie's plan seems to have had a great deal of influence on the details of campus landscape development. It assisted Professor Rowlee in the continuing campaign of landscape improvement which he had started in the middle nineties.

Many of Lowrie's proposals were substantial but respectful revisions of the grand ideas in Carrère and Hastings' plan of 1902. Lowrie demonstrated that significant elements of Hastings' "Beaux-Arts" plan could be executed with respect for the topography, existing planting, and circulation. His report was an important contribution to the shaping of landscape objectives for the Cornell campus.

After the resolution of the confusing struggle over locations for Goldwin Smith and Rockefeller Halls, Carrère and Hastings completed their building plans and supervised bidding on the work. President Schurman and the Trustees decided to take bids for both buildings in one contract because they believed this might result in a better price. Schurman was amazed at the range of the bids and commented to White that there seemed to be as much speculation in the construction business as there was on Wall Street.[23] Neither Rockefeller nor Goldwin Smith Hall (Figs. 160 and 161) was Carrère

and Hastings' best work. The designs seldom appeared in the periodicals of the times when the renowned firm's buildings were published. Budgetary problems harassed Hastings during the design of Rockefeller Hall. The faculty is said to have worked for a reduction of building cost so that some portion of Mr. Rockefeller's grant could be used for equipment. This rumor has never been confirmed, but the interiors were, in many cases, left in a semi-finished state. The exterior has been likened to turn-of-the-century American secondary school architecture; a fair comparison no doubt, but one which may seem too abusive of American secondary school architecture. Goldwin Smith Hall has fared somewhat better in local critical eyes, but it seemed to suffer from over-accommodation to the shape of the Dairy Building. Its hip-roofs seem completely wrong on such a massive building. Professor Corson called it "a Greek temple with bungalow trimmings." But it was a stone building and did complete the stone Quadrangle in a strong, if architecturally confused, manner and it did provide a handsome amount of much-needed accommodation for the faculty of the newly reorganized College of Arts and Sciences.

On 4 October 1904, Professor Goldwin Smith returned to Ithaca, which had been his home during 1868–1872 and which he had visited frequently since then. He came to lay the cornerstone of the building called by his name (Figs. 162 and 163). For Professor Smith this was a happy homecoming. He reminisced extensively and interestingly about the early days of Cornell and the great hopes he had held then for the institution.[24] For White the ceremony marked the achievement of a long-sought goal: the completion of the stone Quadrangle planned thirty-four years previously. For President Schurman the ceremony marked the completion of the first phase of his building program which established the academic and scientific departments of the University in adequate facilities.

[23] Schurman to ADW, 30 December 1903, Schurman Letterbooks, XIII, 575–576.

[24] Goldwin Smith, *Reminiscences*, pp. 368–379.

Fig. 160. Goldwin Smith Hall (1904) by Carrère and Hastings.

Fig. 161. Rockefeller Hall (1904) by Carrère and Hastings.

Fig. 162. Cornerstone laying, Goldwin Smith Hall, 1904. Left to right: Dean "Teefy" Crane, President Schurman, Goldwin Smith, Andrew Dickson White, and Professor Moses Coit Tyler.

Fig. 163. Cornerstone laying, Goldwin Smith Hall; Goldwin Smith and Andrew Dickson White.

He now faced a period of building which probably was more difficult and disturbing to him than the preceding one, which, after all, had been concerned mainly with minor arguments about the location of buildings.

The newly established College of Agriculture was emerging as a powerful force for change at Cornell. Under the strong leadership of Liberty Hyde Bailey it was becoming an important and vigorous part of the Univer-

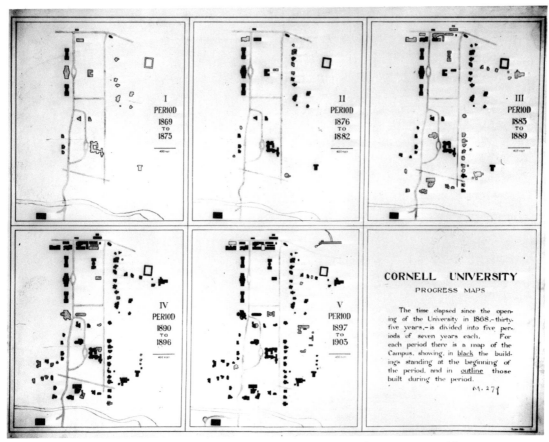

Fig. 164. Cornell University progress maps, 1869 to 1903, drawn by C. J. Tilden.

Fig. 165. View of the campus from South Hill, 1904.

sity. In the years after Bailey's appointment as Director of the College of Agriculture in 1903, Andrew D. White noted several instances of "Bailey trouble" in his diary.[25] The trouble frequently was related to Bailey's ambitious program of expansion—ambitious, not for Bailey, but for the development of agricultural science. The major expansion and academic innovations at Cornell in the decade after 1903 followed new paths mapped in

[25] White, *Diaries,* 4 October 1909; 19 September 1911.

large part by Professor Bailey. President Schurman helped when he could, and that was often. The campus expansion program he had initiated in 1902 following the discussion of Hastings' plans marked the close of thirty-five years of filling in the spaces on the original university site (Fig. 164). A great expansion of the campus was about to begin. From South Hill (Fig. 165) the view of the campus and the rapidly expanding residential area south of it was impressive. More expansion was on the way.

Campus Plans
and Castle Dreams

B Y 1903 THE MAIN ELE-
ments of Cornell's lower campus
were firmly established. The stone Arts Quadrangle was complete and the parklike area
south of it was not to change radically until
thirty-eight years later when Olin Hall, the
first unit of the new Engineering Quadrangle,
was built. In 1903 Liberty Hyde Bailey (Fig.
166) was appointed Director of the College of
Agriculture, and in 1904 the State appropriated $250,000 for its buildings. In 1903 the
Trustees began the slow process of making
decisions on four major components of the
campus—decisions that were to set the overall
pattern of the second half-century of development at Cornell. Seven years later, in 1910,
the decisions on future locations for buildings
of the College of Agriculture, dormitories for
men, dormitories for women, and a new student playfield were finally fixed.

Before 1903 it had been the Trustees' intention to develop the agriculture buildings
around a court fronting on East Avenue. After
this there was new land available to the east,
which had been purchased at Schurman's insistence. With Bailey's ambitious plans for
further expansion of teaching, research, and
extension work in agriculture, it seemed unlikely that the small East Avenue site could
contain all of the buildings that would eventually be needed. In addition to the problem

of siting the new agriculture buildings, plans
for new student housing were also under discussion. Andrew Dickson White was again
dreaming dreams of "Gothic castles." These
would ultimately take form as new women's
and men's dormitories but, before they rose
on the north rim of Fall Creek Gorge and on
the plateau below the completed Arts Quadrangle, he was to see an earlier dream materialize: the development of a carefully studied
plan for long-term development of the entire
campus.

After 1903, the alumni were in active pur-
suit of improved athletic facilities in the field
above the south portion of "Faculty Row."
From 1904 to 1910, two of these three Cornell
interests, the College of Agriculture and the
Cornell Athletic Association, formed in 1889
by faculty, alumni, and students, vied for the
rolling land south of the present location of
Tower Road.

Athletic contests had been removed from
the Quadrangle in 1890 thanks to the gift by
William H. Sage of nine acres of land at the
foot of Fall Creek. The athletic field developed there was named Percy Field in honor of
the Cornellian son of J. J. Hagerman, who
financed its track and buildings. After a decade of descending and climbing four hundred
feet down and up East Hill to participate in
and view sports, many Cornellians had devel-

Fig. 166. Liberty Hyde Bailey about 1903 in a rare moment of inaction on the steps of Morrill Hall. From 1903 to 1913 Bailey was the driving force in expanding the College of Agriculture from a small department to a major component of the University.

oped a great hunger for a playfield on the hill. Liberty Hyde Bailey and his colleagues in the College of Agriculture had an equally great hunger for acres of experimental and instructional farm and garden plots adjacent to the new buildings for their College.

The building cycle and the land debate began with the expansion of facilities for Agriculture. George L. Heins, who had just been appointed the first state architect of New York, wrote President Schurman in May 1904 that he was ready to begin work on plans and specifications for the buildings of the State Agriculture College.[1] The Cornell Trustees had accepted the new college after the passage of an act authorizing it and appropriating State funds for construction. The state

architect was to design the buildings. President Schurman suggested that the professors who would use the buildings list their requirements and that the building committee of the Cornell Board of Trustees review their requests. Then, following such possible "modifications and improvements" as they might make, Schurman would send the requests to the state architect as a preliminary program. The plans were to be reviewed by the building committee of the Trustees and a committee of the faculty.

Schurman, in his usual logical way, had for the first time on record established a formal procedure for communication between faculty, administration, and architect in matters related to building. His office was to serve as the center of communications. Perhaps his confusing experience in connection with the preparation of the plans for Rockefeller and Goldwin Smith Halls had suggested a need to institute such regular methods, but he probably wanted to keep track of Professor Bailey's "empire," too.[2]

Professor Bailey, architect George Heins, President Schurman, Andrew D. White, and members of the Trustees' building committee walked over the upper campus in June 1904 and selected a site for the new buildings on a knoll with a fine view over the rolling hills to the south toward Cascadilla Creek. This seemed an excellent place not only because of the view and the southern exposure but because it was quite near the College of Agriculture's north barn, now the site of Comstock Hall. The site also overlooked the fields maintained by the College of Agriculture. Now there began a dispute over the use of this land. In June 1903, the Trustees had "given the students a playground." According to this decision, Agriculture was to have its farm fur-

[1] Schurman to Heins, 26 May 1904, Schurman Letterbooks, XIV, 511–512 sets the ground rules for planning the buildings; Schurman to Heins, 9 October 1904, Schurman Letterbooks, XV, 38 reconfirms them.

[2] Ibid. Schurman writes that he gives "the first voice to the professors who are to use [the buildings] keeping the ultimate control in the hands of the building committee. . . . For your comfort, however, I will add that all communications will be addressed to the president of the University and, while we have a committee that aids in this work, you will receive all communications from this one source."

ther east. There ensued a seven-year-long argument about the location of the boundary between the playground and the farms. The line was continually being shifted and remained in doubt until 1911. The contending parties were: on one side (the north) the College of Agriculture, led by Bailey and supplied with editorial and political ammunition by the many farm groups in the state; and on the other side (the south) the alumni organizations of Cornell, led by no single general but with many captains, hundreds of whom gave funds for the improvement of "Alumni Field."[3]

In the summer of 1904 Heins developed his sketches for the new buildings for the College of Agriculture: Roberts, East Roberts, and Stone Halls. Three buildings were planned rather than one because the State Legislature had specified that the buildings constructed should "include a principal building, costing not more than $125,000, a hall for agricultural machinery, a stock-judging pavilion, and a horticultural building." By 28 July 1904 Heins had developed preliminary sketches which he sent to President Schurman. The President had given the architect absolute freedom in the design of the buildings, insisting only that the statement of requirements provided by Liberty Hyde Bailey be met.[4] Evidence of the competition for control of decisions on the new buildings for Agriculture is provided in a letter to Heins (9 October 1904). Schurman requested Heins, who had "been corresponding with Professors Hunt and Bailey direct," to send all communications directly to him now that he was back in Ithaca. During Schurman's absence Professor Bailey had campaigned for a shift in the site of the pro-

posed buildings to positions flanking the Veterinary College on East Avenue. Heins had agreed that this adjustment would be acceptable to him. Schurman wrote that the Trustees would not be convinced of the correctness of Professor Bailey's reasoning. The Trustees eventually supported Schurman's views and the buildings were built in the position east of Garden Avenue originally selected.[5] In this exchange between President Schurman and the State of New York, Cornell affirmed its rights to retain control over the location of state buildings on its campus, a

[3] White, *Diaries*, 12 November 1910. White records the main topics of the Trustees' meeting: "Deficit and Athletic Council *vs.* Agricultural Faculty. Long and interesting, tho sometimes rather sharp debate." Then 17 December 1910: "Great question between Agriculture College and athletic interest at last settled, I hope well and finally." See also: *Cornell Alumni News*, Vol. XIV, No. 2 (October, 1911), "Alumni Field."

[4] Schurman to Heins, 29 July 1904, Schurman Letterbooks, XIV, 691.

[5] Thomas F. Hunt, to Schurman, 6 July 1904, Executive Committee Papers. "Report to the Executive Committee, Cornell University from the faculty of the College of Agriculture," 20 July 1904. Executive Committee Papers: Hunt, Comstock, Wing, Craig, Pearson, Tanman, "Memorandum regarding location of State College of Agriculture," 22 July 1904. Executive Committee Papers: Schurman to Heins, 29 July and 16 October 1904. Schurman Letterbooks, XIV, 691; XV, 105. Apparently Bailey was determined to locate the College of Agriculture on East Avenue near the Veterinary College and the greenhouses behind faculty row. This location had been proposed first by White in 1901 and had been incorporated in Hastings' campus plan of October 1902 and Lowrie's campus plan of December 1903. Bailey appears to have convinced George Heins and the Board of Trustees of the advantages of this location sometime during the summer of 1904. This was after Schurman and Heins had settled on the upper site east of Garden Avenue. Bailey then left Ithaca for an extended trip, feeling assured that the College would be on East Avenue. Schurman and the Executive Committee then decided to stick to the upper campus site. In Bailey's absence, Professor Thomas F. Hunt asked reconsideration of the decision. He thought that the upper site required too much grading, that it would require the glasshouses to be located in a spot where they would interfere with the proposed road to the athletic field, and that the site would be too distant from the existing horticultural grounds. Hunt and the College of Agriculture building committee wrote the Executive Committee that "rejection of the [East Avenue site] will bring keen disappointment to the Dean [of the College of Agriculture]." They noted (somewhat threateningly) that "the location of . . . buildings will be watched jealously by those who assisted in the passage of the bill." The Trustees nevertheless voted for the upper site at a special meeting convened on 29 July 1904 to settle the issue. Bailey would not give up. He petitioned Schurman and the Trustees' building committee again in October but they were "not at all convinced by [his] reasoning" and confirmed their selection of the upper site.

Fig. 167. Chi Psi Fraternity House after the fire of 1906. The tragic fire which
completely destroyed the old McGraw-Fiske mansion took seven lives.

control vital to its coordinated development.

During the fall and winter of 1904 work proceeded in Albany and New York City on plans for the new buildings and for renovation of the Dairy Building which was now to house Professor Comstock's entomology department. In the spring of 1905, at impressive and appropriate ceremonies, Jacob Gould Schurman, Liberty Hyde Bailey, and Andrew Dickson White broke ground with a plow and team for the new buildings for Agriculture.

At the other end of the campus the McGraw-Fiske mansion, which had been purchased by Chi Psi fraternity ten years previously, burned to the ground in December 1906 (Fig. 167) in a tragic fire which claimed the lives of four students and three Ithaca firemen. The fire was a grim ending for the romantic "chateau" on which Miller had lavished much of his developing design talent, on which Jennie McGraw had spent much in money and in dreams of a useful life in Ithaca, and on which White had spent much diplomatic skill in the endeavor to make it a university museum of art.

The end of the "chateau" coincided with the beginning of the College of Agriculture in its new home at Cornell. Some parts of its three new buildings were occupied late in the fall of 1906. The dedication of all of them took place late in April 1907. These legislated triplets, Roberts, East Roberts, and Stone Halls (Fig. 168), stood very proudly on their hillcrest. Perhaps they were not as imposing and forcible as the three buildings of the stone row in the Quadrangle, but still they provided a dramatic architectural beginning for the new College of Agriculture campus at Cornell. Roberts Hall, where administrative offices and classrooms were located, was connected by a covered porch to East Roberts, the new dairy building. Stone Hall to the west was occupied by the Department of Rural Education. The group was unified by a southern terrace which also provided a level approach to the principal entrance and for some years a parade area for livestock-judging contests.

Reorganization of the work in agriculture continued with unusual vigor under Professor

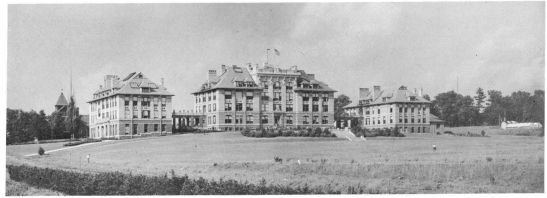

Fig. 168. Stone, Roberts, and East Roberts Halls by George Heins, State Architect (1905). These buildings are the College of Agriculture equivalents of Morrill, McGraw, and White Halls. To the left of Stone Hall is the tower of the North Barn designed by Frank Ayres Wright (1877).

Bailey, with intensive lobbying help from various New York agricultural groups. Professor Roberts had initiated useful joint efforts with the Dairymen's Association, the State Grange, and other influential groups, and Bailey expanded them. Between 1904 (the year after Bailey assumed the directorship of the College) and 1910, enrollment in the various courses in agriculture grew from 296 to 963.[6] In 1910 the Director reported that "in many of the laboratory courses, students had been denied registration for lack of space." In their first and second years the students took much of their work in the College of Arts and Sciences. Now the increased enrollment was working its way through the curriculum to courses in Agriculture.[7] It soon became apparent, to Bailey at least, that additional buildings would be required. In 1910, Bailey arranged to retain the expert services of Warren Manning, landscape architect of Cambridge, Massachusetts. Manning was to work with Professor Bryant Fleming of Cornell's Department of Rural Art and with Professors Martin and Hébrard of the College of Architecture to develop overall plans for additional facilities for Agriculture within the framework of a general plan for the entire Cornell campus. Twenty-five years after he had pointed out

the need for an overall campus plan, Andrew D. White was to see a most effective one prepared by Manning and Fleming. Their campus plan was a substantial improvement over the earlier work of Hastings and Lowrie in content, in quality, and in the extent to which it influenced development.

Cornell was expanding at a rapidly increasing rate in 1910, and though additional lands had been purchased, there seemed some possibility that confinement of the campus within the two stream valleys would not be possible. At the time, the boundary war between the alumni who were raising funds for the new athletic field and the College of Agriculture was still raging. Through the studies of Manning and Fleming, Bailey and the faculty in Agriculture attempted to persuade the Trustees that the new athletic field was poorly located in relation to future building needs on Cornell's campus. While the campus planning study was primarily concerned with the needs of the College of Agriculture, proposals were made for the entire campus. The first approach to understanding the problems of expansion was statistical. Building use by academic discipline and net building floor area per student were carefully analyzed. Ratios of building floor area to the students enrolled in each discipline were then projected as far as 1984, and future building requirements were estimated. The total enrollment of 17,000 pre-

[6] Bailey, Director's report: "Agriculture" in President's report (1910), pp. XLVI–LVI.
[7] *Ibid.*, pp. L–LI.

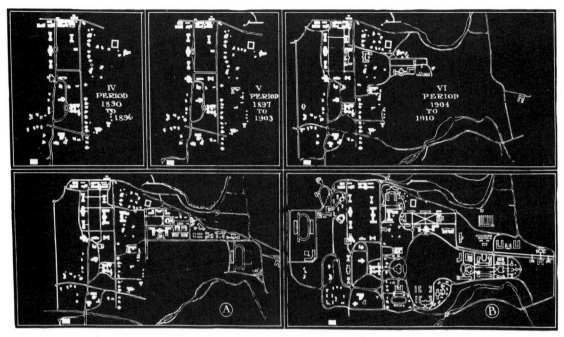

Fig. 169. Studies "A" and "B" for Cornell University by Warren Manning and Bryant Fleming, 1910. The first study was presented to demonstrate that in ten years the College of Agriculture would need more land than was afforded by the triangle between the proposed playfield, Garden Avenue, and Fall Creek Valley. The proposal for what was to become Tower Road appears for the first time in this study. Study "B" shows the major recommendations of Manning and Fleming, many of which were incorporated in later campus plans and development.

dicted by Manning and Fleming for Cornell's Ithaca campus in 1984 now seems a figure likely to be reached by that year.[8]

Using their estimate of long-range building-space needs, Manning and Fleming developed three studies of possible plans for campus expansion (Figs. 169 and 170). They seemed to favor study "B," which located the new athletic field west of the library slope and above Stewart Avenue and so provided ample space between the gorges for all the proposed buildings. Their suggestion for the location of the athletic field was supported by a series of drawings which demonstrated the advantages of nearness to town and public transportation. But this site, alas, was des-

[8] Warren H. Manning and the Rural Art Department, Bryant Fleming in charge, with the assistance of the Department of Architecture and Engineering of the University. *Studies for Cornell University made with special reference to the location of buildings for the College of Agriculture*, November 1910.

tined for the development of men's dormitories. It may even be possible, although we have no proof, that the suggestion of this as a site for sports stimulated the drive to build dormitories. Studies "A" and "C" show several campus improvements later carried out: the straight alignment of Tower Road, a long court around which the principal buildings of the Agriculture campus were to be arranged, and the use of the Kline farm just north of Fall Creek for university buildings. Both of these plans were based on the assumption that athletics would constitute the long-term use of the Alumni Field area.

Manning and Fleming continued from time to time to advise the University on campus development and so had ample opportunity to develop these first campus plan suggestions. Their study "B" of 1910 contained many ideas later used in the development of the campus. It called for the replacement of faculty cottages along Central and East Avenues with academic buildings and the removal of Central Avenue from inside the Quadrangle to a position west of the Stone Row. It proposed the general grouping of the agricultural campus (north of Tower Road and on the east border of Alumni Field) which was to guide its development for forty years. It also suggested the elimination of President's Avenue and an improved alignment for East Avenue at its intersection with Triphammer Falls Bridge. Scheme "B" also shows a revival of Olmsted's concept of a great terrace west of the first three buildings. This seems to have been one of Fleming's most favored projects. He and Manning proposed it for various uses in all of their campus planning studies into the thirties. Figure 169 shows the 1910 terrace proposal most clearly and also shows the proposed development of dormitories below McGraw Hall, a proposed addition to the library stacks, an outdoor theatre on the west slope, and the curving alignment adopted twenty-four years later for Campus Road below Central Avenue.

These plans for Cornell's development and studies prepared by Fleming and Manning in the 1930's are probably the most imaginative and perhaps the most effective overall plans prepared in the history of planning for the development of Cornell's campus. Their research and analysis provided a realistic basis for the proposals. The grouping of the buildings, the disposition of roads, and the carefully conceived presentation of ideas set a high standard for future campus planning. In these plans we can see the first projections of the Cornell of a few years ago. For the period beyond 1960 their power to predict needs and influence development seems limited.

Ex-President Andrew D. White must have been delighted at this development in general planning for the entire campus. His 1885 plea for such studies had finally been acted on. The plans prepared by Carrère and Hastings in 1902 and their refinement and embellishment by the landscape plans of Charles Low-

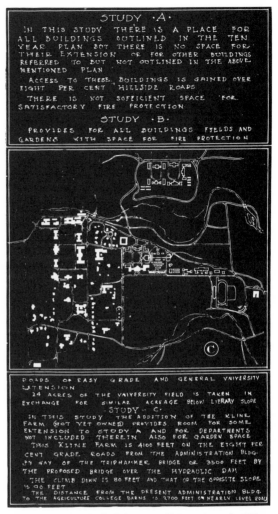

Fig. 170. Study "C" for Cornell University by Warren Manning and Bryant Fleming, 1910. This study shows an alternative to placement of College of Agriculture buildings in the twenty-four acres designated for an "Alumni Playground."

rie were probably not the sort of general plan White had wanted. Carrère and Hastings' plan was too formal and grandiose and Lowrie's plan, although more likely to suit the Ex-President's taste, was limited to the lower campus. The plans of Manning and Fleming probably came much closer to meeting his twenty-five-year-old specifications for a long-range campus plan.

An extensive and varied building program

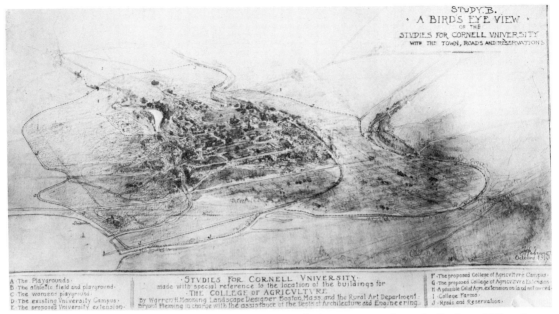

STUDY.B.
· A BIRDS EYE VIEW ·
OF THE
STUDIES FOR CORNELL UNIVERSITY
WITH THE TOWN, ROADS AND RESERVATIONS

A · The Playgrounds ·
B · The athletic field and playground ·
C · The womens playground ·
D · The existing University Campus ·
E · The proposed University extension ·

· STUDIES FOR CORNELL UNIVERSITY ·
made with special reference to the location of the buildings for
THE COLLEGE OF AGRICULTURE ·
By Warren H. Manning Landscape Designer Boston Mass. and the Rural Art Department ·
Bryant Fleming in charge with the assistance of the Depts of Architecture and Engineering ·

F · The proposed College of Agriculture Campus ·
G · The proposed College of Agriculture Extension ·
H · A possible Colof Agri. extension on land not owned ·
I · College Farms ·
J · Roads and Reservation ·

Fig. 171. A bird's-eye view, study "B" by Manning and Fleming, 1910; drawn by Professor Hébrard.

carried out for the College of Agriculture grew from these 1910 plans. Professor Bailey wielded statistics on the enrollment growth and on the research and extension work of the college most effectively in Albany. Over the next three years state appropriations provided for six major new buildings: for home economics, Comstock Hall (1912); for poultry husbandry, Rice Hall (1912); for animal husbandry, Wing Hall (1913); for soils science, Caldwell Hall (1913); for forestry, Fernow Hall (1913); and finally and appropriately, the great auditorium White wanted, Bailey Hall (1913). Bailey Hall (Fig. 172) was not at first so named but it might well have been. It would seem unlikely that a single man could accomplish so much, but in this instance one had. Liberty Hyde Bailey supplied most of the initiative and a great deal of the drive and intelligence behind the expansion of the Cornell College of Agriculture between 1903 and 1913. Bailey was not an easy man to get along with. He believed religiously in the development of scientific agriculture and devoted his life to it. He was a leader in the establishment of agricultural extension courses, was the author of sixty-three books

and five encyclopedias on horticulture, agriculture, farm crops, and farm animals, was editor for over one hundred volumes in various fields of agricultural science, and was the editor of several journals.[9]

Once the first foundations for agricultural extension, research, and teaching at Cornell were laid Liberty Hyde Bailey returned to his first love, research. In 1913, in accordance with a plan for his life which called for twenty-five years of preparation, twenty-five years of work, and twenty-five years of doing what he pleased, he resigned as Dean of the College of Agriculture to pursue his own scientific research. Everyone, well almost everyone, protested his resignation. Some of the agricultural groups in the State were said to have suggested that he be made President of Cornell when it became finally and completely a State University.

Bailey's energy and enterprise built the College of Agriculture, but at the same time they aroused some animosities among the arts college faculty. For example, in 1913 Bailey established a new department of botany rival-

[9] Morris Bishop, *A History of Cornell*, pp. 290–292.

Fig. 172. Bailey Hall (1913).

ing the one in the arts college, and other work he initiated seemed to duplicate work already done in existing departments. Bailey was not one to hesitate when he saw a clear need for research or teaching.

The vast and rapid development of the College of Agriculture after the turn of the century comprised one of the most startling building booms in Cornell's history. Today buildings occupy all of the sites suggested in the 1910 plan for the Cornell campus prepared by Manning and Fleming. These buildings, designed or supervised by various state architects, were and are exceptionally well built of durable materials. They are generally undistinguished architecturally but are generally well suited to the functional needs of the various departments of the College. The "Ag Quadrangle," actually a court, is one of the delightful spots of the campus and several of the smaller courts north of it are, if anything, more perfectly scaled. Most of the buildings are not symbolic nor do they seem to provide (as White would have said) for anything but bare utility. But this, after all, may be appropriate, for from the Colleges of Agriculture, of Home Economics, and of Veterinary

Medicine have come research and teaching of very great utility to mankind.

For one of the significant buildings of this era, Barton Hall, Liberty Hyde Bailey could not claim all of the credit. President Schurman began a campaign in 1907 to get New York State financing for construction of a new drill hall, working in close cooperation with Major John Carlyle of the State Militia, the State Legislature, and the Cornell Board of Trustees. By 1909 preliminary plans had been developed, and an effort was made to obtain a state appropriation for the $260,000 needed for construction.[10] Schurman was disappointed in Cornell's first efforts in the Legislature. He wrote to Major Carlyle in April 1910 that he was sure "that if the State had the money, the committee would vote to give us everything we asked for." [11] In April 1914, the Legislature finally appropriated $350,000 for the building. Schurman and Carlyle, working with the state architect, made no little plans. Barton Hall (Fig. 173), named for Colonel Frank A. Barton ('91), covers almost

[10] Schurman to Carlyle, 10 December 1909, Schurman Letterbooks, XXV, 31.
[11] *Ibid.*, 8 April 1910, XXV, 632.

Fig. 173. Barton Hall (1917) was named for Colonel Frank A. Barton ('91).

two acres and affords possibilities for multiple use which soon made the old armory more useful as a mens' gymnasium. Colonel Barton was one of the first two Cornell students to receive an Army commission in Cornell's Military Science program and was Commandant at Cornell from 1904 to 1908 and during World War I. Barton Hall's great "Gothic keeps" provide an unusually strong contrast to its great glass west wall. The hall's "Gothic Re-revival" exterior features must have been satisfying to White, who was then actively promoting his castle dreams for men's dormitories on the west slope of the campus.

Schurman was continuing to campaign for state building funds. In 1910 he provided a priority list of Cornell's needs in home economics and domestic sciences, and in veterinary medicine. About $365,000, he thought, would be needed to pay for the buildings required by these departments. He asked Major Carlyle as a member of the Committee on Legislative Appropriations to make sure the legislature understood that Cornell wanted a home economics building and "all the other buildings we can get in agriculture

and the hospital in the Veterinary College." [12]

In October 1910, President Schurman received some unasked-for criticism of the new agriculture buildings from F. Ellis Jackson of Hilton and Jackson, an architectural firm in Providence, Rhode Island. President Schurman answered that the buildings of the College of Agriculture were, "under the laws of the State," put into the hands of the state architects and that buildings given the University often had the architect selected by the donor. In reference to a specific criticism of the new memorial at the south end of Goldwin Smith Hall, Schurman noted that when Jackson had seen it, the work was incomplete; it was then simply a hole in the ground. This lovely delicate monument (Fig. 174), a sundial given to the University as a memorial to Franklin Lacy Sheldon ('95) and Charles Lacy Sheldon ('01), had greatly pleased Ex-President White. He thought it quite appropriate to the campus in that location and Schurman thought this represented "pretty fairly the general sentiment on the subject."

[12] *Ibid.*

Fig. 174. Sheldon Sundial (1910) is a memorial to Franklin L. Sheldon ('95) and Charles L. Sheldon ('01).

White was also trying to stir up some "general sentiment" on other subjects. In January 1910, Andrew Carnegie asked White to consider his brother-in-law, Henry Whitfield, as a possible architect for another annex for the Morse Hall chemistry laboratory. The next day White asked Carnegie for $50,000 to build it, which the latter gave at the end of the month. Whitfield was appointed architect.[13] Then, in October 1910, White began his campaign to secure the financial help of Mrs. Russell Sage of New York for the construction of additional dormitory facilities for women.

White's correspondence about this building reveals a great deal about his diplomacy in fund raising, which, in this instance, was remarkably successful. He first wrote Mrs. Sage on 8 July 1910 in response to her expression of interest in women's education at Cornell.[14] Mrs. Sage was associated with the woman's suffrage movement and had a strong interest in women's education. White responded to her inquiry with a history of Sage College and suggested that another "Sage College" would be a fine monument. White concluded that it would give him great satisfaction in his last years to see this fulfillment of his dreams for improved college facilities. After an extended correspondence, Mrs. Sage agreed in February 1911 to finance another "Sage College." She agreed to pay $300,000 for a building to be named Prudence Risley Hall in memory of Russell Sage's mother. White retained William Miller to design it, he wrote Mrs. Sage, because of "his good taste, conscientiousness . . . and familiarity with Cornell."[15]

White sent the architect photographs of Pembroke College, Cambridge, suggesting that something like this might be appropriate for the new women's college. Miller obliged, but the cost proved too high, so by October 1911 White was complaining that they had been forced to change the "hall from a most beautiful, commodious, convenient, healthful, dignified structure, of the very first class into a much smaller, less healthful building." He asked Mrs. Sage to supplement her gift, but she would not. White, though disappointed in the smallness of the building, had succeeded in getting his first "Gothic castle" at Cornell.[16]

A site north or south of Sage College was debated. It seemed, at the time, appropriate and economical of kitchen operations to keep the residential facilities for women in one location on the campus. Less than a year before this decision had to be made, however, Manning and Fleming had completed their studies of the long-range building needs of the University and had prepared plans which showed the difficulties of academic expansion if the University attempted to contain its entire campus between the Fall Creek and Cascadilla Gorges. The building committee and the Trustees engaged in a long debate about where the new women's college should be located.[17] Finally it was decided that a site just north of the Triphammer Bridge should be used. Trustee Emerson McMillin gave the University $20,000 to purchase the site. His gift was the decisive factor in placing Pru-

---

[13] Carnegie to ADW, 3 January 1910; ADW to Carnegie, 4 January 1910; Carnegie to ADW, 29 January 1910, White Papers; Trustees' *Proceedings,* 5 February 1910. At the same time Carnegie refused to give any money to enlarge the Library, stating that the problem of excess books could be solved by storing the infrequently used books in a basement.

[14] ADW to Mrs. Sage, 8 July 1910, White Papers.

[15] Mrs. Russell Sage to ADW, 14 June 1910; ADW to Mrs. Sage, 8, 16, and 25 July 1910; ADW to Mrs. Sage, 12 October 1910; ADW to Col. S. F. Slocum, 21 January 1911; Slocum to ADW, 2 February 1911; and ADW to Slocum, 17 February 1911. Miller to ADW, 4 February 1913. While he was designing the building, Miller and White visited women's dormitories

at Vassar, Bryn Mawr, and Emma Willard School (Miller to ADW, 20 May 1911). All in the White Papers.

[16] ADW to Mrs. Russell Sage, 12 October 1911; Slocum to ADW, 16 October 1911. White Papers.

[17] White, *Diaries,* 8 April 1911; White to Mrs. Sage, 10 April 1911; "Brief for northern site for Risley Hall," 16 February 1911 (Drafts in White Papers). In February and March, 1911, the Trustees considered sites for Risley Hall north and south of Sage College. The objects were to keep the buildings given by Sages together even though Mrs. Russell Sage and Henry W. Sage were not related and to reap the practical benefits of shared kitchens and service areas. White preferred the north site because a building there would, he thought, compose well with Sage Chapel and Barnes Hall in an "open quadrangular court."

dence Risley Hall (Figs. 175 and 176) on the north rim of Fall Creek Gorge and thus establishing the pattern for the location of women's residence halls at Cornell for the following fifty years. Until his last days White continued to dream of Gothic residential towers at Cornell for both men and women students.[18]

From 1885 to 1912 Presidents Adams and Schurman had attempted, unsuccessfully, to secure financing for men's dormitories. In 1905, the Trustees resolved that they would pledge themselves to spend for residential halls out of university funds an amount of money equal to that received as unrestricted gifts. Their limit was $500,000, "it being understood that such halls [should] be of a plain substantial character, fireproof, and as beautiful as is compatible with simplicity and economy."[19] The language of the resolution is Andrew Dickson White's. By 1905 he seems to have been completely converted to the idea of building dormitories at Cornell. Part of his conversion probably took place during several visits to Oxford and Cambridge around the turn of the century. The award of an honorary doctorate by Oxford was the occasion for one of the visits. Shortly after this, the vision of his youth—university towers rising above the shores of one of the Finger Lakes—seems to have returned with great force.[20] In 1911 with the plans for Prudence Risley Hall in the "English Collegiate-Gothic Style" well underway, Cornell's seventy-nine-year-old Ex-President began to work vigorously to achieve a similar "Gothic" architectural environment for Cornell's men students. In this respect Cornell was far behind other major eastern universities. Princeton, Harvard, and the University of Pennsylvania had already built major portions of their projected student housing devel-

Fig. 175. Prudence Risley Hall (1912) by William H. Miller. The second women's dormitory, a gift of Mrs. Russell Sage, fixed the location for construction of women's residences for the next fifty years.

opments. The sight of the "Gothic" quadrangles at Princeton and Pennsylvania must have increased White's desire for similar structures at Cornell. In 1897, White had visited the new campus of the University of Chicago, where the rage for "Gothic" building on American college and university campuses had begun in 1893—the same year that the rage for "Beaux-Arts" public buildings and civic centers was started by the spacious well-ordered magnificence of the World's Fair next door. White told his diary that the University of Chicago campus was "really a wonderful creation and up to [his] ideas architecturally as far as it had gone. Splendid stone buildings in a fine style. Nobly carried out and disposed in quadrangles and courts."[21]

As the 1910 campus plans by Manning and Fleming had indicated, the University was now seriously considering construction of dormitories on the slope west of the main Quad-

[18] In 1916 White sponsored a College of Architecture competition for the design of a dormitory group north of Beebe Lake. Photographs of nine plans submitted in the competition are in the 25 September 1916 White Papers.
[19] Trustees' *Proceedings*, 18 January 1908.
[20] White, *Autobiography*, I, 287–288; White, *Diaries*, 9 December 1904.

[21] White, *Diaries*, 5 February 1897.

Fig. 176. Prudence Risley Hall, dining hall—the realization of Andrew Dickson White's specification of 1871 for a proper English Collegiate hall at Cornell.

rangle. In June 1911, Trustee George C. Boldt asked President Schurman to establish a committee of White, R. H. Treman, Shepard, and himself to develop a general dormitory landscape plan for men's residence halls "below Morrill Hall." The committee was also to devise schemes for money-raising.[22] The firm of Cram, Goodhue, and Ferguson, architects of the new dormitories at Princeton and West Point, was retained to prepare site studies. In July, White wrote an eighteen-page letter to the committee outlining his views. White and the other committee members were satisfied with the general arrangements proposed by Cram, Goodhue, and Ferguson, but Boldt suggested that Day and Klauder could do a better job at a lower cost. During the summer of 1912 the latter firm was retained to prepare the final designs for the new dormitories.

The University's plan of 1905 to finance dormitories by matching the gifts of donors was now abandoned. Boldt favored raising the funds needed by outside subscription.

Cornell's finances were again in crisis. Enrollment had increased to over 5,000 by 1913 (a 150 per cent increase over 1895 enrollment), but income from endowment had not even doubled in the same period. President Schurman wrote a "private and confidential" letter to the Trustees outlining the nature of the crisis. New York State support had increased to ten times the 1895 appropriation. Cornell needed desperately to increase her endowment funds. Schurman noted that if they were a manufacturing corporation he would recommend "doubling the stock and duplicating the plant." [23]

The University's friends—Boldt, Baker, and many others—made their contributions to the development of men's dormitories at this critical time in Cornell's fiscal affairs. Day and Klauder made this easier by designing the buildings to be built in small increments with each unit housing sixteen to thirty students. The architects developed a detailed plan for

[22] Boldt to Schurman, 16 May 1911, White Papers.

[23] Schurman to Trustees, 8 June 1913, "Private and Confidential" letter, Trustee Papers.

Fig. 177. Baker Court (1916), men's residential halls by Day and Klauder. In 1886, President Adams had recommended reversal of the University's policy not to provide housing for men, but it took thirty years to develop strong commitment to the idea and to resolve the problems of financing and location.

the fourteen acres of land purchased in 1902 from F. C. Cornell. The stone "Gothic" residence halls they proposed (Fig. 177) were not simple or economical. They provided student accommodations on the same scale as the Penn and Princeton dormitories of Cope and Sewardson but less luxurious than the new "houses" at Yale and Harvard.[24] Construction of the first unit, later named Founders Hall, began in 1914. White visited the site and found an old Scotch stonemason from Princeton in charge of the work: "a very worthy and capable man."[25]

In August 1914 news of the war in Europe saddened White. At first the Ex-President, who had been United States Minister and Ambassador to Germany for nine years, seemed confused about his position on the conflict; but by the spring of 1915 he noted that he could "no longer sympathize with them"—strong as his leanings in that direction were.[26] The economic recession, caused partly by the outbreak of war, slowed the financing and construction of the men's dormitories. When the United States entered the conflict in 1917, White was very depressed at the sight of thousands of young Cornellians drilling on the campus and marching in the streets (Fig. 178), preparing to fight the men of the country he had loved second best in the world.

In 1915 a statue of White by Karl Bitter was unveiled on the Quadrangle. By this time the Ex-President had ceased being impressed (if,

[24] "Residential Halls at Cornell," *The American Architect* (5 August 1928).
[25] White, *Diaries*, 6 July 1914.
[26] *Ibid.*, 4 April 1915.

Fig. 178. Cadets drilling on Schoellkopf Field in 1917.

indeed, he ever had been) at the generous praise others often bestowed on him. This last was too much. On 16 June he shouted to his diary: *"The unveiling of my statue* on campus." Then he recovered his suave and perhaps somewhat affected composure and continued: "Whole thing rather trying but all seemed to pass off well." [27] Later that summer White bought an automobile (Fig. 179) and so he had the pleasure of living at the beginning of the age of gasoline. One of his first trips in the car was to Taughannock Falls to buy raspberries. The car's speed amazed him—it took only an hour and a half to get to Cortland, eighteen miles distant.[28]

That same summer the landscape architect, Charles Lowrie, presented his "Preliminary Report for the Development of Fall Creek Gorge and Cascadilla Glen" to the University Trustees. His beautifully conceived recommendations for lower-level gorge trails pro-

vided the basic concepts for the trails which were detailed by Bryant Fleming, Carl Crandall, and Charles Cooley during the following twenty years. In the 1920's Colonel Henry W. Sackett ('75) became interested in Cornell's twin gorges and, influenced by the gifts of the Treman family for state parks at Buttermilk Falls and Enfield Falls, was inspired to finance the development of new trails in Fall Creek and Cascadilla Gorges. The beauty of lower-level views of waterfalls and rock formations in these deep gorges, previously available only to the most nimble climbers, were now to be accessible to all.

In February 1916, Andrew White stood with a large crowd observing the destruction of Morse Hall by fire. One suspects he felt some pleasure as well as sorrow at the financial loss as he watched the demise of the out-of-place brick building. That summer he sat through a Trustees' meeting and "uttered not a word." He began the new year in 1917 by writing George F. Baker of Cornell's need

[27] *Ibid.,* 16 June 1915.   [28] *Ibid.,* 5 July 1915.

Fig. 179. Andrew Dickson White in his automobile, about 1916.

for a chemistry building and in April he received the news of declaration by the United States of war with Germany. In November he spent his eighty-fifth birthday quietly at home in the Ex-President's house.

The following year was a very calm one for White. He spent most of his time on the Cornell campus. He attended class banquets, heard the Baccalaureate sermon in May, and attended a few Administration Committee meetings in President Schurman's office.[29] On

[29] *Ibid.*, 18, 19 May; 3 August 1918.

4 November 1918, Andrew D. White died in his home on the knoll above the campus he had done so much for fifty-two years to shape. He will no doubt be best remembered for his innovations in higher education in the nineteenth century. But while he was doing these great things, he always took time to improve campus design, architecture, and art at Cornell. Much of the beauty of the Cornell campus is the direct result of his determination that it be so.

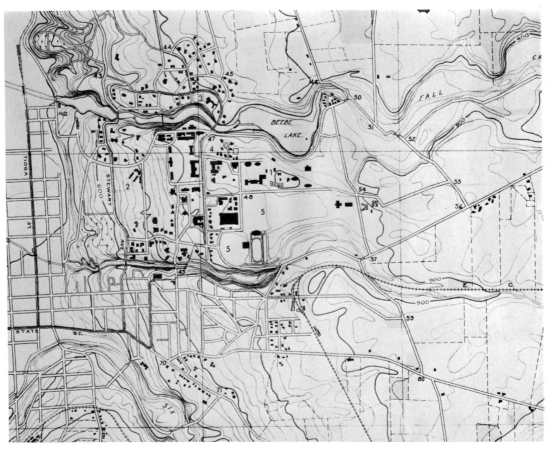

Fig. 180. Map of the Cornell campus, 1918. The principal elements of its structure were established at the end of fifty years of development: new buildings for the College of Agriculture spreading eastward south of Beebe Lake (1); men's and women's residential areas established west and north of the campus (2) and (3); faculty row along East Avenue being displaced by academic buildings—note houses cleared for site of Baker Hall (4); and the men's sports area firmly established south of Tower Road and east and south of Garden Avenue. (5).

Fig. 181. Andrew Dickson White on the Quadrangle outside Goldwin Smith Hall surveying the campus whose planning and architectural development was his especial concern for over fifty years.

XIII

White's Dream Comes True

ANDREW D. WHITE'S PLANS for a great university of a new mold in New York State were the plans of a typical nineteenth-century optimist who believed any reform was possible. The broad features of his academic revolution were realized by the time he retired from the presidency of Cornell in 1885. The dream of a great university campus which came to him as a frustrated freshman at Hobart College in 1849–1850 had essentially come true on the Cornell campus by the time of White's death in the President's House in November 1918.

Ezra Cornell's dream of a great university, where anyone could study anything he or she wanted to, was perhaps even more revolutionary than White's. His ideas of universally available higher education may be realized in this country during the next decades through the growth of community colleges. Even now (1967) the goals of a recent presidential commission include making this opportunity available to all young Americans. A major effort toward the realization of this goal was never and probably should never have been attempted at Cornell. Questions of the nature and quality of university work always intervened. The making of a great university required ever higher standards of achievement for admission. Other methods and institutions have been invented to provide the great variety of vocational education Ezra Cornell envisioned for New York's citizens.

One of Ezra Cornell's dreams for his university, that of a large enrollment, had been realized, however, at the close of fifty years of university development on East Hill. On many occasions Cornell told visitors to the campus that one day (perhaps within a few years) they would see 5,000 students on the campus. That number was reached before 1918.[1] Cornell's visions of future diversity in higher education and numbers of poor young men coming to Ithaca were too far ahead of his times. He would have been pleased, though, at the progress made at Cornell in its first fifty years toward realizing this great dream.

At the close of World War I, the stone Quadrangle at Cornell was completed and was graced with the statues of the two principal founders: Cornell and White (Figs. 182 and 183). They are excellent memorials of the kind White always suggested in the Quadrangle Ezra Cornell planned and Andrew D. White protected. The elms White had planted at the University of Michigan in the sixties were no more beautiful than those which lined Central Avenue, East Avenue, and President's Avenue in 1918. The "informal brick group," was probably as lovely in 1918 as it ever was. It had always been more easily pro-

---

[1] President's report (1918–1919); see table facing p. lxiv. Enrollment first exceeded 5,000 in 1913–1914 (5,015). It dropped below 5,000 during World War I but rose to 5,644 in 1918–1919.

Fig. 182. Library Tower, Morrill Hall, and the statue of Ezra Cornell by Herman Atkins McNeil (1918). Central Avenue was relocated from inside the Quadrangle to the west side of the Stone Row in 1906.

tected from inharmonious building than was the stone Quadrangle because of the lesser expense of brick construction.

By 1918 the College of Agriculture had achieved remarkable success in teaching programs and in research. Its lack of early progress had been one of the great trials of White's presidency and his middle years. Now its campus was filling in rapidly. The State of New York was providing some of the structures White had dreamed of in the 1890's and around the turn of the century: a great auditorium seating over two thousand and a drill hall which could contain the large crowds the University might want to assemble for commencements and other celebrations.

The stone towers of the men's dormitories had already begun to rise below West Ave-

nue. White saw Day and Klauder's plans for some of the most excellent small quadrangles ever built on the Cornell campus. The "society houses" he so long advocated had been built in great numbers; some of them were quite imposing. In fact, President Schurman feared that the expensive construction and elaborate furnishing of such houses was attracting too many sons of wealthy families to Cornell.[2] The original intentions of the

[2] *Ibid.* (1894–95), pp. 63–64. In a discussion of the need for dormitories, Schurman comments that "in the absence of dormitories . . . Greek letter fraternities have been flourishing" and that "in their competition for superior buildings and furniture, which a watchful eye may now begin to discern, they are liable to introduce into the university an element foreign to its comprehensive and democratic spirit and dangerous to its simple, earnest and healthful life."

Fig. 183. Statue of Andrew Dickson White by Karl Bitter (1916).

cation established by Risley Hall, have spread through the area east of Triphammer Road and extend now almost to the border of a development White never envisioned: two groups of housing for married students. Pleasant Grove Apartments and Hasbrouck Apartments, developments of the fifties and sixties, now house over 250 married students and their families.

The Quadrangle is still much as it was when White died. As noted in the preceding chapter, he had been present at the dedication of his own statue, a fine seated figure by Karl Bitter given by Henry R. Ickelheimer ('88) which looks out across the Quadrangle to the three original buildings.[3] He missed attending the dedication of Ezra Cornell's standing statue. It was ready for the ceremony in the month he died, but the dedication was postponed until the following year when Ezra Cornell's only surviving daughter,

Founder were being modified. But as university scholarship aid increased and as special foundations like the Telluride Association were established, White saw the probability that "poor young men" could attend Cornell, too, if they were bright enough.

We may conclude that by the last year of his life Andrew D. White felt that his major objectives for the Cornell campus had been achieved. From that time until the early 1960's most of the development on the Ithaca campus consisted of filling in the basic structure established in the first fifty years. The extension of dormitories to fill the area between West Avenue and Stewart Avenue was completed in 1953. White would probably have been appalled by the architecture of economy employed in these structures. Their red-brick and Ithaca-stone walls and uncertain hip roofs make a group attractive only at night when yellow light through their handsomely proportioned windows makes the architecture invisible. Additional women's dormitories, following the general pattern of lo-

[3] In the White Papers (22 April 1915) there is a drawing in White's hand which analyses four possible locations for his statue: two to the left and two to the right of the portico within fifteen feet of Goldwin Smith Hall. White notes that the head is slightly inclined to the left and therefore should be to the left as one faces the portico. Then it will face those walking up the principal walk from the Library. It was finally placed on the axis of Goldwin Smith Hall about 60 feet west of the portico. White understood the principle followed in classical times of placing sculpture against a building to provide a strong tension between object and its background. But the love for objects on axis—alone in space—was characteristic of the Classical re-revival of the early twentieth century, so White's statute sits foursquare before Goldwin Smith Hall—detached yet worldly, looking out on the Quadrangle from the humanities side. Perhaps this is a proper symbol, even though White's seeming detachment was a carefully studied pose. In 1936, there was discussion of moving White's monument to a position between McGraw and White Halls (Architectural Advisory Board Minutes, May 1936–December 1940, pp. 133, 155, 178). This revision of symmetry failed to occur. White and Ezra Cornell continue to gaze from opposite sides of the Quadrangle they shaped in the University they founded. The statue of Ezra Cornell is the work of Hermōn Atkins MacNeil, a former instructor in industrial art in Sibley College whom Director Thurston encouraged to work at sculpture. In the summer of 1965 the bronze figures of the founders came alive and spoke across the "Quad" in whimsical dialogue during the Centennial Year sound-and-light production.

Mary Emily Cornell, unveiled it as part of the University's semicentennial celebration.

The things that have happened among the red-brick buildings south of the Quadrangle since 1918 have proved the wisdom of Frederick Law Olmsted's advice to the new "National Agricultural Colleges" and specifically to Cornell. The informal arrangement of widely spaced buildings in a park on the south campus has permitted much-needed filling in by new structures. Although the parklike character of this part of the campus is now much diminished, White probably would have agreed with most of the things that have occurred there. In designing the buildings added since his death, some special pains have been taken to respect the landscape and to preserve the qualities of the early buildings. These efforts seem at times somewhat overdone. In Olin Hall, built south of Barnes Hall on Central Avenue in 1942, the architect managed to mingle brick and stone (not unhandsomely) in an unusual accommodation to both the early "Romanesque" red-brick walls of Barnes Hall and the later "English Collegiate Gothic" walls of Willard Straight Hall.

White never dreamed of most of the development that has taken place in the upper campus at Cornell since 1917: the vast assemblage of buildings housing the Colleges of Agriculture and Home Economics, the School of Industrial and Labor Relations, the new Veterinary College, Malott Hall containing the graduate School of Business and Public Administration, and Teagle and Lynah Halls. He would probably have approved the "Gothic" forms of Willard Straight, Myron Taylor, Anabel Taylor, and Teagle Halls. He remained silent about the architecture of the first College of Agriculture buildings that were built during his lifetime, but he must have approved of the towering "Gothic keeps" that frame the façade of Barton Hall. White's dreams for the campus and buildings of Cornell University seem to have come true for the most part. He probably would have been amazed and impressed by overall campus

Fig. 184. Livingston Farrand, fourth President of Cornell University, 1921–1937.

planning efforts and by the complicated procedures of administrative review his successors developed in the 1920's to achieve his and their dreams for the Cornell campus.

After President Schurman retired in 1920 and Livingston Farrand (Fig. 184) assumed the office, extensive plans were initiated for the development of new buildings on the campus. The postwar confidence of the nation was reflected in the plans and programs of Cornell's leaders. But in the fifty-four years that had passed since the University's first building was designed, the institution, the arrangement of the campus, and the practice of architecture had all become more complex. The Trustees decided that the scope of its plans for future development required continuing advice on long-range development and the preparation of overall campus plans. It is safe to assume that White would have delighted in the wisdom of this decision. On 11 May 1922 the Trustees appointed the "University Plan Commission," consisting of Trustee J. Du Pratt White as chairman, President Farrand, Professor F. H. Bosworth, Professor Charles H. Hull, and Trustees Henry W. Sackett and Robert H. Treman. They were to

Fig. 185. Baker Laboratory of Chemistry (1921) by Arthur N. Gibb and Frank Miles Day. This building was the gift of George F. Baker.

study and prepare a plan for the architectural, engineering, and landscape development of the University.[4] Preparation of the plan took three and one-half years. Several preliminary reports were submitted and general advice was given on a number of building projects.

Baker Laboratory of Chemistry, one of the first postwar buildings, was dedicated in 1923. It was constructed before the new campus planning group came into existence. Arthur N. Gibb ('90), who had helped C. Francis Osborne arrange the chemistry laboratories in Morse Hall, worked with the faculty of Chemistry to develop the details of the program, the relationships between laboratories and their layout, and equipment in the new building. Frank Miles Day, of Day and Klauder, provided architectural design services. He used the native Ithaca stone, which had received such acclaim in the construction of the men's dormitories, in panels between the limestone-faced concrete columns of the new laboratory building. Baker Laboratory was made possible by a gift of $1,500,000 from

George F. Baker in 1919. Preliminary plans for this new chemistry building had been prepared by Professor Louis M. Dennis and Arthur Gibb in 1910. These provisional plans were the basis for Baker's decision to finance the building. It was the donor's wish that in the development of the final plans, excellence and completeness of equipment should be given first consideration. It was also decided that the building should be located more centrally on the campus than Morse Hall since work in chemistry was required for students of Agriculture as well as the College of Arts and Sciences.[5] The site selected, north of Rockefeller Hall, also provided easy communication between chemistry and her sister science, physics. This communication has been completed structurally with the building of Clark Hall between Baker and Rockefeller. Baker Laboratory (Fig. 185) was designed to provide for the construction of the additional wings to the east which are now (1967) being completed. The original plan called for two more tiers of open courts surrounded by labo-

[4] Trustees' *Proceedings,* 11 May 1922.

[5] Louis M. Dennis, *The Baker Chemistry Laboratory* (Ithaca, 1925).

ratory units. For this reason the eastern elevation was built of the same pressed cream-colored brick used in the inner court. The laboratory is of fireproof construction and all floors above the basement are reinforced concrete. The original block was probably the finest chemistry laboratory in the country at the time of its construction.

While Day and Gibb were completing supervision of the construction of Baker Laboratory, a number of other architects were commissioned to design buildings for the campus. In 1922, the University Plan Commission was asked to recommend a site for a student union building, Willard Straight Hall, given to the University as a memorial to Willard D. Straight ('01) by his widow, Dorothy Whitney Straight Elmhirst. Their recommendation of a site south of the Library was accepted and Delano and Aldrich were commissioned to design the building. Here in the great high-ceilinged Memorial Room, another dream of Andrew D. White's was realized. He had always wanted a great hall for the assembly of alumni and for other important occasions. His first attempt to have such a hall built at Cornell was made in 1872 when he urged Charles Babcock to enlarge and beautify the dining hall at Sage College with paneling and great fireplaces. This had proved too expensive and White had to wait until 1913, when Prudence Risley Hall was built, to get his great dining hall. But it was too small to come up to his dream. It is almost certain that the Memorial Room of Willard Straight would have satisfied his expectations.

Andrew Dickson White's dreams for a great hall at Cornell were continually being renewed by the proposals of Cornell alumni to develop an "alumni club" on the campus where the "great gatherings and entertainments of the alumni" could be held and where memorials of former professors and students of the University could be displayed. The first resolution in connection with this proposed building was passed by the Associate Alumni in 1888. White offered to give $10,000 for its construction. Indeed, White may have suggested the idea to the alumni, who in turn suggested it to him as Trustee. The committee which was formed to promote the idea and White held several architectural competitions over the years. Some of the programs for these competitions included banquet halls and an auditorium in addition to rooms for group activities. The competitions of 1898 and 1899 called for the design of a building on the site of Sage Cottage (Professor Prentiss' former home). These competitions were held among graduates and students of the College of Architecture. The Trustees were asked to reserve "Prentiss Corner" for the erection of the proposed alumni hall and clubhouse for a period of three years. Open competitions were also held in 1901, 1902, and 1904. But alumni funds were never sufficient to finance construction of a building.[6]

William Gray Purcell ('03) wrote a perceptive and amusing description of the 1902 competition in *Charette* (July 1952). Purcell, who was a junior in the College of Architecture, would not comply with the suggestions of Design Professor Nash, "a Beaux Arts graduate fresh from Paris," so he based his design on respect for the general qualities of the first buildings: basic shapes—windows, doors, and scale of their masonry. The architectural faculty jury (except for "Pa" Martin and "Ma" Phelps) were "nonplussed by such a simple-minded idea." But, according to Purcell's reconstruction, "while the jury was at work judging the drawings and having a lovely time according to their Parisian routine, a shade of Andrew Dickson White drifted across the Atlantic, and stood beside them.

[6] The program written for the competition of 1904 is perhaps typical. It called for a design of an auditorium, banquet hall, and alumni club. The auditorium was to seat 3,500 people including reserved seats for the faculty, Trustees, and President. A monumental organ was to be placed behind the faculty seats. The banquet hall was to seat at least 1,000 and was to be "specially monumental and decorated with pictures, busts and portraits." The alumni club was to include reception rooms, library, dining room, suites for distinguished guests, and "many other rooms for the alumni." This program was written by the College of Architecture's "French Critic," Maurice Jaques Prévot, from suggestions provided by White.

Fig. 186. Willard Straight Hall (1923), by Delano and Aldrich, the first building to be located by the University Plan Commission appointed by President Farrand in 1922. The Cornell Student Union building was a gift of Mrs. Leonard K. Elmhirst in memory of her first husband, Willard D. Straight ('01).

With dismay they began to see that . . . only one contestant had made any real attempt to solve the problem . . . only one design called for a modest building" that was "related to the other buildings on the campus" and "showed a decent respect for the sentiment of the old buildings." Purcell was awarded the prize.

During much of this competing, Willard Straight, soon to become a Morgan partner and to marry a Payne Whitney heiress, was a student in the College of Architecture. We do not know whether he entered any of the competitions, but he surely must have been as aware as any student at Cornell of the great need for an alumni and student gathering place. After Willard Straight's tragic early death, his widow provided a very fine one (Fig. 186) with student meeting rooms, dining facilities, club rooms, reading and game rooms, guest rooms, a music room and an

excellent small theatre. White thought some of the early competition plans had too many smoking, lounging, and billiard rooms in them. Cornell's student union, finally completed in 1925, never seems to have had too many of these or indeed too much of any kind of room. But we must sadly admit that the Memorial Room (Fig. 187), White's main feature for the "Alumni Hall," with its portraits, flags, and trophies, sometimes has a deserted look.

According to an often repeated campus tale (probably not true), the architect for Willard Straight Hall assigned responsibility for design of the great student union building to one of his associates. The architect, William A. Delano, is said to have first visited the campus when the building was almost completed. While walking through the great Gothic hall, he looked out one of the narrow slitlike windows at the Cayuga Lake valley to the north. He then is said to have wheeled on his designer-associate and growled, "Why didn't you tell me there was a view like this from here?" Indeed the hall commands one of the most impressive views from East Hill of the lake. But White would have approved its high wood-paneled walls. In his dream of such a hall they were needed for the portraits of great men including the founders and benefactors of the University.

The Plan Commission continued its preliminary campus planning studies and reviews of current building proposals throughout the twenties. In 1923 it approved the plans for the War Memorial (Fig. 188) and the enlargement of the Crescent. Until then the stadium, built in 1916, had consisted of a rather conventional, straight-topped, tiered arrangement built on the slope of Kite Hill (Fig. 178). The new arrangement, the Cornell Crescent (Fig. 189), designed in 1923, provided a greater amount of seating nearer the fifty-yard line than more conventional stadium designs. It was probably unique in its time.

Late in 1922 Frederick L. Ackerman ('01) was commissioned to design new women's residence halls for the Kline farm property

Fig. 187. Willard Straight Hall, Memorial Room. Willard Straight left instructions that he wanted his estate to "serve in some way to enrich student life and to enlarge the opportunity for human contact" at Cornell.

east of Wait Avenue and Triphammer Road. Ackerman's studies for the women's housing area were carried out under the direction of the University Plan Commission. His thorough analysis of the problems of the site, his development of many alternative solutions, and the careful evaluation of his plans provide good illustrations of the new technical level achieved in campus planning at Cornell in the twenties and thirties.[7] The planning, fund-raising, design, and construction processes for Balch Halls also illustrate the need for continuity of purpose and for continuous review and coordination in campus planning. It was not fortuitous that the interaction of administrative officers, Trustees, Plan Commission members, donors, architect, landscape architect, and builder resulted in the very fine building group of Balch Halls. The achievement was the product of a system which involved all of these actors at appropriate times

in a continuous planning process within the accepted framework of an approved overall campus plan.

Even before World War I it had become apparent that more university housing for women students would be needed. A committee of alumnae started to raise money for a new hall for women. In 1916 the Trustees established a policy that would permit use of university funds for up to one-half of the cost of a dormitory if returns from such an investment would be as large as the average return on other investments. The first university action of a more positive nature was the appointment in 1920 of Trustee J. Du Pratt White ('90) to negotiate with prospective donors.[8] In August 1920 a special committee consisting of Charles E. Treman; James H. Edwards, alumni Trustee; J. C. Westervelt, chairman of the committee on buildings and grounds; J. Du Pratt White; Acting President Albert W. Smith; the Dean of Women, Dr. Grace L. White; and the Comptroller was

[7] Architectural Advisory Board Minutes, 18 June 1923–August 1944 (C.U. Archives) provide an indexed record of these reviews. The Board continued its services until the early 1950's.

[8] Trustees' *Proceedings*, 23 July 1920.

Fig. 188. War Memorial (1923). This addition to the men's residential halls was designed as part of the proposed east-west Library Tower axis which was ultimately to extend to University Avenue. The group is comprised of two residential towers, Lyon and McFadden Halls, and a connecting colonnade.

asked to report on the advisability of using land north of Fall Creek for residential halls for women. The committee's positive recommendation was followed by an exploration of unit sizes and other program questions by a committee of women headed by Dr. White.[9]

Two years of discussions on what was needed and how it was to be financed led to the appointment in late 1922 of Frederick Ackerman to prepare a general plot plan. On 20 January 1923, Ackerman's general plans were approved by the Trustees, and President Farrand was "authorized to present them to the prospective donors." One assumes that the "prospective donors" were pleased with them because with some modifications the plans were placed before a newly formed Architectural Advisory Board in the spring of 1924. During this time both the University Plan Commission and the Advisory Board were preparing the overall campus plan which will be described later. In June 1924, the Architectural Advisory Board pointed out that Ackerman's plans indicated an "extensive encroachment upon land not now owned by the Uni-

[9] Trustees' Papers, 5 August and 2 October 1920.

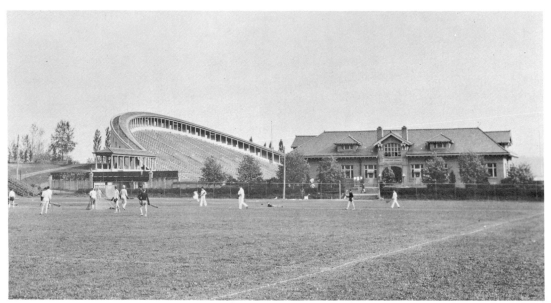

Fig. 189. The Cornell Crescent (1923) and Schoellkopf Memorial Field House (1914). The latter was the gift of Willard Straight ('01) in honor of Henry Schoellkopf ('02).

versity, and even with the removal of the parts which extend over other ownerships, the group is still left so close to the property lines as to be rather unsatisfactory." More than two years passed before agreement was reached on how to deal with the difficulties of the restricted site and the design of the group. Land purchase was authorized and the site and general layout were approved by the Board of Trustees on 13 November 1926.[10]

With the solutions to these basic problems accomplished, Ackerman proceeded with the preparation of detailed preliminary drawings for the buildings and site which he completed in February 1927. These were reviewed and approved successively in the spring and summer of 1927 by the landscape sub-committee, the buildings and grounds committee of the Board of Trustees, and the Architectural Advisory Board. Later that year and early in 1928, President Farrand was authorized by the Trustees to accept the gift of funds for the halls from anonymous donors, contract drawings were completed, more land was acquired, bids were taken, and construction started. Only then was it announced that the gift of $1,650,000 for the new women's residential halls was from Allen C. Balch ('89) and Mrs. Balch, the former Janet Jacks, a Cornell graduate student from 1886 to 1888, of Los Angeles.

The Balches had been involved in the design process, too—had "taken the keenest interest in the development of the plans" and had placed some thoughtful conditions on their gift: Balch Halls were to be used "exclusively to provide living quarters for the women students"; further, the donors expressed their desire that if additions were made they should be "in the same general type of architecture" as the original buildings; and, finally, Mr. and Mrs. Balch hoped that, after maintenance and operating costs and the costs of acquiring additional land were paid, the net operating revenue would be

Fig. 190. Balch Halls (1927) by Frederick L. Ackerman. These residential halls providing room for three hundred twenty women were the gift of Mr. and Mrs. Allen C. Balch.

used "for increasing the salaries of the Professors and Instructors . . . whose services may be deemed most valuable in the instruction and welfare of women students."[11]

The four halls (Fig. 190), each housing approximately eighty students, were formally opened in September 1929. They were built of Ithaca stone and, according to the *Cornell Alumni News*, were in the "English Renaissance" style. Each has an individual entrance off the main court and each has a distinctive style of decoration and furnishing which were at the time the halls were opened styled

---

[10] Architectural Advisory Board Minutes, 16 June 1924, and Trustees' *Proceedings*, 13 November 1926.

[11] Meridian Ltd. to C.U. Board of Trustees, Trustees' Papers, 7 January 1928. The Balches were generous benefactors of American higher education. Another of their gifts was Janet Jacks Balch Hall at Scripps College in Claremont, California.

"Early American, Georgian, English Jaco-
bean, and modern Grammercy Park." [12] The
halls were first occupied some nine years after
the initial negotiations with the donors. The
development of the new women's residential
halls, from conception to occupancy, set no
speed records, but they were typical of the
buildings of the twenties and thirties at Cornell in that the excellence of design, fitness to
site, and attention to detail resulted from an
intelligent, comprehensive, and continuing review by all parties concerned. The product
was clearly worth the pains. Balch Halls still
comprise, without question, the finest student
housing provided by the University.

Creation of the University's Architectural
Advisory Board was triggered by a request to
the alumni of the College of Architecture to
review Ackerman's plans for Balch Halls. In
January 1923, Richmond H. Shreve ('01)
wrote Franke Hunt Bosworth, Dean of the
College of Architecture, that the alumni group
of Cornell architects had met and looked at
the drawings but felt that they could not do
justice to Ackerman's thorough study of the
problems in the time available to them.
Shreve felt that their review, which would be
advisory only, would have little impact on the
development of satisfactory plans for campus
buildings. He suggested that the University
consider appointing an advisory architect or
group of architects who would assist the University Plan Commission with the development of a general scheme for the campus and
with review of specific building plans. The
alumni committee passed a resolution urging
"the formation of a permanent organization
for controlling the architectural development
of the University." They recommended that a
single advisor be appointed to work with the
Plan Commission and the Trustees' building
committee.[13]

[12] *Cornell Alumni News*, 3 October 1929.
[13] R. H. Shreve to F. H. Bosworth, 18 and 23
January 1923, Architectural Advisory Board Papers.
Shreve acted as chairman of the "Alumni Architects
Committee." His recommendation for an Advisory
Board was accepted and the Board was appointed on
18 June 1923.

The University first turned to Warren Manning, one of the landscape architects who had
worked on the campus planning studies of
1910, to fill this role. They soon decided, however, that an advisory board of three members
could do the work more effectively. Manning,
with F. H. Bosworth and Milton B. Medary,
was appointed to this newly constituted Architectural Advisory Board. The group served
in two capacities: setting the overall framework of circulation and building location, and
reviewing and criticizing the plans of architects commissioned to design buildings so that
the whole would achieve architectural unity.
With the assistance of the newly appointed
Architectural Advisory Board, the Plan Commission continued its studies for a long-range
campus plan. After 1923, they received much
assistance from the executive architects appointed to prepare plans for a university library extension, a gymnasium, an extension of
the engineering group, a fine arts building,
and faculty apartments on Thurston Avenue.[14]
The Plan Commission maintained close liaison with these architects as they developed
preliminary plans. At the same time, the state
architect was developing long-range plans
for additional buildings for Agriculture and
Home Economics. Numerous consultations
were held with him. Several of the detailed
preliminary studies which have been preserved in the University Archives (Fig. 191)
show the extent to which detailed liaison was
carried out with various executive architects
and the state architect.

The final report of the Plan Commission,
Plan for Development of the University, was
published 14 November 1925. Figure 192
shows the proposals. Later the plan was approved by two members of the Architectural
Advisory Board, F. H. Bosworth and M. B.
Medary, by Bryant Fleming, who by then had
been named University Landscape Advisor,
and by the Board of Trustees. According to
the published report, it was the intention of
the Commission to produce a plan that would

[14] Architectural Advisory Board Minutes, 18 June
1923–15 July 1931.

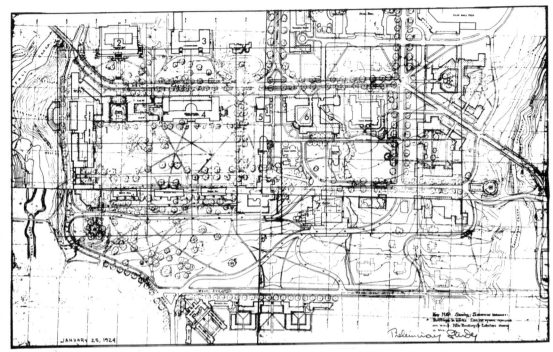

Fig. 191. General campus plan, preliminary study, January 1924. The heavy-line grid represents squares of approximately one minute's walking time. (1) Engineering schools; (2) Baker Laboratory; (3) Rockefeller Hall; (4) Goldwin Smith Hall; (5) Stimson Hall; (6) proposed fine arts building; (7) Willard Straight Hall; (8) proposed gymnasium.

be flexible yet "precise enough to give assurance that under proper guidance in its ultimate execution it would produce a grouping of buildings and a landscape treatment of a character suited to the University." The Plan Commission believed that proper guidance would be best accomplished by the continued operation of the Architectural Advisory Board.

The 1925 plan recognized the already existing division of the campus into two educational areas, an athletic area, and two dormitory areas. It attempted to bind the two educational groups more closely by establishing future building lines. The group's view of the importance of the planning process is nicely summarized:

The Commission has envisaged this plan not as a thing for immediate execution but rather as a skeleton about which to grow. It does not propose the destruction of any existing building or road. It sees this plan as one which will grow into

actual being bit by bit as particular needs arise and only as they arise. It has made free use of many plans which have been made in the past, taking those elements from each which in its judgment were good.[15]

One of the major policy recommendations of the Commission's 1925 plan was to "retain Morrill, McGraw, and White Halls irrespective of their physical condition."[16] A great western terrace was suggested as their setting, "an academic acropolis." Again shades of Frederick Law Olmsted (raised by Manning and Fleming)! The Commission suggested that the design of such a terrace should enhance the sweeping view and provide a dignified setting for the buildings which "represent a tradition and help recall to our minds the original conception of the founders of a university set upon a hill." Such a terrace,

[15] The University Plan Commission, "Report of the Plan Commission" (Ithaca, 14 November 1925), pp. 5–6.
[16] *Ibid.*, p. 5.

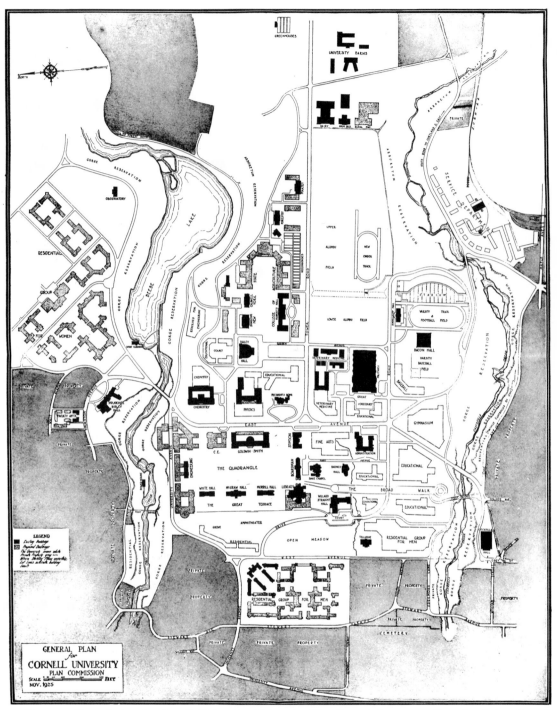

Fig. 192. General plan for Cornell University, University Plan Commission, 1925. Note the designation of Gorge and Arboretum Reservations; the Great Terrace; the Broad Walk; completion of the College of Agriculture Court; a Service Department area; and extensive development of academic buildings around Sage College. Proposed buildings for which fairly detailed studies had been completed are shown in gray.

originally proposed by Frederick Law Olmsted and re-proposed in the Manning-Fleming campus plan of 1910, has been a recurrent idea in Cornell planning. An indication of its long life as an idea for improving the "west front" is the fact that it appears in the campus plan drawings from 1910 to 1948. Recently, in the 1964–1965 studies of the University Planning Office under the direction of Vice-Provost Thomas W. Mackesey, the idea has been brought up to date with some practical proposals that the level below the terrace might be used for parking, for service, or perhaps for classroom space.

The proposals of the 1925 campus plan report accepted the importance of East Avenue as a city thoroughfare linking the city and Cornell Heights. It proposed widening this street to accommodate increasing traffic. The report also proposed the erection of a new Cascadilla Bridge which would provide a direct connection between East Avenue and College Avenue. A recommendation for the relocation of Central Avenue below the "Great Terrace" and west of the Library was shown in preliminary sketches, but the final plan shows Central Avenue completely removed and its space used for "A Broad Walk" for pedestrians to which only emergency vehi-

cles would be admitted. The existing Central Avenue Bridge over Cascadilla Gorge was to serve as the principal pedestrian access to the campus. The report also noted an "imminent danger" to the peace of the campus from through traffic and proposed the improvement of connections between Route 13 and State Street along Dryden Road to divert such traffic away from South Avenue.

The dominant architectural features of the 1925 campus plan were a proposed new College of Engineering group, a massive counterbalancing addition to the Library, a very large fine arts building, an enormous new gymnasium, and further development of both men's and women's residential areas. York and Sawyer were entrusted with the development of detailed plans for the engineering group. Their design (Fig. 193) eliminated all the engineering buildings existing then with the exception of West Sibley and Rand Halls. To provide the required floor area, the architects were forced to use five- and six-storied buildings because of the restrictions of the site. Their design provided for the use of native Ithaca stone in the style set by the residential halls and Willard Straight.

Plans for the extension of the Library were also developed by York and Sawyer. These

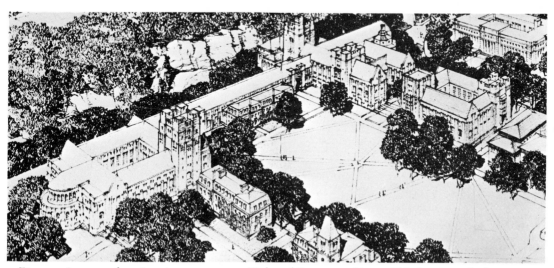

Fig. 193. A proposed engineering group, 1925, York and Sawyer, architects. This drawing is fairly representative of the scale and style of the building designs developed in connection with the Plan Commission studies of the early 1920's.

plans called for the addition of stacks and work space around a large central court. The proposed addition would have extended over 100 feet down the west slope. In architectural treatment the library extension would have echoed the western wing of the engineering group located at the north end of the proposed "Great Terrace." The Library plans also proposed an arch over Central Avenue connecting the Library and Boardman Hall. This link would have provided book space on its upper floors and direct access to additional stack and work space in Boardman Hall. Preliminary studies (Fig. 191) and the final 1925 plan (Fig. 192) show this proposal.

At the same time, preliminary studies for a fine arts building were being developed by Frederick Ackerman. This large structure, proposed for the present site of Day Hall, would have almost completely filled the space between Stimson Hall and Sage College and would have extended from the building line on East Avenue to a line parallel to the front of Sage College. Filling of the stream valley north of Sage College would have been necessary to accommodate it. Ackerman argued that in order to preserve this feature, a building would have to be so small that it would not be of any value as an academic building. Bryant Fleming argued to save the stream valley [17] and fortunately (strongly assisted by the University's inability to finance the building) won the debate that followed.

The men's gymnasium designs for the 1925 plan, also developed by Ackerman, were based on the plan's proposed location for this building at the south end of East Avenue on a triangular site and developed an excellent solution to the difficult problems of the site's shape and slope. Facilities were to be lavishly provided in a location near Hoy Field and the Crescent. But, alas, there were no funds.[18]

Other architectural proposals of the 1925 general plan included the conversion of Sage College to administrative offices, the retention and extension of the agricultural campus court first proposed in 1910, and the development of a service building group in East Ithaca south of Cascadilla Gorge. A general layout proposed for this service area included power and heating plant, storage buildings, stables, laundry, and incinerator. The 1925 study also detailed some major proposals for the improvement of the gorges and the creation of a university arboretum. Colonel Sackett, whose gifts were instrumental in the extensive improvement of gorge trails, was a member of the Commission. The 1925 recommendations included plans for acquisition and informal landscaping of large areas to create a girdle of developed park area around three sides of the University.

The 1925 plan was, in the main, formal. Although it "did not propose any arbitrary symmetry," symmetrical composition was employed effectively in the principal quadrangles and courts and in the Tower Road–Library–men's residential halls axis. The plan was designed to guide future growth on the irregular site and considered the development of bordering lands. It appropriately emphasized the focal aspect of the Library Tower. The proposed fine arts building was probably too large for its site as was the proposed gymnasium, but the other building groupings were well conceived.

The proposal for the creation of a "Broad Walk" had great merit. The elimination of automobile traffic from Central Avenue, which was to have been made possible by the

[17] Bryant Fleming, "Report to Accompany a Tentative Plan for the Development of Cornell University Property Bounded by East Avenue, University Avenue, Cascadilla Creek, Fall Creek and Interrelated Areas, 16 June 1930," pp. 2–4. Fleming admits to sentimentality in his remarks on the preservation of the stream but he continues: "The beauty of the Cornell campus is its admixture of extreme natural beauty and a semi-sense of formality. Were the Campus plan to be completely and architecturally formalized, its primary value, its extreme natural beauty, would be suppressed to a point of possible eradication."

[18] Ackerman's services in connection with planning sports facilities extended over a period of eighteen years. The shamefully inadequate gymnasium in the Old Armory served until 1954, when Teagle Hall was opened. Ackerman's last report on the nagging problem was published in 1939.

construction of a new bridge from College Avenue to East Avenue, would have provided a more restful atmosphere among the academic buildings. Later plans which proposed a relocation of Central Avenue west of Willard Straight and the "Great Terrace" to service the Library and the three original buildings would have accomplished the same objective. Recent proposals for bridging Cascadilla and Fall Creeks on the line of West Avenue and Eddy Street would also accomplish this purpose.

The most noteworthy landscape idea of the 1925 plan was its elaboration of the aged proposal for a "Great Terrace." This improvement, designed to make the impressive view to the Cayuga Lake valley and the western hills more accessible to Cornell pedestrians and to enhance the dignity of the original academic group, seems inevitable—as a proposal.

The economic depression which arrived in the thirties made the realization of most of these plans impossible. But all was not lost. Myron C. Taylor ('94) gave funds for a new Law School in 1930. Its impressive "Gothic" massing and detailing (Fig. 194), and the somber dignified character of its great law library hall give us a good idea of the campus qualities desired by the planners and designers of the twenties. The law school court (a great place for dueling) is one of the most impressive small open spaces on the campus. Funds were never available for most of the buildings sited in the 1925 plan. After the construction of a new central heating plant, Balch Halls for women's residence, the War Memorial including Lyon and McFaddin Halls for men's residence, and Myron Taylor Hall, its specific proposals were abandoned. But many of the plan's general ideas and suggestions were carried over in subsequent development schemes. The painstaking creative work of the 1925 Plan Commission was of great and lasting value to campus planning efforts at Cornell.

While the building plans of the endowed colleges waned, those of the state colleges

Fig. 194. Myron C. Taylor Hall (1930), Eggers and Higgins, architects. This building was a gift of Mr. Taylor ('94), former president of U.S. Steel and later President Franklin D. Roosevelt's personal representative at the Vatican. The axis through the tower was designed to lead down to Stewart Avenue through a group of new residential halls.

waxed. Not much in the way of major building had been done on the upper campus since Liberty Hyde Bailey's last building campaign of 1910–1913. Stocking Hall, a new building for the Dairy Department, was completed in 1923 and a southern wing for the Veterinary College ("English Collegiate Gothic" in deference to Barton Hall) was completed in 1937. The major College of Agriculture additions were built in the early thirties: the gigantic Plant Science Building (1931), and the equally imposing though not so large Warren Hall (1932). These were perhaps exceeded in excellence of facilities if not indeed in size by the College of Home Economics' Martha Van Rensselaer Hall (1933). Over this period of two years the State of New York invested almost three million dollars in buildings for the state colleges. The agriculture court first envisioned in the 1910 plans of Manning and

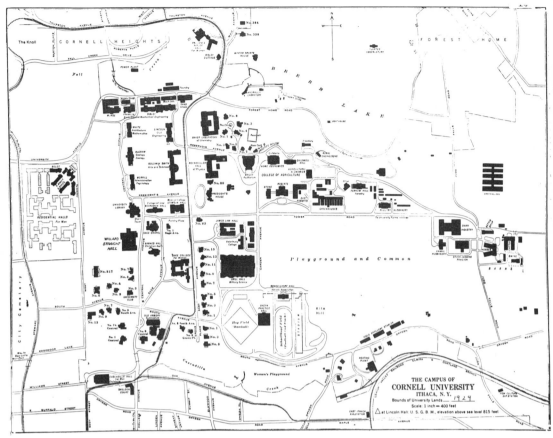

Fig. 195. The Cornell campus, 1929.

Fleming now lacked only its eastern termination.

In 1930 Bryant Fleming and Warren Manning were asked to restudy the campus plan of 1925 and submit proposals for its revision. Fleming's studies dealt chiefly with the principal landscape features and building groups of the lower campus. Manning's studies were concerned with regional concepts and traffic problems.

Fleming's report and plan (Fig. 196) were developed on the basis of the major features of the 1925 plan. He re-emphasized the importance of East Avenue as a main campus artery and the need for construction of a new bridge connecting it to College Avenue. He proposed the establishment of fixed building lines on both sides of the street. He also recommended that Tower Road not be extended west to Central Avenue and was "definitely

against retaining Central Avenue from South Avenue to Willard Straight and the Chapel." "There is nothing," he wrote, "which mars the collegiate peace and quiet more than traffic conditions along the present Central Avenue." [19] In his 1930 report Fleming developed the idea of improving automobile access to Willard Straight, the Library, and Morrill, McGraw, and White Halls in conjunction with the "Great Terrace." The new road he proposed below the terrace was also to provide the access needed for service of these buildings. This road and the proposed retention of Sage Avenue terminating at Sage Chapel made the "Broad Walk" proposal of the 1925 plan a workable idea.

Several years before Fleming's study was prepared, the Franklin C. Cornell property

[19] Fleming, *op. cit.*, p. 4.

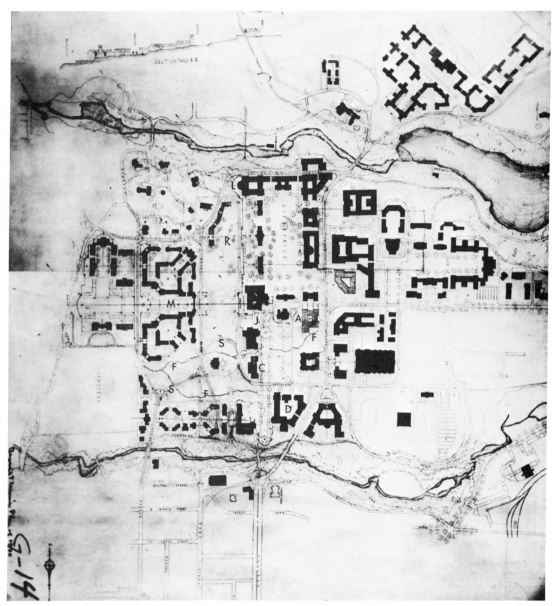

Fig. 196. This sketch for a campus plan by Bryant Fleming, 1930, includes proposals for refinements and extensions of the 1925 general plan: overlook terraces at (*J*) south of the main Library, west of the library addition, and west of the proposed new College of Engineering buildings (*L*); a "secondary quadrangle" west of Sage College; a road below the "promenade" west of the Stone Row; more open and more extensive men's residential halls west of West Avenue (*M*); the landscaping of small stream valleys (*F*) from East and Central Avenues to Stewart Avenue; and a new approach to the campus up the "Libe Slope" south and west of Willard Straight Hall (*S*).

southwest of Willard Straight Hall had been purchased by the University. A new University entrance from the west over this land was now proposed. Fleming's 1930 plan (Fig. 196) shows an alignment for the new entrance (Campus Road) quite similar to that finally adopted in 1932. Other road proposals of Fleming's 1930 plan included one for straightening Stewart Avenue at the bridge over Cascadilla Creek, one for widening College Avenue, and another for a new Cascadilla bridge connection from Eddy Street to West Avenue.

Fleming explained his ideas for the proposed "Great Terrace" very completely:

I would begin this terrace at the north facade of Williard Straight Hall, from there I would create an arcaded loggia connecting Willard Straight Hall directly with the Library, the arcade being a semi-enclosed structure below the level of Central Avenue. This arcade should be so designed as to act as a retaining wall between the two buildings and its roof so planned as to form a platform and parapet to an observation area at approximately the same grade as now established before Willard Straight. I refer to area "J." This could be beautifully handled as a large paved gathering terrace complementary to Willard Straight Hall.

This terrace should then extend out and around the west facade of the Library where it should be developed as an important overlook commanding the fine views to be had from this point. Nothing should in any way interfere with this development, and it would be perfectly feasible to readjust the present plans for the Library to accommodate this idea. . . .

Road "C" could be carried beneath this terrace overlook so giving access to the Library and the three original main buildings, for delivery of freight, etc., tunnelled connections being suggested to these buildings.

From this point north, the road would carry below the base of the terrace above, steps and accents being suggested especially on the axis "K" of McGraw Hall, where an interesting axial line carries up from University Avenue below.

The terrace as suggested terminates in another important overlook at the west end of proposed Sibley College, so giving important emphasis to the Sibley Group at this point. . . .

I will not attempt to go into a detailed explanation as to the designing of this westerly overlook terrace except to say that its parapet should be below a general level of the ground back of the three original buildings, and be paralleled along this entire length by a broad promenade or path from which one would enjoy the view.[20]

[20] *Ibid.,* pp. 7–8.

Fleming also studied several campus open spaces, especially the brook valleys from Stewart Avenue to East Avenue. These were the last remnants of the nineteenth-century topography of the main campus. It was in connection with the preservation of these features that Fleming strongly criticized the size of Ackerman's proposal for a fine arts building. It would have required complete filling of the stream valley north of Sage College. Fleming's study of privately owned areas surrounding the campus led to the suggestion that the land between Stewart Avenue and the city cemetery should be controlled by the University and developed as part of the new entrance off Stewart Avenue. His ideas for the development of the Library slope differed greatly from previous concepts. Among other things, Fleming suggested a formal plaza east of the War Memorial to emphasize the main university axis which runs east and west through the Library Tower, Tower Road, and the Memorial. His suggested observation terrace below the Library was also designed to strengthen this axis.

Fleming's 1930 campus plan proposals included a new quadrangle to be created by the removal of Barnes Hall. It was to be framed by Sage College, Sage Chapel, Willard Straight, and buildings marked "A," "D," and "C" in Figure 196. A large building group at the south end of this quadrangle was suggested as a site for fine arts buildings. Fleming recommended that the remaining faculty cottages eventually be removed from East Avenue and that the "entire avenue be made as a site for university buildings." His report included proposals for the addition of new wings on the east sides of Goldwin Smith Hall and Sage College, similar refacing of Rockefeller Hall's west side, a new building on the site of the President's House, and new academic buildings west of Barton Hall. Here he suggested that two buildings might flank the central axis of the drill hall to emphasize its massive west façade.

An interesting and "radical" afterthought presented in Fleming's report is his suggestion for unifying the two distinct academic groups of the lower and upper campuses along an axis between Morrill Hall and the proposed College of Agriculture library. He thought that developments in the distant future might make possible the modification or razing of Goldwin Smith and Rockefeller Halls, thus permitting a grouping of buildings along this axis leading into the lower campus from the College of Agriculture.

The 1930 campus planning studies prepared by Warren Manning dealt with problems of traffic flow, parking, the Library Slope, regional considerations, arboretum plans, and use of the "Great Terrace" as the roof of a structure to service the Library and other buildings and to provide library storage and covered passage between buildings. Extensive consideration was given to problems of local and regional traffic and the width of roads (Fig. 197). His proposals recommended Stewart Avenue, East Avenue, and Judd Falls Road as the main north-south campus routes. He suggested removing West Avenue because it interrupts the main university axis. Manning proposed the retention of Tower Road to the Library and connecting it with Central and Sage Avenues. Almost every one of his traffic proposals disagreed with those of Fleming. Manning felt that the circuit formed by Central, Tower, and East Avenues was essential for traffic circulation and parking. His recommendation for the relocation of South Avenue, which was necessary to create an adequate site for Myron Taylor Hall, was the same as Fleming's. Its final position (Campus Road) can be traced back to proposals of the 1910 and 1925 campus plans.

Manning also proposed a new use for the "Great Terrace" of the 1925 plan:

I feel that serious consideration and study should be given to the Great Terrace of the 1925–26 General Plan. I would have this studied with a view to providing a building under this terrace to serve as a covered passage from University Avenue buildings to Willard Straight Hall. Such covered passageways are now being established in many large public institutions, especially in the

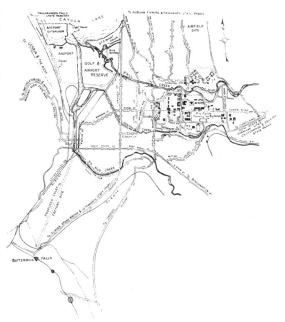

Fig. 197. "Land Units and Direct Ways," a sketch from Warren Manning's 1930 campus planning report.

region of winter snows. This proposed building will, I believe, have a special value as a library extension and as a scientific, industrial and Patent Office model museum.[21]

By far the most radical proposal of Manning's 1930 reports was his suggestion for garages and an access tunnel under the University. The tunnel was to have its entrance in the valley at the foot of East Hill at the intersection of Yates and Linn Streets four hundred and thirty feet below the Quadrangle. Manning's description of it staggers the imagination:

To center automobile traffic, to gain more rapid and direct access to the university centers at all seasons, I am recommending that a study and estimate of costs and of returns from fees be made for an automobile terminal parking space, for a terraced garage on the steep slope, for a tunnel under the university on its axis line with elevators up to such points as Stewart Avenue,

[21] Warren H. Manning, "Reports to the Architectural Advisory Board and the Trustees' Building Committee," 4 November 1930, C.U. Archives, Report No. 762-273.

Men's Residential Group, Central Avenue at the Library, Garden Avenue at Agricultural center, and stadium, and to Judd Falls Road if this is not too far.

If this were found practicable and economic, the whole study that I am presenting would be modified in many ways, with economies in construction and a marked easing up of transportation difficulties.[22]

Another interesting proposal which indicates that Manning's farsightedness was not entirely out of focus was his suggestion for an airfield site near the country club in Cayuga Heights. The site, shown on Figure 197, is not too far south of the present site of the Tompkins County Airport, which was first developed by the University in 1946.

The 1930 reports of Fleming and Manning apparently were used by the Architectural Advisory Board in their work on the 1932 "General Plan of Development, Cornell University" (Fig. 198). Fleming's concepts for the development of East Avenue academic buildings were incorporated with the exception that the President's House was retained and one instead of two buildings were proposed west of Barton Hall. The fine arts building and gymnasium proposals as originally designed by Ackerman in 1925 were retained in the 1932 campus plan. The general layout of the engineering group is also the same as was proposed in the 1925 plan with the exception of a few of the details at the eastern extremity of the group. The layout proposed for the women's residential group remains as it was designed by Ackerman in 1927. The overall plan for the men's residential group was being restudied at the time by Ackerman following his very detailed report of 1930.[23]

Fleming's 1930 suggestions for the Library Slope were included in the 1932 campus plan in greatly modified form. The proposed plaza

[22] Ibid., Report No. 762-274.
[23] Frederick Ackerman, "Housing for Men, Cornell University, Ithaca, N.Y.: Report on an Inquiry into the Utilization of a Certain Tract of Land for Residential Use for Men Students," 20 October 1930.

east of the War Memorial was greatly reduced, and walks changed. His ideas for the "Great Terrace" were also greatly modified and the road he had proposed at its base was now to be placed under the terrace roof.

Following Manning's suggestion, a detailed study of the Library Slope was prepared and discussed in 1931 and 1932. Various planting possibilities and alternative plans for the creation of the "Great Terrace" were carefully considered. The drawings, prepared in the buildings and grounds department, included plans, sections, and a detailed elevation of the project. Apparently, the redesign of the landscape of Library Slope and the terrace idea were abandoned once again shortly after these studies were made.

Manning's insistence on the need to retain the loop formed by Central Avenue, Sage Avenue, and Tower Road and East Avenue was heeded. The "Broad Walk" proposal of the 1932 plan was limited to the stretch of Central Avenue between South Avenue and Cascadilla Bridge. The service area around the heating plant, south of Cascadilla Creek, was developing in accordance with the 1925 plan, and the major features proposed for it in 1925 were retained in the 1932 plan. Following the 1930 recommendation of Warren Manning, East Avenue was widened.

Some of Manning and Fleming's proposals for the extension and improvement of the university arboretum were also carried out in the thirties. The Cornell Arboretum development was established to create a comprehensive plant garden and to enhance the scenic qualities of areas bordering the campus. It was designed "to provide systematically arranged collections of trees, shrubs, vines, and woody perennials which could be studied as they grow in the open." Because of its large projected extent (Fig. 199) it was possible to plan the arboretum as a great parklike area. This was intended to serve as a wildlife sanctuary and at the same time to link the University's various land holdings. The plan, in effect, called for a highly developed greenbelt

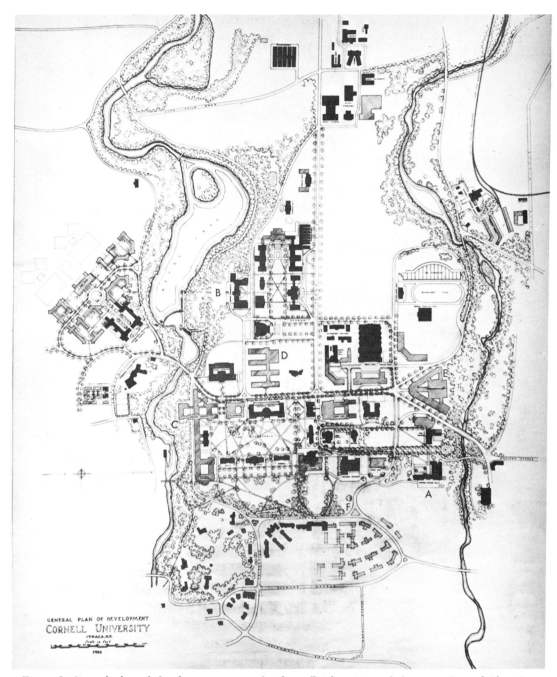

Fig. 198. General plan of development, 1932, the first official revision of the 1925 General Plan. It incorporates approved plans for Myron C. Taylor and Martha Van Rensselaer Halls (*A*) and (*B*); slightly revised plans for the College of Engineering (*C*); plans for a new physics building to replace Rockefeller Hall (*D*); new plans for the men's gymnasium (*E*); and Fleming's proposal for a campus drive (*F*).

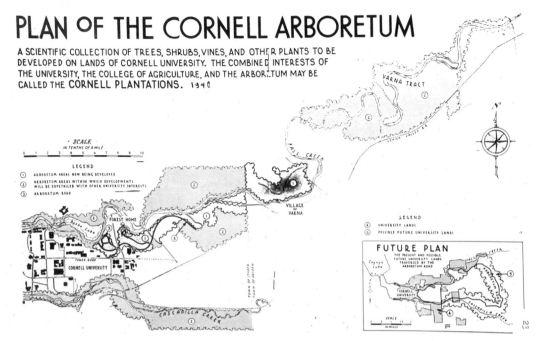

PLAN OF THE CORNELL ARBORETUM

A SCIENTIFIC COLLECTION OF TREES, SHRUBS, VINES, AND OTHER PLANTS TO BE
DEVELOPED ON LANDS OF CORNELL UNIVERSITY. THE COMBINED INTERESTS OF
THE UNIVERSITY, THE COLLEGE OF AGRICULTURE, AND THE ARBORETUM MAY BE
CALLED THE CORNELL PLANTATIONS. 1940

Fig. 199. A plan of the Cornell Arboretum, 1940. The Arboretum, first suggested by Professor A. N. Prentiss in 1877 and afterward by many others, was incorporated in the 1925 general plan. Development work began in 1935 with labor provided by the Civilian Conservation Corps. In 1944 the Arboretum became the Cornell Plantations, administered by a joint committee of representatives from both faculty and administration.

around three sides of the Cornell campus. Two winding drives starting at either side of the campus were planned to extend five miles east of the Quadrangle in the Fall Creek and Cascadilla watersheds. These drives were to be connected by a north-south drive located in the saddle between Baker Hill and Mount Pleasant.

Most of the extensive development of the Cornell Arboretum based on the general plans of the twenties and early thirties date from 1935 when a C.C.C. Camp in the area provided labor at no cost to the University. A great deal was accomplished before the camp was closed in March 1941. One and one-half miles of driveway, several miles of footpaths, a bridge, an overlook terrace, and 850 feet of retaining wall were completed in this period. Many acres of land were cleared, graded, and drained to receive plantings. Continuing improvement of the arboretum, now called the Cornell Plantations, has since then been made possible by generous gifts of Cornell alumni and friends. Its extensive and varied collections, including the superb rose garden, have become a major attraction to Cornellians and campus visitors.

When President Farrand retired in 1937, campus growth and change were at ebb tide. The grand dreams of the mid-twenties had been abandoned, but not before they had left an imprint on the long-term structure of the campus. Morris Bishop concludes that "Farrand's record is an impressive one. But . . . President Farrand hardly touched our education structure." Farrand, Bishop continues, "let the colleges run themselves. Some of them ran themselves very well; and some . . . ran themselves gently downhill. . . . By his very reluctance to make changes [he] endeared himself to the campus. . . . The Cornell of Livingston Farrand became somehow more kindly, more human." Under the gentle guidance of President Farrand in an era of confidence, Cornell developed campus plans that were to have great influence on the future.

Farrand also strengthened Cornell's administrative ability to prepare and revise plans for the well-ordered development of its campus. This increased ability to plan and control the details of development was essential to the maintenance of variety within some semblance of unity during the rapid expansion of the campus that followed his presidency.

XIV

Two Times Cornell

To DOUBLE THE SIZE OF A great university campus in slightly under thirty years is no small feat. To do so in a period when first the great national depression of the thirties slowed the work and then World War II halted permanent construction for four years makes the accomplishment even more remarkable. Yet in the years between 1937 and 1966, under the leadership of Presidents Day, Malott, and Perkins, additions greater in size than the physical plant of 1937 were made at Cornell.[1]

On the retirement of President Farrand in 1937, Edmund Ezra Day (Fig. 200) assumed the office. His style of administration, including decisions on building and campus development, was a marked contrast to his predecessor's. President Day was restless and impatient. He triggered changes, whereas Farrand had waited for them and then either supported or quietly vetoed them. On taking office Day noted the need to improve the University's administration, to provide better library facilities (the Library was woefully overcrowded in spite of new southwest stacks which were completed in 1936) and to over-

haul the College of Engineering and provide it with a new physical plant.

Two new deans took office in Day's first year as President. S. C. Hollister became Dean of the College of Engineering and subsequently played the leading role in providing the college with a new campus; and Gilmore D. Clarke ('13), Professor of City Planning, became Dean of the College of Architecture. As chairman of the Architectural Advisory Council from 1937 to 1950, Clarke played a leading role in the preservation and extension of the excellent quality of the University's landscape and buildings.

Under President Day the Architectural Advisory Board became the Architectural Advisory Council but retained the same functions of supervising the preparation of the campus development plan and reviewing proposals for new buildings, remodeling, and landscaping. The state architect's plans for a library building for the agricultural campus were returned for further study on several occasions in the late thirties. Landscaping details for the development of the arboretum were reviewed and re-reviewed. Proposals for new parking areas seem to have been considered with great regularity and seem to have been disapproved in at least half of the cases. A special committee on traffic control and parking was appointed in 1937.[2]

[1] Cornell University Planning Office, *Gross Building-Area Summary Tables* prepared in 1965. Over three million gross square feet (3,030,000) of building floor area was in place by the end of 1937. From January 1938 to June 1965, the University added over three and one-half million square feet (3,600,000) of building floor area.

[2] Architectural Advisory Council Minutes, 1937–1950. The records show that the Council operated

A series of important recommendations made in 1937 and 1938 required many changes in the overall campus plan. These recommendations are recorded on a schematic drawing prepared in 1938 which shows the campus divided into eleven general use areas: *law school*—Myron Taylor Hall; *engineering*—the area around the Old Armory and Sage College; *religious and social activities*—the area around Sage Chapel, Barnes Hall, and Willard Straight; *fine and liberal arts and pure sciences*—the Quadrangle and Baker Hall areas; *library*—the present site of Rockefeller Hall; *military science*—Barton Hall; *Veterinary College*—its present site at the east end of Tower Road; *agricultural campus; athletics area;* and the two student residential areas.[3]

The decision to provide a new site for the College of Engineering proved to be the most radical and effective proposal of this plan. The south campus project was designed to preserve the capital invested in the original engineering buildings by using them for the much-needed expansion of facilities for the College of Arts and Sciences and at the same time to provide sufficient new space for the current and long-range needs of the College of Engineering. Provisions for the extensive needs of the College of Engineering in accordance with the 1925 plan would have completely filled the north campus site, leaving no room for expansion. Furthermore, in order to accomplish such development, it would have been necessary to remove all of the buildings being used by Engineering with the exception of West Sibley and Rand Halls. The Colleges of Arts and Sciences and Architecture would have been prohibited from expanding at all

Fig. 200. Edmund Ezra Day, fifth President of Cornell, 1937–1949.

by such a development. Moving the entire College of Engineering allowed Arts and Sciences and Architecture to expand into White Hall, Franklin Hall, the Sibleys, Rand Hall, and Lincoln Hall. Since 1950 the gradual shift of Engineering to the southern part of the campus has enabled the other two colleges to expand.

A general plan for the Engineering College prepared by Shreve, Lamb, and Harmon was approved by the Architectural Advisory Council and by the Trustees in January 1938. The first building in the new group, Olin Hall for chemical engineering (Fig. 201) designed

on the principle that those who would serve the general good must do it in the most minute particulars. The smallest changes in paths or the removal or planting of single trees were subject to review and judgment quite as much as were plans for new buildings and major landscaping projects.

[3] Sketch of Campus Development Framework, c. 1938. Department of Buildings and Properties plan files.

Fig. 201. Olin Hall, for the School of Chemical Engineering, by Shreve, Lamb, and Harmon (1941). In 1937 the Trustees decided to relocate the College of Engineering south of Barnes Hall and Sage College. This building was the first unit of the new campus.

by Shreve, Lamb, and Harmon, was started in 1941 and finished in 1942 in time for the wartime Navy program to use some of the space in it. The metallurgy laboratories, Kimball and Thurston Halls, also designed by Shreve, Lamb, and Harmon, were completed in 1953. Since then Phillips Hall for electrical engineering built in 1954, Carpenter Hall for administration and the engineering library built in 1957, Upson Hall for industrial engineering and operations research (1958), Grumman Hall for aeronautical and space engineering (1958), Hollister Hall for civil engineering (1959), the teaching nuclear reactor building (1963), and Bard Hall for materials science (1964), all by Perkins and Will, have completed the relocation of the College. The total construction cost was approximately twelve million dollars.

The proposed use of the southern part of the campus for new engineering buildings had considerable effect on the Architectural Advisory Council's 1942 campus plan (Fig. 202). Although the general framework remained that of the 1932 plan modified by the 1938 diagram, several building proposals were relocated, and new ones added. A proposed new administration building replaced the proposed fine arts building on the site west of East Avenue and south of Tower Road. A faculty club was planned for a site east of East Avenue. The proposed location for a new men's sports building was changed to Hoy Field and an addition to Bacon Practice Cage was also scheduled. The first published version of the plan showed a vast new library on the site of the Andrew D. White villa. A later revision restored the President's House and moved the proposed library back to the "Libe Slope." The 1942 plan showed the contemplated removal of engineering shop buildings north of Sibley Hall to make room for extensive parking areas—a dream now come true. And provision was made for a new building for the College of Architecture to replace the forlorn-looking but still useful Morse Hall. A temporary roof had been placed over the main floor of the burned-out building.

A noteworthy characteristic of the 1942 campus plan in comparison to earlier ones is its extensive proposals for large parking areas and major improvements in the road system. For examples, a new alignment of the road and bridge connecting College and East Avenues was to provide a much better connection to Route 13 than any previous plan; and large parking lots were to be sprinkled liberally about the campus.

The campus development plan prepared under the Architectural Advisory Council in 1942 was the basis for all subsequent campus plans until the early 1950's. The 1946 and 1948 campus development plans (Figs. 203 and 208) incorporated most of the earlier plan's basic concepts. Only the details were changed. So for example, the location of the building being planned to house the new New York State School of Industrial and Labor Relations was shifted in each successive revision. Other modifications included various sitings of proposed agricultural buildings, a variety of proposals regarding additions to the Library, and several schemes for additions to Baker Laboratory and Rockefeller Hall.

But the coming of World War II laid building plans of the late thirties and early forties on the shelf and brought instead an era of seemingly permanent temporary buildings. Plans for the construction of a Statler Inn on the shores of Beebe Lake to be financed by the Statler Foundation for the Department of Hotel Administration were laid aside. President Day's plan to establish a Graduate School of Business and Public Administration was also laid aside for the duration of the war, as were plans for a new agricultural engineering building and the College of Agriculture library.

One project, however, was initiated in spite of the war—and in the nick of time, too. This was the establishment of the Collection of Regional History and University Archives. Morris Bishop reports that wartime "Scrap drives cleaned out University cellars and disposed of, among other things, all the official records of Charles Kendall Adams's presidency." [4] Attics were cleaned out, too. Professor John Hartell of the Art Department found an interesting-looking letter on the floor of a corridor in Franklin Hall. It proved to be a letter from Andrew Dickson White written in 1871 to Charles Babcock offering him the chair in architecture at Cornell. Professor Hartell pursued the truck collecting for the paper drive which had carried away the College of Architecture's old records but, alas, it was too late. The paper had been shipped efficiently out of town. Happily, many other important university records were saved by the activities of the Archives.

After the completion of Olin Hall, wartime construction on campus was limited to temporary emergency facilities: the Navy diesel laboratory intruding on Sage Green established a beachhead, so to speak, for the engineers; a Navy mess hall was located on the recently developed sports field west of the World War I Memorial; and the first edition of the Ivy Room was built to provide dining facilities for Naval cadets on the west terrace of Willard Straight Hall.

But if there was very little building during the war, there was a great deal of planning. The State Assembly Speaker, Irving M. Ives, proposed and the Trustees approved a new state-supported School of Industrial and Labor Relations. The proposed buildings to house ILR were sited first north of Myron Taylor Hall, next on Hoy Field, and, after a

[4] Morris Bishop, *A History of Cornell*, p. 550.

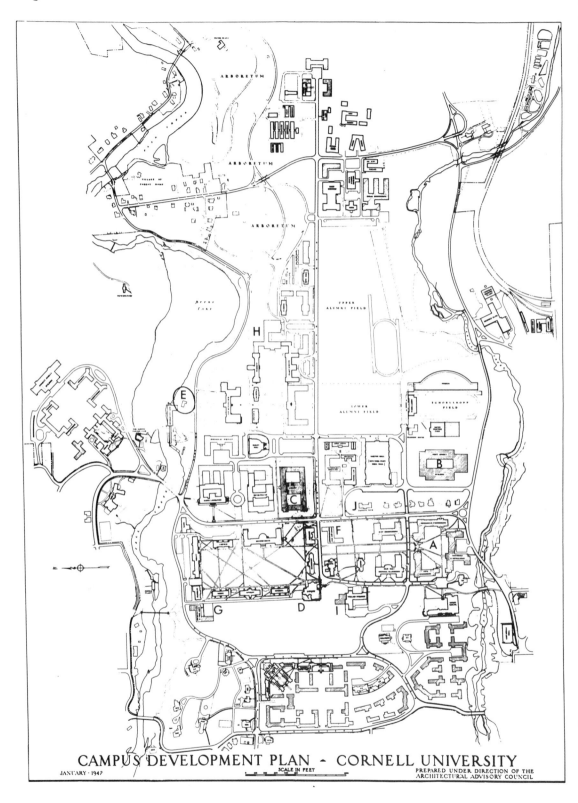

CAMPUS DEVELOPMENT PLAN - CORNELL UNIVERSITY

JANUARY · 1947   SCALE IN FEET   PREPARED UNDER DIRECTION OF THE
                                                                     ARCHITECTURAL ADVISORY COUNCIL

wave of protests by alumni, finally located above East Avenue on the place then occupied by the Veterinary College. President Day developed plans for a School of Business and Public Administration and a site was selected east of East Avenue below Hoy Field.[5] Plans for a new administration building were developed by Frederick Ackerman and plans for the men's sports building were revised and a new site was designated for it east of Barton Hall on lower Alumni Field. Plans for a new women's dormitory and a sports building were prepared by Bagg and Newkirk. The plans for a faculty club were incorporated in Holabard, Root, and Burgee's new design for Statler Inn and the School of Hotel Administration and this structure was allotted its present site on East Avenue. Revised plans for development of the men's dormitory area were prepared by Ackerman, and revised plans for additions to Willard Straight, the Library, Rockefeller and Baker Halls, and new plans for the College of Agriculture were approved. All of the plans for newly proposed buildings, revisions of earlier plans, and revised plans for additions were incorporated in the campus development plan of 1946 (Fig. 203) which, in turn, was to guide a major expansion program after the war.

Edmund Ezra Day's will to build was strong. Most of his plans for postwar expansion at Cornell were realistic; almost all of them have been realized in the last twenty years—and then some! President Day was not afraid to take risks. Morris Bishop calls him an "innovator" and "daring."[6] As World War II drew to a close, the President plunged into action. Some thought recklessly so. Clara Dickson Hall for women was under construction early in the summer of 1945. The University purchased over a thousand acres of land in the Town of Lansing, northeast of the campus, for the development of East Hill Airport; and in perhaps the most daring move of all Day committed the University to building a laboratory for nuclear studies before the funds were in sight and before the Trustees had approved the idea. Fortunately for the President, the University, and the Physics Department, Floyd R. Newman ('12) gave the University a million dollars for the building. Skidmore, Owings, and Merrill were also retained to prepare plans and later to develop preliminary designs for a new building for the Physics Department to replace Rockefeller Hall. Plans for the replacement and additions proposed west of Rockefeller Hall did not get beyond the stage of preliminary sketches, however, and were soon abandoned for lack of funds.

As a rule, Cornell presidents have been faced with only two general classes of problems relating to campus planning: endowed-college buildings designed by architects retained by the Trustees and sited by the University; and State of New York contract college buildings which until 1964 were designed by architects retained by the New York State Department of Public Works and sited by the University. To these, in President Day's postwar administration, were added temporary buildings designed by almost anyone and sited by committees. Eight classroom barrack and quonset buildings and many dormitory barrack buildings were placed on the

[5] Cornell University Development Plan-1946 and Architectural Advisory Council Minutes, 1942–1945.
[6] Morris Bishop, *op. cit.*, p. 589.

Fig. 202. Campus development plan, 1942. Revisions brought about by the decision to relocate the College of Engineering to (A) evoked strong reactions from the university community. The proposed location of the men's sports building on Hoy Field (B) did not receive universal acclaim, and the proposal to build the much-needed new library on the site of the Old President's House (C) was resisted vigorously. Another plan, which revised the long-standing proposal to add library space on the "Libe Slope" (D), was bitterly opposed by other factions. The ellipse sketched south of Beebe Lake (E) indicates some tentative, noncommittal thinking—soon to be abandoned—about a site for a new school of hotel administration. Other proposals of this plan were a new administration building at (F), a fine arts building at (G), the updated version of the College of Agriculture library (H), the addition to Willard Straight Hall (I), the "Great Terrace" (G–D), and a faculty club (J).

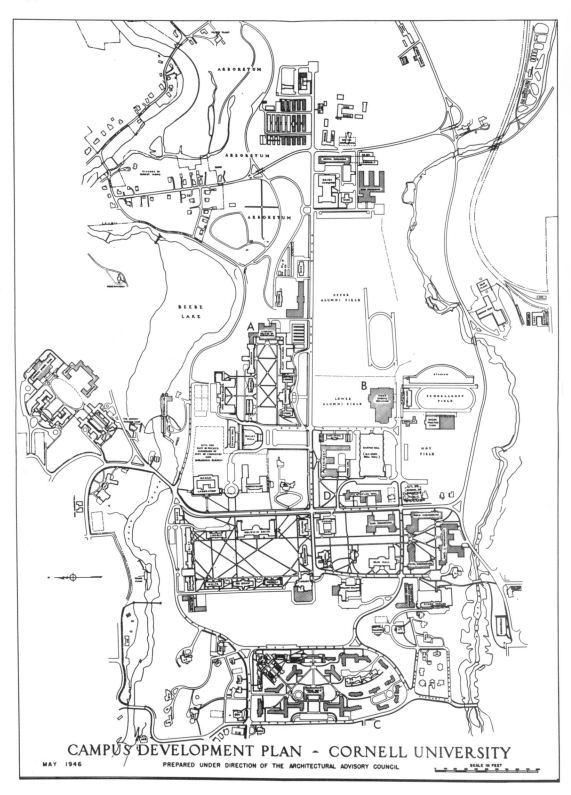

CAMPUS DEVELOPMENT PLAN - CORNELL UNIVERSITY

MAY 1946   PREPARED UNDER DIRECTION OF THE ARCHITECTURAL ADVISORY COUNCIL   SCALE IN FEET

campus in the two years after the end of World War II. Happily, very few are still in place at this writing (1967). They served well in meeting the needs of a swollen postwar enrollment.

Building costs were high and labor short after World War II, so construction of a number of the buildings planned was delayed. Nevertheless, in the period from 1945 until President Day's retirement in June 1949, in the endowed colleges the Clara Dickson Hall women's dormitory, Day Hall for administration, Newman Laboratory of Nuclear Studies, Savage Hall for the School of Nutrition, and Statler Hall for the School of Hotel Administration and faculty club were completed or well started. Five major building projects in the state contract colleges were deferred because of high costs or siting problems. These were the Warren Hall addition, Mann Library for agriculture and home economics, Riley-Robb Hall for agricultural engineering, and new buildings for the Veterinary College and the new School of Industrial and Labor Relations. Several endowed-college building projects which were designed and funded in the late forties and early fifties suffered the same fate. Ground was not broken for Kimball-Thurston Hall, the second unit of the new Engineering Quadrangle, or Anabel Taylor Hall for CURW until 1950. Plans for Moakley House were set aside until 1951. The men's indoor sports building, Teagle Hall, and an addition to Willard Straight Hall were not started until 1952.

When the new administration building, appropriately named Edmund Ezra Day Hall, was occupied in 1947, the President noted these delays and a growing list of additional buildings that would soon be needed. His estimates of needs and costs were: Library expansion ($5,000,000); three additional buildings for engineering ($2,000,000); a new

clinic ($1,000,000); an indoor sports building for women ($3,000,000); additional dormitories ($5,000,000); a student interfaith center ($1,500,000); and the almost completed but still unfinanced nuclear studies laboratory ($1,500,000). In all, Day saw a need for twenty-one million dollars for buildings in the endowed colleges in addition to twelve to fifteen million dollars committed by the State of New York for buildings for the state-supported colleges, but unspent.[7]

In May 1948, the Trustees decided to mount a twelve-and-a-half-million dollar capital funds campaign which would include financing for the major building needs of the endowed colleges. By June 1949 eight million dollars of the goal had been raised, including the gifts of Floyd R. Newman for the nuclear laboratory building, of Myron C. Taylor ('94) for the interfaith center; and Walter C. Teagle ('99) and Mrs. Teagle for a men's sports building. By June 1951 with the goal reached, the first phase of Cornell's postwar building campaign came to a close.

What can we say of these buildings and this phase of campus development? Lacking the perspective which the passage of time supposedly gives critical judgment, we would be well advised to withhold comment. Perhaps it is unfair to conclude that there are no really significant works of architecture among them, and that no great advances for the campus environment were achieved in the first six years of postwar building. While such conclusions are tempting, they would not all be correct. To execute overall campus building plans made in the expansive and prosperous twenties during the expensive forties was in itself difficult. In addition, to maintain the architectural coherence and good landscaping qualities of the campus was a feat in itself.

[7] President's report (1947), p. 13.

Fig. 203. Campus development plan, 1946. The sketches of various buildings are here more detailed than in the 1942 plan: for example, the library for the College of Agriculture (A) is smaller; there are detailed plans for an enormous (and too expensive) sports building on the south end of Lower Alumni Field (B); and there is a new site plan for the men's residential halls area (C). The new hotel school building, Statler Hall, is now shown as being incorporated with the faculty club west of Barton Hall (D).

256 THE CORNELL CAMPUS

Fig. 204. Balch Halls (1927) and Clara Dickson Hall (1946), the latter by Bagg and Newkirk.

Clara Dickson Hall designed by Bagg and Newkirk (Fig. 204) was built to pay its own way. The rich materials and luxurious spaces of Balch Halls could not be repeated. Nevertheless, the architecture of this brick and stone dormitory is very compatible with its neighbor in form and detail and in general fits very well in the dormitory group. Day Hall's

architect made excellent use of the hillside site and provided a generous amount of very much needed space, thereby freeing Morrill Hall for use by the overcrowded College of Arts and Sciences. Its compact, businesslike plan permitted siting that preserved the stream valley to the south and left open a significant space between the new building

Fig. 205. Edmund Ezra Day Hall (1945), the University's administration building, by Frederick L. Ackerman.

Fig. 206. Anabel Taylor Hall, for Cornell United Religious Work, designed by Eggers and Higgins (1950), was the gift of Myron C. Taylor ('94) in memory of his wife.

and the Chapel. If the need for administrative office space on the Cornell campus is best expressed in a frank, economical adaptation, in appearance at least, of the better-class postwar New York City office building, Day Hall (Fig. 205) does the job well.

The other buildings of the postwar construction campaign are so varied in architectural style and siting as to defy evaluation from such close range. All are substantial and useful. Those structures which represent the realization of earlier "castle dreams" are appropriately "Gothic." Of this type there are Anabel Taylor Hall (Fig. 206), a fitting companion for the Law School's Myron Taylor Hall; and Teagle Hall (Fig. 207), a complex

Fig. 207. Teagle Hall (1954), the men's sports building, by Rogers and Butler, was the gift of Mr. and Mrs. Walter C. Teagle.

but low "English Gothic" companion to the simple, massive, high "Gothic" of Barton Hall. The buildings which house new departures in the sciences are appropriately simple, clean-looking, and economical. Of the two structures of this type (Savage Hall for the School of Nutrition and Newman Laboratory for Nuclear Studies), the latter building, by Skidmore, Owings and Merrill, is the most up to date. The clear horizontal expression of alternating brick spandrels and continuous windows and the glass-enclosed vertical circulation make Newman Laboratory an excellent early example of the "International style" in which lie the origins of this famous firm's approach to modern building. The yellow brick used in both buildings is a courtesy nod to their yellow-brick neighbors and continues the Cornell campus theme of variety within unity. Material color provides the uniting force in both, but greater deference of the past is shown in Savage Hall which stands nearer to Bailey and Martha Van Rensselaer Halls than does the Newman Laboratory.

The siting of both buildings is unfortunate. No spatial composition seems to have been intended and none of any quality was created. Savage Hall was originally intended to form the south wing of a U-shaped building for the biological sciences (Fig. 202), but in 1946 its space was rescheduled for sharing with the proposed expansion of chemistry and physics facilities (Fig. 203). Physics arrived first and by 1948 the extension plans for Savage Hall had been reduced to two short north wings (Fig. 208). The desire to preserve several faculty houses on upper Reservoir Road seems to have influenced these decisions regarding sites. In the end, these complications apparently combined with quick decisions to cancel the efforts of the planners to achieve a unified grouping of buildings.

Edmund Ezra Day was a pragmatic "can-do" President. Morris Bishop concludes that he was a "practical man" like Ezra Cornell and one of Cornell's great presidents. At any rate, he coped. And he performed great feats

of leadership in all seasons: in the difficult years before World War II when Cornell was at ebb tide in its fortunes; in the confusing and demanding war years when Cornell responded to the country's needs for special training programs; and in the uncertain postwar years when Cornell was almost overwhelmed with problems resulting from massive increases in enrollment, expansion of the physical plant, deferred maintenance, and rapidly rising costs. The buildings of the Day era, mixed in stylistic approach and architectural quality as well as in function, fulfilled (in a generally satisfactory way) several elements of the campus plans of the twenties and thirties. All of the Cornell campus planning ideas of the postwar era were adaptations in the long evolution of an overall form-idea of the campus. The campus development plans which guided the building of the forties had preserved in modified form many of the proposals of Manning, Fleming, Lowrie, and the Architectural Advisory Board. We may not (and perhaps never will) call the buildings of 1937–1949 beautiful, but they are more than utilitarian additions to the Cornell campus. They respect established forms and in most cases contribute to the continuing evolution of a university campus of great natural beauty in which an elusive formal quality in the relationships between buildings and spaces organizes but does not overpower the scene. In 1948 a revised campus development plan (Fig. 208) was prepared to help guide the evolution of this quality.

An interregnum of two years followed the resignation of President Day in 1949. In these years while Provost Cornelis W. de Kiewiet and Vice-President Theodore P. Wright were in charge, Cornellians saw the ground-breaking or completion of several building projects started during Day's presidency. Statler Hall, completed in 1950, gave faculty and friends spacious club rooms, an economical cafeteria, and a gracious dining room as well as a comfortable library-reading room and an impossibly tiny cloak room. Ground was broken for

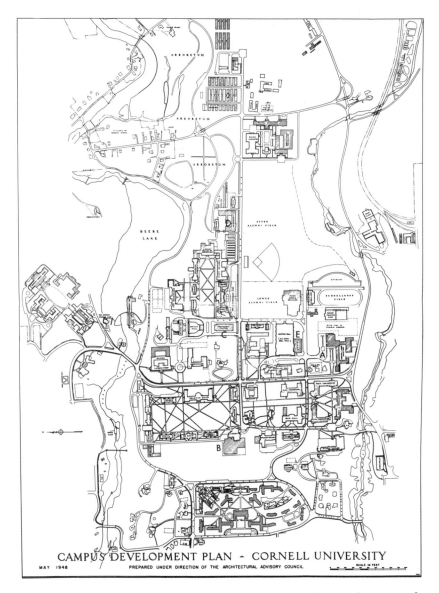

CAMPUS DEVELOPMENT PLAN - CORNELL UNIVERSITY

MAY 1948   PREPARED UNDER DIRECTION OF THE ARCHITECTURAL ADVISORY COUNCIL   SCALE IN FEET

Fig. 208. Campus development plan, 1948—the last published plan prepared under the direction of the Architectural Advisory Council to show specific proposals for new buildings. There are few changes from the 1946 plan: one, the location of the newly established New York State School of Industrial and Labor Relations on Hoy Field (*A*); another, a much larger addition to the main Library (*B*). Other new proposals include a conference center (*C*), an agronomy building (*D*), and an R.O.T.C. addition (*E*). In 1951 the last of the series of campus development plans which started with the 1942 proposals was issued. The name of the Architectural Advisory Council was removed along with most of the specific building proposals. Buildings to be demolished were indicated in dashed lines, and proposals for sites of various Engineering College buildings and the ILR School at the east end of Tower Road were labeled. The era of overall campus planning which had begun in the early 1920's was clearly at its end.

Fig. 209. View of the campus from the west, 1954. University Halls are under construction in the left foreground and at the far end of Tower Road the site of new buildings for the College of Veterinary Medicine is being cleared. Between these two projects little if any construction is underway. Recently completed or almost completed buildings which were started in the late 1940's and early 1950's include Anabel Taylor Hall in the right foreground; Kimball-Thurston Hall, for Mechanical Engineering, at the right; Statler Inn and Hall below Barton Hall; Teagle Hall above Barton Hall; Mann Library, for the College of Agriculture, at the far end of Ag Court; and Riley-Robb Hall, for Agricultural Engineering, above the tennis courts at the east end of Alumni Field.

Kimball-Thurston Hall, the second building on the engineering campus, in 1950. Raising funds for these long-awaited engineering structures was difficult but obviously not impossible. Under the able leadership of Dean Hollister the completion of the group now began to move along at a steady pace. Also, the start of construction for Mann Library (Fig. 209), the long-deferred, much-needed, oft-replanned structure which was to close the east end of the "Ag Court," marked the end of the state-supported colleges' building blockade.

With these buildings of the late forties and early fifties, planning and building on Cor-

nell's campus reaches a point where (with a few exceptions) the evaluation of campus architecture and improvements will be left to future critics and historians. During most of the twenty years following World War II, the quality of Cornell architecture and campus development seems to have suffered under policies which dictated cost-cutting in new construction, remodeling, and maintenance. Great, rapidly changing, and increasing needs, short funds, and rising prices were a constant burden to the administrators and designers responsible for Cornell's environment for learning. It will take some time for the architectural returns to become clear.

Fig. 210. University Halls for freshmen (1952).

One hears arguments on both sides regarding the relations between the problems of cost limitations and architectural excellence. The "correct," perhaps true, and certainly properly idealistic position for a university community is that excellence in architecture and landscape design and therefore excellence in the overall design quality of a campus are much more functions of design skill and hard work for a sympathetic and imaginative client than of budget. The care with which educational programs are designed and the level of utilization of building space are more variable than building budgets. And although it also seems to be more difficult to design a handsome building to be built principally of brick rather than of Italian marble, it is not an impossible task. It is no doubt obvious that the more expensive material may be used in bad designs as well as good and conversely that the common material may be ill or well used. All of which is simply to say that the evolution of the Cornell campus and its buildings in the last two decades could probably have been much better at little greater cost.

Even so, in some cases a somewhat larger budget might have been a wise policy in the long run. Necessity seems to have been the mother of desperation rather than invention in the 1950 decision of the Trustees that "Engineering rather than architectural construction [would be] advisable" for the much-needed men's dormitories. Eighty-five-years of ambiguous and shifting policies on student housing and the press of persistently increasing enrollments plagued the decision makers. They could wait no longer for gifts for "Gothic magnificence."[8] A general mood in favor of economy haunted this decision. The University had accumulated a sizable deficit in the previous war and postwar decade, and had just reached a state of solvency thanks to prodigious efforts on the part of Acting-President de Kiewiet. The Trustees wanted to keep it that way.[9]

The six new "engineering style" men's dormitories (Fig. 210) turned out to be the sort

[8] Morris Bishop, *op. cit.*, p. 597; Trustees' Minutes, 19 September 1950.
[9] Morris Bishop, *op. cit.*, pp. 593–594. The 1949–1950 budget estimated a deficit of over $800,000. The actual deficit was only $69,000.

Fig. 211. Deane W. Malott, sixth President of Cornell, 1951–1963.

of "brick boxes standing on bare plots of ground" which President White in 1885 had so mournfully predicted would appear if Cornell lost her understanding of the educational role played by campus design. What saving or partially redeeming grace has this double echelon of brick boxes? Only one is immediately apparent: their siting respects the great "semi-formal" east-west axis of the University. It may be significant that until very recently the dormitories remained numbered rather than named and that their maintenance costs remain high because of various economies in the selection of building materials and equipment.

But, as President Day wrote in his last Annual Report, "Cornell was on the march." If Cornell's esthetic sensibilities were sleepwalking, as some claimed, still the sleeping senses responded drowsily that the brick dormitory boxes were an improvement over the wood barracks that preceded them on the site west of the World War I Memorial. And so they were, in permanence if not in appearance. Perhaps they will be improved by skilled hands some day and made part of a thoroughly effective composition. President White dreamed and saw fulfilled such dreams for the first buildings on the Arts Quadrangle one hundred years ago. Today's Cornellians could not wish for less.

The University's second greatest period of campus expansion, comparable only to the campus extension and building pace under President Schurman from 1900 to 1920, continued and gained momentum under her sixth president, Deane Waldo Malott (Fig. 211). Cornell alumni and other benefactors gave over $110,000,000 in the decade which began with President Malott's election to office.[10] Much of it was for buildings and other campus improvements. The needs of the state colleges for buildings were also handsomely met. During President Malott's twelve-year administration, over $20,000,000 in state-financed construction was completed or initiated. In total more than $60,000,000 was spent for buildings for the state and endowed colleges in Ithaca over a twelve-year period. When the costs of Medical College buildings, those at the Geneva Experiment Station, road construction, grounds improvements, alterations, and acquistion of new buildings are

[10] President's report (1963), p. 5.

Fig. 212. Law Auditorium and Schurman Hall (1953) are two of the major instructional buildings of the New York State Veterinary College.

added, total capital expenditures were over $90,000,000.[11]

Mann Library and the Warren Hall extension were completed and occupied. New buildings for the Veterinary College (Fig. 212) were completed at the east end of Tower Road in 1958, thereby releasing a site on East Avenue for the much-shifted School of Industrial and Labor Relations. Riley-Robb Hall, the long deferred new home of agricultural engineering named for Professors H. W. Riley ('01) and B. B. Robb ('11), was completed in 1956, and the extensive animal husbandry building, named for Professor Frank B. Morrison, was completed in 1963.

It is good to report that the suitability of space in which to work, solidity of construction, and durability of interior materials and finishes of state college buildings remained at the high levels of preceding decades. The quality of architectural design and imaginative handling of complex design problems also remained at the level previously observed. A surveyor of the vast expanse of buildings erected since the 1920's on Cornell's upper campus might note that its creators followed the building advice given Johns Hopkins' first president by the great scientist Huxley in 1876: "Get an honest bricklayer."[12]

Cornellians may well be grateful that this "no-nonsense approach to building" employed in the upper and middle campus structures of the state colleges encloses so much useful space. Many may also be grateful for the growth of ivy and other planting which clothes some of them so quickly and helpfully under the expert nurture of the Cornellians most skilled in horticulture. There is a persistent rumor that a governor of the State of New York began overturning and restructuring the system of providing design services for state-financed university buildings soon after participating in dedication ceremonies for a recently completed creation of the system.

In any event, the most recent buildings designed for the College of Home Economics and for research in agronomy are likely to be of a very different cast. Ulrich Franzen's designs for the agronomy building will provide a powerful, almost windowless, air-conditioned, brick tower on Tower Road. His designs for a major addition to Martha Van Rensselaer Hall provide for a separate unit having at several levels narrow connections with the north side of the existing building.

---

[11] *Ibid.*, p. 8.
[12] Albert Bush-Brown, "Get an Honest Bricklayer. The Scientist's Answer to Ruskin," *Journal of Aesthet-*

ics and Art Criticism (March 1958), pp. 348–356. Huxley advised Daniel Coit Gilman to save on building costs and spend on faculty and equipment. Gilman, taking the advice, assembled a brilliant faculty for the new university and housed them in second-hand remodeled buildings in Baltimore.

A new look in state-financed buildings at Cornell seems to be in the offing.

During Deane Malott's presidency, the endowed colleges grew at least as much in physical plant and enrollment as the state ones. In addition to and because of the completion of new Engineering Campus buildings between 1953 and 1964 (Fig. 213), the College of Arts and Sciences and the College of Architecture have more and better space. The Sibleys and Franklin Hall were remodeled for architecture, history, and government, and Lincoln Hall, White Hall, and part of McGraw have undergone major renovations adapting them to the needs of the College of Arts and Sciences. The financing and siting problems of Teagle Hall for men's sports were resolved and it moved toward completion in 1954. Lynah Hall was erected in 1958 east of Teagle Hall, and in the same year Gannett Clinic replaced the last remaining faculty houses on Central Avenue, which had been remodeled for clinic use. Helen Newman Hall, completed in 1965, finally provided very adequate facilities for women's sports.

Housing for Cornell's students also received major attention under President Malott. After the completion of the freshman dormitories on the west side of the campus, the supply of apartments for married students was supplemented by the construction of university-financed units west of Pleasant Grove Road and later by the construction of 246 units in the Hasbrouck Apartments. The great growth of graduate programs at Cornell placed heavy demands on local housing available for single as well as married students, and so in 1960 Sage College was converted for use by unmarried graduate students; since then the graduate school offices have also been moved to the southeast wing. In addition, Cascadilla Hall was renovated for graduate student use in 1963. Provision of additional housing for undergraduate women was not neglected. Mary Donlon Hall, Cornell's first "high-rise" elevator dormitory, accommodating 475 students, was completed in 1962. All of these buildings with the exception of Helen Newman Hall and Lynah Hall were located more or less in accordance with the campus development plan concepts of the late forties.

A modest but most welcome addition to campus facilities was realized in 1955 through the hard work of Trustee Allan H. Treman ('21) and the generosity of fifty or so Cornell alumni. This is the "Big Red Barn," a gathering place for alumni made by refurbishing the carriage house built, together with the President's House, in 1874 by Andrew D. White. Apparently, the suggestion that the carriage house be renovated for this purpose was first put forth by President Mallot, and in 1954 Treman decided to surprise him by raising the $30,000 needed for the work.[13] At the time there was considerable pressure to demolish the structure to make room for a parking lot. By the fall of 1955 the amount needed had been raised and work began: new sills, floors, windows, and roof were installed; heating, electrical work, and plumbing were put in; a large fireplace, a kitchen, and paving for the greenhouse were added; and the barn was painted. For many years there had been great need for a special place where visiting alumni could gather. White himself had pointed this out frequently and as early as the 1880's. He wanted a grand one. Now his carriage house remodeled to preserve its rustic character provides a friendly place for reunions.

The John M. Olin Library, completed in 1961, is by far the most significant new building built on the university campus during President Malott's administration. After more than twenty years of overcrowding and many years of storage of parts of the collection in various locations on the campus, Cornell had its long-planned and much-debated central library addition, the Olin Graduate Library (Fig. 214). The interior of the old Library was substantially remodelled at a cost of over $1,800,000 to provide additional reading room space for undergraduates, and the building was renamed the Uris Undergraduate Library.

[13] "Big Red Barn" correspondence, C.U. Archives. By December 1955 the fund was over $33,000.

Fig. 213. Phillips Hall, for the School of Electrical Engineering, by Perkins and Will (1958). The second unit of the new College of Engineering campus was sited east of East Avenue and its extension, Grove Place. The location was based on a restudy of the site plan for the College by Perkins and Will, architects for the next six buildings of the group. Sage College was to be retained, and the Engineering campus to be expanded east of East Avenue to Hoy Field.

Fig. 214. John M. Olin Research Library (1959), Warner, Toan and Lunde, architects. The building provides space for more than two million volumes and, together with the old main Library, forms the central libraries group. Here, in addition to the main research collections, are housed the central administration and technical services for the University's library system, which includes fifteen college and departmental libraries. The Olin Library provides 350 carrels for graduate students, over 100 faculty studies, eleven specialized graduate reading rooms, conference rooms, typing rooms, the unified catalogue for the entire library system, a large reference collection, and several specialized collections.

The placing of Jacques Lipchitz' sculpture "The Song of the Vowels" on its pedestal at the entrances of Olin and Uris Libraries in 1963 marks an event of signal importance on the university campus. For almost the first time in recent history Cornell has the beginnings of a stimulating new civilized composition worthy of a great university. In consequence, to walk through or to pause in this nexus of the campus is a very satisfying experience. And it is not simply the presence of "The Song of the Vowels," excellent and powerful as it is, that makes the place dramatic. The sculpture provides only the initial element for a sympathetic relation of all of the forms there.

Beside it, William Henry Miller's nineteenth-century Library and Tower are visually anchored to the polite but vigorous and somewhat overpowering modern neighbor. The grand staircase that descends from the

podium on top of the Olin Library reading rooms now leads somewhere: down to the sculpture from the east. The stone walls which contain the stairway also extend to frame "The Song of the Vowels." They almost seem to reach out to salute it. Before the sculpture was in place the piers seemed overdone, like Atlas holding up a pea. Now they extend to say: "Look, there is a great work of art." And when the observer descending the staircase raises his eyes from the sculpture they are directed by its upward curve to McGraw Tower, then to the valley below, and finally to the fields of West Hill. Some intelligent tree-chopping would help matters.

In a very pleasing way the new sculpture is partial payment of a debt the university community owes its predecessors and Cornell's first architectural student, William Henry Miller, for the destruction of part of his masterpiece: the Boardman Hall half of the old

Fig. 215. View of the campus from the west, 1963. At the right may be seen the completed College of Engineering campus and at the far right, Charles E. Hughes Hall, the very recently completed residential hall for students in the Law School. Between Baker Laboratory and Rockefeller Hall, the first floors of Clark Hall are under construction. This was the only sign of building on the campus in a relative pause during the year Cornell's seventh President, James A. Perkins, was inaugurated.

Library–Boardman Hall pair. The removal of Boardman Hall to provide a site for Olin Library was explained as a sacrifice necessary to the progress of the University. Those who remember its excellence miss the unity of composition in which the mass of Boardman extended and complemented the main reading room of the Library. It was an excellent building in its own right, in some ways better than its "Square Romanesque" partner; but it was "too small" and "we needed space."

Warner, Burns, Toan, and Lunde, the architects for Olin Library, were appropriately thoughtful about the qualities of Miller's Library in the placement and many of the design elements of the new building. It respects the dominance of the old Library Tower (now McGraw Tower) in its placement, massing, and roof line. The relationship of the south wall to the Tower as one walks between the new building and Sage Chapel emphasizes and heightens the Tower's importance. The proportions of Olin Library's stack windows and the shape of the openings between the stone ground-floor piers and the window wall repeat the shapes of the slits in the Tower and the windows in the old Library. The pattern of the Tower roof is picked up in the surface of the Library's steeply sloped roof. In its attempts to be polite to all of its

Fig. 216. James A. Perkins, seventh President of Cornell, 1963—.

neighbors the new library's roof shape seems to murmur "mansard roof over there" toward Morrill Hall. Similarly, its mass was held respectfully in line with Stimson Hall's north front and roof line and extended the line of Stimson's high windows which when lighted at night make a pretty composition at the south end of the Arts Quadrangle.

But after all of its gracious attempts to be a good neighbor, the new library seems too insistently big and individualistic to appear comfortable beside the delicate east front of the old Library. The Lipchitz sculpture serves as a small-scale but insistent force between them and helps to diminish the incompatibility. In this space between the libraries we find a gracious expectation-raising gate to funnel comings and goings. Now in place are the first elements of a gateway to the Quadrangle that could be superior to the "Triumphal Arch" gateway-building Miller once proposed be-

tween the Library and Boardman Hall. The confusion of small bushes, leftover trees, oddly shaped patches of grass, and inanely placed benches and lights mars what is otherwise good composition. From time to time, Cornell has demonstrated a concern for its landscape equal to the opportunities of its magnificent setting. The new sculpture between the libraries seems to mark a resurgence of this concern and an emergence of the influence of art in planning the environment of the campus. The prospect is as appealing as the potential quality of the new composition.

Another indication of increasing concern for the evolution of the campus came in 1962 when President Malott created the position of Assistant to the President for Campus Planning. Anton J. Egner, who was appointed to the position, began an evaluation of the existing physical facilities and studies of campus traffic, circulation, and parking as well as preparation of preliminary campus development plans. Building programming was also developed on a more formal basis. The increasing concern for decisions on campus planning and development at Cornell in the sixties has been strengthened in recent years by the appointment by President Perkins of Professor Thomas W. Mackesey as Vice-Provost with particular responsibility for long-range planning and by the growth of Mackesey's staff. Both long-range and middle-range planning have been recognized as vital functions in a university whose central campus comprises over 800 acres, whose land holdings exceed 16,000 acres, and whose buildings are valued at over $135,000,000.

The pace of building at Cornell seems to be increasing. The recently completed dormitory for the Law School, Hughes Hall, designed by Eggers and Higgins; Clark Hall for the physical sciences between Baker and Rockefeller Halls, designed by Fouchtbaum, Warner, Toan, and Lunde; and Malott Hall, the center for the Graduate School of Business and Public Administration by the same architects, have been joined by the addition east of

Baker Laboratory and the new agronomy building. Thirty-eight major buildings have been built on the Cornell campus since President Day's inauguration in 1937. As many more appear in the offing in the next twenty years. Vice-Provost Mackesey has projected an enrollment increase from 13,000 to 17,000 and perhaps to 20,000 students in the next fifteen years. To house them, to provide adequate classroom and laboratory space, to build an increasing number of research buildings and new services and to provide support facilities for this medium-sized town will generate a building program costing somewhere in the neighborhood of one hundred million dollars. Some of this construction is already in sight. A $13,000,000 synchrotron in a tunnel under Alumni Field with operating facilities on the north slope of the Cascadilla valley was started in 1965. Preliminary plans

for a number of new buildings are being developed: for more science buildings, for a new social sciences building, for a building for the new division of biological sciences, for many new dormitories, and for a freshmen center designed to mitigate some of the living problems and perhaps some of the architectural imperfections of the freshman men's dormitories.

Parts of the Cornell campus not discussed in this history have been dispersed from Ithaca: the Medical College to New York City; agricultural research to Geneva and Farmingdale, New York; research facilities to the Research Park south of Tompkins County Airport and to East Ithaca; radio astronomy to Arecibo, Puerto Rico; and a part of the Campus Store was moved to Collegetown in 1966. Perhaps even more astonishing is the dispersion of the University's students and

Fig. 217. The Arts Quadrangle in 1965—Cornell's Centennial Year. In a sound-and-light production, the seated statue of Andrew Dickson White "came alive" and spoke with the statue of Ezra Cornell which stands across the Quadrangle. The conversation was about the wonder of the University and its campus after one hundred years of growth.

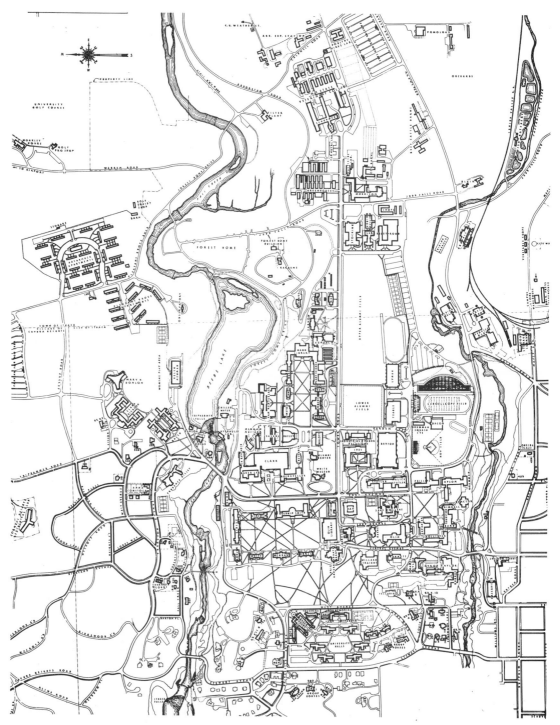

Fig. 218. Plan of the Cornell University campus, 1966, by Professor John N. Tilton.

faculty all over the world in programs of research, training, and support in the United States, Europe, Africa, South America, and Asia.

Still, "in all seasons, from the four corners of the earth" the campus remains a strong magnet drawing Cornellians back to Ithaca. Returns to East Hill are contemplated with anticipation and delight. Will this strong quality of "placeness" be preserved? It is said that more money is spent every day over lunches in the faculty club than Cornell's budget sees in a year. Who knows if planning and building for the vigorous growth which will surely continue will enhance or lessen the rugged, varied, yet subtly ordered beauty of Cornell's campus. The staying powers of Cornell's campus and its landscape setting are great, but so are the forces of change. Yet the signs of the increased concern for the environment give hope.

Cornellians have been promised of late that no buildings will be built in the Fall Creek or Cascadilla Creek Gorges, on the Library Slope west of Central Avenue, in the Arts Quadrangle, or on the site of the White Art Museum; and they rest assured that the worst will not happen.[14] Surely the Library Tower and the "three kingly structures that crown the crest of East Hill" will always be there. Cornell would not be Cornell without them. But change is the order of the next century quite as much as it was during the first hundred years of the evolution of the campus. And change will come with new buildings filling in the spaces between the two deep gorges which define the central campus.

Eminent architects have been retained to design Cornell's major new buildings. The new social sciences building, to be located at the southeast corner of Tower Road and East Avenue, is by Skidmore, Owings and Merrill of New York. Sixteen hundred new units of student housing, located north of Mary Donlon Hall, are the design of Helmuth, Obata and Kassabaum of St. Louis. The new art museum, to be located on the site proposed for a museum in the 1866 campus plan—west of Franklin Hall—is being designed by I. M. Pei.

Cornell's historic structures are receiving careful attention too. The Secretary of the Interior has designated Morrill Hall a National Historic Monument, and the University has agreed to maintain its exterior appearance in an appropriate way and to retain it for educational use. Campus development policy in 1968 calls for the retention of the President's House, Sage College, Barnes Hall and the Chapel.

In a university as large and as diverse as Cornell one hopes there will always be room on the campus for the best of the older, memory-evoking buildings, for green open spaces, long views, trees, walks, benches and gates as well as for up-to-date, forward-looking buildings, for paved spaces, closed courts and quadrangles, sculpture, parking lots and bus shelters;[15] and one expects and hopes that there will continue to be variety within unity, clean unadorned laboratories as well as elegant museums, machinery as well as sculpture, and a sense of formality as well as natural beauty. In short, one hopes that the Cornell of Andrew Dickson White and Ezra Cornell will continue to express beauty as well as utility in the evolution of its campus on East Hill.

[14] Thomas W. Mackesey, Remarks at University Faculty Meeting, 10 October 1965. President Perkins later noted that no plans were being made which would require the removal of the White Art Museum (Minutes, University Faculty, 22 April 1966).

[15] In October 1965, President Perkins suggested the formation of a Committee on Environmental Values as a means of sounding faculty views on the preservation and enhancement of campus values. The Committee was established by action of the Faculty Council in November 1965. Its charge is to advise the Vice Provost and the University Planning Office on matters related to the preservation and enhancement of existing values, to report regularly to the Faculty Council and at least annually to the Faculty.

Documents

1. Report of the Building Committee to the Board of Trustees, 4 March 1866

[This report sets the architectural policy for the first buildings at Cornell and reports, rather despairingly, on the first designs submitted by a number of architects for what was to become Morrill Hall. It is fairly clear that the plan for a great "university square" had been adopted by this time, although it is not explicitly described in the report. Excerpts from the report were included in Hewett's *Cornell University: A History,* but he omitted significant passages about the designs submitted and the issue whether brick or stone was to be used in the buildings. The manuscript of the report in Andrew D. White's hand is in the Trustee Papers in the Cornell University Archives.]

The Committee on Buildings respectfully submit the following report:

At the earliest moment convenient, after their appointment, two of their number in company with an experienced architect visited some of the most noted collegiate buildings in this and neighboring states:—they also consulted and corresponded with several gentlemen in different parts of the country who were prefigured to have valuable experience bearing upon university architecture.

As the result of these investigations the committee have agreed upon the following fundamental ideas regarding the buildings for the Cornell University:

First—As regards style and material, that while they should be tasteful, substantial, and architecturally correct, they should be free from extravagance and from all architectural features not having a basis of useful purpose.

Second—As to disposition of buildings, that the mistake be avoided of connecting all in a single large and pretentious edifice; but that hazard be diminished and convenience as well as architectural effect increased by erecting separate buildings each for its own specific purpose. It is believed that such buildings can be grouped so as to present an appearance far more impressive than any huge structure which it is within our power to build.

Third—As to the progress of the work, that however complete the plans which may be adopted, the buildings be erected from time to time to meet the growth of the university, and that only so much be done now as may be demanded by the undoubted wants of the university on beginning its operations.

The committee are of the opinion that those buildings required by the university in its full scope are mainly as follows: Dormitories, lecture and recitation rooms, laboratories, library, museum, public hall or chapel, farm buildings, workshops, professors' houses, and probably, eventually, an observatory.

As to the first of these classes, the dormitories, the committee generally admit their necessity reluctantly. Experience has shown that better discipline can be maintained without them; that students separated from each other and brought in small groups under the restraints of lodging with quiet families, are generally more easily managed than when brought together in large numbers under a single roof, but the circumstances of this case have left the committee no choice. The university property is so remote from the village of Ithaca, and at such a distance above it, that some provision must be made for the lodging of students upon the university grounds. Moreover, in an institution where the experiment is to be fully tried of allowing young men to engage in agricultural and mechanical pursuits in connection with their studies, it seems a necessity that they should be lodged where they can easily pass from one sort of labor to the other.

As to the construction of dormitories the committee are agreed substantially upon the division of rooms adopted at Yale College. They have investigated the more recent buildings at Harvard College but find them not sufficiently economical of space; the arrangement of rooming at Vassar College they find too complicated; the arrangement at Hobart College, they believe unfavorable to the maintenance of discipline.

The modification of the Yale plan which has been submitted to the architects as a basis provides more effectually than any other plan against too much intercourse between students during the hours of study. By transverse halls very few students are accommodated in each entry in a manner to be alluded to hereafter. The students are to be separated at the Cornell University for the same reason they are at Yale. It also provides simple accommodations for students rooming together in couples under what is known as the "chum" system. These accommodations consist of a small study with adjoining bedroom and coal elevators. It is believed that health and order of habits are provided by separating the room in which the student studies from that in which he sleeps.

The subject of heating and ventilation has also been investigated. Members of the committee have experience with the exterior apparatus in use for this purpose at Vassar College and at the [illegible] Asylum at Northampton and at some other large institutions in neighboring states, but the committee are unanimously of the opinion that no such methods should be tried. They are always exceedingly expensive and rarely accomplish their purpose. The committee believes that a far better system is to have open fires in each study room and to make it the fundamental requirement in all dormitory plans that there be a plentiful admission of sunlight and at need of air through windows—in short—that every study be warmed and ventilated by an open fireplace or grate and that no sleeping room be constructed without at least one window. The committee believes that this simple law will do far more for warmth and ventilation than the most expensive apparatus depending upon the shifting of the winds and the forethought of furnaces in distant parts of a building.

They are, moreover, of the opinion that the style of warming by open fireplaces has the advantage of making the students' rooms more attractive, which is one great point gained in college discipline.

The committee therefore recommend the erection of two dormitories upon this plan for about sixty students, each to be ready at the organization of departments and classes in the university. The buildings to be so constructed also that, if the institution is ever able to do away with the dormitory system, the students' rooms can be connected into lecture rooms for recitations, lectures, and general college purposes.

As to lecture and recitation rooms, the committee believe that those necessary for general purposes can best be placed in a central division of each dormitory building. They are thus easy of access, and have the additional advantage of separating the students of one division of a dormitory from those in the other. The mode of doing this will be seen upon examination of the general plan accompanying this report.

As to size, they should be of such dimensions as to accommodate different classes, ranging from two hundred students down to twenty or thirty.

The committee think that their model is furnished at the new University of Rochester. They should be plain, well lighted and ventilated. The committee are in favor of using our own native woods simply oiled, rubbed and not besmeared with paint.

As to heating in lecture and recitation rooms, the committee recommends furnaces—as to ventilation they are not yet agreed upon a plan and shall ask further assistance.

As to Laboratories, the university will undoubtedly, at an early period, be obliged to erect a separate building on a large scale. Into the department of chemistry nearly all of the branches of the university converge. It is common to the departments of agriculture, mechanic arts, mining, civil engineering, and general science. The institution must possess one of the largest and best, and, if possible, the largest and best laboratory in the country. It should be constructed under the guidance of the head of the department of chemistry. But for the present, the committee do not recommend any separate laboratory building. It is believed that temporary accommodations can be furnished in the basements of the dormitories, or in some of the lecture rooms, until it be more clearly seen what are to be the demands of the chemical department.

As to the library, a building is clearly necessary and on a large scale. Without a large and well-selected library the Cornell University can never take any high rank among the institutions of the country, nor can it attract to itself the best men for instructors.

With such a library, and with provision enabling it to keep pace with the advance of science, the university has a powerful center of attraction for all men of thought and education who are not tied down to cities, and has the means not only of popularizing knowledge but of increasing it. Eventually there must be a large, thoroughly fitted building for library purposes, but at present it is believed that one building can be made to suffice for the library and for the museum.

That the museum is not less necessary than the library will be seen by anyone who considers the scope of the proposed institution. In it must be gathered collections of implements, of grains, of grasses, and of various natural and artificial products bearing upon the department of agriculture. There, too, should be the collection of models and machines bearing upon the department of the mechanic arts. The university must also have a place for her noble collection in geology, for collections in mineralogy, zoology, and botany. Great space will eventually be required for these, but at first they can be accommodated in one building with the library.

But this one building should be so constructed that when the library is removed to a separate building it may be well fitted for its purpose as a museum. To that end the committee have submitted to the architects a plan where the main features are as follows:

The museum and library building should be a single oblong structure about eighty feet in length by forty feet in breadth (or perhaps one hundred feet by fifty feet). It should be in its interior all thrown into one great room without division walls. It should be surrounded by at least two, and probably three, very broad galleries, arranged on some general plan similar to that adopted by the Historical Society in New York or the Agricultural Museum in Albany. On these galleries the different departments of the museum could be dispersed and classified. On the main floor could be temporarily placed the library. The committee recommend that the interior fitting of this building be made as nearly fire-proof as possible. It is believed that this can be done without any expenses not warranted by the great necessity.

This building the committee recommend to be erected at the same time with the dormitories.

The library building to be ultimately erected should correspond in size and general appearance and fire-proof character with the museum building.

The public hall or chapel will also be eventually required. It should have one division—say a first floor—to accommodate meetings of the students. It would also be of great use to have a large public hall above—so large that the people of the State could be invited from far and near to come to the periodical examinations, commencements and public exercises—but this is not an immediate need. The committee therefore recommend that while plans for such a building be considered its erection be deferred.

As to farm buildings, there are some farm houses already upon different parts of the property which are likely to be very useful. What more are required cannot be determined except with the advice of the institution and the cooperation of a Professor of Agriculture.

As to workshops, a building already exists which it is believed can be obtained and which will answer a temporary purpose. The committee recommend that no further plan for such a building be adopted before the plan of instruction in science as applied to industry is more fully developed.

As to professors' houses, the committee are agreed that provision must be made upon the grounds for at least four.

It is believed that they can be made to return a fair interest upon their expense. It is also believed that in organizing the institution they will prove immediately worth more than their cost. If, in calling professors, we are able to offer neat and comfortable houses not far from the field of labor, much smaller salaries will often suffice than when these gentlemen are asked to leave comfortable homes, to rent houses from year to year, illy-constructed, inconvenient, and some distance from the institution. The committee are aware of at least one very strong example directly proving this.

Such houses should be comfortable and well built, and in style such as to form part of the general plan, and should come in as a feature of the grouping.

As to an observatory building, while the committee examined some of the principal buildings in the country, they are not prepared to offer any suggestions at present, but they hope that eventually an observatory will be built which will add greatly to the advance of science, and to give a world wide name of favor to the Cornell University.

In carrying out the plans above suggested the committee have received communications from four different architects and each of them have prepared plans and elevations with more or less adaptation of the requirements laid down.

Of all these plans the most satisfactory are those presented by Messrs. Brown and Nichols of Albany. They are in many respects highly satisfactory—but—the committee have not yet accepted them for the reason that perhaps more competition is desirable. The response by architects to the call of the committee has not been so general as was expected and desired. The committee would therefore recommend that the sum of 500 dollars be placed at their disposal to be used either as prizes or in direct compensation in order to obtain more plans and thus give the committee a wider range for choice.

With such means at their disposal the committee can rapidly come to a decision and they have no doubt that within 30 days they can obtain plans and elevations entirely satisfactory.

As regards the material to be used in the buildings, the board will remember that a resolution was passed at the last meeting declaring that stone should be used. The committee do not as yet see any reason for differing with the majority of the Trustees. In buildings like these, which are to be regarded as public buildings, the seat of probably the greatest educational institution of the greatest commonwealth in the union, it seems appropriate that the material should be of the most noble and the most enduring. The committee are therefore still in favor of using stone, but they ask to be allowed to re-examine the question in regard to economy and in regard to the character of the stone at our command. If so allowed they will at an early day make a more thorough examination than they have yet been enabled to do into the whole question between stone or brick and will agree to recommend brick only in case it be found that the stone at our command is not any more expensive but decidedly inferior to brick on architectural grounds.

The committee having also been entrusted with the location of the buildings have taken into consideration the preparation and laying out of the grounds so far as may be necessary to the effective use of the buildings contemplated. Some of their number have given much thought to the subject and have examined the work done upon the ground of several institutions.

The committee would recommend that they be empowered to select some competent person at a monthly salary to be agreed upon by the executive committee, to make a survey of so much of the grounds as may be necessary, and to superintend the grading and general arrangement of the grounds immediately about the buildings.

In laying out of the farm in general the committee would not recommend at present—they believe that in this the concurrence of a Professor of Agriculture is necessary.

As to the time required for the completion of the work so far as may be necessary for commencing instruction in the University the committee is satisfied that they can have the buildings above specified ready by the time required by law.

As to the expense they are satisfied that by spreading the payments over the time occupied in completing the work and one year afterward, they shall be able to build all that is immediately necessary within the interest of the Cornell fund without touching the principal.

To sum up, therefore, the committee recommend the immediate commencement of two buildings for dormitories and lecture rooms, of a building to serve as museum and library, and of professors' houses not less than two but not more than four in number.

And that to secure plans a sum not exceeding 500 dollars be placed at their disposal.

They also recommend that they be allowed to appoint a landscape gardener at a monthly salary to be fixed by the executive committee and that they be allowed discretion as to the use of brick or stone for the buildings.

AND. D. WHITE
ABRAM B. WEAVER
E. CORNELL
WILLIAM KELLY

2. Letter from Frederick Law Olmsted to Andrew D. White, 12 June 1867

[Olmsted's letter, written immediately after his first visit to the University site in Ithaca, is important because it indicates the force of his arguments for an informal plan—arguments which strongly influenced Andrew D. White's continuing adherence to the need for unity and formality in the Quadrangle and his commitment to an informal arrangement of buildings on the southern half of the campus. The letter is in the White Papers in the Cornell University Archives.]

OLMSTED, VAUX & CO., Landscape Architects
No. 110 Broadway, New York
June 12th, 1867

DEAR MR. WHITE,

I had a very pleasant journey, after leaving you, to Syracuse, with Mr. Fiske. What a nice, excellent fellow he is! I should think he would be of great value to you, but I confess I hope that you will spare him to Hartford a little longer. He would do a world of good there if he could remain a year or two.

On the train we had the pleasure of meeting Mr. Wilcox. I found that he was not at all prejudiced against either shifting your line of buildings to the southward or forming them in echelon. The first plan he thought Mr. Cornell might object to because it must require him to give up his wife's reserve. The second he said he had always thought would be better, as the buildings would group much better and would be much better accommodated to the ground. That is my judgment very decidedly. If you place them as you propose, you will have made the same mistake which all the larger colleges of the country are now repenting. We have twice been consulted within the year as to the possibility of recasting the general ground plan of college buildings from a straight quadrangular system to a more free, liberal, picturesque and convenient one without demolishing the old buildings. You ought to anticipate such a growth of the University as will eventually require ten times the building accommodation that is provided for in your present plan. Do you doubt that far finer buildings than any you are now proposing to construct will be erected for university purposes in the course of a century or

two? I do not. And if so—that is to say, if the university is to be a great success, is to have a healthy, steady growth, is to draw out the affection, the gratitude, the patriotism and the benevolence of other noble men and women besides its founders, then your proposed *line*, complete in itself or the "quadrangle" (which is not a quadrangle) complete in itself and with but one front of dignity, will be simply another monument of shortsightedness, inconsideration and complacency with an [sic] little present, like those at Yale and Amherst. The Treasurer at Amherst told me that the founders of the college took a very fine site for their buildings and put them in a line upon it where a magnificent view was commanded, but when by bequests new buildings were required, no suitable place could be found for them except by entirely disregarding the plan of the founders and destroying the effect which they valued. Accordingly the plan of the present edifices is something as follows:

278

The shaded blocks being the older brick buildings, the others new and mainly of stone. Now they have a bequest of $100,000 which is the basis of a fund for a chapel, and another larger sum for another building, both of which are intended to be much more dignified than any of those now standing. One of the professors strongly advocated placing the largest one of them at the point X entirely ignoring the old line and the half suggested quadrangle. Being the finest building it should be put before all [*illegible*] would go to the rear; certainly it should not be put on the back side of the buildings so much inferior to it as those in the line would be. But X is on the slope of the hill—lower than the old line—so he asked me if a terrace could not be built out there thirty feet high as a foundation for it. You see how in placing the building A which has been lately the pride of the college, the formal effect has been given the coup de grace at one blow. The position very closely corresponds to yours, except that the declivity is steeper and the scale smaller.

This is for your eyes alone, and I shall say nothing of it, professionally, having been informed that it was no longer open to debate, but the more I think of it the more I am impressed with the conviction that you are making a great mistake, and between ourselves, I feel it a duty to tell you so. Your Trustees it appears have decided the question contrary to the judgment, if not to the advice, of their architect. They take a grave responsibility in doing so, for if your architect is fit for his duty at all, his judgment ought to be almost controlling on such a question. If it is open to reconsideration, and your suggestion of shifting the whole line to the southward indicates that you may consider that it is, I would advise you to call a council of architects and if you please of artists. It is a point of great importance and you had better delay another year rather than make what will hereafter possibly be always felt as a fundamental mistake. Don't, I beg of you, if you can possibly avoid it begin by tying yourself to formality and straightlacing. It is obvious already that you will not, would not if you could,

carry out the theme consistently. You are deliberately proposing to arrange half a dozen initial buildings formally and to arrange everything else informally. The result will inevitably be unhappy. You can yet secure picturesque unity, but if you go on, a year hence neither unity nor picturesqueness in high degree will be possible. You will have a little impertinent formality and a great deal of helter skelter.

I don't mean to say that the result will be positively bad, on that point there probably will be difference of opinion, but that a great opportunity will have been wasted, and unless the progress of taste in the U.S. gets a setback or the university fails of a great success I will lay you a wager payable t'other side of [   ] within two centuries some of your buildings will be demolished in order to break up the line and allow new buildings to group in with the hill top and with such old buildings and trees as will be allowed to remain in a manner which shall be just to the architecture of the age and consistent with the comfort of the public eye.

These frankly are my views on that point, and now I have done with it; I have said what I have now and so strongly, in order to get past that point, before I again see Mr. Cornell, from whom I hope next week to receive definite and final instructions as to the limits within which my imagination will be free to work, and with whom I do not propose to discuss the question of site of buildings, which must be the most important of these limits.

Please not to forget to send me copies of the Plan of Organization, as I wish to send it to England.

I found Norton here on my return; he is greatly interested in your enterprise and wants much to see you. He may come to Ithaca with me later in the summer. I shall probably visit him at Cambridge in July. Is there any chance of you being there?

I trust Mrs. White reached home the better for her journey.

Yours very truly

FREDERICK LAW OLMSTED

3. Excerpts from a Report by Ezra Cornell to the Board of Trustees at Albany, 26 September 1867

[This report indicates the great extent of the Founder's attention to the details of financing and construction of the first buildings, and the large scale of the institution he contemplated. Parts of the report which deal with the accounting of the Cornell Fund and the detailed plans for sale of 100,000 acres of Cornell-owned Wisconsin pine lands have been omitted. The manuscript is in the Trustee Papers in the Cornell University Archives.]

TO THE TRUSTEES OF THE CORNELL UNIVERSITY

GENTLEMEN:

Since your last meeting an Act has been passed by the Legislature of New York, fixing the time for the commencement of the educational exercises of the Cornell University in the fall of 1868. This enabled the building committee to be less exacting with the contractor for our first building and they did not press him to the completion of the building by the time stipulated in his agreement which was the 30th of June last. The work is progressing with reasonable dispatch and the contractor gives us assurances that he will complete his contract by the first of November next or early in that month.

The second building which has been commenced, will be a duplicate of the first, and will be located the same distance north of the scite [sic] of the center building, that the first building is south of said scite [sic].

The work on this building has been prosecuted thus far by day labor under the immediate superintendence of my brother, Elijah B. Cornell. It has consisted in quarrying and dressing stones for the walls of the building, excavating the foundation (from which sand enough has been saved to use in the mortar of the entire building) and in laying the foundation walls which were commenced about the first of the month.

The White Medina Sand Stone for the water table, corners and trimmings of the building could not be obtained before next spring owing to the peculiar situation of the quarries from which that stone is to be obtained. This circumstance will limit the progress of our work to the erection of the basement walls, and the preparation of the blue stones for the walls above the basement. I feel confident however, that we shall be able to advance the work so far this fall that the building will be in readiness for occupation by the time of commencement next fall.

I feel constrained to recommend that this second building be erected by the employment of labor by the day, and purchasing the materials by contract in detail rather than to let the whole in a single contract as we did the first building. [By] this policy I am confident we shall secure a better building, at a less cost.

Our resources for the erection of these buildings are as follows:

Income from the Cornell Donation from Nov. 1, 1865 to Nov. 1, 1867, two years	$ 70,000
The appropriation from the State to be paid over on completion of first building	25,000
One year's Income from the Cornell Donation up to Nov. 1, 1868	35,000
	$130,000

280

Less Contract price of first building	$ 58,425	
Probable extra charges of contractor	3,000	
Cost of fitting up lecture and recitation rooms, and furnaces	5,000	$66,425
		$63,575
Cost of second building as above	$ 66,425	
Cost of necessary grading and filling around buildings	1,000	
Water closets	500	
Supplying water for immediate use	500	
Furnishing the two buildings $50 each room	3,200	$71,625
Deficit to Nov. 1, 1868		$ 8,050

. . . This statement contemplates the stopping of our building after the completion of two buildings which will furnish us with dormitory room for 128 students as the rooms were placed, but will accommodate 200 students without uncomfortable crowding; two large lecture rooms which will seat 800 students; eight or ten recitation rooms of about 20 by 40 feet in size; and the basement rooms of both buildings which may be used temporarily for laboratories and such other purposes as room may be wanted as they are dry, light and airy.

This policy is proposed so that the income from our building fund may be applied to the support of the Faculty and enable the Trustees to open the Institution to the public upon a scale that will inspire confidence and command the respect of the people, and fill the University with students.

It will also hasten the demand for more room, extended facilities, and better accommodations. We shall want separate buildings for laboratories, libraries, cabinets, observatories, for armories and military exercises, farm buildings for the accommodation of stock and other farm uses, workshops and appliances for mechanical instruction and illustrations, dwellings for professors, teachers and the various employees of a large establishment, which with the improvement of the farm and ground will cost much money, and require much time to provide. This money can be obtained by the sale of our lands, and it was with a view of providing for this demand that I recommended the sale of 100,000 acres of pine lands at the very low price of $5.00 per [acre] to a company which might be organized with sufficient capital to properly handle that amount of land, and to reap the rich reward it was sure to return if properly handled.

I have commenced the formation of such a company with fair prospects of success. I have not had the opportunity yet of presenting it to our Trustees generally. Several of those to whom I have presented the subject have encouraged the enterprise with very liberal subscriptions, and I trust that each will aid in some form, if with nothing more than a kind word. This sale must be effected, and the income from its invested proceeds added to our available means for supplying the numerous wants that will press upon us. . . .

4. Excerpts from a Letter from Andrew Dickson White to Ezra Cornell, 19 June 1868

[White left for Europe in April 1868 to collect ideas, faculty and books for the University. While he was away, Ezra Cornell, working with Professor Crafts, devised a plan for a large wooden laboratory building to be located about 250 feet east of the site of McGraw Hall. White's reaction to the proposal in this letter is as characteristically sharp and bold as it continued to be for fifty years on all issues related to the development of the campus. A copy of the letter, written in Paris, is in the White Papers.]

. . . Among the letters from America was yours giving general plans of the new workshop, laboratory, etc. I must confess my feelings regarding it were very much mingled. I was rejoiced to think of the college of the Mechanic Arts being placed on an excellent footing as regards buildings and equipment. But as to the carrying out of the plans in the manner you propose I have serious doubts.

1st. I doubt whether it is the best plan to place laboratories and workshops in the same building even temporarily in case of fire.

2nd. I decidedly demur to the site you have chosen. I fear it will spoil the whole plan on which we have been working. All our plans for buildings have been based upon the idea of a large area surrounded by substantial buildings in a style of Architecture befitting such a university as ours will be. All this you destroy by planting right in the center a great wooden workshop—not harmonized either with the general plans or the style of the buildings. If not too late I beg of you to place the building at one side, say on the street north or on the south line—better however on the north line of the university square near the house already erected. . . .

But after all my great objection is to the site as defacing the whole plan. We must make our grounds attractive. We must have a substantial style about them and your great wooden factory in the center will, I fear, render all attempts in that direction futile.

5. Excerpts from Andrew Dickson White's Annual Report of 1885

[White's final annual report, submitted to the Board of Trustees on 17 June 1885, includes the following extended remarks on the building needs of the University and on the need for a general plan of development. Also in the report is "A Final Statement of Views on General University Policy, Internal and External." The last section of this statement (12) is reproduced here.]

Buildings

The principal buildings erected during the past year are the addition to the main structure of Sibley College and the Sibley Annex. Beside this a house has been erected for dairy purposes in connection with the agricultural department; the chapel of the University has been improved by memorial windows, placed by various individuals, one of them being in memory of a beloved graduate of the University; the Founders' Chapel has been completed and beautified; and the Cascadilla Building has been improved within and without by the refitting of the upper story, by the addition of a new entrance, and by the large oriel window on its front; Sage College under the direction of Mrs. Derkiem has received various additions to its fittings which give it more of the character of a home, and the same may be said of the room set apart in Morrill Hall for the use of the lady students. Two additional cottages have been erected under the usual arrangement, and both do much to make our grounds more beautiful and attractive. The completion of one of the fraternity halls upon a piece of land assigned it upon the University property has added to the beauty of that part of the grounds and to the facilities for the proper housing of students. My views in favor of allowing the erection of such halls were fully presented in my last report and remain unchanged.

As to additional buildings more immediately needed it may be well again to remind you of the permanent library building which must be erected within a few years, of the temporary remodeling of the south room in the McGraw building as a reading room for the present library, of the enlargement of the small class rooms in White and Morrill Halls, and the exchange of the present class rooms occupied by the Professor of Greek for one adjoining his private rooms in White Hall. So, too, the building for the veterinary department, referred to in my discussion of that part of our organization, should be provided for this year, and the final annex to the gymnasium which will complete that structure, should receive early attention. I would also here impress again upon the Trustees, the necessity of looking forward to a proper receptacle for a collection of casts, illustrative of classical art and archaeology, history, sculpture, and plastic art in general. Every great university and technical school in Europe has such a collection either of its own, or in some institution in its neighborhood. The same is true of several important institutions in this country, especially Yale College and the University of Michigan. In no other way can an education of the eye and taste in the principles of beauty be secured. This subject is naturally suggested to me by the beautiful gift to the University made by the graduating class of this year. It is a cast of full size, made at Rome, from the colossal statue of the Emperor Augustus, discovered within a few miles of that city some twenty years since. I trust this may prove the first of a long series of such casts. I have no recommendation to make as regards an immediate outlay, but would urge the Board to keep in mind, whenever plans of a new library are presented, the importance of providing for a suite of rooms where such a collection can be accumulated. A very small appropriation each year would soon make it most valuable and interesting.

The provisions for the safety of our buildings, including arrangements with reference to an outbreak of fire, are still under charge of the Superintendent of Buildings and Fire Warden, Professor Morris, and are believed to be as good as we can make them with the appliances at our command.

And now before closing this subject allow me to present certain general considerations, and a practical suggestion resulting from them which seems to me worthy of immediate attention. The University has in Ithaca a splendid domain, and a large number of buildings. As time goes on there will be erected more and more edifices to meet the needs of various departments, and to carry out more successfully the various purposes of such an institution as ours is to be. The expense of such buildings will doubtless be defrayed partly by the University, but, in my opinion, more largely by individuals. This has been the case in the past history not only of this, but of many other important institutions in the land, and there is no reason to expect the future to differ from the past in this respect, save that, in my opinion, the increase of munificence is to go on even in a greater degree than heretofore, in accordance with the increase of wealth in the nation. It is of the utmost importance then that our plans be made with reference to this inevitable increase in buildings and means of instruction.

Perhaps the mistake that most immediately strikes the eye on visiting any of our older American universities is the short-sightedness of their authorities in days gone by, in this respect. In hardly any case has there been any proper general plan beforehand. Each building has been erected as it has been wanted, in accordance with the supposed necessity or even whim of the moment, with reference solely to immediate needs, with hardly any large thought of future needs, or the slightest regard to harmony and general effect as to position and style of the entire mass of buildings. The result has been that on the grounds of the various leading universities we find buildings huddled together upon no general plan, in no effective style, and in a way which not only offends the eye, but subjects both those giving and receiving instruction to perpetual inconvenience, discomfort, annoyance, and consequent waste of power. There is no difficulty in our American institutions more universally recognized at present than this. Very rarely in these institutions has there arisen a man with the foresight of Thomas Jefferson when he planned the scheme of accommodation for the University of Virginia. In view of these facts I would suggest that the time has arrived for the calling in of the best architectural talent obtainable to make suggestions and prepare plans with reference to the position of our future buildings. This will certainly save us a large expenditure in the long run; but what is more important, it will save us from those evils which have been entailed upon similar institutions by a different course. The time will come when on this University hill will stand a very large library, a gallery for casts and pictures, a building for the departments of civil engineering and architecture, a hall for the alumni, a laboratory or laboratories for biological and kindred researches in natural history, similar to those recently erected at Johns Hopkins University and elsewhere, a school of mines, a large special assembly room for University purposes, like those at Harvard University and the University of Michigan, an observatory, a law school, a preparatory medical school, a veterinary school, a conservatory of music, and various other edifices. Certainly it is none too soon to begin devising a general plan as to the positions of such buildings as these. I do not mean that we should set apart distinct pieces of ground for each of these buildings, some of which may come in five years and some in fifty, but that a general plan and scheme be adopted in accordance with which such structures may be brought into proper relations to each other and to the buildings already erected. In taking leave of my work here permit me to say that there is hardly anything short of the most essential matters directly pressing upon us which relate to instruction and government on which I should lay greater stress than this. I submit a resolution referring the matter to the Building Committee authorizing and directing them to take measures for the securing of at least general sketch plans, having in view the best possible arrangement of our new buildings. . . .

12. In conclusion, the Trustees should not forget that the atmosphere of sentiment which gathers about the University is a most powerful factor in its real success. If all be hard, dry, and unattractive, its buildings mere boxes, its grounds a mere plot of earth for such boxes to stand upon—if all this be as devoid of interest as an attorney's office in a city block, then the University will fail in one of the highest parts of its mission. Fortunately all its surroundings are such as to create love for the place even in hearts least susceptible to natural beauty. A good beginning has been made also in stimulating a healthful sentiment by the erection of buildings other than mere boxes, in the attractive application of landscape gardening, in placing windows, portraits, and memorial tablets to those who have been identified with us. The chimes, the memorials, the bits of carving here and there, the walks among the groves and along the ravines and streams, have their value in creating an atmosphere which shall make our students something more than machines. I would lay stress here again on the educating value of all these things. The memorials, especially, serve to show students that there is a fame which outlasts that of the demagogue, the politician or the stock jobber. They maintain the dignity of the University, the self-respect of its Faculty, the affectionate sentiment of its Alumni and Students. I would again insist upon the vital efficiency of these things, and urge that in buildings and adornments this fact be not forgotten, but that the University steadily enrich itself as time goes on with buildings which shall quicken the sense of beauty, in memorials which shall arouse love and veneration, in works of art which shall stimulate manliness, and in a general development of the treasures of beauty lying all about us, which shall make its Faculty and Students cherish their connection with the University and the Alumni cherish their remembrance of it. . . .

6. Letter from Henry Van Brunt to Charles Kendall Adams, 1 May 1886

[This letter indicates that Van Brunt was very sensitive to the ideas on campus planning and architecture expressed in White's 1885 Annual Report to the Trustees. His analysis of the two most favored sites for the new library building shows an ability to deal positively with the "givens" in each situation. Adams favored the selection of Van Brunt as architect for the new library. It seems that Van Brunt evolved some general plans for the campus along with his many preliminary plans for the library building. So far as I know, there are no extant copies of these "general plans," which Adams refers to in his lament to White (30 November 1888, White Papers) after the rejection of Van Brunt's final plans for the library building. A copy of the following letter is in the White Papers.]

Office of VAN BRUNT & HOWE Architects

May 1, 1886

60 Devonshire Street
Boston, Mass.

PRESIDENT ADAMS,
DEAR SIR:

As suggested, I submit a few preliminary observations regarding the proposed new Library Building for Cornell University for such use as you may think proper to make of them as a member of the committee having this special interest in charge. In doing so, I shall find it necessary to report much of what I mentioned to say to you under the impulse of first impressions while on the site with you, adding the results of subsequent reflections on the subject.

As a primary consideration, not only in respect to site but character and materials, it seems to me very important that the new building should not antagonize the structures already erected, but, so far as possible, should justify them, and, by taking up the architectural suggestions which they supply, should supplement the group and give to it a higher character as a work of design. The misfortune of our University buildings, whenever I have had opportunity of studying them, is that the new are apt to be added to the old without due consideration of existing conditions. The

college campus therefore is generally surrounded by structures in different styles, of different materials, and with mutual relations as to site so accidental that the result of incapacity is evident to the most uncultured eye. The main buildings of Cornell are perhaps less open to such criticism than those of some of the older institutions of learning, but the note of discord has already been struck, and the difficult task is now given to the architect of the next new structure of importance to devise a building which should not only be perfect in itself once on a high plane of architectural thought, but shall rise to the dignity of peacemaker by placing itself in harmony with the old works and in some sense reconciling their contentions of style and colour.

I had a very instructive view of the general aspect of the University buildings from the railway on the opposite side of the valley. Whatever of dignity there is in the existing group, as seen from this distant point of observation, is plainly to be attributed to the effect of the central group of buildings with its tower and the separate but flanking masses of White and Morrill Halls. The other elements of the architectural display do not, from this point, add to its effectiveness as a congruous whole. If in their nearer aspects, these gray buildings are not committed to a distinct architectural character as to details,

286

and are somewhat uncompromising and unimaginative in their severe adjustment to practical uses, their symmetry (or rather their balance of parts) is a very important contribution to the general effect of repose.

It is evident to me therefore that the new building which may occupy the area south of this group, should, if practicable, in some way fall in with those gray structures and at the same time serve as a balance or pendant to the red and gray building that stands north of the same group [the Chemical Laboratory], thereby excusing and extenuating the more distinct architectural character of this building, and making it at home on its site.

This, of course, seems to suggest for the new member of the group a red and gray effect, the mass of its walls being in the local greenish blue or gray random rock-faced stone of the old structures, pointed with red and relieved with red sandstone in such proportions as to compose well in respect to the architectural colour of the building itself and to have relations of comity with the other members of the group. Such a combination is practicable and not inconsistent with due vigor, gravity, and breadth of effect. If, from any practical point of view, the local stone is objectionable, the natural alternative would be the Onondaga stone, of which we made a study when together in Syracuse. Much of the local stone required could be blasted away from the immediate site of the proposed building, thus avoiding the cost of transportation, and thus seems, from cursory inspection, to be no reason why it should not be jointed and fitted in such a way as to produce a good piece of masonry. Fully one quarter of the area of such walls, including all weatherings, should however be in red stone, like that from the Saemby or Albion quarries. The proportion and character of the admixture of these colours would constitute a fundamental part of the composition as a work of architecture. It is my opinion that the local stone would compose rather more harmoniously with red sandstone than the Onondaga stone.

The alternative to some such arrangement as this would be to get the red effect in brick laid in red mortar on the facing corners with Onondaga stone trimmings, thus in some degree allying the group of principal frontage, which we have been contemplating, with the other and more distant college buildings on the southern part of the grounds. According to my judgement, this alternative is not to be preferred unless the authorities should be forced to it by considerations of economy. It would be difficult to make a binding treaty of peace between such a brick building and those of stone, with which, by reason of proximity, it must always challenge comparison.

The site which we are now considering is certainly very beautiful indeed, and very inspiring. But when we study the proper site for the Library building we should of course first be controlled by considerations of practical use. Prima facie, the Library, in a group of University buildings, being a place of general resort, should occupy a central position if possible. The adjustment of an architectural composition to the practical service of a Library naturally results in a building of which the external characteristics must differ fundamentally from those adapted to other uses. The work spaces must be larger, and the general features, notably the fenestration, must assume a more grandiose aspect, fitting in to become the central member of a group made up of smaller subdivisions. These exceptional external aspects also suggest the obvious difficulty of making such a building a pendant, or correspondent of any other building. We should take into consideration also the necessary external character of the bookstack, which, under conditions of economy, it is not easy to make ornamental and at the same time "capable of indefinite extension." All the facades of such a building on such a site would be conspicuous. We are not permitted here to hide such a feature of utility behind a mask of buildings as in the Library at Ann Arbor. I am suggesting difficulties which may not be insurmountable. Indeed, it is possible that because of just such difficulties, including those connected with irregularities of grade on this site, under vigorous study, a building of exceptional interest and of most striking character may be evolved. It is a question which can only be valued by experimental sketches. There is no obvious solution save on another site.

You may now understand why any inclination at present leans towards placing this building in a position where there are fewer embarrassments of adjustment and correspondence, and where the design could be developed more independently, i.e., more distinctly from within outward. You are prepared for my suggestion to place the building opposite McGraw Hall, and to make it the central member of a *"corps du bâtiments,"* of which the subordinate wings should extend continuously northward and southward with lower skylines, terminating at the ends opposite Morrill and White halls with partitions of greater height, the whole forming the eastern boundary of the campus as the discontinuous gray buildings are the western boundary. This continuity of structure comports both with dignity and economy. It would protect the University from the danger of incongruity in future buildings and the designer would be left comparatively free in respect to choice of materials. In such a position the necessary isolation could be secured to the Library building by fire walls, and the bookstack could develop itself eastward behind the masks of the main building, with ample opportunity for extension upon a plan to which external considerations would offer fewer impediments. Such a continuous building could be divided by fire walls into sections which could be constructed as they might be needed, but always in general conformity with a preconceived architectural composition so devised as to be elastic to conditions of convenience. Each of these additives would be in other respects independent of the others, and would each have one less exterior wall to be built in order to fit this building to the eastward slope of the table land. I would suggest placing it on a continuous terrace which should overlook the campus. It is sub-

mitted that a sketch of such a building, with the completed Library in the centre and so composed as to be capable of various adjustment without loss of essential architectural character and balance according to the future needs of the University, would, if discreetly used or published, invite or give direction to the generosity of wealthy friends of learning and result in the present completion of the building. My experience with the buildings of the Episcopal Theological School at Cambridge, comprising chapel, dormitories, library, recitation halls, refectory and deanery, seems to justify this assumption. A plan of a continuous series of supposed buildings was drawn up in order to justify the location of chapel; all of these were built in substantial conformity with this general scheme within a few years by various benefactors of the institution. This scheme in fact was the father of the buildings as they stand. I venture to suggest that the wings, connecting the pavilions at the extremities of the facade with the central structure might be made useful as dormitories, the aspect being favorable from a dormitory point of view. The [*illegible*] might be adjusted for the Law School and Engineering School. If necessary, archways could be provided through the building to facilitate communication between the quadrangle or campus and the buildings behind or to the eastward.

I enclose a general sketch of the arrangement proposed. If you think it desirable, or at least not intrusive, we will prepare rough tentative sketches submitting studies of both alternatives. These sketches to be preliminary to the more careful drawings which would follow the ultimate determination of your committee as to site. In fact those preliminary sketches would have for their object mainly the determination of this point, and would need to be carried only far enough to illustrate my propositions and to facilitate the conclusions of your committee. In this case we should require a general plan of the college campus and a plan of the site south of Morrill Hall with levels.

Many thanks for the Document which I have this moment received. It will be safe to write to me at Kansas City until May 24th.

Very truly yours
HENRY VAN BRUNT

P.S. I have read President White's report, since writing the above, and am greatly pleased that his views regarding future buildings entirely coincides.

7. "A Plan of Development. What Cornell University Now Needs," by Andrew Dickson White, September 1891

[It appears that White started this draft, which is in the White Papers, with publication in mind. I can find no evidence that it was ever completed and published. After a brief introduction the paper discusses building needs and proposed locations under Roman numeral I. I take this as evidence that White intended to write additional sections, presumably on such topics as endowed chairs, fellowships, and the like. The draft is incomplete and undated but a phrase crossed out by White dates its preparation in September 1891.]

It is now a quarter of a century since, at the first general meeting of the Cornell University Trustees, I submitted a "Plan of Organization" for the institution about to be created. Having been published by them it met with very severe criticism in many influential quarters, and there was more than one apparent demonstration that the plans it suggested could never be put into practice. The whole University system proposed in it was denounced, not only in many parts of this commonwealth, but in many of the surrounding States. But Cornell University in its development has followed that plan in almost all its essential points. Over thirteen hundred students are now in actual attendance. Not only has the general system advocated in the "Plan of Organization" been successful here, but in its most important features it has been adopted in many other institutions, and in one case by one of the oldest and largest universities of our country, under the direction of a very eminent authority who once wrote a book mainly to prove that the principal features of the plan, and especially university education free from sectarian control, liberty of choice between various courses of study, a considerable range of options in courses, equality between various courses, thorough provision for modern studies, especially those in greater modern languages and literatures, and honor to leading studies in science equal to that hitherto accorded to studies in classics,

were chimerical.

Having recently been re-elected a Trustee of the University, I now propose as supplementary to that "Plan of Organization" a "Plan of Development" for the institution as it stands today. To this I would respectfully invite the scrutiny of all connected in any way with the University.

This plan of development is based upon close observation, and study during more than twenty-five years, of this and other of the higher institutions of learning at home and abroad, and is made in view of what seems to me the clearest needs of this University and of our own land and time.*

I. Buildings

1. The Agricultural Building

The importance given to Agriculture in our charter is well known. Until recently our Agricultural Department has developed slowly, but now it is showing itself in full proportions, and the time has come when a proper building should be erected upon the University grounds in recognition of the great interests involved, and for the greater efficiency of the work here to be done in furtherance of them.

* As suggestion is made of gifts and bequests to Cornell University, I may mention that the restriction in the original charter as to the amount which the institution may hold has been entirely removed by the State Legislature, so that no limit is now imposed.

290

What should such a building be? First, it should bring together the various departments which go to make up the College— which are now crippled and curtailed because scattered through various buildings. Scientific and Practical Agriculture, Horticulture, Economic Entomology, Veterinary Medicine and Surgery, and the like, should all be thus brought into helpful contact with each other, and the rooms set apart for each of these departments should include such lecture-rooms, recitation-rooms, laboratories, operating-rooms, and rooms for special collections, as are in each case needed.

Secondly, in the midst of all there should be an Illustrative Museum, upon which each department may draw for the means of exhibiting to individual students and to classes what is necessary for their better instruction. Such a Museum should be on a large scale: it should include the best examples of recent specimens of agricultural implements and products, with the more important examples of machines and implements; thus showing the development of agricultural invention in the past, and indicating the lines on which it may best act in the future. The University has already a considerable collection of models, implements, and materials: it has for example, the great collection of cereals and grasses presented to the University by the British Government; the very extensive collection of plough models made at the German Agricultural College of Hohenheim; a large herbarium; a small collection of recent English and American implements of the best construction, models from the Patent Office, etc., etc., samples of various products; and a considerable number of models and preserved specimens in the Veterinary department; but it is certain that if a proper Museum building on a large scale were established, the best makers and producers of the United States would greatly increase the existing collection, and hasten to fill the building with the most approved examples of their work and products. We have already seen such a display of generosity in the contributions of leading manufac-

turers to the Sibley College of Mechanic Arts, where the accommodations are comparatively small, and we may be quite sure that a far larger collection would be speedily secured in agriculture, if we had proper Museum accommodations. Such accommodations, it need hardly be said, should be in close proximity to the lecture-rooms of the Professors, in order that any illustration needed may be used easily and at once. To have a Museum at a distance from the lecture-rooms is simply to cripple instruction in the whole department.

With the wonderful foresight which Ezra Cornell always showed regarding the future of the University, such a Museum was one of the earliest objects of his care; he frequently dwelt upon it, and had he lived it would doubtless have been established long since. Such an idea has been carried out in various institutions in the Old World and at some in our own country. The value of such a combination of illustration with instruction will doubtless strike all who give attention to the subject.

Such a building complete, would cost from eighty to one hundred thousand dollars. Situated in the very center of this great State of New York, its influence upon the agricultural progress of the State and country would be great and far-reaching. The funds of the University are so absorbed in carrying on the work already undertaken in various departments, that so large a sum could hardly be taken from the funds of the institution without diminishing its power for its ordinary work. Who, then, will provide this building? No nobler monument could be erected by any man interested in the great fundamental industry of Agriculture. Such a monument would stand here in the heart of this great commonwealth for hundreds of years bearing the name of its donor;—a monument of his public spirit and an example to all men of means as to the best uses of money. Is there not some one who will rise to a true conception of duty to the State and Nation in this respect? And if the University shall erect it, is there not some public spirited citizen who will endow it with a sum sufficient to carry on the work done in it and so attach his name to it?

2. *Additional buildings and other facilities for Sibley College*

While various other parts of the University have been developed in the most satisfactory manner within the past few years, all cognizant of the facts will agree that none has grown in such a remarkable manner as has the Sibley College of Mechanical Engineering, and no growth has been more legitimate. It has gone on under the direction of the Director, Professor Thurston with the co-operation of Professor Morris and their able assistants, until it has outgrown not only its original buildings, but all the large additions made to them. Everywhere throughout the country its efficiency is recognized by leading men in the profession, and everywhere its graduates are doing the best of work. But this very success is now imposing a very serious burden on the University. It is a question whether the Trustees must not shut its doors to a large number of talented young men who wish to fit themselves at the College as leaders of the great army of mechanical industry in the country.

While the site for future buildings in connection with Sibley College has been carefully guarded, and all has been planned with reference to such future buildings, it seems impossible at present to erect them from University funds. There is needed a large lecture-room which can accommodate the whole body of students and even more, in order that the lectures by eminent leaders in mechanical industry which are given here throughout the year, may be heard by all those who would profit by them. So, too, more laboratory and drafting rooms are needed, also rooms for special pieces of apparatus, testing machines, dynamos, and the like. Even moderate outlay extended through a series of years, the erection of one part of the buildings needed after another, would be of the greatest possible service, and would redound vastly to the credit not only of the University, but to that of any person thus aiding us.

3. *A University Auditorium and Hall for Music*

Every great University ought to have some fitting hall large enough for the assemblage of its entire body of Trustees, Faculty, students, and invited guests. Not only is such a hall valuable on the greater public occasions, like Commencements, exhibitions, contests in oratory, essay-reading, and the like, but it is often of the utmost importance in carrying on the more ordinary University work. It is not unfrequently very desirable to summon all connected with the University to a general meeting at short notice. Cornell University has now, beside about a hundred individuals connected with its governing and instructing body, over thirteen hundred students, and will probably, within a short time, have nearly two thousand. There is no room upon the grounds large enough to contain all these save the Gymnasium; this is at the best very poorly adapted for the purpose, and the use of it involves various difficulties, in addition to breaking in upon the work of an important department.

But the ordinary assemblage of the students is by no means the only thing of importance: a secondary use, and in some respects a use even more important, of the great hall, would be for entertainments of the kind which civilize, enlighten, define and elevate the whole body of students and the community in which they live. For lectures, readings, and the like before the whole University body, such a hall would be exceedingly useful: but there is yet a higher use; such an auditorium containing a great organ, would be fitted not only for public University exercises, but for concerts, organ recitals, and the like. The success of such entertainments upon the University grounds thus far, even on the very small scale possible hitherto, has been most remarkable. It has shown a real hunger on the part of the students and community for the highest and most ennobling music, and for those better forms of entertainment which not only give needed rest and change to the minds of those engaged in study, but which lift all to higher and better realms of culture than they could otherwise attain. Any one who has entered the great Auditorium of the University of Michigan, seating as it does three thousand students, and especially, any one who has heard the noble concerts given there by the Musical Department of the University,—any one who has entered the similar Auditorium built by Archbishop Sheldon at Oxford, or that which bears the name of Sanders at Harvard, will understand the great influence for good which may be exercised by this means in various ways upon Trustees, Faculty, students, and the whole body of citizens of a University town.

Besides this, such a building would tend to make the University more and more a center for the more important Conferences, Associations, and Conventions of the greater historical, literary, and scientific societies of the United States. It would afford in connection with the other facilities offered here, a constant attraction to these great and influential bodies, and would thus extend, not merely the name and fame, but the efficiency of the University throughout the country.

Such a building should be monumental in its character; it should stand in a central position; say in the center of the line of buildings forming the west side of the northern quadrangle; its architecture should be massive, its adornments simple and noble. Here, too, is a great opportunity for some public benefactor. Who will do for Cornell University what Sheldon did for Oxford and Sanders for Harvard? Who will erect a monument of this sort which shall be for ages a great center of ennobling influences, and which shall at the same time perpetuate the name of him who establishes it, and bring upon him the gratitude of generation after generation of young men and young women going forth from these halls during the coming centuries?

4. *A Hall of Fine Arts and Gallery of Casts*

More and more the greater Universities of the world are seeing what a bearing studies in the development of Art have upon the history of Civilization in all its fields, and what a powerful means they afford for the better development of Civilization. Hence it is that almost every great institution is accumulating illustrative collections in these studies. Cornell University has already begun to make collections of painting and statuary; has received as gifts a considerable collection of medallions and engravings illustrative of the history of Art, beside perhaps the most important collection in the United States of large photographs, illustrating Architecture and Sculpture throughout the world. More than this, it has the pledge of eight thousand dollars for a collection of casts illustrative of the history of plastic Art,—this sum to be available just as soon as any proper gallery can be afforded to contain such casts. Here again, is a noble field for munificence. Such a Gallery might indeed be connected with the Auditorium above named, either directly or indirectly. In any case the erection of such a building, which might cost from sixty to eighty thousand dollars, would be a benefaction of the very greatest importance to the University and to the State. Here is an opportunity for some individual to place in our commonwealth a monument which will for ages tend to substitute higher for lower tastes and enjoyments among our people. There is nothing chimerical in this: the success of the beautiful Slater Memorial Building in Norwich, Connecticut, with its collection of casts, in exerting a wide spread influence for good is well known.

5. *A Biological and Sanitary Laboratory*

Although the University has been doing admirable work in Biology ever since its foundation, and has contributed much directly and indirectly to the development of Sanitary Science, it has been sadly crippled by want of suitable rooms, and, with the increasing number of students, must be more and more unable to fulfill its proper function in this respect. The material already in possession of the University for the work of such a department is very great, so far as collections, preparations, and the like are concerned, but what is especially needed is a building for their proper use by Professors and students. Such a building, of stone, standing between the McGraw and White Buildings, connected with the Biological Museum and Laboratory in the former, would be of the highest use. It should be fire-proof, and would perhaps cost sixty or seventy thousand dollars. It would be the theatre of fruitful investigation and research for hundreds of years. More and more the researches made in such laboratories, especially in Microscopic and Comparative Anatomy, Bacteriology, and kindred sciences are enabling us to combat diseases, against which the world was formerly powerless. Who will make this provision for the good of humanity?

6. *A Law School*

The Trustees of the University have felt that to establish, in the heart of New York, a Law School, is to aid in the elevation of a profession which in every country has to do more than others with constitutional, legal, and administrative development. Lawyers every country must have: the question is, whether they shall be worthy of the name of lawyers—thorough-bred, imbued with historical and social studies, inspired from the great leaders of their profession, and so making their profession a noble one, and contributing constantly to the better development of the laws under which we live—or whether they shall be left without such better influences, and simply become pettifoggers—making of the profession a parasitic growth for evil upon the body politic.

The success of the Law School thus far has been very great. But the time is rapidly coming when it must have more suitable accommodations. At present it is carried on in rooms upon the fourth floor of a building never designed for any such purpose, and which is in every way very ill fitted for this new use. Who will link his name with a great Law School in the heart of the State of New York, as the name of Nathan Dane is immortalized in connection with the Dane Law School at Harvard?

A building for this purpose should contain the Law Library, lecture-rooms, offices for the Professors, sundry other rooms for various purposes, and, in view of the future of the department, it should be made commodious and convenient with reference to four hundred or five hundred students. It may be placed either in the upper quadrangle, in which case, under the policy adopted by the Trustees, it should be of stone, or in the great southern group of buildings, in which case it may be of brick. In view of the fact that it is to contain the Law Library, already valuable and sure to become much more so, it would be well to have the building fire-proof, but this is not essential. Such a structure should cost from seventy to ninety thousand dollars.

7. *A College of Medicine*

In very many of the leading universities a medical college forms an important part. Never was there a time when research in medicine was producing more surprising and beneficent results than now. Cornell University has already provided a preparatory medical course designed to train men intending to study medicine thoroughly in the principles and methods likely to be fruitful of good.

I must confess that with all my ambition for the future of Cornell University, I have no great desire to see a medical college established in connection with it upon the ordinary basis. Of proprietary medical colleges there are too many already. That many of them have done good, great good, is certain, but many of them are certainly doing harm by admitting and graduating masses of young men unfit to practice so noble a profession, simply for the purpose of swelling the fees of Professors. A great service will be rendered to humanity when there shall be fully endowed a medical department for this or any other university, so that its professors may have salaries mainly derived from invested funds and not from students' fees. In such an institution alone can education in medicine be raised to the point where it ought to be.

The location for such a medical college should be doubtless in one of the larger cities, and so far as Cornell University is concerned, my opinion is that it might best be placed in the city of New York. The connection of such a college with Cornell University would be beneficial both to the University and to the college. This is no individual opinion of my own: the University has several times been approached by eminent members of the medical profession on this subject, who have expressed themselves substantially in the terms above stated. Hitherto an establishment of the kind has been thought premature, but the time has now arrived when it may well be considered. The sum required for such a college would of course be very large. There would be necessary a very complete building, with lecture-rooms, laboratories, museums, and all the usual provisions in a medical college. Beside this there should be an endowment for a sufficient number of Professorships, Instructorships, Fellowships, and the like. With less than half a million of dollars nothing could be done which would warrant beginning instruction in this field in connection with the University. The University has been informed frequently that such a sum could be raised by a combination of eminent men in the profession at some of our great city centres, and in my opinion it would be well for the authorities to enter into communication with such leaders at some day not far distant, with reference to this matter.

8. *An Observatory*

Among the things especially dwelt upon by Mr. Cornell in the early days of the University, was the establishment of a fitting Observatory. It may well be doubted whether this university town, in a belt so largely swept by clouds rising from the great lakes, is one of the best fitted for astronomical observations on a large scale; but an observatory of moderate size and well equipped for the illustration of Astronomy and the astronomical training of special students, the institution ought certainly to have. Thus far it has been obliged to make shift with a very inadequate provision in this respect. A modest observatory with an Equatorial, say, of nine inches, with a Transit perhaps somewhat larger than that in present use, and two or three accessory instruments, with a house for an observer and care-taker, would be a most beautiful addition to our means of general and special instruction.

Such an observatory could be built, furnished with instruments, and equipped in all its parts for from thirty to forty thousand dollars. Here too, is an opportunity for a noble monument which shall be a means, not only of advancing science, but of cultivating the religious spirit in its highest sense. If "the undevout astronomer is mad," what better provision for the higher religious thought in the midst of a great body of young men interested in scientific pursuits, than an observatory which will lead them to study the wonders revealed to us by Astronomy.

9. *Fellows Buildings and Dormitories for Students*

Cornell University has not in days past thought it wise to provide dormitory accommodations for its students on any very large scale; but the increasing number of those seeking its advantages, and the importance of having the Assistant Professors, Instructors, Fellows, and Resident Graduates in the immediate neighborhood of the newly erected Library and of their class-rooms, make it desirable that something should be done in this direction. A Fellows Building in which unmarried Professors, Assistant Professors, Lecturers, Fellows, and Resident Graduates, could have comfortable accommodations near lecture-rooms, recitation-rooms, and library, is becoming more and more a necessity. The present President of the University in various Reports, has again and again called attention to the importance of such a building. Such accommodation would be exceedingly useful in many ways, would adorn the University grounds, and would prove an excellent investment. Any person wishing to endow a Professorship, Fellowships, Scholarships, or any building for general University purposes, could do nothing better than to invest from fifty to seventy thousand dollars in a building of this sort. As such a building on the University grounds would require no expenditure for a site, and would not be taxable, it would return an excellent income for the outlay, and this income might be appropriated to any worthy purpose which the donor should indicate, such as maintaining a Professorship, or carrying on a building.

But smaller sums can be admirably used in this same direction. The history of the smaller dormitory buildings erected by the various Greek letter Fraternities of the University, shows how much may be done in this way with moderate sums. It is proved by the care and good order of these buildings in the hands of students, that student dormitories on a smaller scale would be of very great use. I strongly favor, so far as the general body of students is concerned, the erection of a certain number of small dormitories each accommodating from fifteen to twenty-five students, and costing from twenty to twenty-five thousand dollars. Each of such buildings could be leased to a Club of students formed for this purpose, the whole Club to be held responsible for each of its members and for the good order of the building. These buildings, while relieving the pressure for the accommodation of students in our immediate neighborhood, would afford an excellent investment for funds which any individual might give for any specific purpose to the University.

10. *Public Adornments, Bridges, Gates, and the Like*

As time goes on, at the various Universities of the world, men see more and more the uses of beauty in the surroundings of students. The latest examples of this have been shown at Harvard University, where two different gifts of about ten thousand dollars each have been made by individuals for the erection of beautiful gateways at different points on the University grounds. A much older and very striking example of this same feeling is seen in the noted gateways erected by Dr. Caius at the English University of Cambridge.

The grounds of Cornell University, already becoming known throughout the country for their exceeding beauty, afford many opportunities for enrichment of this sort. The present entrances, north and south, are utterly unworthy of such an institution and of its beautiful Campus. Moreover, other very striking opportunities are presented: for, say, ten thousand dollars a beautiful bridge of stone might be thrown over Cascadilla Gorge where the main avenue of approach to the University crosses it by the present temporary iron bridge. A single stone arch spanning the Gorge at this point above the Falls, would be not only of high use for centuries, but would be a most beautiful object in the landscape, attracting the admiration of all visitors. It should bear the name of him or of her who gives it. Are there not some men or women who would be willing to make gifts of eight or ten thousand dollars to link their names forever with monuments so fitting and beautiful?

8. Memorandum from Andrew D. White to Governor and Mrs. Stanford, 26 May 1892

[Andrew D. White was perhaps the single most influential figure in the evolution of higher education in the United States during the last half of the nineteenth century. In the case of Stanford University his involvement was extensive and effective on both academic and architectural issues. He nominated Stanford's first president, David Starr Jordan, and suggested Frederick Law Olmsted as planner and H. H. Richardson as architect for the new university. It is clear from the contents of this memorandum that Mr. and Mrs. Stanford's memorial to their son was developing along academic and architectural lines of which White heartily approved. A copy of the memorandum is in the White Papers.]

Ithaca, N.Y., May 26th 1892
To GOVERNOR AND MRS. STANFORD,

MY DEAR FRIENDS:—

At various times you have done me the honor to consult me, and recently you have asked me as to my impressions regarding your University. It is on this account that I now take the liberty of sending you a memorandum resulting from my recent visit:

Surroundings of the University:

First, as to the Location: I was astonished and delighted at the position of the institution and the beauty of its surroundings. I had not imagined a region so attractive, nor had I supposed it so easy of access. Still less had I expected to find in all the country about it evidences of so much progress, and especially of a community prepared so fully to profit by the work which such an institution as yours is to do. During the month of my residence at Palo Alto I have been brought under the charm of the situation and surroundings with ever-increasing interest.

Buildings: I can imagine nothing more perfect, whether as regards utility or beauty than the general plan of the main educational structures which hangs in the University library. The part already completed, the interior of the main quadrangle, is certainly far more beautiful than any other group of University buildings in the United States. It seems to me ideal as regards its fitness for the work proposed, richness of material, and beauty and dignity of style. It was a most happy thought to adapt the early Spanish construction to modern uses, and it could not have been better carried out. Evening after evening, I have walked under its archways and along its corridors, fascinated by the blending beauty of the sky, landscape and buildings. Day after day, as I walked there, to and from lecture room and library, I have been more and more impressed by the vision of the young men and young women who for centuries to come shall throng its courts, and go forth over the whole Pacific coast, owing to your dear son and yourselves the impulse and power to make the world better than they have found it.

I am familiar with the principal university buildings of our own and other countries, and have thought much upon university architecture. May I not venture then one or two suggestions?

First: I hope that whether the two end groups are ever completed or not, the great central group may be completed at an early day, so that you and I may enjoy the sight of it during our life-time. The front row of buildings, besides being very useful, as giving space for library, museum, etc., will add immensely to the effect, especially to all approaching the institution, and with the interior courts which will be formed between it

297

and the existing buildings, will greatly enhance the beauty of the whole.

Secondly: While the original style should be carefully maintained, I think there should be a slight modification in the proposed "Chapel." It should be made large enough to serve as an auditorium for the whole body of students, with accommodation, say, for fifteen hundred on the ground floor, and, say, five hundred on each of two galleries, thus giving room for about twenty-five hundred in all. This is no mere advice at a venture. All great universities have felt greatly the need of such an auditorium. Oxford, Cambridge, Harvard and Princeton, and many others, have provided them, while others have used large adjacent halls or churches, as is the case at Yale and Cornell.

Thirdly: One little thing, very small in cost compared with the outlay on the buildings, would be an exquisite addition to the whole,—giving it a *voice* by day and night; and that a chime or peal of sweet-toned bells, which should be rung at stated times, and chimed by the clock at the hours and quarters.

Such a chime of, say, ten bells or even a peal of four bells, properly tuned, and especially with a clock for chiming them, and marking the time on four dial faces, would be useful and beautiful. We find that our chiming clock at Cornell University, while of practical value in keeping professors and students aware of the flight of time, is ideally useful in developing the sense of beauty, and attaching Faculty, graduates, students and visitors to the place. Think of the voices of sweet-toned bells, sounding from the quadrangle during the day, giving warning of the flight of time, and then during the night echoing under the arches, and floating over to Menlo Park, and the surrounding villages. It is the only thing needed to complete the beautiful impression made by that whole creation and its surroundings.

I am aware that there has been talk of a subscription among the students for this purpose, but I cannot advise waiting for this. Such a subscription will take a long time and when raised it is a grave question whether it will be expended wisely. I would advise placing the bells, either peal or chime there at once. A good peal of four bells could be bought in this country of C. H. Meneely of Troy, for about $3000 to $4000; a good chime of nine bells, like ours at Cornell, in the key of G, with a large bell on D below, bought of the same firm, would probably cost about $7500. But your surroundings are so exquisitely beautiful, and your aim is so evidently to have the best, that I cannot avoid suggesting to you to order your bells at the best place in the world,—the establishment of Van Aerschot at Liege in Belgium. The tone of their bells is exquisitely beautiful. Those of the "Holy Trinity" Church in Philadelphia, which they made, are far superior to any ever cast in this country. Meneely's bells are decidedly good, but there is a sweetness in those Belgium bells which our makers cannot yet attain to, and I think it would be a patriotic service to give the makers on the Pacific coast an example of the best that can be done in that line. If bought in Belgium a chime would probably cost $10,000 to $12,000, including duty.

As to the place for them: It might easily be obtained by building a belfry on one of the end towers, placing the four clock faces on its sides. The tower might also include a room for the ringer. At Cornell, we select every year a needy and meritorious student, of musical talent, who for a very small compensation takes care of the clock and chimes the bells, and I know of nothing which better repays the outlay. There are always a number of students musically inclined to choose from. As to raising one of the towers and placing a belfry upon it, if done under the direction of a good and tasteful architect, it would help the general effect rather than hurt it, giving variety and an additional and interesting break in the sky-line of the buildings.

Other buildings: I noticed while at Palo Alto designs of wooden buildings for various departments of instruction, to be placed somewhat in the rear of the stone edifices. The erection of these seems to me wise, and their design perhaps satisfactory.

As to cottages for the faculty: Having had much experience in living in them, and in planning them, allow me to make a few suggestions. It is very important that they be fairly commodious, convenient and attractive. We have had these three qualities in view in all our plans for cottages at Cornell, and yet I am satisfied that it would have been wiser for us as a rule to favor the erection of a somewhat better class of cottages than we have done. An increased additional outlay, of which the interest is a very small sum, represents frequently the difference between a house in which a professor's wife can live comfortably and contentedly, and one in which she cannot. The want of a few small conveniences which make house-keeping comparatively easy may make a valuable professor's household unhappy, and lead him to accept a call elsewhere which he would otherwise decline. Even the presence of an attractive little veranda or bay-window may hold a wife against an advanced salary for her husband elsewhere.

It is on this account that I have steadily at Cornell sought to provide everything which might make the lives of the professors and their families attractive and diminish household cares as much as possible, and the comparatively small additional investments required for this purpose have certainly been wise. I am glad to note that the second range of your professors' cottages is a decided improvement on the first, but I think it would still be wise to remove their sheds for wood and coal so that they will adjoin the kitchens, and to give back-stairs to the upper floor and cellar wherever possible.

Dormitories: Your two dormitories are exceedingly attractive. Encina Hall is certainly the most beautiful building for students' residence in the United States; but if you were to furnish more accommodations for students, I would urge you not to repeat the Encina plan. For a family hotel it is perfect, and the time is coming when excellent families will be glad to pay well for such accommodations on your grounds, to be near their sons and daughters, but the fundamental principle in erecting dormitories for students is separation and segregation. This is no mere theory. It is the practical outcome of all experience here and at all the other universities in the world. In all these institutions, old and new, the plan is now adopted of having "entries," with short cross halls and stairs from top to bottom of the building, and only two to four double rooms at most on each landing. This makes it difficult for students to do too much visiting with each other. With long halls making it easy for each student to run to and fro and call on every other, making assemblies in various rooms, on the slightest pretext, a thing of course, the temptations to too much social enjoyment, with its waste of time and suggestions of mischief, are greatly increased. So, too, the difficulty of controlling such a hall and keeping it quiet is greatly diminished when students are thus separated. A student is comparatively little likely to go down two or three flights of stairs, to go out into the open air in the evening, and then climb up two or three flights of stairs, to talk with companions. I have lived as a student in both sorts of college buildings and I know that the disorder consequent upon long halls is far greater than in dormitories where the cross halls and entries make the running together of students difficult.

I do not mean that the fault showed itself to any marked extent at Encina Hall during the month I lived there. On the contrary, I found the students exceedingly well behaved. It must be borne in mind that you have few if any sophomores or upper classmen yet. The main difficulties in university government generally arise in dormitories. So fully is this fact recognized, that at Cornell we have gradually got rid of them almost entirely, so far as the young men are concerned. True, students are better than they were formerly. The new system of greater range of choice in study has vastly increased the percentage of these who really take interest in their work, but there must always be some few worthless young fellows, city bred, sons of rich parents frequently, who feel no need of work, and only heed the desire for "a good time," and a few of these in a dormitory where they can easily get access to all the other students may make much trouble.

Should you desire it, I can send you tracings of some designs for students' dormitories, made in the light of the best experience on that subject.

Naturally, an experienced professor like myself has accumulated some knowledge regarding this subject; just as an experienced machinist has regarding the construction of shops, or an experienced manufacturer regarding factories, or an experienced railroad man regarding railroad building.

Material: I was especially struck by the beauty of the stone used in the construction of your buildings. I have heard many speak of it and have frequently spoken of it myself since my return. The fineness and richness of its color, harmonizing as it does with the color of the tiles adds new beauty to the architecture, and indeed, to the whole landscape. Therefore it is that I hope that at least all your central group of buildings will be made of this beautiful material. No artificial material can ever be as beautiful; and certainly none can have that *character* which is given by stone.

Supervision: But, in my view, absolutely the most important thing of all is to have near the university a consulting architect of the highest class, to advise and direct regarding the whole system of buildings. Without this, your present plan, beautiful as it is, will certainly deteriorate. A single mistake might detract enormously from the impression made by the whole. Such a supervising architect should be one who has proved himself good both from the constructive and artistic side, and all persons employed on plans should work under his direction. In the long run such a man will save the university much money. At Cornell inferior architects have cost us far more than superior ones.

Now you are fortunate enough to have in California one of the most talented young architects in this country. I have given much attention to the subject and have had much experience practically with architects, but I

have seen no recent work which has pleased me more and no man whose ideas have seemed to me more promising than those of Mr. Page Brown of San Francisco. He distinguished himself first in our architectural department at this university; then he went abroad to the great government school of architecture in Paris; then returned to San Francisco where he has been architect of the Crocker building, opposite the Palace Hotel, of the new Trinity Church, of the California building at the Chicago Exposition, and of the remodelling of the University Club, as well as various other things which show remarkable talent and even genius. Now I have no interest in this young man further than that aroused by my admiration for his talents and character, and my desire to see your beautiful creation kept beautiful, and developed according to the ideas and plans already adopted. I think if you speak with Mr. Crocker he will agree with me in my estimate of this young man. Mr. Brown, as supervising architect, would, as it seems to me, prevent mistakes which men of less experience and ability are sure to fall into.

President and Faculty: Looking very carefully over your instructing body, including the president;—discussing various matters with them, and inspecting their modes of teaching, I am satisfied that this most important part of the work is going thoroughly well. More than that, I am convinced that you have made no mistake in the choice of your president: more and more I am satisfied that he is exercising a great and growing influence on general education on the Pacific coast, and that he is selecting as his colleagues bright young men of character and brains who have a reputation to make and can make it.

Students: I also had a good opportunity to look over the student body, and was greatly pleased with it. Looking into the faces of about two-thirds of them nearly every day for three weeks, and talking with many of them at the Encina dormitory, I found them as good a body of men, in every respect, as can be found on any university in the land. Better material no instructor could wish.

The Library: An excellent beginning has been made in the way of books but there are various departments in which additional equipment of this sort is greatly needed. I do not advocate at all the collection of "learned lumber," but every professor needs the books, which show him the progress of his science or art thus far, preparatory to his developing it further. If there is one truth which the great doctrine of evolution has in these days forced into men's minds, it is that great improvements in civilization are rarely if ever sudden and complete creations; they are generally developed out of the past by a constant process of improvement; hence it is, that, in every department, the professor to do thoroughly good work, needs the accumulated thought and work of those who have gone before him on which to base his own. In Mr. Woodruff you have an admirably competent librarian, and the sum of $7000 to $10,000 expended very soon under his direction would be money well laid out from every point of view.

Art Gallery: Among the things which I especially admired was the gallery which Mrs. Stanford has provided for the fine arts and objects of interest. I have said more than once since my return that it is the most sumptuous and complete art· gallery connected with any university or college in the United States, indeed, one of the most perfect in the world. While there will be ample space in it for the rare and beautiful things of interest that you have already collected, especially those relating to your son and yourselves, its main purpose should be to contain a *gallery of casts* representing the whole development and progress of sculpture from its Egyptian and Assyrian beginnings through Greek, Roman, Mediaeval and Renaissance art, down to and including modern times. Such a gallery, supplemented by a collection of large photographs, would be of immense value in connection with historical studies, and would be of ever-increasing interest to students generally, and to the public at large. All the great universities of the world have shown their appreciation of this fact during recent years by the establishment of such galleries. We

here are now making a beginning; I having given over three thousand large architectural and artistic photographs, and Mr. Sage having made us a gift of $8500 for casts. These casts are ordered under the direction of our Professor of Archaeology from Bruciani in London, the modelling establishment of the Louvre in Paris, and the similar establishments in Berlin, Rome and Athens. Your Instructor in Art, Mr. Bolton Coit Brown, is abundantly able to draw up the schedules required. Should you wish to see a very fine gallery of architectural casts and photographs, you can do so at the French government collection in the Trocadero Palace at Paris. For from $20,000 to $25,000 a superb gallery of casts and artistic photographs could thus be had at Palo Alto. Each costs but little, but each represents exactly and fully some great work in the history of art. My suggestion would be that the casts be ordered so that they can be shipped in one or at least in a few cargoes directly to San Francisco, and not examined by the custom-house officers until they arrive at Palo Alto, thus avoiding all difficulty as regards breakage. We have made this arrangement here. In fact at this moment a large collection of boxes filled with these casts is awaiting the arrival of the custom-house officer from New York, to go through the formalities required by the government.

Conclusion: In conclusion I trust that you will pardon what might so seem under other circumstances a volunteering of advice. I should not venture it but for your kind questions at various times, and I am emboldened especially by my desire to see your great and noble plans worthily carried out, as well as by my admiration for what you have already achieved.

With all good wishes, I remain,

Most respectfully and truly yours,
AND. D. WHITE

(In letter to Page Brown I have offered to contribute $5000 to $10,000 toward a chime if a rapid subscription is made among the Gov.'s friends in San Francisco.)

9. Excerpts from a Letter from Andrew Dickson White to Waterman T. Hewett, 1 October 1895

[There have been several versions of the story about the selection of the university site and the design of the first buildings. This letter gives White's account of these events. It seems to correspond fairly well with the reconstructions given in Chapters II and III, which were developed from various sources before this document was discovered. It is in the Hewett Papers in the Cornell University Archives.]

. . . On pages 475 and 476 [i.e., of Hewett's draft of *Cornell University: A History*] I note your discussion of the architecture of the University, and will not seek to "fight our battles o'er again," in the matter of a series of quadrangles, though I hold as fully to that plan as ever—indeed more fully since within the past few days I have seen how beautifully the Yale quadrangle has been developed, and how eagerly the Harvard authorities have done everything to produce a similar effect on their grounds by a series of academic courts. My remembrances also of the beautiful quadrangle and adjacent courts at Stanford University have increased this feeling. But, as regards the style of the architecture adopted at the outset, in the first buildings, I do not think you appreciate the difficulties under which we labored. The time allowed us was very short and the plans of a more academic character satisfied no one. Though two architects, who at that time took the lead in American Gothic architecture, did their best for us, the Trustees would have none of their work and really as I remember it I cannot blame them. We were forced to fall back upon the simplest plans submitted, which I thought then and still think may one day in the hands of a better architect be so modified as to produce a thoroughly good effect.

When I mention the fact that from our first buildings we deliberately left out sash weights from the windows in order to save a few hundred dollars for books and equipment, you will see what the dilemma was in which we were placed. . . .

The question of the location of the University buildings is not stated I think with exactness. The facts in the case, as I remember them, are that after a meeting of the Board of Trustees, Mr. Cornell brought the entire Board, with some citizens of Ithaca, upon the grounds. We visited first the lower site, near where the quarry now is, just above the new Cornell mansion. That site struck the Board favorably, and was favored by Judge Finch and myself, but we then came upon the higher grounds, and viewed the landscape from the spot now occupied by the Chemical laboratory. It was a beautiful day and the panorama was magnificent. Mr. Cornell urged the reasons on behalf of the upper site, the main one being that there was so much more room for expansion upon it, and all the Board agreed with him fully except Mr. Finch and myself. I confess freely, that while the development of the University would have in some respects been more easy upon the lower site the upper site has on the whole proved the better.

10. Letter from Andrew Dickson White to Professor T. F. Crane, 3 February 1899

[Professor Crane had been appointed Dean of the Arts College in 1896 and was made Acting President in January 1899, when President Schurman left the campus to serve as president of a commission to recommend United States policy in the Philippines following the Spanish-American War. As this letter indicates, Andrew D. White lost little time in informing the temporary boss of his concerns in matters of campus architectural development. In this letter and elsewhere White refers to "a sketch of the campus" with proposed sites for buildings which is, he says, in his house. A thorough search of the Archives has failed to turn up the sketch. This letter is in the Crane Papers in the Cornell University Archives.]

EMBASSY OF THE UNITED STATES
OF AMERICA
Berlin, February 3rd, 1899.

Professor T. F. Crane,
Acting President, &c., &c.,
Cornell University,
Ithaca, New York.

Dear Professor Crane:

Referring to your kind letter of January 17th, the news it contains pleases me greatly, and I have no doubt that under your administration all will go satisfactorily. Trying hours will come no doubt, but your experience will carry you successfully through.

Among the things which I hope you will bear in mind is the importance of preventing irreparable injury to our beautiful campus in the placing and in the architecture of buildings. One or two very bad mistakes have already been made, but on the whole we have preserved most of the magnificent views.

By all means in each case let the men really and deeply interested in such things and fully competent to discuss them, examine, study, and carefully report before a decision is made.

For example, I should lament the placing of any building on the small open space across the road opposite west of the Gymnasium for the reason that it would cut off what little remains of that exquisite vista or series of glimpses of the lake which one gets on arriving at the top of the hill.

So, too, in placing buildings upon the Campus, pains should be taken to carry out the original plan of having the upper group a great quadrangle or hollow square of stone buildings in architecture which, if not the same throughout, should at least not be made up of utterly discordant parts.

If you can get a moment to write me I would like to know how the interior of the new Chapel strikes you, including the Memorial Apse, and whether any of the Memorial Windows or Tablets had to be sacrificed. Such a sacrifice would be a great pity.

To tell you the plain truth I was much disappointed in the plans which were sent me of the proposed Alumni Hall. What I have always dreamed of and looked forward to is a *HALL* in the true sense of the word as understood at Oxford, Cambridge, Harvard, Yale, and elsewhere—a noble oblong room with mullioned windows giving places for memorials to be placed by different classes, the windows placed high so that there would be room for portraits of university worthies below them, and at least one great fireplace; this to be the place for the assemblages of the Alumni, and especially for their annual banquets, and to be used for fitting university purposes during the year. To these other

303

buildings could be attached as needed, probably one or two reception rooms, writing rooms, and possibly a reading room; but I was greatly discouraged at seeing in the plans so much stress laid on "lounging" rooms, "smoking" rooms, etc., of which, Heaven knows, there are enough on the Campus already.

As to a great Auditorium, that is a totally distinct matter. Like the "Sheldonian" at Oxford or the University "Theatre" at English Cambridge, the Sanders at Harvard, as well as the "Aulas" of the great European Universities, its purpose should be to contain large university assemblages, and the best model I have ever seen is the Carnegie at Pittsburgh, which is beautiful, dignified, holds on the floor and in the galleries I should say 3000 people, and every one within easy hearing distance of a person speaking on the stage. Some day I trust some one will give us a Department of Music which shall include such a Hall.

Among my papers at my house is a sketch of the Campus with the sites which after very careful study I thought most fitting for such buildings, and measured to a scale and filled in with them.

Bear in mind, I beg of you, and urge the Executive Committee to bear in mind that one University Campus after another in the country has been absolutely spoiled by carelessness as to the placing and material of buildings. Harvard has gone to great expense in rectifying the matter, and Yale has now to tear away all its old buildings in order to carry out the plan of a great interior court or square which ought to have been the plan from the first. The University of Michigan is an awful example of the same thing: buildings of every sort stuck down anywhere and everywhere.

Do what you can, I beg of you, to maintain in the Executive Committee and in the Board a proper feeling in this respect.

11. Letter from Andrew Dickson White to President Jacob Gould Schurman, 12 February 1903

[Andrew D. White played a major role in the long debate over the location of Rockefeller and Goldwin Smith Halls. This letter, which summarizes his position in early 1903, also contains interesting comments on Ezra Cornell's conception of the first campus plan and White's reaction to the campus plan of 1902 by Carrère and Hastings. The letter also gives evidence of the Ex-President's heavy commitment to the development of excellence on Cornell's campus. His detailed descriptions of the advantages of various sites and the character of building appropriate to them is obviously the result of long thought. He also volunteers to give up other travel plans to rush back to Ithaca to argue for his ideas. A copy of the letter is in the White Papers.]

The Chalet, Alassio, Italy,
February 12, 1903.

J. G. Schurman, LL.D.,
Ithaca, N.Y.

My dear Mr. President:

Returning to Alassio after an absence of three weeks, I find your letter of January 24th.

I rejoice especially to learn that the Trustees have bought farming land east of our present domain, and most earnestly hope that they will purchase any land necessary to connect the two properties already ours which can be obtained at anything like a fair price. The examples of many other universities—to say nothing of our own—urge us strongly to do this, and, much as I abhor debt, I would gladly vote that the University incur liabilities for the full extent allowed by its charter in order to secure all the necessary land east of us before it is too late; and this is the only thing for which I would be willing that the institution incur a debt.

Now as to your question. Mr. Cornell's original idea, to which the Board of Trustees agreed in the first days of our organization, was that there should be an upper campus, in which all the buildings should be of stone, and that the enclosure should be a single large quadrangle. I feel sure that it never occurred to him that it would ever be divided by lines of buildings running from east to west.

The earliest buildings on the west side of this great quadrangle were separated from each other in order to diminish the danger of a sweep along the whole row by fire; but he always thought favorably of an eventual plan which should place fire-proof buildings to fill the main gaps in the west row, namely, those between McGraw and Morrill and McGraw and White. His idea was that such buildings would not only be useful—being at the very center of University activity—but that they would serve as a much needed windbreak to protect students and others from the gales of winter, which sweep with such force across the unprotected part of the hill. There was some talk at a later period of a line of buildings parallel to Sibley, running from a point between McGraw and White and the southwest corner of the Civil Engineering building; but I do not think that he ever dreamed of this as desirable or possible. From time to time I have thought not only of such a line, but of a second line parallel to it, extending from the space between McGraw and Morrill on the west directly eastward across the campus and joining any buildings which should form the east side of the campus. This would

305

give two quadrangles of good size, one at the north and the other at the south end and a third quad or—more properly—court between them, this smaller court being bounded on the west by the McGraw building.

But on reflecting upon the whole matter, especially in the light of Mr. Sibley's objections, I hope most earnestly that some way may be found to obtain a proper site for the Rockefeller building other than erecting it in a line from east to west across the campus. While I agree with you that there may be circumstances under which we should withstand the wishes of donors of buildings as regards cutting off portions of the campus from the view of such buildings, still, in this case, when Mr. Sibley's wish is added to the misgivings which we must all naturally feel at dividing such a beautiful campus as we now have, it seems to me that every effort should be made to find another site for the Physical Laboratory.

In the rough sketch which I enclose, I have indicated two which seem to me, on many accounts, better even than that which has been proposed. The first is on a site directly east of Garden Avenue and south of the Reservoir back of the houses occupied by Professors Law, Hewitt, Hammond and myself. There would be ample space for buildings of any size, accommodating not only the proposed Physical Laboratory to-day and for the far future, but for the Department of Architecture, giving a northern exposure for its drafting-rooms, which it so much needs. The main advantages of this site are, that the ground is there level; that there is ample room, both as regards the present and the future; and that it may be built of brick in a simple but good and massive style at a price vastly less than a stone building running across the campus. I remember that last summer, when President Gilman and I, as Trustees of the Carnegie Institution of Research at Washington, were examining the Government Physical Laboratories and Experiment Stations at Charlottenburg near Berlin, the Director told us that, in view of the rapid progress and

constantly changing demands of experimental physics, laboratories should be rebuilt every ten or fifteen years. There is great force in this remark, and this site to which I refer would enable the Department to expand in any manner and to any extent hereafter found desirable. For the sum at your disposal, you could erect on that site in brick an immense building around three sides of a very spacious court, leaving the fourth or north side open for an Architectural or other building, as might be found necessary. The position is very accessible, near the center of things, and, if adopted, the electric railway could be left where it is, which seems to me a very great advantage.

The only objection to the site that I can think of is the possibility of tremor from the Beebe Dam and Triphammer Falls, which are not very far from that point.

But if this be an objection, there is another site which seems to me to present very great advantages, namely, one on the west side of Central avenue, facing Sage College. This would also have all the advantages above named and be still farther removed from the tramway and from all possibility of tremor from Fall Creek. The expense of obtaining the site would be small, since we already own the firetrap known as Sage Cottage, regarding which I doubt not we have all had serious misgivings.

An advantage in this site additional to those named above is that it works perfectly into the plans of the entire University property made by Messrs. Carrere and Hastings, as I understand them. On this site—which in the sketch I have marked "B"—extension could be made—north, south or west—and to any extent. If necessary, Prof. Caldwell's house could be acquired later; but it would be hardly needed at first. This building, if erected in brick in a simple Romanesque style, not conflicting with Barnes Hall opposite its northern end, could certainly be made a very effective architectural addition to your campus. The adoption of either of these plans would, of course, enable you to adjourn indefinitely the running of buildings across the upper quadrangle, which adjournment I think all of us would rejoice at. I have tried hard, of late years, to convert myself to the idea of such buildings and, for a time, succeeded; but in view of the impressive building which Mr. Sibley has given us, my old doubts and misgivings have returned. Could not the whole matter be allowed to lie over until the annual meeting of the Trustees next spring? I have, as you know, given the location and the architecture of the future buildings on the campus much thought and study, and would esteem it a very great favor if I could look over the whole matter with you this spring, before a final decision is reached. If this can be done, I am willing to give up sundry excursions in Switzerland and Spain which I had planned for May & June, and to sail for America in time to be with you at the annual meeting, which I understand to be June 17th—even if my family are obliged to come later. I most sincerely hope that this arrangement can be made, and then, as Mr. Sibley would probably be present, the whole matter could be arranged satisfactorily.

I have lately been studying the plans of Messrs. Carrere and Hastings, and, while I find some features excellent, I find some others which, I am sure, would prove a very serious misfortune to the University. I would greatly like to sit down with you and discuss the whole matter. I think that I could suggest a few modifications which they would accept, and which both you and they would see to be to the best interests of the institution.

I cable you to-day as follows:

"Can you not defer whole building matter until spring trustee meeting? Am sending sketches. White."

I remain, my dear Mr. President,

Yours faithfully,

P.S.—You will note that I have inserted roughly the connecting links between McGraw and Morrill and McGraw and White, namely, fireproof structures a little less than the width of those buildings, which is about fifty feet; and as each would be 112 feet long, you would get, at very small cost comparatively, buildings for lecture-rooms, recitation-rooms, etc., buildings equivalent to a single building 224 feet in length. Of course such a structure should be fire-proof; but it would need no corner-blocks of stone, and the ends would be of rough brick. It would, in fact, consist merely of east and west walls, two floors and roof.

This would, in my opinion, necessitate the change, which I have roughly sketched, in the front of the McGraw building, namely, the taking down of the present tower, which, as you know, has subsided and is badly cracked, and reerecting it with another as a companion to it on the west side of the same building, thus making twin towers with a gable or monumental stone dormer in the roof between them. This would give the building character and be really, I think, impressive, and the sky-line would be especially good, since we have at one end of the line the great campanile of the Library and at the other the tower of Franklin Hall.

I have also sketched in at a venture an octagonal annex of say two stories to the Library, which will certainly be needed some day as a Bibliographical Museum, Seminary rooms, etc.

P.P.S.—In case whole matter of buildings can be deferred as above requested, I will regard it an especial favor if you would cable me, "Deferred," addressing me, "White, Alassio, Italy"; and if it cannot be deferred, cable to same address, "Not deferred." I ask this for the reason that, if the whole matter can be postponed as above until June 17th, I should at once arrange for my passage.

A. D. WHITE

12. An Excerpt from the Annual Report of President Jacob Gould Schurman for the Academic Year 1919–1920

[This was President Schurman's last annual report. In it he gives a fairly detailed account of his successful efforts over the years to expand the land holdings of the University, which he felt was "cribbed, cabined and confined." Schurman also enters a plea for cutting down trees to open up vistas from the campus, a policy first suggested by Charles Lowrie and prosecuted with handsome results during the third President's administration. The report indicates that Schurman was quite conscious of the fact that the principal elements of the form of the campus were fixed during his twenty-eight years in office.]

Buildings and Grounds

I have already mentioned the expansion of the University grounds from 200 acres to 1456. The first step was taken in 1902. About that time a field of some sixteen acres below West Avenue, which then formed the western limit of the University domain, came into the market to be sold for building lots. I recommended that the entire tract be purchased by the University as a future site for residential halls for men students. But the University had not at that date committed itself to the policy of housing its students, and the Executive Committee referred the recommendation to the full Board without endorsement. At the next meeting of the Board I pointed out, in support of the proposal, that many of the leading universities of the country, from Harvard, Yale, and Columbia, the oldest, to Chicago, one of the newest, had made the mistake of not securing land enough for development and had in the course of time found themselves hemmed in by alien ownership, through which they could not expand without great and in some cases prohibitive expense. The Board, on my motion, then took a short recess to inspect the tract in question and on re-convening voted unanimously to purchase it. This is the field on which Baker Court and Founders Hall now stand—fireproof buildings constructed of local stone, in the Gothic style, as beautiful as they are commodious and well appointed—and it is destined in the not remote future to be covered with other halls which will, I trust, maintain the high standard set by Baker and Founders.

For further expansion we turned to the east and secured two or three farms. The development of the State College of Agriculture later reinforced the reasons I had urged for expansion in this direction and additional farms were purchased. This enlargement of the University domain might be visualized as a fan extending away to the east and beyond the north and south gorges, between which the original grounds of the institution lie like a flat handle.

The next step in expansion came in connection with the location of the hall of residence for women students, the gift of Mrs. Russell Sage. It was proposed, with very general if not indeed universal approval, to locate that building immediately to the north of Sage College. I opposed that location and advocated the purchase of land as a site for the new hall immediately to the north of Fall Creek Gorge. I pointed out that, while the site of Sage College was very suitable for a women's hall at the time of its erection in 1872, it had been rendered unsuitable for the purpose by the general development of the campus and especially by the location in the immediate neighborhood of the men's playground, athletic field, and drill hall. I also urged the consideration that in the future the University would need all the land in and about Sage

308

College for buildings devoted to instruction and research. At the meeting of the Board of Trustees in which the question was to be settled I moved that the Board take a recess and examine the merits of the two sites proposed. On re-convening, the Board voted unanimously for the site to the north of Fall Creek Gorge and one of the Trustees, Emerson McMillin, was so impressed with the advantages of the site that he presented the University with the money to purchase it. I then urged, with the support of one or two other Trustees, the purchase of the adjoining tract along the north bank of Fall Creek Gorge up to Forest Home as a site for future halls and grounds for women students, and in a short time this was accomplished, the addition embracing over fifty acres.

Just as the first expansion below West Avenue has provided an ideal site for residential halls for men students, the erection of which began with Baker Court and Founders Hall, so this expansion of the University campus to the north of Fall Creek has provided a beautiful, convenient, and yet secluded site for the location of women's halls, and it is adequate for the indefinite future.

The location of the original buildings of the State College of Agriculture was a difficult problem. The faculty and friends of the college were practically unanimous in the wish that they should be placed on or alongside the original Campus. I pointed out that such a location would afford inadequate space for future expansion and recommended instead the farm field east of Garden Avenue and north of the University playground and common. It was strongly objected, not without feeling indeed, that this site involved banishment from the rest of the University and even discrimination against the College of Agriculture. Fortunately the State Architect, the Hon. G. L. Heins, who had charge of the plans, favored the site, and eventually the Board adopted it. The policy has been abundantly vindicated by the expansion of the College. Not only are its buildings now close to the other University buildings, but it is

already obvious that its future growth will call for all the land from the University common and playground to the highway along Fall Creek Gorge.

The gorges between which the University Campus lies are wonderfully beautiful and constitute one of the best assets of the institution. It has been no easy task to preserve them from utilization for material purposes which would greatly impair if not entirely destroy their beauty. Of course the streams are used for the water and power supply of the University, and by the purchase of land a few miles up Fall Creek provision has been made for an almost indefinite enlargement of that water and power supply in the future. In the construction of the present power plant some of the ablest experts on the Board of Trustees recommended the use of a large pipe in the Gorge, but, in deference to the objections which I and other Trustees urged against that plan on aesthetic grounds, it was finally abandoned and the water was conveyed to the power house through an underground tunnel to the north of the Gorge.

The main lines of development of the Campus are now firmly established. East of Garden Avenue and its prolongation to the road along Fall Creek Gorge the entire area to the north of the playground and common and athletic fields will, as just stated, be required for the buildings of the College of Agriculture which already dot a considerable portion of it. Between Garden Avenue and West Avenue and Fall Creek Gorge and Cascadilla Gorge the entire area will be needed in the course of future generations for class rooms, laboratories, and other structures devoted to purposes of instruction and investigation. The professors' houses on this tract are destined to disappear rapidly; four or five were displaced by the Rockefeller Hall of Physics and still more will be displaced by the new Chemical Laboratory. No new lots either for professors' houses or fraternity lodges within this area have been granted in the last quarter of a century.

Within the campus there are a number of

interesting and important problems connected with the buildings and grounds. It has already been decided on my recommendation to locate the new Chemical Laboratory on the tract between Fall Creek Gorge and Rockefeller Hall, in line with this latter building. There is no finer and more commanding site on the campus. That arrangement, however, will prevent the expansion eastward to any appreciable extent of the College of Engineering. It is also limited on the north by the road along Fall Creek Gorge. Unless the quadrangle is divided by an east and west building to the south of Lincoln Hall there is no place for additional buildings for the College of Engineering except to the south and west. Of course the present shops will be demolished to make room for modern well-lighted laboratories like Rand Hall, and the ruins of Morse Hall, on which the fire insurance for the entire group of buildings has already been collected, will in time be removed. It would be a fortunate circumstance if Franklin Hall, built in 1883, which in its exterior is an eyesore to the campus and in its interior the darkest and most inconvenient building on the campus, could also be removed. I look forward to the time when this area will be covered with modern buildings for the College of Engineering. Let me also add that if Lincoln Hall, built in 1888, which is very poorly adapted to the needs of the division of Civil Engineering and which in the opinion of the Building Committee cannot be advantageously altered or reconstructed, were removed altogether it would have the happy effect of bringing the new and stately Chemical Laboratory into the main quadrangle of the University.

The planning and disposition of the new buildings authorized last winter by the Legislature for the College of Agriculture at a cost of three million dollars will have most important architectural effects for the campus. Fortunately the matter is being carefully studied by the State Architect, the Hon. L. F. Pilcher, whose imagination has grasped this opportunity of combining useful buildings with fine monumental effects. He will of course have the support of the University Committee on Buildings and Grounds and particularly the valuable assistance of its sub-committee, Chairman Edwards and J. C. Westervelt. When this building scheme has been completed I trust that the Agricultural quadrangle may be connected with the main quadrangle of the University not merely by a footpath but by a broad and stately mall.

It is not difficult to foresee that new University buildings will in the future be located on the southern half of both East Avenue and Central Avenue. When the new gymnasium comes it will undoubtedly be located in the neighborhood of the Drill Hall, playground, and athletic field. For further development there would remain the area between Central Avenue and West Avenue which, apart from certain fraternity houses, is now altogether intact.

While the University through the enlargement of its grounds has secured the upper reaches of the gorges in addition to the sections adjoining the Campus, the lower portions still remain in private hands. I trust that either through gift or purchase these also may come into the possession of the University; for the gorges are of incomparable beauty and they would be much better preserved by the University than by a number of different owners with interests limited to their own particular holdings which in most cases they value only for utilitarian purposes. I venture to express the hope that these gorges will be kept in their wild natural condition.

No other university has so beautiful and romantic a situation as Cornell. We owe it to the alumni and old students who know and love it and to the endless generations of students who will come here in the future to preserve these beauties unimpaired and inviolate. If, however, their refining influence is to be fully felt in the aesthetic education of students these beauties must so far as possible be visible from the Campus. They are, however, becoming rapidly obscured. To some extent this is due to the erection of new buildings.

But the principal cause is the growth of trees which were set out, sometimes indeed on a plan, but oftener than not at random and by chance. Every lover of nature mourns the destruction of trees, but even at the risk of the charge of denudation the cutting down of trees and the opening up of vistas in numerous places is an absolutely imperative necessity if the members of this university community while going to and fro on the Campus are not to be shut out from the wondrous beauty by which they are encompassed and which in previous years it was our good fortune to enjoy.

13. Report to Accompany a Tentative Plan for the Development of Cornell University Property Bounded by East Avenue, University Avenue, Cascadilla Creek, Fall Creek, and Interrelated Areas, by Bryant Fleming, 16 June 1930

[Bryant Fleming was one of the most imaginative of the parade of landscape architects who served the University in the first half of the twentieth century. As the report shows, he knew the campus well and was keenly aware of its most significant landscape values. The report describes proposals sketched in his plan of 1930 (Fig. 196). The capital letter symbols used in it refer to the symbols on that sketch. Some of its most radical proposals, including the recommendations to remove the President's House and Barnes Hall, were not incorporated in the official 1932 General Plan of Development. Nevertheless, many of Fleming's ideas on the landscape development of the campus were and are valuable, especially those dealing with the "great terrace" and its extensions south to Willard Straight Hall. A photostat of the campus plan sketch and a copy of the report are in the Campus Planning Papers in the Cornell University Archives.]

To The Committee on Buildings and Grounds
Cornell University, Ithaca, New York.

Gentlemen:

In accordance with the request made me in April 1930, by the Chairman of your Grounds Committee, Mr. R. H. Treman, I am submitting a general, but still somewhat tentative study and report for the further development of the University property within the area bounded by East Avenue, on the east, University Avenue, on the west, Cascadilla Creek, on the south, and Fall Creek, on the north.

In presenting this plan and report to you, I am taking for granted that we are all more or less agreed upon the major facts and ideas presented and discussed in the several earlier reports submitted; witness the agreed strategic location of Ithaca and the University; the already studied and apparent interrelation between the City and the University to the surrounding country; the important and definite values of the natural scenery; the beauty and controlling value of the gorges; all of the above having been analyzed and reported upon.

I assume too, that the Report of November 14th, 1925, made by Mr. Medary, Mr. Bosworth and myself is accepted in its major features, at least in part sufficient to afford a basis for a general scheme, deficient only in its more detailed recommendations.

I also assume that the several reports made by Mr. Warren H. Manning, especially with reference to the outlining [outlying] districts and their relation to the University problem, are agreed upon as majorily fundamental to the University Plan.

Therefore I shall not go into a discussion of the many controlling and obvious facts and conditions which have already been reported upon, but instead accept, in general, these earlier decisions and endeavour to give you a more specific and detailed series of thoughts within the area which has been suggested.

EAST AVENUE is unquestionably the acknowledged important north and south traffic-circulation-axis of the University, connecting at the south with the proposed new circulation to College Avenue and Eddy Street, and to Varna, Dryden, and the East; and at its north end with the Forest Home Road, Easterly, and to the north via the bridge over Fall Creek to the Heights, and beyond.

This Avenue at present is one given over to both University and residential use. Residences should be eliminated and the entire Avenue be made one as a site for University buildings. East Avenue is unquestionably the acknowledged important north and south axis. The principal break in this Avenue is

312

Documents 313

Tower Road leading to the east and serving as the major circulation to the State College of Agriculture. Its junction with East Avenue should therefore be recognized as am [an] important focal point.

Considering the importance of this intersection, new buildings could and should be located in a position to emphasize Tower Road which would mean the use of a building site to the front of the present Veterinary College, and a complementary building site occupying the location of the present President's House. Buildings in these two locations should be so located, blocked, and clipped at their corners, as to create a plaza feeling at this junction.

A new building to reface the present west facade of Rockerfeller [sic] Hall is suggested on an alignment with the proposed two buildings at the Tower Road junction. Other buildings following this newly created building line are suggested as a group addition or facing to the present Drill Hall now much in need of focalization from East Avenue and as a continuation of buildings along East Avenue to South Avenue extended, otherwise known as Schoellkopf Road.

As mentioned in earlier reports the east facade of the present Sage College could be added to in a manner to aligne [sic] with a refacing of Goldwin Smith, the present east facade of Stimpson [sic], and such other proposed buildings as have been suggested along the west side of the Avenue. In this manner, and through this development, East Avenue would pass from a residential street to one given over to College buildings.

The present discussed location for College of Fine Arts, namely the area just north of Sage College, is a most valuable and interesting site for a building of considerable importance. Regardless of the use to which this site might be assigned, nothing should in any way interfere with the now existing and beautifully controlling contour or valley to the north of Sage College. You may feel that there is a bit of sentimentality in this remark, but the beauty of the Cornell Campus is its admixture of extreme natural beauty and a semi-sense of

formality. Were the Campus plan to be completely and architecturally formalized, its primary value, its extreme natural beauty, would be suppressed to a point of possible eradication.

A College of Fine Arts has been suggested, and, in fact, designed for this location, the building as now designed, however, being far too large for and unrelated to the site, completely destroying all evidence of this natural valley. If a building is to occupy this site, its plan and design should unquestionably be so studied as to bring out and express the beauty of the natural conditions at this point, which means that the southern facade of such a building should be carefully designed and related to the present existing conditions. Especially does the site call for a smaller building than was proposed for Fine Arts or Architecture.

As to whether this site should be given over to Fine Arts, is still a question in my mind, the situation not being quite imaginative and inspirational enough for devoting to such a use. The major merit, however, of this site as a location for Fine Arts is its close proximity to Stimpson Hall, the use of which as a medical building will probably be cancelled. Stimpson Hall might then be used as a connected addition to Fine Arts, its laboratories, etc., being somewhat easily converted to drawing and drafting rooms. Stimpson Hall, I grant, is not an ideal piece of architecture, or one showing nicety of design suitable to Fine Arts or architectural use. In summary, it is not architecturally inspirational, but is possible of improvement and modification. Too, were it architecturally tied to a new building on site 'A', the group as a whole could be so designed as to form a most interesting architectural terminal to Tower Road, considering the group to be so planned as to possibly provide a large archway leading into an interior court between the two buildings and focusing through to the Library Tower beyond.

Such a western terminal to Tower Road could be developed most interestingly and a recession or broadening of East Avenue before this group could be so arranged as to give proper access to the group as well as form an important widening in East Avenue at this point, so facilitating traffic and parking. In summary, regarding East Avenue there is no question in my mind as to the satisfactory terminus of this Avenue at the south, the proposed Gymnasium providing a splendid focal. I am a bit concerned, however, with the northerly terminal of East Avenue and its relation to the Forest Home Road, the bridge over Fall Creek and the proposed easterly terminal of the Sibley group. Specific study should be given this particular portion of the problem or plan. It has been tentatively studied in the November 14th, 1925 report, but not to the point of complete satisfaction.

TOWER ROAD—I am still quite adverse to Tower Road being extended west from East Avenue to Central Avenue, and definitely against the retaining of Central Avenue from new South Avenue to Willard Straight Hall and the Chapel. I feel that the November 1925 report made a most excellent recommendation when it proposed that a Mall be substituted for Central Avenue. There is nothing which mars the collegiate peace and quiet of the Campus more than the traffic conditions along the present Central Avenue. With the circulation which has been provided to the west of Willard Straight, and which we are further developing in the present plan submitted, and with the continued use of the present roadway between Sage College, Barnes Hall, the Chapel and Site 'A', it seems to me that all necessary motor access can be provided to these concerned buildings. I therefore suggest the retention of the roadway between Sage College, Barnes Hall, the Chapel and site 'A', this roadway to be so altered as to provide an ample turning court to the east of the Chapel: the Chapel being the principle building this roadway would serve.

SECONDARY QUADRANGLE B—Upon the plan I am submitting Barnes Hall has been removed. I appreciate that this will not be accomplished immediately, but I believe it should be eventually. I have suggested its removal to better create a secondary quadrangle B, framed by Sage College, proposed building site 'A', Sage Chapel, Willard Straight Hall, proposed Building Site 'C' and proposed Group 'D' at the southern end of this area. I appreciate that Barnes Hall is an endowed building and still usable, but the open space gained by its removal will prove the value of this suggestion.

Regarding suggested Group 'B', I consider this site as one of the most important undeveloped areas yet unassigned. The block as shown is, of course, merely suggestive and makes use of the present Armory and Gymnasium outlines, the value of their being kept as buildings depending entirely upon the detailed development of Group 'D'.

The site is important in that it most conveniently relates to the entrance circulation leading from College Avenue to East Avenue; has the beauty of relating to quadrangle 'B' and the Mall and the possibility of the group being so designed as to compose well with the Law Group to the west. It has the added beauty of overlooking Cascadilla Gorge to the south.

While I do not assume to assign this group 'D' to a specific use, the convenience, beauty, and size of area suggests the possibility of an interestingly designed Fine Arts Group here, or at least a school or college of equal importance and size. The site has the advantage of circulation by the public to the group as well as the possibility of quiet and beauty on its south, west, and north sides.

THE LIBRARY OR WEST SLOPE— Regarding the treatment of the so-called Library or West Slope, and the areas to the west and below this slope my thoughts and feelings are quite definite, and may appear somewhat radical. Relative to the development of this area, the purchase of the Frank Cornell property has been of the greatest importance, providing as it does the possibility of a most beautiful somewhat domestic and park entrance to the University at the junction of Stewart Avenue and the present South Avenue.

With the building of the War Memorial, conditions relative to the Library Slope have changed materially, a strong east and west axis having been created by the position of the two Memorial Towers and their connecting cloister. Too, the location of the War Memorial has materially decreased the apparent distance between this building and the University Library above. The result has been a desire to create more or less of a formal tie between these two buildings, and to bring out and emphasize this now very apparent axis. The Library, especially in its proposed enlarged form, becomes a very dominant and focal building, not only to the West Slope, but to the entire University Plan. The Dormitory Groups below and the University Quadrangle above become two strong units, one superimposed above the other, in need of a strong interrelated axis or tie, to design and bring together or compose two now unrelated areas. The present neutral zone, the Library Slope, is perforce disappearing as a great meadow or meadow slope, and in its stead is developing an open unit 'E' to the north of the Memorial-Library axis and a complementary open and parked area 'F' to the south of this axis. To emphasize the axis mentioned and to create a tie between the upper University Quadrangles and the Dormitory Groups, I suggest that a plaza or court be created before the War Memorial. I would gain this plaza be [by] a widening of West Avenue at this point, and in addition, extend a strong retaining wall into the grade of the Library Slope, so creating an open space before the Memorial Building, this plaza to be established at the grade of West Avenue.

An architectural motif such as a fine piece of memorial statuary could interestingly focal this open space. Steps on the axes of the towers would lead to the upper level, and penetrate these retaining walls, and from these, on across the meadow I would extend broad paths leading up the hillside which fortunately is comparatively flat at this point, these paths terminating in a terrace which would connect in turn with a great observation terrace to the west of the Library.

This brings me to a discussion of the Drive circulation from Schoellkopf Road, or South Avenue extended. I have chosen to accept Schoellkopf Road as now planned, to and as far as the court already designed for the lower approach to Willard Straight Hall. Regarding a continued road to the north from this point, road 'G' I wish to recall or cancel my earlier suggestion of extending this road diagonally across the slope to Stewart Avenue, and instead suggest that the road be carried north and parallel with the Library, Morrill, McGraw, and White Halls. At a point H, just west of White Hall, I would continue the road into University Avenue over an easy grade at this point.

The location and thought regarding this northerly extention road 'G' is strongly interrelated to an idea which I have long cherished and discussed many times, namely, the creating of a definite terrace 'I' upon which to rest or support the Library, Morrill Hall, McGraw Hall, White Hall, and proposed new Sibley.

If such a terrace is ever to be considered, as indeed it should be, the present proposed additions to the Library should not be accepted as now designed. I refer to their detailed design, not to their architectural character. Instead, the west facade of the Library should be restudied with relation to the establishing of such a terrace.

I would begin this terrace at the north facade of Willard Straight Hall, from where I would create an arcaded loggia connecting Willard Straight Hall directly with the Library, the arcade being a semi-enclosed structure below the level of Central Avenue. This arcade should be so designed as to act as a retaining wall between the two buildings and its roof so planned as to form a platform and parapet to an observation area at approximately the same grade as now established before Willard Straight. I refer to area 'J'. This could be beautifully handled as a large paved gathering terrace complementary to Willard Straight Hall.

This terrace should then extend out and around the west facade of the Library where it should be developed as an important over-look terrace commanding the fine views to be had from this point. Nothing should in any way interfere with this development, and it would be perfectly feasible to readjust the present plans for the Library to accommodate this idea. The proposal will mean modifica-tion of the present proposed Library plans, but the value to be gained is worth any amount of restudy of these plans.

Road 'G' could be carried beneath this ter-race overlook so giving access to the Library and the three original main buildings, for de-livery of freight, etc., tunnelled connections being suggested to these buildings.

From this point North, the road would carry below the base of the terrace above, steps and accents being suggested especially on the axis 'K' of McGraw Hall, where an interesting axial line carries up from Univer-sity Ave. below.

The terrace as suggested terminates in an-other important overlook at the west end of proposed Sibley College, so giving important emphasis to the Sibley Group at this point. It is also here that I would have located the Ezra Cornell memorial statue.

I will not attempt to go into a detailed explanation as to the designing of this west-erly overlook terrace except to say that its parapet should be below a general level of the ground back of the three original buildings, and be paralleled along this entire length by a broad promenade or path from which one would enjoy the view.

As mentioned above, the Library Slope di-vides itself into three areas, a northerly area 'E', a semi-formal area 'L', connecting the War Memorial with the Library and a south-erly area 'F'. Area 'E' can reasonably be en-closed along its north-westerly side by a row of semi-detached buildings devoted to any use necessary; these buildings however,

should relate in grade primarily to University Avenue and be built into the garde [grade] of Area 'E'. It is suggested they be tied to Uni-versity Avenue and to McGraw, White and Morrill Halls by important axial paths. The remaining portion of Area 'E' I would leave open and parked, at least until the extreme necessity calls for its occupation by buildings.

Area 'F–F–F' I consider of even greater im-portance than area E, it being possessed of more natural beauty and composing more successfully with the grouping of buildings to the south. I have suggested the eventual re-moval of all of the present buildings within this area with the possible exception of Tellu-ride, and I doubt the real wisdom of this building in its present location, when consid-ering the future plan. This building, however, is not harmful in its location or design for some time to come. The remaining buildings in this area could be made use of temporarily, by the University in their present state, but their location should be considered as temporary.

My thought relative to these areas 'F–F–F' really begins at the Stewart Avenue bridge. The City and the University should consider Stewart Avenue as a most important approach to the Dormitory sections of the University holdings. It will always be a domestic or resi-dential entrance way from city to the University.

Stewart Avenue should be re-aligned from William [sic] Street to its junction with present South Avenue, and the bridge be re-built along more architectural lines in ac-cordance with the re-alignment of the Avenue. I believe the City is contemplating this change. Edgemore Lane should be developed as a beginning of the Marginal Road along the north side of Cascadilla Gorge, approxi-mately in its present position.

An important entrance-way 'M' should be created at the intersection of Stewart Avenue and the present South Avenue. South Avenue should be abandoned in its present location and in its stead a new road, following the slightly higher contour to the north should be created connecting with West Avenue and Schoellkopf Ave. above. Stewart Avenue would continue on about as now, except for a bettering of its general alignment between present South Avenue and Cornell Road.

The above arrangement could be made the formative beginning or part of a magnificently parked section, taking full advantage of the interesting valleys, stream beds, and contours of the area, one important valley (South Avenue removed) extending from Stewart Avenue easterly to the Mall, and giving setting to the new Law Group and its possible extensions westerly to Stewart Avenue; and the other valley to the north of relocated South Avenue following its way up past Telluride, Willard Straight Hall, thru the suggested south Quadrangle and on between Sage College and Group Site 'A' from where its continuation would be Tower Road.

There is the possibility of a wonderful system of penetrating park areas were this scheme adopted and developed. It is nothing more than a reversion to original conditions, and the play and recreation areas it would offer would be incomparable.

In discussing the above arrangements, I have passed by rather lightly the suggested development to the west of the new Law Group. A tentative grouping or block is sketched below and to the west of the new Law School, merely suggesting the possibilities of the area, developed either as University or Dormitory building groups, depending upon need. I do wish to go on record, however, as insisting upon eventual complete University control of all of this area and especially should this relate to all of that area to the west of Stewart Avenue and along the present cemetery property, an especially fine site for further graduate or faculty dormitories.

Incidentally, I should like to see the University extend its holdings to include all of the land between Cascadilla Creek and William

Street from Eddy Street to Stewart, so guaranteeing unquestionably the gorge development along this section and aiding in the tieing in of the Andrew D. White Entrance and Eddy Street into the scheme of things.

Regarding the Major Dormitory Group between Stewart Avenue and West Avenue, I am showing a somewhat revised blocking of the Dormitory Group, especially to the south of the east and west axis irrespective of plans as already proposed. My reason for this is largely to obtain what I feel might prove a better relation to the suggested new east and west axis and the parked areas 'F'.

I am especially anxious to see the University obtain control of all of the land to the west of Stewart Avenue and bounded by University Avenue, Stewart Avenue and Cornell Road, so acknowledging University Avenue as the westerly boundary of the University property.

Considering this land to be eventually available, the east and west axis should carry through to University Avenue, where at 'N', the top of the bluff, it should be terminated by an important overlook to the city below, this eventually acquired land, to be allotted to possible further dormitories and possibly the President's House, Llenroc being obtained and remodelled for this purpose.

As Stewart Avenue traverses this Dormitory Grouping, I would semi-restrict its civic character or treatment by gates at the north and south ends, and walls or balustradings parallel in the roadway, the easterly wall or balustrade being upon the upper level, so forming a base or setting to the upper groups, and the westerly wall being established at the level of Stewart Avenue, so gaining an expression of width, restriction and privacy, and a strong tie between the upper and the lower groups.

Cornell Road I would leave as now, the Baldwin Memorial acting as complement but secondary to the more important overlook end terminating the east and west axis.

I shall make no mention of the semi-privately owned area 'O' to the north of University Avenue except to again say that this entire area should in some manner be brought under University control and designing or planning. It is I am sure agreed that these lands should never have been omitted from University holdings. Semi, if not complete control, should be contemplated.

Too, the City and the University should seriously consider and cooperate in the obtaining of the entire westerly side of University Avenue to a point south as far as Cascadilla Creek. I refer to the obtaining of the westerly bluff of this street sufficient to act as a westerly parking strip to the University, but City controlled, and to University Avenue so becoming a city park approach to the University, the City Cemetery in its present condition interrelating with this scheme.

For similar reasons of better interrelation between University and City development, College Avenue, Eddy Street, Stewart Avenue, and East State Street with its connection, Mitchell Street, should be civically studied. The interests of the University and the City are strongly interrelated via these city arteries.

Especially would I like to see College Avenue widened and extended to a City terminal overlooking six-mile creek. College Avenue could easily be widened, especially along its easterly side so creating an important thoroughfare, devoted to good uptown shops well designed in unit form, especially from East State Street or Mitchell Street north; a fine terminal plaza being possible with Sheldon Court and the present Lutheran Church as components.

Eddy Street, I feel, is less important, but not to be neglected, especially as it relates to a possible rejunctioning with Dryden and the University Entrance at this point. Here too, a most interesting City spot could be developed.

A very radical suggestion and yet one upon which I would like to go on record as proposing, concerns the far eventual possible axial relation between the University proper and its main quadrangle and the State College of Agriculture Group, and I am submitting with this report a most tentative rider-sketch suggestion incident to this subject, the result of continued thought upon the part of one of the designer's in my office.

I believe we all acknowledge the ill-planning and design of Goldwin Smith Hall, irrespective of its being a fairly new and costly building. I believe there will come an eventual day when it will be razed or markedly remodeled. The same somewhat applies to Rockerfeller Hall in inadequacy more than ill design.

Were these buildings wholly or even partially removed a very strong interrelating axial treatment could readily be developed between the University proper and the State College main group, this axis focusing on Morrill Hall and the terminal easterly building of the Main Quadrangle of the College of Agriculture. I could discuss at length the possible readjustments of Goldwin Smith Hall, Stimpson Hall, Rockerfeller Hall, and the building on the site of the President's House at this time, but it does not seem proper other than to bring to your attention this possibility. Nothing could do more for the improvement of the University, as a whole and complete design, than to find some way possible to architecturally and visually tie these two now distinct and important units together. My thought is radical and probably too far reaching, but, as any plan made for the University must take into consideration the eventual future, proposals such as this are permissible.

In closing, may I say that many of the suggestions in the above report may appear extreme and far reaching, but in thinking over a development of this character, one must allow their mind to think rather distant and progressively and not be too closely concerned with immediate facts and conditions, which too often are allowed to spoil or make impossible more broadly conceived developments.

Respectfully submitted:
BRYANT FLEMING: *F.A.S.L.A.*
A.I.A.
June 16th, 1930.

Copies to—Dr. Livingston Farrand, President.
Mr. J. Du Pratt White, Chairman, Building & Grounds Committee.
Mr. R. H. Treman, Chairman, Grounds Committee.
Cornell University, Ithaca, New York.

14. Excerpts from a Report to the Buildings and Grounds Committee of the University Trustees by Warren H. Manning, 4 November 1930

[The notion that a "pedestrian campus" is a worthy goal in the motor age is not a recent one. The previous document and this report urge elimination of many internal campus roads at Cornell. In the campus planning studies of the early 1930's Manning's principal assignment was to prepare recommendations for a more efficient circulation system that would free large sections of the campus from automobile traffic. The full report and some of Manning's sketch plans are in the Campus Planning Papers in the Cornell University Archives.]

. . . This summing up of units and ways from which will come a constantly increasing number of vehicles and people to and by the "Heart of the University" clearly indicates the need of broadening the essential public traffic ways through the University lands, and a more adequate protection of the faculty, students, equipment and activities of the University from the undesirable intrusion of people in automobiles who regard the University as a place of casual tourist interest, and also from the bus traffic promoters. . . .

THE UNIVERSITY'S PUBLIC AND LOCAL ROADS

There are only [three] easterly and westerly, and [two] northerly and southerly public ways through the University building areas, and they lie from 1500–3000' apart, and they must carry much of the traffic that enters from about thirty roads that lie about 300' apart as they lead in from valley and upland units.

Stewart Avenue lies about 200' above the town. It has a 50' right-of-way with about 25' in traveled way and electric tracks. It should be given an 80' right-of-way on which there shall be no buildings.

East Avenue lies about 200' above Stewart Avenue. Its width is given as 50'. The traveled way and tracks occupy 25'. This road could be made 80' to give more room for passing and parking.

Judd Falls Road is 100' above East Avenue. This should be made 80' wide from the State Road to and beyond Forest Home Village. Buildings should be set back 50' from the road center if possible.

On all these main roads, there should be a travel-way to provide for four lines of vehicles with parking areas at intervals on one or both sides when this can be brought about. Walks may well be on varied levels to fit the lay of the land, the buildings, and the parking strips. Where it is feasible, land should be set aside to provide for the separation of path and road grades at heavy traffic points. The difficulties of accomplishing this on steep grades to gain a connection between the two roads are such that I am making no recommendations on my plans.

The broadening of the Stewart Avenue bridge over Cascadilla Gorge is not as serious a problem as is the indirect and crooked way over Fall Creek. This needs special study. To the north of Fall Creek a direct line road is indicated on plan #762–197, by dotted lines from Stewart Avenue down to Lake Street on good grades, that seemed to be quite practicable to Mayor Bergholtz' administrative staff as we went over the ground together in the spring.

From Stewart Avenue an entrance is indicated to the Men's Residential Group on the main axis line of the University. I am indicating an arrangement of the buildings here to permit this, and to give a dignified tree-shaded mall to the Memorial steps and arch.

From Stewart Avenue a most important

east and west road is indicated and called Edgemoor Road. It is a broadening to 60' over the westerly end of South Avenue, and the southerly end of West Avenue, and it is continuing to the state highway by the southerly end of the Stadium. Edgemoor Lane passes into this road from Stewart Avenue.

From this road will pass a road to Taylor Hall forecourt and parking space, and to the Willard Straight parking space. The Stadium service and auto outlet road that climbs the slope to the back of the stadium passes out of this road around the back of the stadium to connect with the proposed South Avenue extension. This road may be made to serve as a southerly outlet from the big play field where 4,000 cars may be parked, and from a parking area that may be made by grading down Kite Hill back of the stadium.

Taylor Hall has made a relocation of a part of South Avenue essential. The new South Avenue as indicated will offer an easier grade, and will connect up with the road around the stadium. This relocation and the abandonment of the present road north of the gymnasium will give a large open space for future buildings.

The easterly-westerly roads at either end of the State Drill Hall and Garden Avenue will doubtless be retained.

Central Avenue from the new South Avenue southward to and over the bridge is indicated as a wide walk. To the north of South Avenue, Central Avenue is given a width of 40' to connect with the Tower Road, and to provide for parking in either side to supplement the parking area back of Willard Straight Hall.

My recommendation is that West Avenue as a through traffic road be eliminated as it crosses the most important axial foot traffic way. It is recommended that all public vehicle traffic across the campus areas be confined to Judd Falls Road, Stewart and East Avenues.

The indicated bridge of the General Plan of 1925–6 from Eddy Street to West Avenue should not be undertaken if the East Avenue

and Stewart Avenue bridges are to be made adequate, and the road of this plan between the proposed Willard Straight parking space to West should also be omitted.

My recommendation is that several of the easterly and westerly entrances to the "Heart of the University" unit be made loop-road parking areas, to be carried far enough into the grounds to give short walks to the important buildings.

To serve the Morrill, McGraw and White Halls, a loop road and parking space is indicated on the proposed Great Terrace of the College Committee's General Plan of 1925–6. This, with Central Avenue and Tower Road should serve the Library.

These vehicle loops should eliminate roadway connection across the southwesterly corner of The Quadrangle to which an important Library slope path will come. Some roads may be made paths wide enough to give automobile service when this is essential.

The proposed Fine Arts building and other existing structures on East Avenue can be served by parking spaces along this Avenue.

University Avenue is really the only present easterly-westerly trunk line heavy traffic road through the University. It is much crowded at times now, and will be increasingly inadequate as time goes on. Its lower end to Stewart Avenue is so hedged by houses and high walls and memorial structures, that broadening here for future traffic demands will be difficult, but a study and estimate of cost should be made. The right-of-way should certainly be made as wide as possible to East Avenue bridge, even though a strip of Fall Creek bluff reserve be included, and all proposed buildings north of the avenue be eliminated. Heavy traffic to a high-class residential, club and probable future air field district will pass over this East Avenue bridge.

The state and city are now developing a main thoroughfare on Dryden Road for heavy through traffic on a northeasterly and southwesterly direction outside of the built up and highly cultivated farm areas of the University. The proposed Edgemoor Road will help University Avenue by diverting traffic from it. This diversion helps the recreational interests of Beebe Lake, to both shores of which there should be a free and safe movement of students. Let me add here, that the slope above the road south of Beebe Lake should be reserved for the increase of recreational uses.

Another relief road for the lower part of University Avenue may be made by modifying the dangerously steep Lake Street that now passes by the Gun Works to the Fall Creek lower level bridge. The grade may possibly be decreased by increasing its length on curves through the Gun Works and adjacent properties, or preferably by carrying a road down the unoccupied slope southward to Linn and Yates Streets.

Another relief is offered by Cornell Street [now Avenue] which passes up from University Avenue, by the Memorial terrace, and along the north line of the city cemetery to Stewart Avenue.

Tower Road was planned to go to the Library Tower on Central Avenue. It is indicated as a 40′ road. Its importance as a part of the circuit road by Central, Sage and South Avenues, and as a road upon the sides of which automobiles may be parked, justifies its retention and broadening. This Tower Road is also indicated for an extension eastward to the new state highway where an important University entrance may be established.

The importance of the central University axis line first established by the Tower Road is now emphasized by having it made the central line of the Memorial Cloister Arch and of the Residential Groups for the Men. A continuation of walk and steps on this axis line is proposed down to the town level. It happens that the view of the University Boat Club house on the Inlet lies nearly on this axis line. . . .

LIBRARY SLOPE LAWN AND PATHS

The paths through the great oval lawn from the War Memorial Tower and Cloister, and the Residential Group to Willard Straight

Hall, the Library and The Quadrangle and the Arboretum rose plantations on either side, will form a University Plan unit with great inspirational and educational value and beauty. This should be studied with the greatest care, with the aid of all departments of the University to secure the most exquisite results in both construction and maintenance. There should also be a presentation of the study to show present, proposed, and actually accomplished conditions that will give all observers and students a valuable object lesson. If the terrace building that I am suggesting is constructed, the walk connections to and through the structure will be of great importance as indicated. The central walk and its terminal terrace will emphasize and dignify the University axial line. This path, with its steps and seats may be used as a restful way up the slope. The diagonal paths are essential "short cuts."

There is now standing in this slope a scattered plantation of deciduous and evergreen trees on which are some fine tall plume-shaped Elms that could be transplanted to the Residential Group buildings in such a way as to give them a well-established foliage setting instead of waiting 50 years for young trees to mature. There are also groups of evergreens, some of which have very picturesque forms, which could be used very effectively about the more recent buildings in this vicinity to give them pictorial foliage values that they do not now have. The present planting is now largely ineffective because it is scattered and crowded in a way that tends to destroy the breadth of this foreground for fine buildings and distant views from this, the "Heart of the University.". . .

BUILDINGS

I feel that serious consideration and study should be given to the Great Terrace of the 1925–6 General Plan. I would have this studied with a view to providing a building under this terrace to serve as a covered passage from University Avenue buildings to Willard Straight Hall. Such covered passage ways are now being established in many large public institutions, especially in the region of winter snows.

This proposed building will, I believe, have a special value as a library extension and as a scientific, industrial and Patent Office model museum.

The new building that is proposed on the site of the old Chemical Laboratory will doubtless have a high and beautiful tower by reason of its dominant location as viewed from the important northwesterly and westerly entrances to Ithaca, from the Lake and elsewhere.

On this study is indicated a repetition of the present men's dormitory group to the north of the War Memorial, and we have added the proposed buildings of the first group study with modifications to provide for the entrance loop.

AN AUTOMOBILE CENTER AND A TUNNEL AND ELEVATOR ACCESS

To center automobile traffic, to gain more rapid and direct access to the University centers at all seasons, I am recommending that a study and estimate of costs and of returns from fees be made for an automobile terminal parking space, for a terraced garage on the steep slope, and for a tunnel under the University on its axis line with elevators up to such points as Stewart Avenue, Men's Residential Group, Central Avenue at the Library, Garden Avenue at Agricultural center, and stadium, and to Judd Falls Road if this is not too far.

If this were found practicable and economic, the whole study that I am presenting would be modified in many ways, with economies in construction and a marked easing up of transportation difficulties.

BROAD LANDSCAPE AND FINE ARTS VALUES

As a nation we are approaching a period when the beauty of living landscape pictures in which buildings and plant life play such an important part will soon be as appreciated as the painted pictures have been appreciated in the past. The time will come when ideal pictures created by landscape, architectural and sculptoral artists will be as reverently preserved from defacement and cherished as painters' pictures are now cherished. If the University can secure the highest pictorial values in this unit that I have referred to as the "Heart of the University," it will be then bringing landscape standards up to the architectural standards that are being established in your finest buildings.

It must be recognized that one of the difficulties in [accomplishing] such a result will come from the attitude of so many people who object strenuously to the cutting of any trees. The beauty of the best Elm trees in The Quadrangle is largely due to the cutting of crowding trees that I helped to bring about a dozen years ago.

With the highest standing of Cornell's Engineering, Fine Arts and Landscape instruction, it should take a well-advanced position in the creation of the highest type of beauty about its courts and buildings.

A CONSENSUS OF OPINION

Recognizing that such an important study as this must be founded on a concensus [*sic*] of well-informed opinion, I have had conferences in offices and on the grounds with President Farrand, Chairman Treman, Dean Bosworth, Messrs. Curtis, Crandall, Cooley, Blanche, and Ward. On city problems that in part pertain to the University, I have gone over the ground with Mayor Bergholtz and Messrs. Feller, Dahmen, Euston, and Baker, of his administrative staff, and I want to herein express my appreciation of the knowledge, the open-minded and helpful attitude and cordial appreciation of all these people.

WARREN H. MANNING

WHM:DEA
November 4, 1930

15. A Policy for Architectural Design at Cornell, 11 June 1966

[Late in 1965 Vice-Provost Thomas W. Mackesey, chief administrative officer for planning at Cornell, began drafting a policy statement on architectural design to be used as a guide for University decisions and for architects commissioned to design campus buildings. The Buildings and Properties Committee of the Board of Trustees adopted the following policy statement on 11 June 1966.]

June 11, 1966

The education of the student is the sum of his experiences in and out of the classroom. The quality of the environment in which he lives, pursues his studies, and finds his recreation, contributes to that education. Cornell University is committed to excellence in its academic programs. It is equally committed to excellence in the design of new buildings to house those programs and to support the academic enterprise. Buildings are more than enclosures of space. They are the physical elements which can guide the life and movement of the academic community and which can suggest the character, purpose and philosophy of the institution as a whole.

It is expected that each new building will not only represent a functional solution of special requirements, but will also be an aesthetic statement of lasting significance in itself. The buildings of the Ithaca campus have been built over a span of one hundred years. Each represents something of the conditions and values of the times that produced it. In this sense each building was modern in its time. New buildings added to this complex should reflect the spirit of Cornell as a pioneering institution and should be of the time and place.

While the importance of direct and vigorous architectural solutions is paramount, it must be remembered that each new building will be placed in a setting that has evolved over a century. It will not stand alone as an isolated monument, but will contribute to, and become part of, a total environment. This

environment, with the older buildings, the spectacular gorges, the views across the town to the west, of the Lake to the north, of the valley to the south, the symbolism of the Library Tower, must be not only recognized but embraced by the architect. Each new building must in itself be a statement of the architect's talent and vision, and at the same time contribute to a coherent whole.

As more and larger buildings find their place on the campus, it is inevitable that the open aspect of the campus will be modified. As this happens, more attention must be given to the relationship of buildings one to another, and particularly to the spaces between buildings. A campus is a particularly appropriate place for an architect to be concerned with "outdoor rooms." Outdoor space must not be simply the incidental space left over between buildings nor may campus planning concern itself only with the siting of individual buildings and efficient circulation. The entire campus must be thought of as a site, partly roofed and partly enclosed. Outdoor spaces should be dimensioned to human scale, related to the students who will walk and lounge and talk, individually and in groups, within the spaces created.

More building will undoubtedly mean higher building in some locations in order to hold down land coverage and to preserve that sense of spaciousness which is a fortunate characteristic of Cornell. The upper floors of high-rise structures will look down on the campus patterns and also on the roofs of lower buildings. The architects of lower buildings where this may occur should give

324

concern to the developing roofscape, remembering that their buildings may be seen from above as well as from the ground.

Finally, the architect must consider the contribution of each new building to the profile of the University as seen from the town below and from the hills to the west and south.

Acknowledgments

THE IDEA OF WRITING about the history of the Cornell campus was first suggested to me by Professor Thomas W. Mackesey in 1952. His favorable reaction to my first efforts and the cooperation of Robert Mueller, Richard Mac-Dowell, and C. A. Thompson of the Cornell Buildings and Properties Department made it possible to complete the first paper. This earnest but sophomoric work lay dormant for ten years until my interest was renewed by Albert Bush-Brown's casual reference to the importance of expanding and improving it.

Several generous grants from the Cornell Faculty Research Grants Committee in 1962 and 1964 made possible research assistance, typing help, the reproduction of documents, plans, and photographs, and the redrawing of old plans. I am much indebted to Damon Boynton, Thomas Rogers and the Committee for this help. Without it many of the materials in the Cornell University Archives would have been difficult if not impossible to use.

President Deane W. Malott generously provided additional support for research assistance on two occasions when this part of the work seemed about to run aground. I am deeply grateful for his interest and his substantial help.

My greatest aid in research was Keith Sutherland who worked as research assistant for two and one half years. His skilled and diligent efforts in the University Archives was done with enthusiasm, patience, and a wry Maine sense of humor. I must confess that I did not know how valuable an intelligent, talented, well-trained research assistant could be until Mr. Sutherland appeared from the far reaches of Cornell's Department of History. His extensive and excellent knowledge of the

White Papers, his thorough searching, and his suggestions were major factors in sustaining my efforts to throw the light of documentary evidence on the people and events which have shaped Cornell's buildings and its campus. I am deeply grateful for Mr. Sutherland's contribution.

Vice-President Thomas W. Mackesey and Professors Stephen W. Jacobs and Morris Bishop have read most of the manuscript and have offered excellent suggestions and very helpful criticisms. Burnham Kelly, Dean of the College of Architecture at Cornell, has provided intellectual encouragement and material help on several occasions.

Among the other colleagues and friends at Cornell who have helped generously in various ways are John W. Reps, Stuart W. Stein, Barclay G. Jones, A. Henry Detweiler, Glenn Beyer, George Healey, Frederick Marcham, Paul Gates, Paul McKeegan, John Marcham, Walter Stainton, John Summerskill, H. Peter Kahn, and John N. Tilton. Their help and encouragement and the stimulation of other Cornellians who have listened, sometimes patiently, to my rough approximations of the history of the place are gratefully acknowledged.

I owe a profound debt to the biographers, chroniclers, and historians who made earlier soundings of Cornell's past. I have enjoyed and learned much from the long and fascinating *Autobiography of Andrew Dickson White,* Alonzo Cornell's admiring *Biography of Ezra Cornell,* Goldwin Smith's urbane and witty *Reminiscences,* Waterman T. Hewett's definitive and thoroughly researched *Cornell University: A History,* Albert W. Smith's *Ezra Cornell: A Character Study,* Paul Gates's fine scholarly volume *The Pine Lands of Cornell*

University, Philip Dorf's masterful *Liberty Hyde Bailey: An Informal Biography* and *The Builder: A Biography of Ezra Cornell*, Carl Becker's thoughtful book, *Cornell University: Founders and the Founding*, and Morris Bishop's very thorough and very delightful centennial volume, *A History of Cornell*. These surely comprise the minimum reading for "Cornellophiles."

Mr. Jackson Towne of Michigan State University very kindly let me read his manuscript on Charles Kendall Adams' role in the planning of the University of Michigan and Cornell University library buildings. Professor Paul F. Norton, Editor of the *Journal of the Society of Architectural Historians*, encouraged and sustained my interest in the history of campus planning and architecture at Cornell by publishing a short version of the material now expanded in Chapters I, II, and III. The historian of the New York State Capitol, Cecil R. Roseberry, provided excellent and useful background material on John Snaith and on Louis J. Hinton, the English building craftsman of Ithaca and Albany.

For their useful leads and encouragement I am grateful to Mark Beach, Laura Wood Roper, L. Bancel LaFarge, Frederic Mayer, Martin Kramer, and Frederic C. Wood. Robert Sena and Paul A. Curtis did the drawings of President White's villa and the McGraw-Fiske mansion. Mr. G. J. Requardt ('09) with the help of Thomas R. Silcox reconstructed the plan of the McGraw-Fiske mansion. Mr. Requardt, who survived the Chi Psi fire of 1906, and other Chi Psi alumni apparently enjoyed this detective work. I appreciate their interest and assistance.

Deep thanks are also due many very helpful librarians: to Stephen A. McCarthy, Director of the Cornell University Libraries, for his interest and encouragement and for the use of a quiet study in Cornell's John M. Olin Library; to Edith Fox, Curator of Cornell's Regional History collection and the University Archives, for suggestions and comments during the course of the work and for the excel-lence of this collection; to Barbara Shepherd, Assistant Curator of the Archives, and to Robert R. Jones, who were always helpful in making the use of the collection efficient and pleasant; to David Shearer of Cornell Fine Arts Library for his willingness and ability to meet many special requests; and, finally, to the following librarians who provided assistance at various times during the research—Laura S. Greene, Helen Wurthman, and Joan Carpenter of the State Education Department Library in Albany; Katherine McNamara of the Library of the Graduate School of Design at Harvard; Robert W. Hill, Keeper of Manuscripts, The New York Public Library; and David C. Mearns, Chief of the Manuscript Division of the Library of Congress.

Drafts of the book and early articles based on the research were typed in Ithaca and Albany by Rosina Mason, Louisa Massicci, Helen Fuller, Lori Myer, Kathy Chandler, Geraldine Yerdon, Nancy Jarman, Carol Farkas, and Jacquelyn Haskins. Hawley MacDermid, Mae Gleason, Mary Adesso, and Marilyn Aiken typed the final manuscript.

Many of the photographs and drawings are from the Cornell University Archives. I am grateful to them for access to their large collection. Ralph Smith, a prodigious collector of early Ithaca and Cornell photographs, was generous in spending time identifying and dating many of his photographs and in granting permission to copy them. The DeWitt Historical Society of Ithaca and Tompkins County, and its erstwhile curator William Heidt, also provided numerous early views of the town and campus. Photographer C. Hadley Smith spent long hours "bringing back" faded views and "magically" removing the creases and tatters of time from photographs of old drawings and prints.

Last and most my gratitude goes to my wife, Janice Patten Parsons, to whom this book is dedicated, for her encouragement, patience, and help, and to our children, John and Stephen and Katherine.

CREDITS FOR ILLUSTRATIONS

C. Hadley Smith: Figures 4, 9, 12, 20, 23, 30, 33, 40, 42, 80, 91, 92, 98, 102, 116, 122, 132–135, 144, 150, 155, 158, 169, 170, 171, 191, 192, 202, 203, 208, and 215; *C. Hadley Smith from Cornell University Archives Picture Collection:* End Papers, Figures 31, 32, 34, 36–38, 44, 47, 48, 50, 51, 64, 71, 79, 82, 95, 104, 113, 127, 131, 157, 196 and 197; *C. Hadley Smith from the Collection of Ralph Smith:* Figures 2, 21, 24–26, 45, 74, 75, 77, 84, 86, 89, 93, 109, 124, 148, 149, 166, 167, 178; *C. Hadley Smith from Cornell College of Architecture Slide Collection:* Figures 46, 55, 156 and 198; *C. Hadley Smith from DeWitt Historical Society Collection:* Figures 62, 81, 94, 99, 100, 101, 110 and 111; *C. Hadley Smith from a drawing by Robert Sena:* Figure 14; *C. Had-ley Smith from a drawing by John Tilton:* Figure 218.

Cornell University Archives: Frontispiece, Figures 1, 3, 6, 8, 13, 17, 22, 27, 41, 49, 57, 58, 59, 60, 61, 63, 66–70, 72, 73, 76, 78, 83, 85, 87, 88, 90, 96, 97, 103, 105–108, 112, 114, 115, 118–121, 123, 125, 126, 128–130, 136–143, 145–147, 151–153, 159–165, 168, 172–177, 179–190, 193–195, 199–201, 204, 205, 207, 209, 211–213; *Cornell University Photo Science Studio:* Figures 5, 7, 10, 11, 15, 16, 18, 29, 35, 39, 43, 52–54, 56, 65, 154, 206, 210, 214, 216 and 217; *Cornell University Library:* Figure 117; *Paul Norton:* Figure 19; *Russel Wright:* Figure 28.

Letters or numerals have been added to Figures 156, 180, 191, 196, 198, 202, 203, and 208 for purposes of identification.

Index

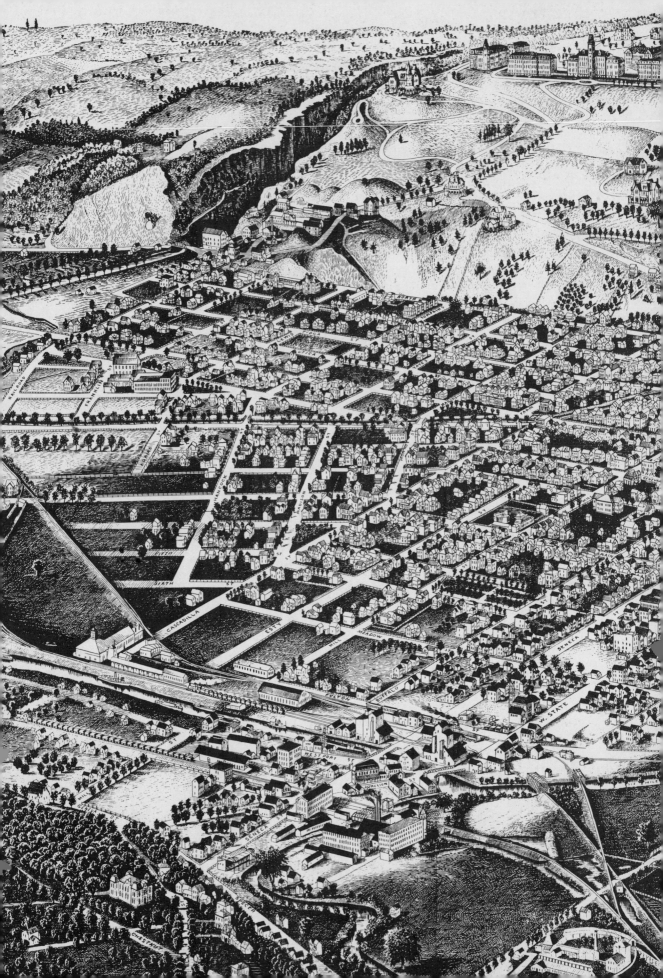